Successful Manager's Handbook

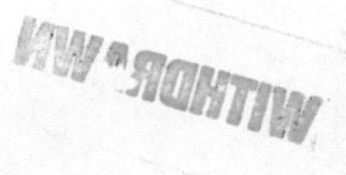

> ▸ 8TH EDITION ◂

SUCCESSFUL MANAGER'S HANDBOOK

Develop Yourself
Coach Others

Susan H. Gebelein ▸ Kristie J. Nelson-Neuhaus

Carol J. Skube ▸ David G. Lee ▸ Lisa A. Stevens

Lowell W. Hellervik ▸ Brian L. Davis

and the Consultants of PDI Ninth House

North America ▹ Europe ▹ Asia Pacific

Australia ▹ Middle East ▹ Latin America

PDI Ninth House
GLOBAL LEADERSHIP SOLUTIONS

Interior Design and Production: BookMobile
Editorial Services: Lynn Marasco
Indexing: Terry Casey Indexing
Reasearch: Karin Murphy
Managing Editor: Linda VanDenBoom and Kristie Nelson-Neuhaus

www.previsor.com

PreVisor ISBN: 978-0-972-5770-3-8
PDI Ninth House ISBN: 978-0-972-5770-4-5

Printed in U.S.A.

10 9 8 7 6 5 4 3 2

Contents

Using financial data goes beyond reading a spreadsheet or creating a budget. We talk about measuring performance, recognizing and managing risk, investing wisely, and achieving aggressive financial goals.

The global economy affects every manager, regardless of the industry. We cover a range of issues: developing a global mind-set, understanding global business models and markets, working across cultures and borders, and executing global initiatives.

We help you better understand your customers and their businesses, raise the bar for customer service, and develop an approach that helps your company exceed customer expectations.

Business plans are just words until people take action. As a manager, you often act through and with other people. So we focus on the key elements of delegation and facilitating meetings, plus setting expectations, measuring performance, and accountability.

Without realistic plans, it's difficult to accomplish your objectives. We help you build plans that support the organization's vision and strategy, coordinate efforts with individuals and groups, and plan for contingencies.

Processes save time and limit variation—both of which can be costly. Processes also enable organizations to deliver high-quality results. Here we offer tools to help you design, improve, and measure your processes.

People may appreciate the results of change, but the anxiety leading up to it can slow or stop necessary action. We talk about how to get people on board, plan for and implement change, and reinforce both progress and success.

The value of ethical business leaders has become evident in recent years. We focus on both personal and organizational trust, from modeling high levels of integrity to responsible use of resources.

Ambiguity, stress, setbacks, mistakes, crises—life as a manager can be challenging. We help you adapt appropriately to people, shifting demands, and changing priorities; cope with frustration and stress; and maintain a positive outlook in the face of it all.

Lifelong learners see a payoff for their efforts, whether it's knowledge, skills, or sheer enjoyment. Because time is usually the biggest obstacle, we tell you how to learn efficiently, concentrate on what counts, and incorporate feedback to stay on track.

Acknowledgements

We would like to thank the individuals and groups who helped make this book possible. *Successful Manager's Handbook* is the result of true partnerships within and outside of PDI Ninth House.

Introduction

Welcome to the eighth edition of *Successful Manager's Handbook!* You're about to join more than a million leaders who have relied on the handbook since 1984.

During the past 25 years, management fads have come and gone. Leaders in all industries hopped on and off of bandwagons. But through it all, they had one thing in common: when they were ready for substance, they turned to *Successful Manager's Handbook*.

Like all smart leaders, you don't have time or patience for simplistic answers or formulaic solutions. You need proven ideas and strategies that you can use to be more effective at work.

That's exactly what you'll find in these pages. Whether you're a novice or an expert, you'll find information geared to your level and your situation, from the basics to fine-tuning highly sophisticated skills. Some ideas will be immediately helpful and useful, some might apply to your next project or job, and others will prompt you to think more deeply about your current situation.

The PDI Ninth House edge

▼

At PDI Ninth House, we know what it takes for people to learn and to change their behavior. For four decades, our consultants—using a combination of experience, cutting-edge research, and a keen awareness of the practicalities of a situation—have helped managers and executives become more effective. The result: we know these ideas work, because real people have used them.

Included in *Successful Manager's Handbook* are 28 leadership competencies that PDI Ninth House has identified as being important to the four responsibility areas of leaders: results, people, thinking, and self-management. Here you will find for each competency a chapter that offers specific suggestions and tips for improving your skills and ideas for coaching others.

Using the book in your work

▼

Successful Manager's Handbook is a library of practical suggestions, ideas, tips, and resources. It's the place to turn to when you're put in charge of something you've never done before, when you want new ideas, or when you want to help one of your people develop.

The handbook isn't meant to sit on your shelf; it's meant to be used. Most people don't read the whole book cover to cover; they find and read what they need. Here are examples of how other leaders have used *Successful Manager's Handbook* at their organizations:

▸ "I look for new ideas when my approach isn't working."

▸ "We give a copy to each person promoted into management to show how important the job is."

▸ "I recommend that my direct reports read a few pages when they need to learn how to do something new."

▸ "I've never read the whole thing. I just dip in and out when I need to."

Make it your own! Bend the pages, write in it, and flag your favorite parts. The more ways you find to use it, the more it will help you.

- ▶ Write notes and comments in the margins.

- ▶ Put start and completion dates next to activities.

- ▶ Use colored Post-it® notes or flags to designate low-, medium-, and high-priority activities.

- ▶ Use highlighters—one color to call out your strengths and another to note development needs.

- ▶ Put stickers next to ideas you want to remember.

Planning templates

▼

We've included plans that you can use for yourself or for someone you're coaching. Choose your plan (see descriptions below), go to the relevant section of the handbook and find ideas or suggestions, fill in the template, and add details like deadlines and the people you will involve. You'll find four templates:

1. Learning plan (short-term goals)

   When you need to develop a skill ASAP, use this form. Be as specific as possible, especially about your action steps and deadlines. Make sure you build in activities you can do each day.

2. Development plan (medium-term goals)

   When you and your boss identify development areas during performance reviews or when you review your 360 feedback report, use this form to plan your learning.

3. Career plan (long-term goals)

   Most careers don't follow a straight path, especially during economic downturns. Even if you don't know exactly what you want to be doing in five or ten years, you can still plan your career. You probably have a strong sense of where your interests are and how you'd like to spend your time. This form can help you fill in the details and give you some structure without restricting your ability to respond to opportunities that arise along the way.

4. Coaching plan (for each person you coach)

This form will help you keep track of individuals' learning objectives and determine how you can support them and create learning opportunities.

www.pdininthhouse.com

Visit our Web site to learn more about PDI Ninth House, our offerings, and our learning solutions. While you're there, send us an e-mail. We look forward to hearing from you!

PDI Ninth House
Successful Manager's Handbook
Leadership Wheel

Successful Manager's Handbook

1

Analyze Issues

The ability to analyze issues in a clear, consistent, and objective manner is a skill that is critical to your success as a manager. The key to analyzing issues is the process you use to examine facts, obtain information, and expand your thinking beyond your normal limitations, experiences, and cultural beliefs.

Successful analytical thinking involves developing the ability to separate emotions, preconceived beliefs, assumptions, and personal bias from the issue at hand; to probe for answers beyond the obvious; and to tactfully involve colleagues, direct reports, and key stakeholders in evaluating and resolving issues.

Some people are naturally gifted at analytical thinking, while for others it may take learning, practice, and willingness to look at issues from multiple perspectives. No matter where you are in the process, strengthening your analytical skills will increase your success in your managerial role and in your overall career.

In this chapter, we will cover the following areas:

▼

- ▸ Evaluate your analytical skills
- ▸ Break down problems into manageable parts
- ▸ Focus on the most critical information you need in order to understand problems
- ▸ Look beyond symptoms to identify causes of problems
- ▸ Identify and test assumptions
- ▸ Become more open to ideas and perspectives
- ▸ Analyze issues from different points of view
- ▸ Apply accurate logic in solving problems
- ▸ Recognize the broad implications of issues
- ▸ Integrate information from a variety of sources to arrive at optimal solutions
- ▸ Define reasonable alternatives to resolve problems or make decisions

Evaluate your analytical skills

▼

If you have specific concerns about people's ability to analyze issues, discuss your concerns in terms of how they could improve their process.

To evaluate your current strengths as an analytical thinker, answer yes or no to the following questions:

Do you look for multiple ways to define problems?	Yes	No
Do you look for more than one option or solution?	Yes	No
Do you look for implications and effects of behaviors, solutions, and actions?	Yes	No
Do you anticipate other people's concerns?	Yes	No
Do you usually see connections and interrelationships between things?	Yes	No
Do you approach work from a systems- and process-oriented point of view?	Yes	No
Do you figure out ways to get your ideas accepted?	Yes	No
Do you plan for reactions and responses from others?	Yes	No
Do you ask for the assumptions that underlie strategies and plans?	Yes	No
Are you curious about why others see things differently?	Yes	No
Do people see you as open to the ideas and perspectives of others?	Yes	No
Do others give you feedback that you are flexible and adaptable?	Yes	No
Do you regularly change your mind when you are given new information?	Yes	No

Break down problems into manageable parts

▼

If you want to craft a successful solution or course of action, you must take time to clearly define the issue. How an issue or opportunity is defined is critical. It governs what information you gather, how you evaluate it, and whom you involve in the process. Consider the following suggestions:

Ask people to identify a critical path through a situation. Help them break it down into steps.

▶ Recognize that a problem or issue might be seen in a number of ways. For example, outsourcing can be seen as:

▷ An effective way to save money.

▷ The cause of job losses.

▷ A way to stay in business by offering more competitive pricing.

▷ A loss of quality control.

▶ When you face an issue or opportunity, consider:

▷ What is the issue or opportunity?

▷ In how many ways can you define or identify the problem or issue?

▷ If it is a problem, when does it occur? Just as important, when does it *not* occur?

▷ Who is involved? What role does each person play?

▷ If it is a problem, what is the root cause?

▷ If it is an opportunity, what is the opportunity? Why is it an opportunity?

▷ What are the positive elements or consequences of this issue or opportunity?

▷ What are the negative elements or consequences of the opportunity?

▷ How might the problem be seen in other cultures? Is it even a problem to others?

▶ Your first responses to these questions are likely to be somewhat tentative or general, especially if the issue represents something new, complex, or subtle. As you gather information, review and revise your initial responses to reflect your increased awareness and understanding.

Focus on the most critical information you need in order to understand problems

▼

Having the correct information is essential for effective analysis. When you analyze an issue or opportunity, your first step is to determine what information is critical. Consider the following suggestions:

▶ Before you gather information, list what you would like to know in order to analyze and resolve the issue. Rank the items on your list according to how critical they are to resolving the issue.

▶ Avoid wasting time collecting unnecessary or marginally useful information. Weed out information that is tangential, or is too difficult or time-consuming to collect in light of its potential value. Some information may be interesting but won't help you move forward. Be pragmatic.

▶ Build on existing knowledge to avoid reinventing the wheel. Ask:

▷ Has the organization faced a similar issue in the past? If it has, who was involved and how was it handled? What were the results? What has changed since then in the organization and in the industry?

▷ How have other organizations handled similar issues?

▶ Incorporate others' viewpoints. When other people in the organization will be affected, you need to know their views to reach a workable, wise, and accepted solution. For example, people might have several views on the best way to launch a new product or service. In this case, talk to people in several groups and regions, and also obtain customer and supplier input when appropriate.

Ask people to identify the most critical information they need on an issue and what critical information they are missing.

▶ Determine how, where, and when you will gather the information. Sources might include conversations, written materials, interviews, group discussions, written or online questionnaires, surveys, online chats with work groups, video chats with regional managers, Web-based searches, Wikis, and direct observation.

▶ If you are not sure how to obtain the information you need, ask your manager, your peers, or your team for ideas. They may use sources that differ from those you typically consider.

▶ Determine whether your conclusion stems from facts, not just your personal beliefs. Also make sure the facts truly support your conclusion. Discuss whether the data could point to any other conclusions.

▸ Be careful throughout the process not to get bogged down in unnecessary details. You will most likely uncover a lot of information—some of which will be relevant to the problem and some that will be based on people's personal opinions, biases, concerns, and agendas. Limit your time frame for gathering information and making a decision. Focus on the actual problem and sort out the information that is directly related and most critical to solving it.

Look beyond symptoms to identify causes of problems

▼

Ask people at least five "why" questions to help them do a deeper analysis and to realize how much they do or do not know about the situation.

If you handle issues and problems at a surface level, you will face them over and over. On the other hand, if you identify root causes, you can get to the bottom of them and take effective action. Consider the following suggestions:

▸ Describe the problem. Be careful to describe only the problem—not possible solutions. Define it in terms of needs.

▸ Develop a theory about why the problem occurs. Include the role that you play or your team plays.

▸ Ask team members to describe their experiences with the problem. Write down common themes. Look for patterns.

▸ Create a graphic showing the occurrences and consequences of the problem. If others are involved in resolving the issue, you may want to demonstrate the problem and related factors in a PowerPoint presentation or in a shared work space online.

▸ Summarize the problem or issue: when it began, when it occurs, when it does not occur, who is involved, who isn't, when/how it gets better or worse, what affects it, what does not.

▸ Identify root causes by using a "five whys" approach. Uncover layers of cause and effect by asking why the issue occurred, why that condition existed, why that was so, and so forth.

For example, a problem may be that materials did not arrive on time. *Why?* The vendor had the wrong ship date. *Why?* The person who ordered the materials put the wrong ship date on the form. *Why?* The person filled out the forms online and couldn't verify the information.

Why? The system froze and he couldn't print an order confirmation. *Why?* The vendor was migrating to a new system and still working out bugs.

This example illustrates the power of this process; it surfaced many issues to deal with, rather than one person to blame.

▶ It's important to realize that most issues stem from a number of factors and/or complex relationships within and between organizations, business units, systems, vendors, suppliers, and customers. It's easy to assume that a failed outcome (problem) can be attributed to a single factor or person. Remember that you are operating within a system, or multiple systems, and that whatever you do will affect others. Be careful to look for all the causes and dimensions.

Identify and test assumptions

▼

Effective analyzers recognize that assumptions made while looking at issues govern the analysis. Therefore, it's important to identify and test assumptions. Consider the following suggestions:

▶ When you hear about a problem, opportunity, or issue, identify assumptions. For example, if a customer complains about poor service, what is the customer assuming? That service should be better. That someone should care that he or she received poor service. That if he or she complains, it will make a difference. Given those assumptions, it is easier to see why people feel anger and frustration when a complaint is not handled well.

Remind individuals involved in the problem-resolving process that people generally begin with assumptions and that assumptions often are missing information.

▶ Look at the implications of each assumption. For example, if a help desk assumes that 10 percent of customers will complain and 50 percent of the complaints will be from people who do not use the product correctly, how might they react to customer complaints?

▶ Ask others to identify the assumptions you have made about an issue.

▶ Notice when people make assumptions different from yours. Pick up on cultural differences. For example, in some cultures, problems are to be endured, not solved.

Become more open to ideas and perspectives

▼

Your mental model—personal picture of the world—not only guides how you think about issues, it also governs the type of information you notice in the first place. Unless you make a conscious effort to broaden the range of ideas and perspectives you hear, your thinking necessarily will be limited. Consider the following suggestions:

► Adopt the attitudes of effective analytical thinkers. They are curious, adaptable, future focused, positive, and open to new ideas. Their knowledge is broad and they cultivate a wide range of interests.

► Recognize that analytical thinking involves the following:

▷ *Critical thinking:* the ability to objectively analyze a situation and evaluate the pros, cons, and implications of any course of action.

▷ *Conceptual thinking:* the ability to grasp abstract ideas and put the pieces together to form a coherent picture.

▷ *Creative thinking:* the ability to generate options, visualize possibilities, and formulate new approaches.

▷ *Intuitive thinking:* the ability to factor hunches into the decision-making equation without allowing them to dominate the final outcome.

When you hear people dismissing others' points of view, challenge them to look seriously at the possibility that they could have missed something important.

► Ask people for feedback on how well you demonstrate these characteristics. In instances when you don't demonstrate them, determine why you are being less open, less flexible, or less positively focused than you want to be.

► Approach other people's ideas with curiosity and an open mind. Constantly ask:

▷ How else can this situation be viewed?

▷ How do others view this?

► Practice these different kinds of thinking by reading books about creativity, intuition, and thinking, and by playing thinking games in newspapers, magazines, and creativity books.

Analyze issues from different points of view

▼

A major recurring obstacle to high-quality analysis is the tendency to look at an issue only in the way it most naturally appears to you, and then to analyze only your view of the issue. This approach not only limits your view of the situation, but also affects the ensuing analysis, recommendations, and decision, which will contain pronounced biases and preconceived notions of the issue and its parameters. To bring in other perspectives and points of view:

Ask people to look at a situation from the point of view of each constituency involved to give them a broader perspective.

▸ Consider the issue from stakeholders' perspectives. How would internal customers view the problem? Your manager? An external customer? The union? A process expert? The CEO?

▸ Map out the process. It may have a flow, loops, and decision points rather than follow a simple cause and effect pattern.

▸ Consider whether the issue represents a change that is actually part of some larger-scale transformation. What is the larger context? What does it indicate for the product, department, organization, or industry? Recall how things looked six months ago, a year ago, and three years ago, and then extrapolate what that could mean in the future.

▸ Find out how different regions view the issue. An issue is defined by and depends on the values, attitudes, business culture, and expectations of the people involved in and affected by it. A company office in London might see a problem that needs fixing, while the Singapore and San Francisco offices might be happy with the status quo.

Apply accurate logic in solving problems

▼

Facts can be bent, shaded, and shaped to fit several versions of a story. To be as accurate as possible in your logic and reasoning, consider the following suggestions:

Provide feedback when you believe that people are using poor or inaccurate logic.

▸ Identify your mental model as it relates to the issue or problem. Your mental model is your personal picture or theory about the world, people, teams, and organizations. For example, you probably have a mental model of how customers should be treated.

▸ Recognize that your mental model affects what you see, what you pay attention to, and what options you generate. Therefore, to detect flaws in your reasoning, identify the potential flaws in your mental model. It is easiest to do this by involving other people, since it may be difficult to be objective about your own mental model.

▸ Ask other people to challenge your assumptions, the inferences you make from information, and the options and limitations you see.

▸ Check your inferences using the chart below.

Facts	Conclusions	Alternative Conclusions

If you cannot find alternatives by yourself, ask your team or a colleague to help. How do these additional views affect your view of the issue or problem, and the options you generate?

▸ When people explain their reasoning, identify the assumptions that underlie their proposed solutions or points of view. Ask them for evidence that the assumptions are true.

▸ Try a change of venue. Role-play your issue as a court case. Take on the role of the advocating attorney and ask trusted colleagues to play the roles of judge, jury, opposing counsel, and journalist. Analyze your reasoning from each perspective. What constructive criticism can the group offer? Where do your arguments need fine-tuning or a different focus?

Recognize the broad implications of issues

▼

Leaders with strong analytical skills are able to see the big picture. They operate from a systems perspective and see a broad, long-term perspective rather than taking a narrow view or focusing only on short-term implications. To gain a broader perspective, consider the following suggestions:

▶ To understand an issue or opportunity, investigate the following:

▷ The business process in which it is nested.

▷ The purpose of that business process.

▷ The people involved—their roles and responsibilities for parts of that business process and the relationships among them.

▷ The goals of the people.

▶ Work with your team to identify all the stakeholders potentially involved in the issue.

Ask someone who has a reputation for seeing the big picture to discuss an issue and its implications with your team.

▶ Gather information from the different stakeholders. As you discuss the issue, probe beneath the surface; ask many open-ended questions.

▶ Define problems from the perspective of each stakeholder. If you are not able to talk to stakeholders directly, ask team members to put themselves in the role of those perspectives and explain the issues from their points of view, straightforwardly and without sarcasm.

▶ Listen carefully to understand the underlying issues. Link the information you receive so you can more fully grasp the issue and understand connections or interrelationships.

▶ Identify potential solutions or actions. In considering alternative actions, evaluate how they will affect each stakeholder and other parts of the process.

▶ Think about whether the action being considered will help you achieve your goals or those of the organization. Is it consistent with strategy? How will stakeholders react?

▸ Use your team and the stakeholders to determine what will be needed for the solution to work. What are the pitfalls? How can you anticipate potential problems?

▸ Communicate the decision, rationale, and plan to all who were involved in the process of identifying the issues.

Integrate information from a variety of sources to arrive at optimal solutions

▼

Remember how you felt when you first wrote term papers? You may feel the same sense of information overload after you research a problem. Having some guidelines can help you sort and integrate your information. Consider the following suggestions:

▸ Categorize the information into key issues and subissues. A key issue should be truly unique from other issues. Think of it as the top of a pyramid; there will be a lot of information underlying it, but the key issue will rise to the top.

▸ After you categorize your information, determine whether you have all the data you need for each category. What are you missing? What new questions do you need to pursue?

Ask people which information sources they used to research an issue. Ensure that these are useful and appropriate for the topic.

▸ Guard against identifying patterns and themes that don't truly exist. Check whether a trend or pattern is simply a short-term deviation.

▸ If you get caught up in details, revisit the purpose for your research. Focus on what you are trying to achieve, not on interesting details you may have discovered along the way.

▸ Make your synthesis meaningful and useful to other decision makers. Present your analysis and recommendations in a concise and clear format.

Define reasonable alternatives to resolve problems or make decisions

▼

Inquire about options that people considered regarding an issue, especially when you think they settled too quickly on an answer.

Generating several reasonable options will help you make more effective decisions. Involving other people in this process will give you more alternatives to choose from and give you additional buy-in for the decision or solution. Consider the following suggestions:

▸ Brainstorm possible solutions with others. Use idea-generating questions such as: If we had unlimited resources, what could we do? Technical limitations aside, what would be the best solution?

▸ When a team is generating ideas, intervene whenever team members begin to evaluate alternatives. Remind the group that the focus at the moment is to gather as many options as possible, not to critique them. You may have to say this more than once, but it's important because criticism of at this time can stop the flow of ideas.

▸ Think of alternatives that people in different areas of the company might generate. This approach will challenge you to understand the situation and try to find a solution that would work from their perspective.

▸ Talk to people who will give you divergent opinions about the issue. List each viewpoint, and beside it note the reasons the person gave for his or her opinion.

▸ List all the ideas for alternatives you have generated or received, noting the rationale behind each one. Discuss this list with your team members and debate the merits of each possibility.

2

Make Sound Decisions

Making sound decisions in a timely manner is a key skill for managers. What constitutes a sound decision? How do you know if you have all the necessary information and are involving the right people? Whether you make decisions alone or work collaboratively, learning how to break down the decision-making process into actionable steps can help you make better, more informed, and, ultimately, more accurate decisions that have a positive impact on your organization and the people you work with.

Too often, decisions are made hastily or based on emotion and personal assumptions. When managers take the time to involve the right people, think through issues from multiple perspectives, and use a logical, sequential approach, they increase the likelihood of making the right decision at the right time. Your ability to make sound decisions can increase your credibility and help you earn the trust of associates, key stakeholders, and direct reports.

In this chapter, we will cover the following areas:

▼

- ▸ Establish clear goals for decisions
- ▸ Determine criteria for decision making
- ▸ Gather the information you need to make decisions
- ▸ Analyze information in relation to decision-making criteria
- ▸ Take all important issues into account when making decisions
- ▸ Consider strategic issues in making decisions
- ▸ Base decisions on sound logic and rationale
- ▸ Make decisions in the face of uncertainty
- ▸ Curb impulsiveness in making decisions
- ▸ Take responsibility for your decisions
- ▸ Act decisively
- ▸ Choose the best alternative based on consideration of pros, cons, trade-offs, timing, and available resources
- ▸ Make timely decisions
- ▸ Make sound decisions on complex functional issues
- ▸ Seek appropriate input before making decisions
- ▸ Clarify decision-making responsibility and methods
- ▸ Test the practicality of decisions

Establish clear goals for decisions

▼

Remind those who are making decisions to determine the key goals for the outcome.

Before making any decision, you need to determine your goals. Obviously, you want to make the best decision, and to do that, you need to address several criteria that serve as the foundation for sound decision making. Consider the following suggestions:

▶ Recognize that sound decision making balances two types of needs. First, you need to consider whether you are making the right decision (the quality of the decision). Second, you need to know whether you can get commitment from people to implement the decision, even if they are not involved in the decision-making process.

▶ Ensure that you cover a range of decision-making criteria. For example:

▷ Simultaneously address both short- and long-term issues.

▷ Resolve issues in a way that the organization can afford.

▷ Resolve issues so that operations are not disturbed.

▷ Resolve issues so that those involved find the decision acceptable.

▷ Resolve issues or make decisions in such a way that relationships among the people involved are not harmed.

Determine criteria for decision making

▼

Discuss how the person determined which criteria were most important for a decision.

Sometimes the criteria on which a decision is based are obvious and people agree with them. Other times, people may have different criteria, and thus have different ideas about what constitutes the right decision. Consider the following suggestions:

▶ Recognize that a hallmark of sound decision making is clear criteria for making a decision.

▶ Before making a decision, determine criteria for evaluating the options. This is particularly important when a number of different constituents are involved.

▶ Recognize a range of criteria for decision making. The following are typical criteria:

▷ Has minimal impact on current operations.

▷ Is logically sound.

▷ Helps achieve important business priorities.

▷ Reflects business priorities.

▷ Is consistent with values.

▷ Is acceptable to those involved.

▷ Can be implemented within the constraints of the situation (time, resources, other priorities).

▷ Incorporates data analysis, intelligent speculation about the future, and related people concerns.

▷ Considers any and all pros, cons, and risks.

▶ Be aware of the type of involvement you will need from people to execute the decision. Sometimes leaders think only about the quality of the decision and forget about the support they will need to carry it out. Even though it may take some time to gain buy-in, it will save you time in the long run.

Gather the information you need to make decisions

▼

To make a sound decision, you first need to gather enough information from those involved and those who will be affected. Consider the following suggestions:

▶ Begin by assessing whether you have enough information to make the decision. Also consider whether others involved believe that you have the necessary information and whether they believe you should make the decision.

Ask people to share their plans for gathering information before they make a decision.

▶ People typically want to be involved in decisions that affect them. Even though you may be able to make a logical and sound decision yourself, whenever possible, involve those who believe they need to be involved in the decision-making process.

▶ Look at the issue from all points of view, so you can be certain that you are getting all of the relevant perspectives.

▶ Make sure to ask for and listen to people's concerns and preferences when you are gathering information; this helps build trust and shows you care. Build in their ideas when possible. After you make a decision, use active listening to hear people's reactions. Look for ways to show support for them personally even if you cannot support their preferences in your decision.

Analyze information in relation to decision-making criteria

▼

Help others to understand that people may want to be involved in defining a problem as well as in coming up with solutions.

Information is useful only if you analyze it in terms of the goals you've identified for your decision. Consider the following suggestions to ensure that you are appropriately analyzing and synthesizing information:

▶ Carefully identify, define, and review the issues.

▷ What is the problem or issue? Describe it in one clear sentence. State it in terms of a need rather than a solution.

▷ What important, critical facts are known?

▷ What is unknown? Who knows that information? How can it be determined or gathered?

▷ How do people feel about the situation and potentially changing it?

▷ What related problems are present? If something changes, what else is likely to change with it?

▷ What assumptions—about people, technology, systems, funding— have been made that might need to be challenged?

▶ Organize the information according to its relevance for each of your goals. For example, if one of your goals is to resolve the issue in a way that the organization can afford, then combine all the information you've gathered about costs and possible solutions so you can clearly see how it relates to your goal.

▶ Analyze the relevant information for each goal. For each goal, ask yourself:

▷ How does the information affect this goal? Does it support it or present obstacles?

▷ Do you have all the information you need to ensure that you meet this goal? If not, what do you need and how can you obtain it?

▷ How does the information give you new perspectives on this goal?

Take all important issues into account when making decisions

▼

As a manager, you need to study all relevant issues before making a decision. Consider the following suggestions:

▶ Consider whether you fully understand the current situation. It may be tempting to put the situation into a familiar category so you can use a familiar solution. Take care not to make erroneous assumptions.

▶ Categorize information into key issues and subissues. A key issue should be truly unique from other issues. Think of it as the top of a pyramid; there will be a lot of information underlying it, but the key issue will rise to the top.

Ask people to explain which issues are relevant and why. Remind them to seek input from people in other functions who could be affected by their decision.

▶ As you study a critical need, challenge yourself to identify patterns, trends, and themes. On the other hand, guard against identifying patterns that don't truly exist. Determine whether a trend or pattern is simply a short-term deviation.

▶ Draw on the expertise of people within and outside your organization. Ask questions and seek advice on important issues. Let them teach you; you will learn a great deal and develop stronger relationships.

▶ Don't rest on your laurels; continue to increase your knowledge. Learn more about your customers, the market, your organization, industry trends, and other issues. Set up a schedule for reading, take a class, or interview industry experts.

Consider strategic issues in making decisions

▼

Effective leaders have a vision, goals, and strategies for their part of the business. For strategic thinking to have impact, it must be integrated into daily activities. Consider the following suggestions:

Encourage the person to obtain input from key stakeholders on how this issue intersects with the organization's strategic plan.

▶ When you're making a decision, always look at both short- and long-term consequences.

▶ Ask for feedback from others about whether you make decisions inconsistent with strategic priorities.

▶ There may be times when you feel compelled to focus on short-term priorities at the expense of strategic priorities. Consult your manager or more experienced leaders on how you can address short-term issues in a way that won't hurt strategic initiatives or make them more difficult to carry out.

Base decisions on sound logic and rationale

▼

Have the person take you through the logic behind a decision, and together look for leaps or gaps.

Good decisions are based on sound logic, and people are more comfortable with a decision when they understand why it was made. Consider the following suggestions:

▶ Carefully identify and define the issue. This is central to getting the right decision. For example, if you define an issue as a customer service problem, you will probably look to customer service to fix it. However, if the problem actually involves a lack of understanding of the client's need, customer service won't be able to solve it.

▶ Define the issue in a number of ways. In a group meeting, use a flip chart and list the different ways in which the issue can be viewed. Look at it from each definition. This will give you a better understanding of the issues.

▶ Ask questions that begin with *who, what, where, when, why,* and *how.* Who is involved? What is occurring? Where is it taking place? When did it occur? Why is it happening? How are people addressing it?

▶ Identify your assumptions regarding the issue. Test whether each assumption is valid before you make a decision.

▶ If you use a model to structure your thinking, be aware of its flaws and biases. Try using more than one model on difficult issues to uncover new perspectives.

▶ Be careful not to manufacture or magnify information to support your conclusions. Test your conclusions by inviting a colleague to be a skeptic and ask targeted questions.

▶ Evaluate the pros and cons of your options. Weigh each option in terms of meeting the need, and in terms of the acceptance and support of those who will implement the solution.

▸ Discuss your options with your team. Encourage each person to point out potential errors in reasoning.

▸ Ask trusted colleagues to evaluate your analysis skills. Ask for examples of when you used solid analysis skills and when you did not. Also ask them to differentiate between errors in logic versus an inadequate explanation of your reasoning.

Make decisions in the face of uncertainty

▼

Because uncertainty is always present, every decision involves an element of risk. The ability to recognize and take calculated risks is a skill required of all managers. Consider the following suggestions:

▸ Determine whether information is missing. Identify who can provide missing information and how quickly.

▸ Assess the risk of making, delaying, or not making a decision.

Discuss the risk factors involved in the decision and how they can be managed.

▸ Figure out how to mitigate the risks of a decision. Develop contingency plans for the risks you know, and decide who you will consult if you encounter unexpected risks.

▸ Determine how you will know a wrong decision. For example, other people doubt that it will work, people won't carry out the decision, unintended negative consequences occur, or you discover that you hadn't thought about some aspect of the decision.

▸ Analyze your implementation process and determine the points at which it could be halted—the "go/no go" decision points. Inform others of these points so they will not be surprised if you decide to discontinue the process. If the risk becomes too great, stop at one of these points.

▸ Talk with others about how they account for risk factors in their decisions, and study the way they make decisions. Then apply what you have learned to your own decision-making process.

▸ You may feel uneasy about the level of risk because you haven't clearly identified the pros and cons of each alternative. List each alternative and its associated risks and benefits. Then choose the one that provides the greatest benefit along with an acceptable level of risk. Manage the risk by anticipating problems, planning for contingencies, and dealing with problems as they arise.

▶ Ask yourself, "What is the worst thing that could happen as a result of this decision? How much impact could this 'worst thing' have on me personally, on the organization, or on the work?" Determine what you could do if the worst-case scenario occurred.

Curb impulsiveness in making decisions

▼

If you often make decisions and later have to backtrack, or if you realize you should have waited until you had more information, you're probably making decisions too quickly. This can lead to wasted time and effort, diminished effectiveness, and reduced productivity. Knowing the reasons for your tendency to rush can help you avoid it. Consider the following suggestions:

▶ Understand whether the issue is about information. Do you make rapid decisions because you believe that you have the necessary information, only to find out that you acted prematurely?

▶ Do you value quick action at the expense of working more methodically through an issue? If so, create a plan that will efficiently lead you through the decision-making process and clearly result in action. Identify who will be involved in the decision-making process, the types of information you will need, the criteria you will use to judge solutions, and a time frame for action.

Discuss what needs to occur before the person can make an informed decision.

▶ When you feel pressured into making decisions that you are not ready to make, learn to "buy time." If possible, tell the person applying pressure that you need more time and why; name a date by which you will announce your decision.

▶ You may find that it is not feasible to get enough data within a specified time. The best option may be to postpone the decision if the consequences of making an imperfect decision would be worse for the organization and the people involved than making the decision too early.

▸ Although feelings are an important consideration, determine whether your decision-making process is driven too frequently by emotion. For instance, do you make choices when you are upset or angry? Next time, wait until you calm down. You can then judge better whether the decision is truly the best one or simply one that felt right at the time.

Take responsibility for your decisions

▼

Give examples of decisions you made that you had to fix later because of unintended consequences.

Sometimes leaders have difficulty accepting responsibility for the decisions they make or need to make. If they are defensive, people may perceive them to be unwilling to accept responsibility. Consider the following suggestions:

▸ Recognize that people expect you to be responsible for your decisions. When people question your decisions, resist explaining the reasons for them; explaining makes you appear defensive. Instead, listen to others' concerns and summarize what you hear.

▸ If you find that one of your decisions was wrong, deal with the consequences as well and as quickly as you can.

▸ Assess whether you have a history of blaming others. If so, practice accepting responsibility for your part in making a decision. Resist saying "They gave me the wrong information" or "No one told me" or "It wasn't my fault."

Act decisively

▼

It is important to make decisions when they need to be made. Indecisiveness may result in the perception that you cannot make tough choices or take a stand on issues. Consider the following suggestions to increase your decisiveness:

▸ Analyze your concerns about making decisions; find common patterns. For example, you may be uncomfortable making decisions involving technical areas with which you are unfamiliar, or you may delay making decisions on issues important to your manager.

▶ Consider whether any of the following indecisive behaviors apply to you. Then try the suggested action to become more decisive.

▷ If you have difficulty determining which of several alternatives is best, don't go to others for a decision. Instead, challenge yourself to choose one of the options and develop a rationale for why that alternative is best. Then seek input: describe the alternatives you've identified and your recommendation, and ask for opinions.

▷ If you turn to others immediately before you've formulated options, ask yourself why. For example, you may believe that you don't have enough information and you don't have time to find it, or you're not sure where to start.

▷ If you tend to procrastinate, set a deadline for making a major decision. For minor decisions, make your judgments within a few minutes.

▷ If you have a tendency to second-guess yourself, stand by your decision once you have made it. Avoid reopening the decision-making process unless new information strongly indicates that you should.

▷ If you tend to push your decision-making responsibilities upward, get into the habit of presenting recommendations, rather than problems, to your manager.

Have the person set a firm deadline for making a decision. Focus on best, not perfect.

▷ If you use tentative language in describing your ideas, other people may view you as indecisive. Get a better sense of how you come across. Tape-record yourself as you state your decisions. Also get feedback from others on the style you use to communicate your ideas.

▷ If you are concerned that taking a stand will cause others to dislike you, remind yourself that it is impossible for everyone to like you and that even if people don't like you, they may like your ideas. Likewise, accept that when people reject your ideas, they are not rejecting you.

▷ If you look for approval before implementing your decisions, ask yourself whether it is really necessary. Constantly seeking approval can give others the impression that you lack confidence.

▷ If you are unclear about when you can make decisions independently, meet with your manager to discuss your span of control—where you can make decisions independently and where you need to seek approval.

Choose the best alternative based on consideration of pros, cons, trade-offs, timing, and available resources

▼

Ask the person to make a comparison grid showing the pros, cons, and trade-offs of each alternative.

Successful leaders choose from alternatives that have the greatest impact by evaluating the costs, risks, and benefits. Consider the following suggestions:

▸ Generate several alternatives by brainstorming with others, by considering how colleagues have solved similar problems, and by asking questions such as "If we had unlimited resources, what would we do?" and "If technical issues were not an issue, what could be done?" Think creatively and then evaluate your alternatives against what's workable.

▸ Determine the fundamental assumptions underlying each alternative you're considering and whether the assumptions are valid. Assumptions might include: Our large customers will continue to buy from us; We'll have adequate materials for manufacturing; Consumers will rapidly adopt our new product.

▸ Involve your team and financial support people in determining the pros and cons of alternatives. Using the chart below, list strategic criteria, financial considerations, trade-offs, available resources, and the impact on other initiatives. Share these criteria with everyone in your area.

Alternative	Pros	Cons	Who Will Support It	Who Will Resist It
(1)				
(2)				
(3)				

▸ Conduct a sensitivity analysis. Select some key data, alter them, and determine the impact that changing those factors would have. For example, what if sales volumes were 10 percent lower than your best estimate? What if they were 30 percent lower? Work through some best- and worst-case scenarios.

▸ Use a variety of data sources (internal and external, industry-specific and general business) to research your decisions. When it is practical, increase your accuracy by obtaining the same information from two or more independent sources.

▸ If you receive conflicting information, ask probing questions to evaluate the accuracy, underlying assumptions, and reliability of your sources and the information.

▸ Identify items that are most prone to estimation errors and seek ways to reduce this risk. You may want to use alternative estimation methods such as consensus estimates from experts or trend analysis.

▸ Ask which assumptions and estimates are "solid" and which are "soft." For each soft item, consider how much the actual numbers could differ from your estimates.

▸ When you are faced with substantial uncertainty, look for ways to keep your options open without sacrificing potential returns. Avoid being indecisive; take calculated risks when necessary.

Make timely decisions

▼

When leaders do not make timely decisions, they miss deadlines, hold up projects, waste resources, and frustrate people who are counting on them. Some leaders procrastinate because they want to be absolutely sure they collect enough information; others, concerned about being right, spend a lot of time analyzing information. Although the intent is positive, the result can be missed market opportunities, lower morale and motivation, or other negatives. Consider the following suggestions:

► Avoid "analysis paralysis." Understand the urgency of the situation and set a deadline for analyzing your information. Prioritize your greatest concerns and spend your time on those issues.

► Ask yourself:
  ▷ What information is absolutely necessary?
  ▷ What additional information could be collected? How long would it take?
  ▷ What information would make me feel better, but probably would not cause me to change my decision?

► Rather than insisting on certainty before you make the decision—which is likely to be impossible in any case—anticipate possible problems and plan for contingencies.

► Once you've made a decision, stand by it. Reconsider your decision only if new information drastically changes your analysis.

Ask for a description of the consequences of a delayed decision, adding any the person missed.

Most people do not procrastinate every time they make a decision; rather, they tend to delay decisions under certain circumstances. It's useful to identify those circumstances and determine how you can handle them in the future. Consider the following suggestions:

► Each time you find yourself delaying a decision, pinpoint the reason for the delay.

► Once you've determined why you procrastinate, look for a solution. For example:
  ▷ When a course of action is unclear, choose what appears to be the best plan and implement it on a temporary basis.
  ▷ If you lack sufficient time for focused, concentrated thought, block out time on your schedule.
  ▷ If you fear negative reactions, face your fears. Seek the involvement of those you believe would resist your decision.

Make sound decisions on complex functional issues

▼

When you deal with complex issues, you need to think about how a decision made in one area will affect all groups within the organization. You need to sort through opinions and facts, determine what information has merit, and understand the impact on the organization. Consider the following suggestions:

Ensure that the individual identifies not only the right functional issues, but also the right questions about those issues.

▶ Work with your team to identify all the stakeholders potentially involved in the issue. Gather information from each stakeholder group. As you discuss the issue, ask open-ended questions and clarify any murky issues.

▶ Define problems from the perspective of each stakeholder. If you are not able to talk to the stakeholders directly, ask team members to put themselves in those roles and explain the issues from their perspectives.

▶ Identify underlying issues. Gather a small group of people and list issues on a white board or flip chart. Then draw lines between connected items. This can help you see hidden or subtle connections.

▶ Identify the work processes that are involved in a problem or opportunity. Illustrate the process with a flow chart or Gannt Chart— whatever will help you see all the pieces.

▶ When you spot an opportunity, look at it from a systems perspective.
  ▷ What is the opportunity?
  ▷ Who needs to be involved?
  ▷ Who is affected?
  ▷ What business processes are needed for the opportunity to achieve its potential?
  ▷ What are the obstacles to success?

▶ Identify potential solutions or actions. As you consider your options, evaluate how each action would affect other parts of the organization.

▶ Think about whether the action being considered will help you achieve your goals or those of the organization. Is it consistent with strategy? How will stakeholders react?

- Use your team and the stakeholders to determine what will be needed for the solution to work. What are the pitfalls? How can you anticipate potential problems?

- Communicate the decision, rationale, and plan to everyone involved in the process. E-mail or blog regular updates as you implement the decision. Establish an online forum where people can post their questions and concerns.

- Make sure that you are basing your decisions on adequate information. Your decision should take into account:
  ▷ All relevant facts and issues
  ▷ A solid understanding of the business and its priorities
  ▷ Analysis of hard data
  ▷ The pros and cons of alternatives
  ▷ The input of people who are necessary to the process

Seek appropriate input before making decisions

▼

A collaborative approach to decision making often produces the best results because so many perspectives and ideas are considered. In addition, those involved in making the decision are more likely to be committed to carrying it out. Thus, the increased time required in the decision-making process is often regained during the implementation phase.

Talk about whom people are involving in the decision-making process and why.

Group decision making is not appropriate or necessary when decisions need to be made immediately, when the issue is confidential, or when buy-in is assured. The following steps will help you identify appropriate situations for collaborative decision making and ways to get others involved in the process:

- When you first learn that a decision must be made, determine if the decision is solely your own or if it requires input from others. Collaborative decision making is useful when:
  ▷ Other people have information you need.
  ▷ The problem is complex or ambiguous, and you need other people to clarify and define it.

▷ Other people are needed to implement the decision, and they want to be involved.

▷ The situation can be used to train other people in problem analysis or decision making.

▶ If you determine that the decision should be made collaboratively, use the group to define the problem, determine criteria for making the decision, look for alternatives, and/or actually make the decision. The group may be the same for each phase of the process, or you may want to use a larger group for getting input and a smaller group for making the decision.

▶ When you are using a collaborative approach to decision making, keep the following in mind:

▷ Involve others in the process by talking with them one-on-one, e-mailing them for input, chatting online in work groups, or calling for an on-site or virtual meeting.

▷ You can effectively make collaborative decisions during well-run meetings, especially when participants are informed of the issues in advance.

▷ Use consensus decision making, rather than taking the majority view. Ask the group to consider "Can I live with this?" rather than "Do I like this?"

Clarify decision-making responsibility and methods

Inaction often results when it is unclear who is responsible for making a decision. When a decision involves new areas, people may be especially uncertain about who has the authority to make it. To help clarify who is responsible for making a decision, consider the following suggestions:

▶ Talk to your manager to confirm his or her view of who should make the decision, how, and via what process.

▶ If the decision is yours to make, develop an action plan.

▷ If you have all the necessary information, and those involved will commit to a decision if you make it, then simply make the decision.

▷ If you need more information and/or the involvement of others for commitment, set up a process that appropriately involves people.

▷ Involve not only the people whose information or commitment you need, but, whenever possible, also those who believe they should be involved.

▶ If you establish a decision-making team, use the following steps to ensure that you reach the best decision:

1. Enlist the group's help to determine what is known and what needs to be known in order to make a sound decision. This effort will encourage others to step forward and allow them to practice leadership skills and gain experience. Make sure the group stays on track and distinguishes between information that is truly necessary and important, and what is merely good to know.

2. Once you have obtained the necessary information, use it to redefine the problem or opportunity as clearly as possible. You may decide to have multiple definitions.

3. Before making any decisions, generate multiple alternatives. Look for those that satisfy the multiple facets of the problem.

4. Together with the other group members and stakeholders, develop criteria for evaluating alternatives and selecting the best solution.

5. Make the decision.

6. Develop contingency plans in case the solution doesn't work out.

Talk with people about when they should make a decision themselves, consult with others first, make a decision with others, or let others make a decision.

Test the practicality of decisions

▼

Alternatives might look good on paper and initially sound feasible but turn out to be impractical, difficult to implement, or ineffective. Here are several ways to test your decisions to increase their probability of success:

▶ Get into the habit of asking at each stage of the decision-making process whether the decision is workable. Consider the specifics of your situation. Think through possible results of the decision to ensure that you've covered all your bases. Identify potential problems and plan ways to deal with them.

▸ Before making your final decision, ask those who will be affected to assess the practicality of the decision, the impact of the decision on them, and whether they would be likely to accept it. Remember to consider people in other units who might be affected by the changes you initiate. These people can be as instrumental in determining the success of your plan as those within your own group.

Ask people to check in with the people who will carry out the decision and confirm the feasibility of the plan.

▸ Because many good decisions fail in the implementation phase, be sure to develop a sound, specific plan that details the correct sequence of steps and assigns responsibility for the success of each step. Get input from all groups or departments that will be affected. If you understand how best to implement the change from their points of view, you will increase the likelihood that they will accept and support your plan.

▸ Despite careful analysis and planning, a seemingly sound solution sometimes proves to be unworkable. In such cases, you need to be flexible and adapt your decision to eliminate efforts that are not working out. Be aware of this, and don't let these situations hinder your future efforts to choose and implement the best solutions.

3

Act Strategically

Strategy is the key foundation for organizational success. Financial markets, customer needs, competitive threats, breakthrough technology, new markets, process innovation—all have an impact on strategy. As a manager, you need to stay on top of your organization's short- and long-term strategies and, in turn, to formulate effective strategies for your business unit or function. You play a direct role in determining how your area of the business can achieve its objectives in the most effective possible manner.

It's vital that you learn not only how to think strategically, but also how to act and react so that your daily decisions consistently align with your organization's overall strategy.

In this chapter, we will cover the following areas:

▼

- ▶ Demonstrate understanding of key industry, market, resource, technology, and regulatory trends and conditions and their implications for the business

- ▶ Have a historical perspective about the industry, its growth, and its trends

- ▶ Have a deep understanding of your customer value proposition

- ▶ Know your target customers well

- ▶ Understand current and future customer needs

- ▶ Identify issues related to emerging customer and market needs

- ▶ Understand needs of your customer's customers

- ▶ Know the strengths and weaknesses of competitors

- ▶ Spot potential competitors and threats to your market position

- ▶ Stay abreast of key competitor actions and their implications for or threats to the business

- ▶ Identify competitive differentiators

- ▶ Bring cross-disciplinary knowledge to bear on issues and opportunities

- ▶ Understand the organization's mission, strategies, strengths, and weaknesses

- ▶ Understand the role you and your area play in the success of the business

- ▶ Convey a thorough understanding of your area's strengths, weaknesses, opportunities, and threats

- ▶ Develop a vision and strategy for your group consistent with its role in the success of the organization

- ▶ Integrate organizational strategies to achieve and sustain competitive advantage

- ▶ Pursue initiatives to capitalize on strengths and market opportunities, and to counter competitive threats

- ▶ Identify the business processes that are key to the success of the strategy

- ▸ Know the pivotal roles necessary to execute the strategy
- ▸ Ensure that initiatives and priorities are integrated with one another and aligned with the direction and strategic priorities of the broader organization
- ▸ Create measures that accurately reflect the success of the strategy and execution of the processes needed to drive it
- ▸ Evaluate and pursue initiatives, investments, and opportunities based on their fit with broader strategies
- ▸ Create strategies to balance short-term requirements with long-range business plans

Demonstrate understanding of key industry, market, resource, technology, and regulatory trends and conditions and their implications for the business

Discuss the top three changes that occurred in your industry over the past year.

Your business operates in a dynamic environment that has an impact on you—and, in turn, you can influence this environment. Whether your market position allows you to shape the environment or requires you to work within it, you need a thorough understanding of the forces that affect your organization now and those that may influence it in the future. Consider the following suggestions:

▸ Identify the external factors—industry trends, existing and new competitors, customer requirements and expectations, technology, governmental policies and practices, global and local trends, availability of resources—that most affect your organization.

▸ Chart industry context by examining the following:

  ▷ *Growth of the industry.* What is the rate of change? What drives change in the industry?

  ▷ *Bargaining power.* Look at the relationships between suppliers and buyers. Which are the most constrained? What bargaining power does each have? For example:

    – Single vendors have more power than multiple vendors because the organization is reliant on the single vendor.

    – In a commoditized industry, buyers have a lot of power because they can choose among many vendors. Price is the most important consideration until someone offers a differentiated product.

  ▷ *Labor force issues.* How available is the right talent? What are the collective bargaining trends?

    – Lack of talent may be a serious constraint to growth.

    – Bargaining agreements might be up for negotiation.

  ▷ *Competitive threats.* Who are the competitors now? Who are the potential competitors? Are substitutes for your product or service available?

  ▷ *Government regulations.* What government regulations—both in and outside the home country—affect the industry?

  ▷ *Other strategic issues.*

- Systematically track external factors and changes in them. Regularly review what you know.

- Challenge your assumptions that you know enough, that your sources of information are adequate, that you are listening to your market information, and that you are collecting the correct data.

- Keep track of internal factors and conditions that are critical to success of the strategy. For example, note changes in leadership, quality, retention, and work processes. What impact are they having or might they have on execution? For instance, more turnover requires more training, and you may need clearer work processes. In a customer-intimate model in which your relationship with customers is key, retention of employees is a critical success factor. High turnover does not allow you deep relationships with customers.

- Continually do environmental scans to ensure that you are picking up signs of change in the marketplace. Closely watch what your competitors are doing and listen to what your customers are saying. Study your customers' customers as carefully as you study your own.

- Identify the assumptions—customers will remain the same, no new competitors will come into the market, turnover will stay the same, yours is the best way to meet the customer's need—upon which your strategy relies. Now figure out how those assumptions could be wrong. (Right now, one of your competitors is likely to be finding a way to remove an assumed constraint.)

- Based on the competitive analysis, identify areas in which you are vulnerable. For example, if you know that your competitors are investing heavily in technology and you are not, you may soon be in trouble. If you are a knowledge-based business, your greatest threat may be that you don't have the people you need with the necessary skills.

- Conduct customer reviews to gather information about their requirements, anticipated changes in their requirements, their perception of your organization, their perception of competitors, and their recommendations for improvement.

- Identify factors that are broader than those you typically consider. For example, if you typically focus on your part of the organization, look at what is happening in the region, your section of the industry, and the industry as a whole.

▶ Gather information from multiple sources. Don't rely on a single source or allow yourself to be overly influenced by startling findings. Read national, regional, and local newspapers and magazines, trade and industry publications, general business publications, Web sites, blogs, white papers, books; listen to podcasts and attend webinars by industry experts. How are your sources of information about the industry and the marketplace limited? Perhaps you have information from geographic areas that were your source of growth in the past, but where you do not anticipate growth. Is your customer base aging, or are demographics changing in some other way?

▶ Challenge others to identify what you might be missing or assumptions that are dangerous to make without sufficient analysis and questioning.

▶ As you look at information from other cultures, be aware of who is analyzing its meaning. Ensure that people who know the culture are telling you what it means.

▶ Network with other leaders in your city and region. Pay attention to what is happening in their industries and discuss factors they are watching.

Have a historical perspective about the industry, its growth, and its trends

▼

An industry's history can help you understand some critical issues that often continue to influence matters today and perhaps in the future. For example, consider fresh food in markets. The size of stores, the cost of energy, the amount of room for refrigeration, and shoppers' income levels have influenced and will continue to influence number, variety, and packaging of products. Consider the following suggestions:

Discuss how the industry, competitors, and trends have affected your business over the past decade.

▶ Talk with people in the organization and the industry to find out what they know about their history. Ask:

▷ How and why did this industry or company get started?

▷ What problem was it solving or need was it addressing?

▷ How has the industry or company changed over time?

▷ What contributed most to change?

> ▷ Who were the important people in the history of the industry or company?

> ▷ How have needs changed over time?

> ▷ What have been the important industry or company lessons?

> ▷ What was the biggest impact on the business over the past two years?

> ▷ Which of the industry's greatest challenges or problems have not been fixed yet?

> ▷ What one problem or opportunity could be solved that would dramatically increase the success and growth of the industry?

▶ Find the organization's historian—someone who has been associated with the organization for a long time and knows a lot of history. Sometimes this is a formal role, but more often it is an informal one. People in HR or communications may know who these people are because they tap their knowledge.

▶ Reflect on historical information and discuss it with your team. Ask yourselves:

> ▷ What have we learned that has an impact on us today?

> ▷ What important lessons were learned or should have been learned by an individual or the organization?

> ▷ What does history tell us about the future?

Have a deep understanding of your customer value proposition

Ask people to explain how your organization adds value to your customers. Discuss what is required to build deep knowledge of customers.

Your customer value proposition is at the heart of your organization's strategy. It answers the question of what value you provide to your customers. Therefore, it is critical to understand who your customers are, who your best customers are, and what value you provide to each customer segment. Consider the following suggestions:

▶ Understand the value you provide to customer segments by understanding their needs, how they use your products or services, and the value your products or services provide to your customers' customers. Your marketing group should have this information, or talk with customers yourself.

▸ Define customer segments by looking at what different customers have in common:

　▷ The benefits or value they want, or their relationship to the organization.

　▷ Use intensity, value sought, loyalty, or attitude (often used for business to business).

　▷ Demographics, geography, or lifestyle (especially in consumer markets).

▸ Identify and understand what is believed to be the sustainable, competitive advantage to customer segments. Remember that you are looking for elements of value or differentiators that cannot easily be duplicated or replaced, or for which your customers cannot find a substitute.

　▷ Ask your customers what they value in your products or services and whether anyone else offers anything of similar value.

　▷ Ask your customers to differentiate you from your competitors and to compare your competitors with one another.

▸ Challenge your organization to identify flaws in your knowledge or logic that may threaten your assumptions of how much value you create, how sustainable your advantage really is, and how loyal your customers will be when they are presented with a competing value proposition. It is easy to be lulled into complacency and get blindsided by a smart or unexpected competitor.

▸ In your own area—a support group in the organization or a group directly providing value, such as customer service or manufacturing—identify the work processes that deliver the value of your group to the customer. How you extract the value from internal business processes and how much value you can generate determines whether you are able to add value for the customer. For example, if you promise to be a low-cost provider but your costs continue to increase, you will be unable to deliver on your value proposition.

Know your target customers well

▼

Organizations are more successful when they identify target customers—the primary customers they want. They are the customers who value what you can provide; the customers you can satisfy, retain, and grow; and the customers who are profitable to your organization. Consider the following suggestions:

▸ Talk with your marketing or sales group about your high-value customers and your target customers.

Ask people to identify the best customers in your industry and discuss why they're considered the best.

▸ Find out how high value is defined. High value is usually based on, but is not limited to, profitability. Some customers may be high value because they are market leaders and will attract other organizations to use your organization's products or services. Others may be high value because of the volume of business they do at acceptable margins. Figure out how to retain and grow high-value customers.

▸ Identify customers you want to target based on research on current customers, your strategy, and your competitive differentiators. Include customers who would value your services or products, whose future needs map closely with the value you intend to provide in the future, who are profitable, who have potential for growth, and who can help you get more customers.

▸ For all targets, create customer portraits: the customer's business, its goals and strategies, its challenges, needs, customers, and key people. Understand the criteria target customers use to select services and products.

Understand current and future customer needs

▼

As you consider strategy, understand both current and future customer needs. Future needs affect your future strategy. From a strategic standpoint, you want to deliver value to customers over the long term. It is much easier to grow the business you do with current clients than to get new ones, so stay close to customer needs and anticipate future ones. Consider the following suggestions:

Ask the person to pick a top customer and track how the customer's industry has changed. Discuss what is likely to happen next.

▸ Understand your customers by talking with them:

Your Customers
What are their needs now?
How do they anticipate that their needs will change?
What are the key drivers of their decisions today?
What do they anticipate will be the key drivers in future decisions?
How will technology change the industry?
In what ways are their customers changing? What is happening in their industry and in their customers' industries? How will this affect their requirements of you?
How do your customers view your competitors? What are your competitors' strengths?
How do they compare the value you provide to the value provided by your competitors?
From your customer's point of view, how could you add value or help them improve?
What do your customers wish you could do?

▶ Continue to explore with your customers the value you provide. Listen carefully so that you hear what they say rather than what you expect or want to hear.

▸ In addition to gathering information from your customers, talk to people outside your company and pay attention to their interpretations. Consider their perspectives when you plan future strategy.

▸ See your products or services in action. Talk with people who use them. Get suggestions for improvement.

▸ Attend industry and professional conferences, webinars, and teleseminars; listen to podcasts; create a Google alert; add your customers' blogs to your reader (e.g., Bloglines) to learn about their issues, plans, and concerns.

▸ Gather information from people who deal with customers. Ensure that customer feedback and evaluations are used throughout the organization. Ask how customer feedback has influenced decisions; groups that are paying attention to customers should have an answer to that question.

Identify issues related to emerging customer and market needs

▽

As you analyze internal and external trends, review current and future customer needs, and look closely at your customer value proposition and current business strategy, you will discover emerging customer and market needs and issues associated with them. Consider the following suggestions:

Encourage the person to read articles and listen to podcasts of trend watchers. Discuss what the person is learning and how it could affect your customers.

▸ Focus energy on understanding emerging customer and market needs and their implications.

▷ Get information from sales and marketing, or analyze your part of the business yourself.

▷ If other people are gathering information, look at the questions they plan to ask and the information they're looking for so that you know the strength and depth of the information you will receive. Find out who will conduct interviews and assure yourself that that person has the knowledge and skills to get the information you need. You need to be comfortable with the process and the people doing it so you will trust the analysis.

- ▶ Examine the impact of customer needs on your current value proposition. Will you continue to have value, increase in value, or decrease in value? Ask:
  - ▷ How do emerging needs affect the value the customer perceives in your service or product?
  - ▷ Will emerging needs change priorities for your customers, so that you no longer provide value to their most pressing needs? A customer segment may have valued one-stop shopping but now prefers to spread purchasing across many vendors. Your value proposition of easy to buy, one-stop shopping may no longer have value.
  - ▷ Will emerging needs add value to your differentiation, or will they diminish it in some way? A customer may have valued your product because it uses a particular technology. Now the customer has changed to a new technology platform. What happens to the competitive value you provide? In this example, it probably decreases.
  - ▷ How do changes in the marketplace affect the value you can provide? For example, a customer in a tight financial situation may decide a 70 percent solution is good enough or may be satisfied with a less costly solution than you provide.
- ▶ If changes mean a threat to your competitive advantage, you will need to determine how to sustain your competitive advantage or create new differentiation:
  - ▷ Use the information you gathered about customer needs and market trends.
  - ▷ Gather information about competitors and their plans.
  - ▷ Systematically work through customer needs and the potential value you can provide.
  - ▷ Test your assumptions about value and sustainable advantage to ensure that you have a customer strategy that will last.

Understand needs of your customer's customers

▼

In the business-to-business market, it is helpful to stay on top of customers' needs by understanding how your product or service fits into their value chain.

▸ Do your customers use your service or product in their own organizations, or it is part of a product or service they provide to *their* customers?

▸ What is the impact on your customers if your product or service does not meet their requirements? Does it mean that they cannot meet their customers' needs? How much down time does it mean for them?

Encourage people to take their team to a customer site to see their products and services in action.

▸ Understand each requirement in order to understand why each is a priority and the consequences of not meeting needs.

▸ Go see your product or service in operation at your customers' sites or at their customers' sites. Most customers appreciate vendors who want to understand how to meet needs and improve products and services, and are therefore willing to provide access.

▸ What are the consequences for your customers if they do not meet their customers' requirements? A heavy financial penalty for a missed deadline? Parts rendered unusable by deviations from requirements?

▸ Ask your customers what needs they are meeting for their customers. Also find out other ways those needs are being met. For example, how do their competitors meet those needs? You may discover new ways to meet your customers' needs that you have not yet considered.

Know the strengths and weaknesses of competitors

▼

Thoroughly understanding your competitors is a fundamental business practice. This is a challenge for organizations that focus internally rather than externally. Your competitors' value propositions, their strengths and weaknesses, their rate of improvement, and their strategies for growth are all critical and can have a considerable impact on your strategy and your sense of urgency. Consider the following suggestions:

▸ Determine who your competitors are.

Ask people to research the company's top five competitors and report a summary of the competitors' key strengths and weaknesses.

▷ Ask sales and marketing who your competitors are.

▷ Ask your customers who your most challenging competitors are and why.

▷ In which markets do your competitors play? In which do they dominate?

▷ Who are the competitors in the geographic areas in which you sell or plan to sell? Are they local companies or global companies?

▶ To analyze value propositions and strengths and weaknesses of competitors, determine how players in the industry differentiate themselves. Each industry has somewhat different elements of differentiation.

▷ Porter's general dimensions of differentiation include differentiated versus low-cost, and focused versus broad.

▷ Treacy and Wiersma use customer intimacy, product leadership, and operational excellence.

▶ List your competitors and identify how they compare with one another on these dimensions of differentiation.

▷ In which areas are your competitors strongest?

▷ In which areas are they vulnerable?

▶ Assess your information about the strengths and weaknesses of your competitors and how your organization stacks up.

▷ What are the major differences among your competitors in terms of their strengths and weaknesses?

▷ Which activities give your competitors a key advantage?

▷ What are your competitors' unique products or selling angles?

▷ Do your competitors dominate a certain market segment?

▶ Based on this information, decide what you believe your competitors' value propositions are and what their competitive strategies probably are. Go to their Web sites. If there is a strong alignment between value proposition and Web site, you should be able to see the value proposition in action. It also should be reflected in the information you gleaned from customer interviews.

▸ Review your own and your competitors' value chains by answering the following questions:

▹ How do our products and services compare with our competitors'? What are our strengths and weaknesses?

▹ What activities and processes give us a competitive advantage? What do we have or do that is special and cannot easily be duplicated?

▹ What activities and processes give our competitors an advantage?

▸ Pay attention to media coverage about your competitors. Comb the articles for information about their plans and strategies and learn more about their customers, potential customers, suppliers, and vendors.

▸ Ask your customers how they view your competitors. Although it may be painful to ask, it is critical to know. Find out what your customers think your competitors do better.

▸ If you are invited to supplier or vendor events, go. This builds your relationships with your customers and also allows you to see whom they are doing business with.

Spot potential competitors and threats to your market position

▼

Challenge people by asking, "What actions could our competitors take to hurt us and our plans?"

The competitors you need to fear the most are the ones you don't see. Successful managers look for potential competitors; they don't limit their competitive analyses to current and known competitors. Competitors who redefine the business in some significant way pose the biggest threats. They often are not even from the same industry as you are. Consider the following suggestions:

▸ Learn who is talking to your customers about their needs. Salespeople and customer service people may not always realize the value of the information they hear.

▹ Notice salespeople in your customer's lobby or offices. Casually ask who they are and whom they are calling on. Find out whether your customer knows them.

▹ If a customer mentions that he or she met with a competitor, find out what they talked about and what your customer liked about what the competitor had to offer. Use this as a time to gather information, not defend your organization.

▸ If you are asked to respond to a request for proposal (RFP), ask who else received the RFP and why they were chosen. Pay special attention to unexpected organizations and find out why they are on the list.

▸ Ensure that your technical experts and professionals attend conferences within and outside of your own country in order to stay intellectually competitive and know what is going on in the profession and the industry. Your home country may not be the most up to date.

▸ Challenge teams working on strategy to identify potentially competitive industries, technology, and methods. For example, look at how Apple turned the traditional music industry upside down. Discuss how the oil and gas industry might be changed by the entry of alternative energy competitors. Now determine who could change your industry.

▸ Identify potential competitors by listing the "givens" in an industry might be changed. What factors are taken for granted in the industry? What would happen if they were no longer givens? For example, if there were no compliance issues with medication, how would that affect health care businesses?

▸ Guard against the ethnocentric assumption that innovation comes only from your own or a few countries. Note that advances in technology and business processes are coming from all over the world.

Stay abreast of key competitor actions and their implications for or threats to the business

▼

Competitors do not stand still—and they may move faster than your organization. To stay ahead of the competition, take off the blinders and learn about your competitive environment and your vulnerability:

▸ Pay attention to what your competitors are doing in the marketplace. Investigate:

▷ *Financial health.*

> *Velocity:* how fast the competitor is growing, changing, or improving. Make sure that you spot increased velocity in these areas:
>   – Market growth and new clients.
>   – New geographic areas or new businesses.
>   – Introduction and success of new services and products.
> *Messages to the markets* (if the company is publicly traded).
> *Internal messages.*
> *Web sites:* a great source of quarterly market reports and other public information.
> *Changes in leadership and implications of the changes.* For example, did a cost-cutting expert assume leadership, or was it someone known for growth?
> *Hiring patterns.* For what roles are they hiring? Is this because of retention problems, expansion, or a change in strategy?
> *Large purchases.* Did your competitor just acquire part of the value chain that previously was outsourced?
> *Media coverage.*

Have people analyze how sustainable your competitive advantage truly is.

▶ Notice particular changes. For example, did a competitor win a bid with an offer that was substantially different from one they had before? Have you heard that the sales force is all going to mandatory training?

▶ Once you learn important information, get it to the appropriate people within your organization. For example, if you know your competitors are trying to hire people in a specific function, hire a larger number of people, or hire a certain person, give this information to your HR department. Together, figure out what, if anything, that means about their strategy.

▶ Consider using a cross-functional team or an action-learning team to analyze information. Although this is probably the responsibility of a number of functions in the organization, it is sometimes helpful to have a new perspective. Use this strategy when you are concerned that others have missed things.

- ▶ Consider your sources of information about competitors. If you are using the same sources everyone else is using, you won't learn anything your competitors don't want you to know.

- ▶ Network with industry peers from other geographic areas. Because they do not view you as a direct competitor, they may be willing to share information.

- ▶ Determine what your competitors are doing now or are likely to do in the future to capitalize on opportunities. (These are the threats.)

- ▶ Identify areas in which you are vulnerable. For example, if your competitors are investing heavily in technology and you are not, you may soon be in trouble. If you are a knowledge-based business, your greatest threat might lie in whether you have people available with the necessary skills.

Identify competitive differentiators

▼

If you offer no differentiable value to your customers, they could bolt at any time. To increase your organization's value, create clear differentiation from your competitors. Consider the following suggestions:

- ▶ Identify competitors in the markets in which you currently operate and those in which you intend to enter.

Discuss the differentiators of the top five companies in your industry.

- ▶ Identify the ways in which competitors distinguish themselves: breadth and depth of services, global reach, price, levels of service provided, linkage with other products and services.

- ▶ Compare your competitors to one another against these criteria. Then, by yourself or with a group, identify what your organization can do better than its competitors. Another way to look at this is to ask how you use your resources and strengths to deliver value that is unique and addresses client priorities. Your advantages may lie in relationships with customers that allow you to be part of their planning processes, with your efficient distribution channels, or with your global sales force.

▷ Determine where in your value chain you are exceptionally good at doing something. These are the business processes that may be differentiable.

▷ Consider asking your customers to describe what they see as your differentiators.

▷ Look at your resources. Which can you leverage to provide exceptional value to your customers? For example, your worldwide distribution may decrease cost of sale. Your marketing database may be leveraged to expand the business into new product lines.

▶ When you come up with what you can do better than your competitors, challenge your organization to understand whether these are sustainable differentiators. That is, do the differentiators clearly set you apart from your competitors in your customers' eyes?

▷ How valuable is this differentiator to your customers?

▷ Will it be valuable in the future based on your understanding of your customers' future needs?

▷ Can it be protected or not easily replicated?

▷ Are there possible alternatives to this differentiator that will minimize the advantage?

▶ Recognize that the best differentiators are highly valued by the customer and are not easy to duplicate or substitute.

Bring cross-disciplinary knowledge to bear on issues and opportunities

▼

Today's business challenges are complex. Effective leaders are able to bring cross-disciplinary knowledge to bear on issues and opportunities, and they have a wide-angle perspective of the company as a whole. Managers must develop cross-functional knowledge and maintain good working relationships with other areas in order to execute strategy. To develop your understanding of other groups, consider the following suggestions:

▶ Learn the business from the perspectives of people in other functional areas. When you work with experts in other fields, discuss issues such as:

Connect people with peers from several functional areas so that they can get a wider perspective on the organization's challenges.

  ▷ How do they view the business? How is their perspective the same as or different from yours?

  ▷ What is their role in executing strategy? How do they fit into the value chain?

  ▷ What do they see as the current and potential future differentiators?

  ▷ If they are part of the support system, what organizations do they support?

  ▷ What are their goals and strategies, and why are they significant?

  ▷ What do they believe the organization could do to be more effective?

  ▷ If they work closely with you and your group, what do they think you could do to improve?

▶ Ask peers what they measure and why. Measures typically point to the critical variables that underlie effective business processes. Spend some time in other areas to get a feel for the work, the people, the pace, resources, and so on.

▶ Use cross-disciplinary teams to work on complex or recurring problems, and to pursue business opportunities. Provide an open forum to enable experts in other areas to contribute their ideas to the team.

▶ Learn about your organization through newsletters, online forums, white papers, presentations, podcasts, blogs, and so on. This will give you information about what other divisions and business units are doing.

▶ Conduct learning sessions as part of the cross-functional team's work. Regularly ask team members what they are learning. Pay attention to what individuals from various functions talk about. Is it the same? Different? To solidify learning and promote better understanding of each function, determine how they will apply what they learned.

▶ Seek out assignments in different functional areas and in both line and staff positions. A line assignment provides good, solid strategy and execution experience. A staff assignment develops organizational savvy, cross-boundary competence, and interpersonal skills.

Understand the organization's mission, strategies, strengths, and weaknesses

Without a clear understanding of your organization's mission and strategies, you will be unable to set a clear direction for your group to support them. Too many organizations have business areas and teams pulling in their own directions instead of in a unified direction. To develop a better understanding of your organization's mission, strategies, and strengths and weaknesses, consider these suggestions:

▶ Review all the strategy documents that have been sent to you. As you review the material, list any questions you have.

▶ Study analyses that were part of the strategy process. Look for:

▷ Industry and market trend analyses.

▷ Competitor analyses.

▷ Information about current and future customer needs.

▷ Identification of target customers.

▷ Analyses of your area's and your organization's differentiators.

▷ Determination of your customer value proposition.

▷ Strategic resource analyses.

▷ Ideas for improvement in business processes needed for success.

▷ Talent assessment, including constraint analyses.

Ask the person to conduct a strategic analysis of your organization and take you through it. Note where the person has a strong grasp of the material and where more work is needed.

▶ If this information is not in the documents, talk with your manager; if he or she does not have the information, go to the strategic planning group or person.

▶ Be able to answer these questions:

▷ What is the strategy?

▷ Why was it chosen?

▷ How will it create competitive advantage?

▷ What is needed for the strategy to succeed?

▶ Discuss the strategy with your leadership team. Presenting the strategy to them and answering their questions will help you to develop a deeper understanding of the strategy. If you do not have the knowledge or experience to do this, ask someone in your management chain to do it.

- ▸ Read or listen to presentations the CEO has made to the board, investors, and others. CEO presentations typically communicate direction and progress toward both short-term business goals and long-term strategic initiatives.

- ▸ Read your organization's annual report, particularly the CEO's message to stockholders, which typically includes a clear statement of company goals, recent progress toward longer-term objectives, and future challenges.

- ▸ To check whether you understand the strategy, explain it to someone.

- ▸ Talk with leaders in the organization to understand the organization's approach to strategy and the reasons for that approach. Approaches may differ in the degree of planning and the role that analysis plays. Knowing about different approaches is helpful when the organization's strategy is difficult to figure out.

- ▸ Use strategic theorist Michael Treacy's work to understand your organization's strategy. Identify which of Treacy's strategies your organization is following. He describes three types of strategies:

Total Cost	Best Product/ Technical Excellence	Total Solution
This strategy emphasizes operating excellence. Operations are standardized, simplified, tightly controlled, and centrally controlled. Low cost, efficiency, and speed are optimized. Management systems are focused on integrated, reliable, high-speed transactions and compliance with norms.	This strategy focuses on the core processes of innovation, product development, and market expansion. This strategy emphasizes product excellence rather than cost. Its business structure is flexible, so it can respond to entrepreneurial efforts. Its management systems are results-driven and measure product success, and its culture encourages creativity, innovation, and outside-the-box thinking.	This strategy concentrates on customer intimacy. It focuses on the core processes of relationship management, solution development, and results management. Its structure moves decision making down close to the customer, and its management systems are geared toward developing specific relationship and customer-service competencies.

- Ask your manager to tell you about corporate planning sessions that he or she has attended.

- To get an external perspective of the organization's vision and strategies, obtain research reports on your company prepared by industry analysts.

- Assess how you are communicating the strategy to your team and to others in the organization. If people hear the strategy only once, they may not understand it or its implications.

- Assess whether your employees can explain the strategy and the role of the work group in executing the strategy. Ask them:
  - Why was the strategy chosen?
  - How is your organization differentiated from the competition?
  - How does the strategy influence what you do and how you do your job?

- Make sure that you and your employees attend company meetings in which strategies and results are discussed. Doing so keeps you on top of changes and gives people a clearer idea of how they fit into the big picture.

- Keep a wide-angle perspective on how your organization operates as a whole. Take the time to get to know people in other functions and ask them about their work, processes, and challenges. Understand how the whole organization operates so you can make decisions that create more efficiency and effectiveness for your group.

Understand the role you and your area play in the success of the business

▼

Have the person do a mini-survey of the group to gauge understanding of the organization's strategy.

Each business unit and function contributes to overall execution of organizational strategy. Some contribute directly by finding and retaining customers, manufacturing goods, or delivering services; others support the business through IT, legal, or financial expertise.

Successful managers understand the role they play in the success of the business. To understand your role and that of your work group, consider the following suggestions:

- Ensure that you thoroughly understand the vision, goals, and strategies of the organization.

▷ Review all the documents, including online sources you have.

▷ Talk with leaders involved in the strategy process to understand the thinking behind the strategy: the analyses, the options discussed, the rationale for the strategies selected.

▷ If you don't understand something, ask questions. It's better to ask questions than to get it wrong. Your questions may help leaders pinpoint areas of the strategy that need clarification.

▷ As you listen to the strategy and the plans, think about what they mean for your group.

▶ Think about the role your organization or work unit plays in accomplishing the goals of the organization. Usually this is reasonably clear, because you have responsibility for a particular function, a business process, or a work unit. The more difficult challenges are to figure out specifically what you need to do well and to find opportunities to deliver more or better results.

▷ Ask your boss for his or her view of the most critical work processes in your area. Also ask about opportunities for improvement.

▷ Determine the specific actions that make a difference and are needed to successfully execute your strategy.

▷ Use your team to identify key processes.

▶ Talk with your boss about the role of your group in the business. Are there additional contributions your group could make, given the resources of the group and the direction of the organization?

Convey a thorough understanding of your area's strengths, weaknesses, opportunities, and threats

▼

Successful managers are keenly aware of their own area's strengths and weaknesses. To maintain that awareness, they assess the performance of the business processes key to success in their area. They also focus on people—their performance and capabilities in pivotal roles and whether the talent pipeline is preparing people for roles in supporting processes and systems. In addition, when they are considering a change in direction, effective leaders identify constraints to success and ways to address those constraints. Consider the following suggestions:

▸ Regularly evaluate the strengths and weaknesses of your strategy and your value proposition, your business processes, your talent, and your execution of strategy.

Ask people to identify the strengths and weaknesses of their work unit. This will give you insight into how thoroughly they understand their group.

▸ Conduct competitive analyses and customer reviews so that you are keenly aware of the marketplace and customer needs. Do not allow yourselves to be lulled into complacency. Stay on top of emerging needs and possible competitors so that you are not blindsided.

▸ Provide people with access to customer satisfaction data and analyses of current and future needs. Find out what others have done about the issues raised by the data.

▸ Use action learning or cross-functional teams to identify opportunities and threats in the marketplace. Adopt the practice of questioning and challenging the analyses and findings of groups that have worked in an area for a long time. People sometimes unintentionally get stale, cut corners, or neglect to question long-held assumptions, resulting in important strategic mistakes.

▸ Ask a cross-functional team or action learning team to put itself in the role of your competitors. What would the team do to overtake you in the marketplace?

▸ Identify the business processes and actions at which your work unit needs to excel in order to achieve its goals. What do the unit's strengths need to be to achieve your goals?

▸ Understand the people constraints to the success of your strategy. Identify the pivotal talent pools. These are the roles in which having an A or a C player makes a big difference. For example, let's say that your organization has key account managers who are responsible for large accounts that make up over 60 percent of your revenue. They are critical to the success of your strategy if your organization intends to retain and grow large customers. In a second example, if your organization promises to provide technology that is so simple and easy to use that customer service is not even needed, then engineers are pivotal.

▸ Find the gaps in your most necessary talent pools. Focus on attracting, deploying, developing, and retaining these people.

- Set the expectation that your team will regularly assess business processes. Ask to see these assessments. Periodically review progress on areas for improvement.

- Talk with customers about why they use your products or services. Find out how they see your competitors. Also pay attention to people and companies who are not your customers. Why are they choosing another firm?

- Define "opportunity" and "threat" for your area. Analyze how you view them.
  - At what point do you take note of these opportunities and threats, and at what point do you take action?
  - Has your timing so far been on target or too late?

Develop a vision and strategy for your group consistent with its role in the success of the organization

▼

Ask the person to show the connections between the organizational strategy and the strategy of his or her group. Discuss the rationale for any areas that are not in alignment.

Work group visions and strategies flow from the corporate and business unit vision and strategies. Effective managers thoroughly understand the organization's vision and strategies and understand the role of their group or groups in accomplishing the organizational goals. Consider the following suggestions:

- Make sure that you understand your organization's vision, goals, and strategies.
  - Review all available information about vision, goals, and strategies including CEO messages to the organization or the investor community.
  - Learn more about the thinking behind the strategy by talking to the leaders and strategic planners involved in the strategy process. Make sure you understand the analyses, the options discussed, and the rationale for the strategies selected.
  - If you don't understand something, ask questions. Your questions may help leaders pinpoint areas of the strategy that need clarification.
  - Present and discuss the vision, goals, and strategies with your employees. This is an excellent opportunity to communicate information they need to know and to test your own understanding.

▸ Work with your team to determine how the team can contribute to the success of the organization. What business processes is your team responsible for, and what resources do you have that can be leveraged?

  ▷ In light of the organization's strategy, value proposition, and competitive position, determine which business processes and which team actions are most critical to the success of your work group's role in executing the strategy. For example:

    – Your group is responsible for online marketing for a technology firm. Your Web site is crowded with too much information, hard to navigate, and not continually updated. How does that affect your organization's brand image? Will you look like you're on top of market trends and a leader within the industry?

    – If you are in HR, what is the impact of having 50 open manufacturing positions for six months if the area is supposed to produce 10 new products this year?

  ▷ Determine what else your group can do to leverage its resources to support or drive the organization's strategy.

▸ Look at the roles that are necessary for the business process to work well and to leverage the work unit's resources. Excellent performance in those jobs is key.

▸ Based on your analysis, concentrate on driving excellence in both business process and individual performance.

Integrate organizational strategies to achieve and sustain competitive advantage

An organization's strategy operates at many different levels, as corporate, business unit, and product line strategies. These strategies should be integrated with and build on one another if you plan to leverage core competencies. Consider the following suggestions:

▸ When you are developing distinctive strategies, determine the level of strategy on which you are working. Ensure that the executive team has developed corporate strategy that clarifies:

  ▷ The businesses you are in, will stay in, will leave, and will enter.

> ▷ The markets in which you plan to play and the customers you will target.

> ▷ The organization's value proposition and how it intends to create and sustain competitive advantage in the markets in which it operates.

> ▷ The business processes and strategic resources the organization will leverage to create strategic value.

> ▷ The pivotal talent needed to execute the strategy.

> ▷ The systems, processes, and management of talent needed to support the excellent execution of the business processes.

Have the person identify which strategies need to be integrated with other groups, and check for understanding of interdependencies.

▶ Look for a corporate strategy that is more than the sum of the business unit strategies. Corporate strategy not only guides the allocation of resources among business units, it also must add value to the strategies created at the business unit level.

▶ Expect to see indicators in the corporate strategy of whether the mix of businesses should change, whether the business processes need to change to leverage more value, whether there are common corporate initiatives to improve value, and whether business processes will be centralized or decentralized to leverage value.

> ▷ Organizations that need to cut costs often centralize some functions to avoid redundancies. These same organizations may decide later to decentralize some functions to enable the organization or those functions to get closer to customers.

> ▷ An organization undergoing a lot of change may have a corporate initiative aimed at developing change management as a core leadership competency and standardizing some change processes to make the organization more nimble.

▶ Look for opportunities to leverage the work done in other businesses or groups. Work groups can learn a lot from one another. Ask people to stay in touch with people in other businesses and functions and learn what they are doing.

▶ When you plan an initiative, always check to see who has done something similar. Talk to your boss, your peers, direct reports, and people in your network. Also read your organization's intranet, blog, and all-organization e-mails.

▶ Meet with people from other groups that affect you. Present your strategies to one another, and then discuss synergies, timing, and coordination. In what ways do you need to work together to make your groups' plans successful? What can you learn from one another?

Pursue initiatives to capitalize on strengths and market opportunities, and to counter competitive threats

Countless initiatives vie for attention in organizations. Successful leaders focus on the key initiatives that will have the greatest strategic impact. The key to strategic success is the ability to analyze the current situation, determine how to gain sustainable competitive advantage, and execute the plan. Whether you are responsible for the corporate strategy, business unit strategy, or your team strategy, the process is similar.

▶ Identify and pursue opportunities using the following process:

1. Identify your current key strategic opportunities by answering these questions with your team:
   ▷ What is the mission of your organization or work unit?
   ▷ Who are your customers? What are their current and anticipated needs?
   ▷ What have the industry's chief limitations been in the past?
   ▷ Which barriers to entry will no longer exist in five years?
   ▷ What changes in technology, resources, legislation, and public policy will influence your industry?
   ▷ Who are your competitors and anticipated future competitors?
   ▷ What activities and processes give your competitors an advantage?
   ▷ What are the major differences among your competitors?
   ▷ What are your competitors doing to capitalize on opportunities?
   ▷ What competitive threats must you address?
   ▷ How do your products and services compare with your competitors'? What are your strengths and weaknesses?
   ▷ What activities and processes give you a competitive advantage?

▷ What do you have or do that is special and cannot be easily duplicated?

▷ How can you leverage your strengths to gain sustainable advantage?

2. From this information, identify your strategy for gaining competitive advantage.

▷ Ask your team to identify opportunities you and the team have for improvement, including new strategies and better execution of business processes.

▷ Determine what you need to know in order to decide which opportunities you should pursue.

3. Gather information about your competitors so that you are not surprised by their actions and can anticipate their moves.

▷ Talk with your competitors' customers to understand why it made sense from their point of view to choose your competitors.

▷ Conduct these conversations so customers understand that you are not suggesting that their choice is wrong or trying to convince them to become your customers. Focus on seeing their point of view.

▷ Review competitive information and challenge assumptions. Ensure that the data and the analyses, including the practical analysis, are sound. Even if the analyses were done by the marketing department or an agency with a good reputation, challenge assumptions and ensure the analyses are sound.

▷ Thoroughly understand your competitors' value chains and their competitive positioning. This will help you predict their next moves. For example, a competitor who competes on the basis of low price can be expected to make price-based moves.

▷ Watch what your competitors are doing. Where are they investing? The adage "follow the money" will help you understand what your competitors are doing.

▷ Charter an action-teaching team to put themselves in the role of your competitors and determine how they would compete with your organization. This exercise will provide insight into what your competitors might be thinking.

▷ When you plan a course of action, create scenarios to anticipate what the competitive response will be. Business is a lot like chess: success goes to those who can plan several moves ahead.

▷ As part of a strategic planning session, deliberately anticipate your competitor's next moves. You may also want to ask marketing to do this. To anticipate moves and limit the number of surprises, analyze the information you gathered, your understanding of the marketplace, and customers' needs.

▷ Charter an action-learning team to figure out where unexpected competition will come from. You may also want to do this as part of a strategic planning session. Pay particular attention to competition that could come from unexpected directions, like another industry. When new industries enter the marketplace, both value propositions and the industry change dramatically. These quantum changes require you to look at your own strategic positioning which often will not survive another industry entering the marketplace unless you anticipated the move.

If people miss significant segments of the environment in their competitive analysis, provide examples of what they should look for.

▷ Identify areas in which you are vulnerable. For example, if you know that your competitors are investing heavily in new products and you are not, you may soon be in trouble. If you are a customer service business, your greatest threat may be that you don't have people with the right skills.

4. Respond to competitive moves without throwing the organization off its competitive positioning or strategic course of action.

▷ Your competitive positioning is based on your analysis of how you can win business. Therefore, when a competitor takes an action that looks like a potential threat, analyze the threat before you respond, and respond in a way that is consistent with your positioning.

For example, if a competitor lowers prices, don't assume that you need to respond by lowering your prices. A response that reinforces the value you provide may be more consistent with your positioning.

▷ Pay close attention to customers' reactions. While your positioning is based on sound analysis, you need to understand when the assumptions you made are wrong or have changed. If the competition lowers prices at the same time your customers institute a strategic purchasing function whose charter is to cut costs significantly, your assumptions about the importance of value may change.

▶ Remember that good customers are anticipating what you will do. Think about in doing something unexpected. For example, an organization welcomed its chief competitor into a country in which it had been the sole supplier for more than 10 years.

▶ Identify efforts that will have the greatest impact. Challenge your team to keep learning about your customers, their needs, and how your company can better meet those needs.

Identify the business processes that are key to the success of the strategy

▼

Competitive advantage results from identifying how you can use your resources to deliver value to customers in a way that is different from what your competitors can do. A strategy for creating advantage is empty without day-to-day execution of the work that is necessary to create this advantage. Consider the following suggestions:

▶ Once you have identified the role you and your group play in achieving the organization's goals and have chosen your strategies, specify the work or business processes that are necessary to deliver the needed results.

For example, in an organization that plans to grow through acquisition, the acquisition process is critical to the success of the strategy. The organization needs this business process to operate as well as it possibly can.

Review one long-standing business process to assess its timeliness, cost efficiency, and quality.

▶ Ask the team to identify critical work processes. Identify others who would have valuable input in regard to these work processes: other parts of the value chain, other groups you interact with, customers, your boss.

▶ Figure out the components of the critical work processes and what is most important about execution of them. Use workflow charts to identify the full processes.

For example, if you're focusing on acquisition, what is most important? Finding the acquisition targets? Developing relationships with the acquisition targets? Negotiating the deal?

▶ Use your teams to identify parts of the processes that are most vulnerable and in need of improvement, and focus improvement efforts on those parts. Look for how things can be done better, faster, or more thoroughly.

   ▷ In the acquisition process: Do you have enough acquisition targets? Are the rate and volume of acquisitions high enough? Do the results of the acquisition match the original plan?

   ▷ Does customer service work as planned? When the process is used, how often are customers satisfied?

Know the pivotal roles necessary to execute the strategy

▼

Challenge people to think about whether they have the right people in critical roles.

While all employees are valuable, some roles within a work unit are more pivotal to success of the strategy. Know what these roles are and take special care to select the right people for them. Consider the following suggestions:

▶ From your work group strategy, identify the resources you plan to leverage to create advantage and the work processes that are necessary to create this advantage. Next identify the roles that are needed to leverage these resources and execute work processes.

For example, in the pharmaceutical industry, if your strategy is to develop new drugs, then the discovery process is critical, and researchers and product managers are in critical roles. If your strategy is to acquire new drugs, then acquisition and product management are critical roles, and the business processes of integration and product introduction are critical.

▶ Work with your team and others in the value chain to identify the most critical roles. Consider the roles in which having an A or a C player in the role will make a big difference to the outcome of the work process.

   ▷ Strategic account managers assigned to the organization's most important clients are by definition in critical roles. It is their responsibility to retain and grow customers.

▷ If a retail store's brand promise is customer service, the personnel on the floor will be in critical roles because their treatment of customers makes a big difference. If a retail store's brand focuses on low prices, the people who negotiate the price of goods will be in the critical roles.

▸ Work with your HR department to identify the experience, skills, knowledge, and attributes necessary for success in critical roles. Develop a recruitment and selection process that ensures that you have the right people.

Ensure that initiatives and priorities are integrated with one another and aligned with the direction and strategic priorities of the broader organization

▼

Unless you are at the top of the organization, others set its vision and direction. Your responsibility is to bring the corporate vision, goals, and strategies down to the next level. You and your team or business unit need to develop a vision, goals, and strategies for your area that are consistent with the direction and strategy of the level above.

In the process of creating and confirming the vision, goals, and strategies for your group, consider the following suggestions:

▸ Obtain copies of the corporate and/or business line's vision, goals, and strategies. If you were not involved in developing them, talk with people who were involved to better understand the company's direction.

▸ Share your understanding of the vision, goals, and strategies with your team. Provide background information. Knowing the strategic options that were discussed will give the team a richer understanding of the direction that was chosen.

▸ Discuss your expectations with the group, including the methodology you want to use to arrive at the vision, goals, and strategies for your part of the organization. The vision, goals, and strategies should address what your unit needs to do to accomplish its part of the overall organizational strategy. Provide the model of strategy used by the organization and some information about strategy so that team members approach the task using a similar methodology.

▸ Once you have decided on the vision, goals, and strategies for the business unit or team, review them against the criteria your team should be using to ensure the accomplishment of corporate and business unit goals. Ensure that your goals and strategies are aligned with those of the organization.

If you already have goals and strategies, consider this process:

▸ Review the team or business goals and strategies against the corporate or business unit goals and strategies. Where is the alignment? Where are there differences?

▸ Look at the rationale for the differences. Bring areas that lack alignment into congruence with the corporate strategy.

Review assumptions about why the current strategy was chosen.

▸ Investigate what type of interaction and synergy you need for the goals and strategies of your team, and ensure that coordination takes place.

▹ Ask people to work together to identify contingencies and coordination points. Make sure that plans have adequate resources and that different people are not counting on the same resources at the same time.

▹ When projects are long and complex, use common project planning processes and software.

▹ Use cross-functional teams to plan work whenever the accomplishment of goals involves units working together.

▹ Identify the coordination points between your group and others so you know where to have joint planning and execution.

▸ Monitor the team's work over time for consistency with the plan and the priorities.

▸ View your business strategy as a living document. Regularly review progress against the plan. Use it to focus and guide your actions and the actions of your team.

Create measures that accurately reflect the success of the strategy and execution of the processes needed to drive it

▼

Review how people intend to measure the success of strategy and the effectiveness of the processes used to execute it. Ensure that they are focused on the right things.

It is smart leadership to evaluate the success of the work processes and the individual performance that deliver your group's results. This evaluation can also tell you whether your strategy is working. Consider the following suggestions:

▸ Check that you and the team have clearly identified the activities and work processes that are needed to deliver the intended results. The work processes need to be defined clearly enough that you and others know what they are and whether they are being used. The actions need to be clear enough that people know what is expected and do what is needed.

▸ Work with the people who do the work to identify ways to evaluate processes and performance: Is the process used? What is its result? For example, do employees consistently follow the process for handling a customer complaint? What is the result of this approach?

▸ After strategies are identified, also identify indicators of success. How will you know that the strategy is working? That it has accomplished what was intended? Interim measures help you gauge the success of the strategy, provide encouragement to the organization, and allow you to make midcourse corrections.

Evaluate and pursue initiatives, investments, and opportunities based on their fit with broader strategies

▼

The purpose of strategy is to help you make choices and keep you focused. Effective leaders use strategy regularly to help them decide where to invest critical time and energy—an organization's most limited resources. Consider the following suggestions:

▸ As part of the strategic planning process, your organization, business unit, or function will probably have identified strategic issues, developed strategies to address them, and planned initiatives. This framework provides rationale and criteria against which to evaluate other initiatives, investments, and opportunities.

- When you make decisions, ensure that they are consistent with the organization's direction and priorities. For example:
  - ▷ If a key competitive issue is time to market worldwide, discuss translation issues early in the planning process so you can get the resources necessary to address them.
  - ▷ If a strategic issue is to develop leadership talent from within the organization, keep that in mind as you develop criteria for new hires. Hire people who have potential in addition to their ability to do the current job.

- When decisions are made, discuss the rationale behind them. Basing your rationale on strategic issues will help people view those issues as important.

- Ask teams to establish decision-making criteria that take into account the strategic framework. For example, if the need to improve the organization's speed is a strategic issue, people should use that as a criterion for decision making.

- Evaluate investments based on their fit with strategic direction and strategic priorities. Look at how the investment will advance the strategic goals.

Encourage people to work on a strategic project with others who excel in strategy. Periodically review what they are learning.

- Review three major decisions made by you or your team in the past year.
  - ▷ Were they aligned with strategy?
  - ▷ If they were not, why did you make them? Understand what takes you off track. How did the decisions affect your team or the organization?

- Meet with your direct reports to:
  - ▷ Convey the organization's priorities.
  - ▷ Review their priorities.
  - ▷ Give them feedback when their priorities do not align with overall strategic priorities.

Act Strategically

Create strategies to balance short-term requirements with long-range business plans

▼

Success depends on effectively executing both immediate short-term objectives and plans and long-term strategic plans. Pursuing one without the other is unwise and risky. For example, organizations need to achieve short-term goals that please investors and meet employee bonus plans, and also address long-term issues that keep them competitive. Consider the following suggestions:

▶ Review the work that you and your team have done in the past quarter to determine what has been accomplished on both short- and long-term issues. If the balance is not right according to the priorities of the business, set new priorities for how you and your team spend your time.

▶ If you have attempted to set new priorities and it has not worked, consider assigning some team members to short-term objectives and make others responsible for executing long-term plans.

▶ Ask your teams to look at how they can make progress on long-term issues while addressing short-term needs. For example, a goal may be to understand more about a customer's industry. Ask the team to figure out how to make progress on that goal while they are serving the customer.

Some managers allow day-to-day activities to capture their attention, while planning and strategy fall by the wayside. If feedback indicates that others have this perception of you, consider the following suggestions:

Ask people to compare priorities to how their group is spending time. Provide feedback and talk about changes that may be needed.

▶ Establish goals about what big-picture work you want to do (strategic thinking, developing a new approach, developing bench strength). Each month, evaluate your progress against your objectives.

▶ Keep a log to determine how you spend your time. Evaluate whether you are giving proper time and attention to the big picture.

▶ When you face competing priorities, determine which are the most important and make them your first priority. When an urgent matter arises, determine how it fits into your daily plan (is it urgent and important, or simply urgent?) and act accordingly.

4
Leverage Innovation

Innovation drives successful businesses forward, while the lack of it holds others back—often leading to their decline. Organizations need people who can see things from a new perspective, look at problems from multiple angles, and together come up with the ideas, solutions, products, and delivery that keeps them leaders in their market.

As a manager, you need to develop the ability to recognize people's gifts for innovation and foster an environment in which creative thinking and new ideas are welcomed, encouraged, and received warmly. Asking open-ended questions, challenging old or outdated processes and assumptions, and motivating people to be open-minded all contribute to innovation.

In this chapter, we will cover the following areas:

▼

- ▶ Determine when to use creative thinking

- ▶ Use logical and intuitive approaches

- ▶ Approach problems with curiosity and open-mindedness

- ▶ Generate innovative ideas, solutions to problems, and opportunities

- ▶ Stimulate creative thinking in others

- ▶ Challenge the way things have always been done; look at problems, processes, and solutions in new ways

- ▶ Identify novel solutions to old problems

- ▶ Use brainstorming to generate innovative ideas

- ▶ Routinely try out new ideas, methods, and technologies

- ▶ Leverage fresh perspectives, breakthrough ideas, and new paradigms to create value in the market

- ▶ Find ways to extend and apply innovative ideas to enhance business results

- ▶ Identify significant cost-saving or revenue opportunities

Determine when to use creative thinking

Recommend that people choose team members with complementary skills when they need to solve problems.

Creativity is always helpful to the problem-solving process; at times it is essential. At these times, traditional, rational, reductionist problem solving actually wastes time. Use the following guidelines to determine when you should employ a creative-thinking process:

Creative problem solving is essential when:	Use traditional problem solving when:
▸ Problems keep recurring.	▸ Problems are well defined.
▸ Problems are ambiguous.	▸ Causes are definite and defined.
▸ Causes are unknown.	▸ Facts are central to the process.
▸ Facts are unknown; feelings abound.	▸ Incremental solutions are acceptable.
▸ You are not sure how to evaluate the problem.	▸ Problems seldom recur.
▸ The standard "way it has always been done" is no longer working.	▸ All essential criteria for evaluating the problem are known.
▸ Something that has not been a problem has become one.	▸ You want to do things better.
▸ Unpredictable and risky solutions are acceptable.	
▸ You want to do things differently.	

Use logical and intuitive approaches

Review people's analytical process to ensure that it is logical. People sometimes draw conclusions from faulty assumptions.

Both logical and intuitive thinking are necessary for creating the optimum climate for innovation. Logical thinking is a sequential process, while intuitive thinking tends to be holistic. The following information will help you learn more about each approach.

A *logical*, or linear, approach provides structure and a sequence of steps for generating alternative solutions. Here are some examples:

▸ *Matrix analysis.* Use a two- or three-dimensional matrix to help identify where to look further for new ideas.

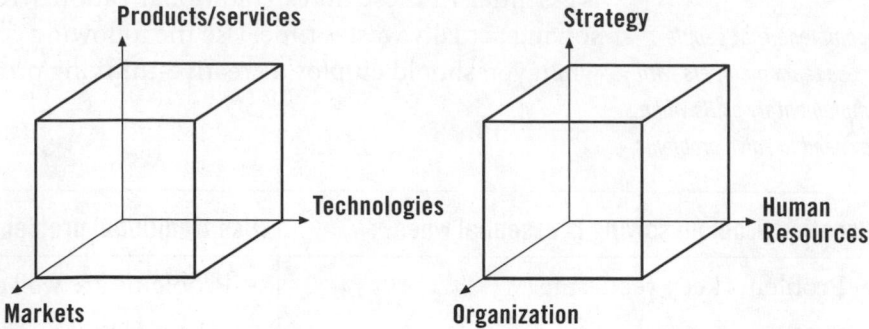

▷ Draw a three-dimensional box and label each of the three axes. For example, your axes could be products/services, markets, and technologies.

▷ List on each axis the items pertaining to the category, from core (close to the origin, lower back corner) to peripheral.

▷ After you complete the list for all three axes, it will be easier to identify a number of combinations that have not yet been used.

▸ *Attribute listing.* Define all the attributes or components of a procedure or product that you wish to improve. Then look at each attribute for possible ways to improve it.

▸ *Force-field analysis.* Write an objective statement of the problem you wish to solve, and then describe the factors blocking and the factors supporting a successful outcome. Analyze the positive and negative forces to identify ways to strengthen the positive forces, weaken the negative forces, or add new positive forces.

Problem Definition _____

Blocking Factors	Forces	Supporting Factors
Negative (–)		**Positive (+)**
1.	1.	
2.	2.	
3.	3.	

▶ *Reframing questions.* View your problem from a different perspective. Ask questions about your problem in a way that lets you examine it from a broader perspective and identify its less-obvious aspects. An example of a reframing question is "What are the facts of this problem or situation, and how can each of these facts be challenged?" If you apply this question to a delivery problem, for example, you may determine that one of the facts is that you must ship to your customer on Tuesday mornings. By challenging this assumption, you might find that your customer would be equally satisfied with shipments on Tuesday evenings or Wednesday mornings, which would ease your delivery person's tight schedule.

▶ *Mind map.* Map ideas around a concept or idea that you wish to expand upon.

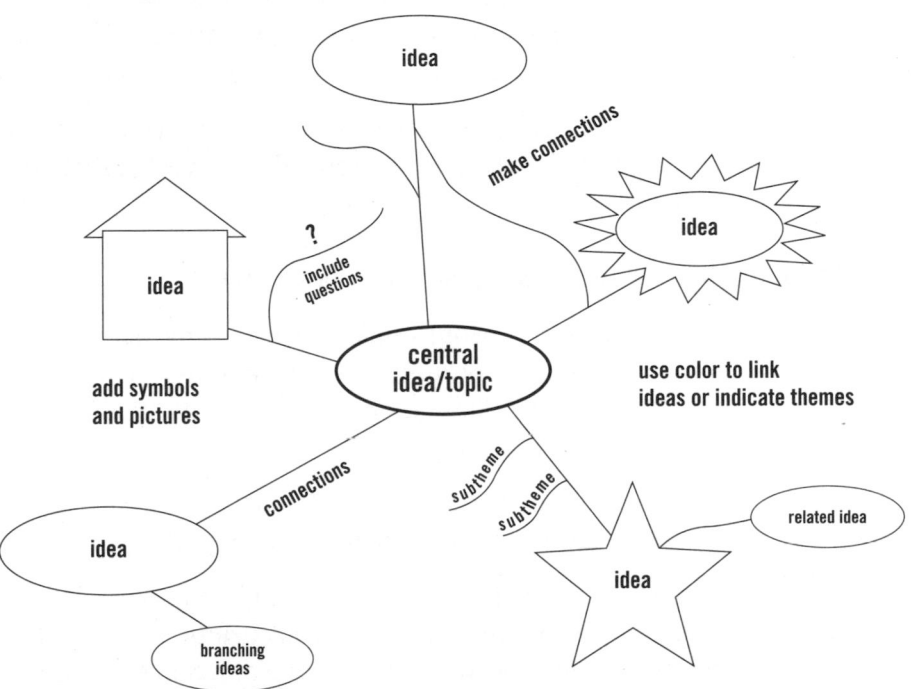

An *intuitive* approach focuses on the issue as a whole rather than on the parts. Solutions often arrive in one larger step rather than in a sequence of steps. Here are some examples:

▸ *Analogies.* Find similarities or parallels between familiar and unfamiliar issues or situations. Look to other fields—for example, science, literature, visual arts, film, sports, politics.

To get started, complete the sentence "This is like . . ." or "This reminds me of . . ." or "This is different from . . ."

▸ *Imagery.* Generate ideas by imagining experiences, scenes, or symbols. Describe each one in detail. Then determine where links exist between your words or descriptions and the issue at hand.

▸ *Drawing.* Draw a picture of the issue. Drawing is an effective way to bring out intuitive processes by communicating through impressions and symbols rather than words.

▸ *Feelings.* Think or talk about when another situation made you feel the same way you feel about the current problem. This technique enables you to identify core themes or conflicts in interpersonal situations.

▸ *Dreams.* Pay attention to dreams, which may produce images and key words that can be applied creatively to real-world situations.

Approach problems with curiosity and open-mindedness

▼

Creative people engage in open-minded, somewhat undisciplined thinking throughout the problem-solving process. Remaining open-minded allows them to generate more alternatives. Consider the following suggestions:

▸ Be more open-minded and creative by challenging yourself to see problems as challenges and opportunities.

Provide specific feedback about what gives you the impression that people aren't open to new ideas.

▸ Look at your style to see if there are certain kinds of situations that excite you, that make you curious and enthusiastic, and others that are unappealing. What are the differences? Frame situations in a way that will make you more eager to address them.

▸ Build your intellectual curiosity by developing your knowledge of the world around you. Pay attention to new ideas and trends, and figure out how they could affect your organization or industry.

- Ask *why, where, what, who, when,* and *how* as you analyze situations. The answers will increase your understanding of the challenge and its relation to other issues.

- Identify creative people in your organization. Ask them to be involved when you need more creativity.

- Make an effort to deliberately and systematically understand how others see a situation. This will help you see that there is more than one way to perceive something.

Generate innovative ideas, solutions to problems, and opportunities

▼

Provide people with learning opportunities in innovation and creativity.

One of your challenges as a leader is to help people think differently about the situations and opportunities they encounter. Managers often need to take the lead in this activity by offering unconventional solutions that are still feasible. Consider the following suggestions for generating innovative approaches:

- Develop your personal creativity. Start by setting aside time to be creative. If you schedule every hour of every day, you will not have time to think, let alone dream. Creativity is often the culmination of a process, not a flash of inspiration.

- Break out of your typical patterns. Whenever you think in a different way, you build brain capacity. Explore ideas in different industries and disciplines. Read or listen to books, magazines, blogs, e-zines, white papers, and podcasts about new topics. Do simple, small things that change your routines.

- Apply creativity to many phases of the problem-solving process:
  ▷ Look at different ways to view a problem.
  ▷ Think about who, beyond the obvious, should be involved in defining a problem, generating alternatives, or designing solutions.
  ▷ Generate different options.
  ▷ Think creatively about how to decide what you will do.

- Continually challenge yourself to think of innovative approaches: "In an ideal world, I would . . ." or "If cost were no issue, I would . . ."

▸ Change your scene. A different physical environment may help you break out of your routine and generate innovative ideas.

▸ Approach the problem differently. For example, instead of describing your problem in words, draw a picture of it. Drawing stimulates images, concepts, and intuition, while writing lends itself to facts, numbers, and logic.

▸ Believe that a solution is possible. When you face a problem, you may feel overwhelmed. Believe that every step you take will bring you closer to an effective solution.

▸ Turn your ideas into action. Be relentless about putting your ideas into practice so you can see what works and what doesn't. This will help you put failure into perspective, increase your confidence, and help you see more possibilities.

Stimulate creative thinking in others

▼

You can't think of all the creative ideas yourself. You need people who think creatively. To switch from a corporate culture that endorses conformity and compliance to one that fosters creativity and initiative, you need to show that you support innovation in others. Consider the following suggestions for encouraging creativity in others:

Encourage people who come up with creative ideas: If they have trouble getting their ideas accepted, strategize on how they can get organizational buy-in.

▸ Give people time to think. Creativity typically is not produced on demand. Reflection is part of the creative process.

▸ Find out whether people think you encourage and support creativity, or stifle it. Listen carefully to feedback, even though it may contradict how you see yourself. Discuss issues until you understand how others are seeing and interpreting them.

▸ Ask people to be creative.

▸ Thank people for their creative ideas.

▸ In a brainstorming session, stop yourself and others for criticizing or evaluating ideas.

▸ Allow people opportunities to learn new ideas. Support them as they attend conferences, join or start study groups, and read widely.

- Bring in people to talk about new thinking, discoveries, products, and services. Creativity spawns creativity.

- Protect "idea people," who can cause a certain amount of angst within a group when their ideas rock the boat and force people to break out of comfortable routines. Be a champion and advocate for them. Communicate why ideas are important for the success of your group and organization.

- Reward people who suggest creative solutions by giving them both tangible rewards (merit salary increases, promotions) and intangible rewards (recognition, public credit for their ideas, more challenging projects).

Challenge the way things have always been done; look at problems, processes, and solutions in new ways

"The way it has always been done" is a perennial obstacle to making positive changes in an organization. Some people think it is wrong and inefficient to change things that don't need to be changed. Others do not want to do things differently because of the time and energy involved. They need to believe that it's worth their effort, and they need confidence in the process and structure they're going to use. Consider the following suggestions:

- Identify reluctance to challenge "the way it has always been done." Common concerns include:
  - ▷ It's working, so why change?
  - ▷ There isn't a better alternative.
  - ▷ It will be too disruptive or costly.

Ensure that people clarify whether a situation calls for an improvement or an entirely new approach.

- Then figure out how to remove obstacles:
  - ▷ Demonstrate why a change is important.
  - ▷ Demonstrate the cost of not changing.
  - ▷ Challenge the idea that "it's working."

- Identify organizational barriers to innovation. For example:
  - *Policy barriers.* People are often encouraged to analyze their suggestions in terms of existing procedures and policies. This may discourage them from proposing solutions contrary to current guidelines.
  - *Lack of funding.* Financial plans frequently do not include the cost of promoting an innovation.
  - *Silo thinking.* Because specialists may overlook relationships outside their area of expertise, combine people from various areas when you are developing new ideas.
  - *Micromanagement.* Hovering, second-guessing, and tinkering will smother people's desire to be innovative.
  - *Hidden agendas.* People may be motivated to maintain the status quo.

- Involve new and different people so that you and your team will become aware of new ways of seeing situations.

- Challenge people to regularly improve business or work processes. Choose something that will truly make a difference if it is improved.

- Support individuals who challenge assumptions and question the way things are done. Organizations typically reward people who avoid rocking the boat. Instead, promote innovation and motivation by actively encouraging questions and positive challenges.

- Encourage your people to talk with and visit people in other organizations. Seeing what others do gets people to think.

Identify novel solutions to old problems

Some problems almost become old friends. People get so used to creating workarounds that they no longer feel any urgency to solve the underlying problems. To reenergize people and identify novel solutions, consider the following suggestions:

- Quantify the extent to which the problem is a problem. You need to know whether it's worth your time to find a new solution. If it is, this will motivate you to fix it.

▸ Recognize that people may not want to solve the problem. They may not even see it as a problem anymore. To make your case for solving it, you need to show that they will benefit measurably from fixing it.

Ask people to list their "go-to" group for ideas. Challenge them to add new voices to the mix.

▸ Invite people who are new to the organization or people from other functions or departments to troubleshoot. They may recognize aspects of the problem that you overlooked.

▸ Review what people have done in the past to solve a problem. Have any of the circumstances changed since then? For example, you might have access to a new technology, or you may have hired people who have expertise in this area.

▸ Try bold ideas. Instead of making an incremental change, considering making a substantial change. It may energize people to envision something that is significantly better.

▸ Anticipate whether using a novel solution to an old problem will create entirely new problems. You may start a chain reaction that causes more problems than it solves. Involve people from several areas to analyze a proposed solution.

Use brainstorming to generate innovative ideas

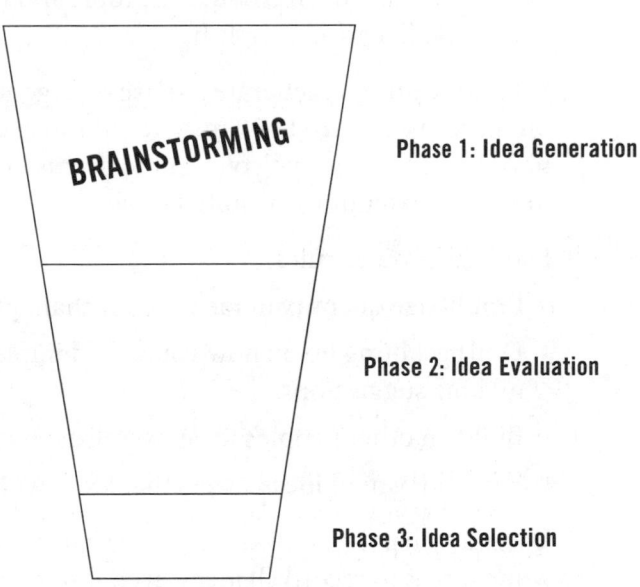

BRAINSTORMING

Phase 1: Idea Generation

Phase 2: Idea Evaluation

Phase 3: Idea Selection

When a number of people gather to solve a problem, they can build on each other's ideas. To start brainstorming with your group, consider the following guidelines:

▸ Choose an issue for which you need new, fresh ideas. Frame it clearly and specifically. For example, brainstorm "How can we communicate the strategy throughout the organization?" rather than "How can we improve communication?"

Watch a team brainstorm and pay attention to their process. If they evaluate as they go, they will limit the number of ideas.

▸ Based on the topic, choose who should be involved in the session. For example, you might want to invite individuals from other departments or divisions, regions, or even a key customer. Sessions can be conducted in person or through video conferencing. A brainstorming session can serve as a team-building exercise and give people a head start when it comes to implementing ideas. Think creatively about this.

▸ Limit the number of participants to ensure that everyone will have a chance to participate. Typically, five to eight people is an optimal-size group.

▸ Find a place to work where you won't be interrupted. Display people's ideas as they generate them. For example, use flip charts, a whiteboard, PowerPoint, or an interactive electronic whiteboard.

▸ To start the session, introduce the topic and be very clear about what you would like to accomplish.

▸ Set a time limit to generate a sense of urgency. A group usually runs out of ideas after 20 to 30 minutes of intense brainstorming. If you have related issues that you want to discuss, hold subsequent meetings instead of extending the initial session.

▸ Establish ground rules:
  ▷ Emphasize quantity of ideas rather than quality.
  ▷ Don't get hung up on how you would implement an idea. Just keep making suggestions.
  ▷ Build on other people's ideas as well as suggesting new ones.
  ▷ Ban criticism of ideas. Stress that ideas will be evaluated later.

▸ Use a flip chart, Web slides, desktop sharing, or online collaborative work spaces to record all ideas, even if they are mentioned more than once. If a sketch or drawing would clarify a point, invite the individual with the idea to make the drawing or upload an image. Share the results so people can track what has been suggested so far.

▶ If you are the facilitator, keep people on track, make sure you focus on building ideas, not evaluating them, and encourage everyone to participate.

▶ Let everyone know what you plan to do with the ideas. For example, you might want to sort through them as a group, or review them later yourself or with a subset of the group.

▶ Choose ideas that you would like to explore further. Move to the next stage by assigning people or teams to flesh out the selected ideas.

▶ If you want to involve more than eight people, here are some ways to get ideas from more people:

▷ Interview people individually or in groups.

▷ Ask two groups to debate an issue with others listening. Then ask the entire group for ideas of how to see the issue and possible solutions or opportunities.

▷ Do brain writing—brainstorming in a written form. Create a Wiki for sharing ideas or do a group chat session online.

▷ Send questionnaires.

▷ Ask groups to generate ideas, share them, and build on each other's ideas.

▷ Ask people or groups to draw pictures or schematics of an issue, opportunity, or solution.

Routinely try out new ideas, methods, and technologies

▼

Successful organizations depend on leaders who can turn original ideas into reality. This involves developing concrete action plans and implementation strategies for your ideas. Consider the following suggestions:

▶ Try experiments or pilot projects before deciding to fully implement a plan.

▶ Clearly define the parameters for piloting a new idea, method, or technology.

▷ What will be piloted?

▷ What is the purpose of the pilot?

▷ How will you know if you have succeeded?

Challenge people to think of unexpected ways their ideas could go off track or be blocked.

▶ Determine who needs to be involved in the pilot.

▷ Whose work will be affected?

▷ Who will benefit from the idea?

▷ Who can get things done?

▷ Whose participation will influence others?

▶ Form a core team dedicated to implementing the new idea. There can be strength in numbers, especially when the action goes against the status quo. Choose your team members carefully to include both people who immediately favor the idea and people who are initially skeptical. They can help you anticipate problems and create a solid action plan.

▶ Secure resources early in the process. Look beyond your area. Would other people or groups be interested in your ideas? Are people interested in pursuing cross-functional projects?

▶ Investigate forming a partnership with other leaders. Their political support may be crucial if your test is successful and you want to expand the project.

▶ Research how original ideas are typically received in your organization. Are people supported and encouraged, or are they left to struggle on their own? Knowing the likely response will help you prepare yourself and form a realistic expectation of the experience.

Leverage fresh perspectives, breakthrough ideas, and new paradigms to create value in the market

▼

Competitive strategies require innovation, especially if an organization wants to create a competitive advantage. If your organization's strategy is to be the product leader, then innovation is the foundation of your competitive advantage. If you are after customer intimacy, then you will focus creativity on understanding and meeting customer needs. Consider the following suggestions:

▸ Based on your strategy, decide where creativity is most critical.

▸ Look at the value chain to spot constraints and opportunities for improvement.

▸ Identify the "givens" in your organization or industry. Challenge your team to eliminate them. For example:

  ▹ How could you reduce your employee turnover rate?

  ▹ How could you double profit margins?

  ▹ How could you reduce time to market by 25 percent?

▸ List needs that are not being met within your organization or industry. What could your organization do to meet them? Brainstorm ideas that are not solely dependent on current personnel or technology.

When people talk about new ideas, discuss whether they're building on existing ideas and pushing them to the next level.

▸ Regularly challenge yourself and your team to look at your business from perspectives outside of your organization. You may find new opportunities to create value.

  ▹ How do your suppliers describe their relationship with your organization? How do they describe the value you add to your customers?

  ▹ What changes would make customers' experience with you more favorable?

  ▹ What was the biggest change you made this year that had a positive impact on your customers?

▸ Make sure people in your work unit have a clear, solid understanding of how the business works. This will help them understand when a new idea has potential.

▸ Set the expectation that a larger percentage of revenue will come from new products.

▸ Require regular measurable improvement in business processes.

▸ Ask a team to figure out how to extend a product or process innovation in their area.

▸ When team members have an idea, challenge them to pursue it. After they have developed their thoughts, have them report back to you. Listen to their ideas, encourage them, and ask how you can support them.

▸ Consider how you would compete against your organization.

▸ Study past innovations in your organization, industry, and marketplace. What prompted the innovation? How could this apply to the current environment?

▸ Assess whether you have enough new ideas. If attempts at leveraging new ideas are not working, bring in creative individuals or people who have worked in innovative companies. Sometimes you need an influx of talent to stimulate or challenge your existing talent.

▸ Write down five to ten emerging trends that are most likely to affect your industry. Share your ideas with your staff. Work together to determine how your organization could capitalize on them.

▸ Draw on the ideas and experiences of others. Instead of waiting for radical breaks with current thinking, consider moving ideas one step forward.

Find ways to extend and apply innovative ideas to enhance business results

▼

Ask people to identify one improvement they could make in the next three months that would directly affect the results in their group.

Businesspeople don't search for innovative ideas as an academic exercise. They want to do things better, smarter, and faster. They want to enhance their business results, to serve their customers better and increase revenues. Consider the following suggestions:

▸ Develop a clear understanding of the priority placed on product development and product excellence in your competitive business strategy. If you intend to be successful because you have the best products, you need to emphasize stimulating creative ideas that meet or anticipate customer needs, and you must bring new services and products to market regularly and quickly.

▸ When product development is a priority, ensure that management systems and processes support it. Also make sure that you place a high priority on developing infrastructure to support new products or services. This includes:

▷ Support for research and development and product marketing.

▷ High-performance teams to create new services and products and bring them to market.

▷ Incentive plans that reward creativity, innovation, product introductions, and new-product success.

▸ Establish knowledge-sharing and learning systems so that teams and people can learn from one another rapidly and move quickly from idea to product. Ask your team to apply what was learned rather than repeat old mistakes on new projects.

▸ When a new product or service is created, identify line extensions. While you introduce the first product in the line, develop and manage the line extensions.

▸ Decide what percentage of revenue should come from new products. Then manage the business processes to support this direction.

Identify significant cost-saving or revenue opportunities

Organizations depend on leaders who can funnel innovative ideas into cost-saving and revenue opportunities. As you work with your group, consider the following suggestions:

▸ Align your efforts with the organization's strategic direction. Is the organization trying to cut costs? To increase profits? Focus your efforts on areas that are already supported.

▸ Set specific goals. For example, instead of saying that you want to cut costs, specify that you want to cut them by 3 percent during the next nine months. This will give people a measurable target.

▸ Make sure people have a solid understanding of how the business works. This will make it easier for them to determine whether an idea will save money or create a revenue opportunity.

▸ Give people examples of the type of results you're looking for. Motivate people by sharing stories of companies that made measurable changes.

As a group, discuss how they did it, and how you could apply similar ideas at your organization.

Have the person study a company known for cost saving. Discuss which ideas could transfer to your company.

▸ Anticipate the consequences of making a change. For example, will reducing costs in one area increase them in another? Involve people from several areas to analyze a proposal.

▸ Examine what it will take to realize a revenue opportunity. Determine whether the additional revenue will offset the costs of creating and maintaining the product or service.

5

Use Financial Data

Learning to evaluate, interpret, and incorporate financial data in your daily decisions is an essential element in your success as a manager and in your ability to understand your organization's financial goals and focus your efforts on them.

Managers must develop financial acumen to understand not only where the organization is headed but also their group's role in meeting financial goals. They need to know when to spend and when not to spend. While many managers have a foundation in financial data, expanding your understanding of how your organization measures financial performance, strengthening your ability to include more accurate or robust financial analysis and reports in your proposals, and evaluating your competitors' financial indicators all deepen your grasp of what it takes for your organization to succeed. With careful study and the help of a trusted adviser, you can develop stronger financial acumen that will benefit your group, your organization, and your career.

In this chapter, we will cover the following areas:

▾

- ▸ Understand the organization's financial environment
- ▸ Set aggressive yet achievable financial goals
- ▸ Grasp the full meaning and interrelationships of key financial indicators
- ▸ Demonstrate understanding of how your work unit's performance contributes to the overall organization's financial results
- ▸ Conduct regular reviews of financial performance
- ▸ Identify levers to improve financial performance
- ▸ Develop an early-warning system to spot unusual trends
- ▸ Learn to read and interpret annual reports
- ▸ Draw accurate conclusions from financial reports and other quantitative information
- ▸ Use reporting formats that track key metrics and financial indicators
- ▸ Communicate financial information so that others understand it
- ▸ Create accurate forecasts
- ▸ Understand your company's investment policies and practices
- ▸ Evaluate the viability of proposed investments before making recommendations or taking action
- ▸ Strive to maintain the highest quality while managing costs
- ▸ Make prudent decisions regarding significant expenditures
- ▸ Identify and document decision-making criteria up front
- ▸ Review assumptions underlying financial analyses
- ▸ Employ appropriate analytical techniques
- ▸ Perform a sensitivity or "what-if" analysis
- ▸ Conduct post-audits of previous decisions
- ▸ Develop contingency plans

- ▸ Identify ways to manage risks in making financial decisions
- ▸ Create a budget
- ▸ Readily identify soft spots in budgets and profit plans
- ▸ Get your budget approved
- ▸ Assess the relative profitability of products and product lines
- ▸ Work with a knowledgeable financial adviser as your mentor

Understand the organization's financial environment

▼

Pay attention to the types of financial questions the person asks, and determine whether they are at the right level.

All organizations operate within environments that they create themselves and also are shaped by macroeconomic conditions, the industry, competitors, government policies and regulations, new advances in technology, and so on. The more you understand the environment, the more helpful you can be to your organization. This will help you understand top management moves and priorities, anticipate what will happen, and shape and influence the environment and realities for your group. Consider the following suggestions:

▶ Read or listen to top management's briefings to the financial markets and investors. These briefings include messages to investors and answers to concerns that investors or financial market representatives may have about the organization and its future.

▶ Understand whether the organization is highly leveraged and has debt that needs to be paid in the short term. In these circumstances, you can predict that cost savings will be a priority.

▶ Note the targets set by top management: percentage of growth, percentage of organic growth, percentage of growth through acquisition, profitability targets, amount of cost reductions. These metrics are indicators of priorities.

▶ Pay attention to your competitors so that you understand where your organization stands in comparison. For example, your organization may be growing at a rate of 10 percent per year, which you might think is substantial growth, but your competitors may be growing at a much faster pace.

▶ Note whether your organization manages multiple metrics, such as a balanced scorecard. If the organization has a balanced scorecard, understand why. Often an organization turns to a balanced scorecard or a multiple metrics approach when an area needed for success of the business has been neglected, or when the organization has decided to pursue a new strategy that calls for a focus on a new or different area.

For example, an organization that is losing customers might decide to adopt a customer measure that includes customer satisfaction, customer retention, and customer growth. This new measure, now one of the organization's key metrics, signals a new or renewed focus on customers.

Set aggressive yet achievable financial goals

▼

Some organizations set financial goals from the top, others from the bottom; some use a combination approach. It's important to understand how your organization sets financial goals and how to operate effectively within that system. Successful managers know how to set goals, know how to give their management information so that goals that are set are reasonable, know how to push back against goals that are unreasonable or unattainable, and know how to help others go after goals that seem to be a very large stretch.

When you set goals:

▶ Use historical, market, competitive, and industry information.

▶ Set goals within the context of the organization's goals and the goals in the value chain. For example, if you are in human resources and your part of the organization plans to open 50 new stores, your goals will include hiring people for those new stores. If you are in marketing, your goals will include the percentage of market share you intend to take from the competitors in each location where you are opening stores.

Have people explain the rationale behind their financial goals. Coach them on how to challenge assumptions.

▶ Link goals to organizational strategy and work unit strategy. Clearly articulating the links will help your work group and organization achieve the goals.

▶ Set aggressive yet achievable goals. Goals need to be aggressive to ensure maximum possible performance, but they need to be achievable or they will lack credibility. If people believe goals are unattainable, they won't be as motivated to pursue the goals and their results will suffer.

▶ Communicate the goals to your work unit and translate them into individual action plans. Every manager and team member should know how to answer the question "What do I need to do to ensure that we reach our goals?"

When goals are set for you:

▸ Never let yourself be handed goals that you have not influenced.

▸ Always give your boss information in a way that makes sense to him or her, so that the goals he or she sets will be attainable.

▸ Prior to goals being set, brief your boss about your work unit, its work, the issues you see, and your goals. Even if goal setting is top down, you can suggest priorities and goals. Provide rationale and understanding for your boss, so that the goals make as much sense as possible.

▸ Remember that you will not always have a boss who wants to understand you and your work unit. It is your job to influence your boss as much as possible for the good of the organization. Figure out what is important to your boss so you can influence him or her with the best information or approach.

When you want to push back:

▸ First, thoroughly understand the background of the goals. Assume that your boss is smart and is not deliberately setting you and your group up for failure. Be a detective and ask enough questions so that you understand why the goals were set.

▸ Check to see if your boss thinks the goals are attainable. If so, talk together about ways to reach the goals. Ask for help.

▸ If your boss has doubts too, treat the situation as a problem for the two of you to solve. Ask if your boss pushed back on the goals. If not, find out why, and together consider whether pushing back is an option. Involve your team so that you have several minds working on the problem. A change in the usual way of operating may be needed.

▸ Consider contingency planning. If you are correct and the goals are not attainable with the current resources and methods of operating, figure out options for what you are going to do. Organizations are interlocking systems that count on each part to deliver what it is supposed to deliver.

When you need to motivate your team to pursue goals they believe are unattainable:

▶ Realize that teams will not try to attain goals they do not believe can be reached. They may try, but without the necessary energy and creativity.

▶ Work with team members to figure out how to attain the goals. The key here is that the team may be right: the goals may not be attainable unless something is changed. You need to have them on board about the importance of achieving the goals, and then harness their creativity to figure out how it would be possible.

Grasp the full meaning and interrelationships of key financial indicators

▼

Share with people your perceptions of their financial acumen. Let them know what skills they need to learn or develop.

Most organizations use several key indicators to define and communicate success to the financial markets. Because management expects to be held accountable for achieving the stated financial targets, these indicators have a strong and far-reaching influence on management policies and practices, ranging from resource allocation decisions to incentive compensation plans. Consider the following suggestions:

▶ If you are not aware of the financial metrics of your part of the organization, talk with your manager about how he or she uses metrics to evaluate the work unit. Ask how the work unit metrics fit into the metrics of the organization. Ask to see financial reports that your manager reviews regularly. If you do not understand them, ask for an explanation from your manager or a finance person.

▶ Research the company's Web site, speeches, annual report, newsletters, and press releases to find out which indicators are emphasized by management in communications to investors. Key financial indicators can vary substantially by industry and company, but most fall into the categories of growth, profitability, liquidity, and productivity.

▶ Identify indicators (sales per square foot, inventory turns, for example) your company uses to help everyone in the organization understand how the goals will be achieved. Review internal financial reports, the corporate balanced scorecard, strategic planning documents, Web sites, annual reports, and employee communications to learn about these indicators.

▸ Learn the meaning of each indicator, how it is calculated, and why it is significant. Then identify the ways in which your work unit contributes to these indicators. Determine whether your work unit is measuring the activities that contribute most to the organization's success in terms of these indicators.

▸ Determine whether your company uses industry-wide metrics, which many companies report on. These indicators are often thought to foreshadow future performance, and they also enable investors to compare your organization's performance with its competitors. Become conversant in these industry-wide measures: what they are, how they are calculated, the meaning ascribed to them, how your organization compares to your competitors.

▸ Study leading companies to find out which indicators they track. Consult books, trade organizations and their publications, conferences, Web sites, blogs, podcasts, and industry reports. If you find indicators that you are not tracking now, select the few you think are most important and start tracking them in your work unit.

Demonstrate understanding of how your work unit's performance contributes to the overall organization's financial results

An understanding of your work unit's contribution to the organization's overall performance can help you set direction and priorities for the work unit and motivate team members. Consider the following suggestions:

▸ Look at what your work unit is responsible for. Some work units are part of the primary value chain that creates, sells, and delivers products or services to customers, while others are part of the functions that support this value chain. Both are important.

   ▹ What does your group do?

   ▹ What happens if the group does not perform its role?

   ▹ What happens to other groups if your group doesn't do what it is supposed to do?

▷ What happens to the organization's results if your group does not perform to expectations? Some functions or work units have direct and immediate effects, while others might have subtle or longer-term implications. For example, if sales targets are not met, revenue will be lower. If a legal function does not do its job well, the organization could be at higher risk of a lawsuit that could substantially affect the bottom line.

Discuss the consequences for other groups if the person's work unit doesn't make its numbers.

▸ Talk with the groups with whom your group interacts or is connected. Understand the impact on the groups downstream if your group does not meet its goals, is late, or does not follow the agreed-upon business processes. Note what happens to your group when the groups upstream do not follow processes, achieve their goals, or act in a timely way.

▸ Ask your internal customers what you can do to improve and how you can add more value for them.

▸ To understand your work unit's contribution, review the historical performance of your unit:

▷ What role does the work unit play in creating value for customers? For example, it might create a product, deliver a service, provide customer service, or hire designers for new products.

▷ Is this role increasing or decreasing? When a work unit's role is more pivotal to the value creation process, it typically gets more resources. For example, if an organization switches from discovering or developing its own technology to acquiring it, the roles of strategic acquisition and legal advice become more important. In addition, the organization might create an integration function to integrate the acquisitions better and faster. On the other hand, discovery group funding might drop because new products are supposed to come from acquisitions.

▷ How has your work unit's contribution to the organization's results changed over time? What have been the major implications of these changes? For example, a customer service group might have been started to fix products that had a lot of defects; when reliability of the product improves, they will focus on how customers can use the product in other ways and on new customer needs.

▶ Understand your organization's value chain and your role in it.

▷ An organization creates value for its customers. An organization that produces no value will not stay in business.

▷ An organization's value chain consists of inputs (such as components for a machine or ideas for a new drug), the process via which the organization transforms them to create value for customers (such as parts becoming a machine or ideas becoming a life-saving drug), and outputs (the product or service).

▷ All of the work units in an organization contribute something to the value chain or the value creation process.

▶ Use the value chain to identify the key business processes that your work unit contributes to and is responsible for. For example, you might source materials, engineer the product, combine a group of products or services into a solution, sell the services, or hire the agency that markets the products.

▶ With an understanding of the role your group plays in the value chain, it is possible to identify the ways in which you can add the most value to the organization.

▷ Figure out whether your group is one of the pivotal units. While all work units create value, some create value that is pivotal and that is the differentiator for the company. For example, if the company's point of differentiation is that it offers total solutions to its customers, then the group that integrates the products into solutions is key to the value creation process.

▷ If the work unit addresses a key constraint to the organization's success, that can also be a source of value. For example, if an organization has decided to grow sales through strategic alliances, the work unit managing the strategic alliances is pivotal.

▶ Attend conferences sponsored by industry or professional associations where you can learn about new directions or contributions your area could make. For example, marketing managers could find new ideas about how to contribute value by learning more about the role of branding global products.

Conduct regular reviews of financial performance

▼

Observe people doing financial reviews with their direct reports. Ask them to critique themselves, and offer your thoughts.

Financial reporting systems are fundamental measurement and feedback tools. To develop or fine-tune your and other people's skills in this area, consider the following suggestions:

▸ Develop a standard format for financial performance reviews, focusing on what people need to know to make better decisions.

▸ After each review, conduct a debriefing session to note opportunities for improving the quality of the presentations.

▸ If some team members lag behind others in financial knowledge, hold a separate session at which people have an opportunity to ask even the most basic questions.

▸ Review all of the periodic reports you and your team produce. Consider whether any of these reports could be strengthened by the addition of financial information.

Identify levers to improve financial performance

▼

Challenge people to identify how they can achieve greater growth. Add your ideas when it's appropriate.

Successful managers understand the business model or models of their organizations. This allows them to identify the levers they can use to improve business performance. Consider the following suggestions:

▸ Ask your boss or a financial colleague to explain the business model(s) to you.

  ▷ Note where the organization makes its money. For example, the organization may make more money on service contracts than on the sale of products.

  ▷ Understand whether the business is based on selling a lot at low margins or selling less at higher margins.

  ▷ Understand the role of different distribution channels so that you know which channels provide more volume and which provide more profitable business.

▸ Determine what part of financial performance needs to be improved. Next, examine the constraints to improvement in that area. For example, if you need to increase sales of new products, look at what is constraining the sales. Do customers know about the new products? Do they trust that the products work? Are the salespeople comfortable selling them?

▶ Do not pull levers before you look at what will have an impact. It will do no good to increase sales incentives on new products if customers will not trust new products from your organization until early adopters have used them for a year.

▶ Use value chain analysis or some form of process analysis to understand which parts of the business process need to be addressed. Chart the process so you can identify each part and understand its impact.

▶ Get ideas from others about what needs to be improved.

▶ Measure the current state before you make a change. Then make the change and measure the difference so that you know what is actually happening.

Develop an early-warning system to spot unusual trends

▼

Unforeseen and unexpected events affect your business and organization, making it impossible to predict the future accurately. Also, your business is based on a series of assumptions. It is important to know what those assumptions are, challenge them, and have systems to warn you when they are incorrect. Consider the following suggestions:

▶ Develop a comprehensive list of danger signs that will alert you to unusual or unfavorable trends and immediately trigger further investigation.

Ask people how they determine if an indicator has become a warning sign.

▶ Show the list to your team and financial specialists, and ask for their input.

▶ Periodically review and update the list to reflect changing circumstances.

▶ Integrate financial and nonfinancial indicators of business performance. Nonfinancial indicators (customer satisfaction data, market share data, progress on key initiatives, customer traffic, merchandise return rates, capacity utilization statistics, employee turnover, quality data) often foreshadow problems before they are reflected in financial statements.

Learn to read and interpret annual reports

▼

Financial statements and other data in annual reports represent the public face of the company and, in turn, have significant implications for how the company is managed. To develop your proficiency at reading and interpreting annual reports, consider the following suggestions:

▶ If you are a novice at reading financial statements, read John A. Tracy's *How to Read a Financial Report: Wringing Vital Signs Out of the Numbers* (Wiley, 2009) or Richard Stutely's *The Definitive Guide to Business Finance: What Smart Managers Do with the Numbers* (FT Press, 2008).

Have the person read the organization's past three annual reports. Discuss questions the person has.

▶ Obtain the most recent annual report for your company. Review the financial statements, accompanying notes, and management's discussion and analysis section. Answer the following questions:

  ▷ What is your company's current financial health? Is it improving, deteriorating, or relatively stable?

  ▷ How are the results of your work unit or organization reflected in the financial statements?

  ▷ What is the company's capital structure? How much and what types of debt is it carrying? What is the ratio of debt to equity? What are the implications of this capital structure for your organization?

  ▷ From what perspective does management present operating results and significant events?

  ▷ How are investors and other stakeholders (customers, suppliers, creditors, for example) likely to view the company?

▶ Obtain annual reports for key competitors. Review the reports with the following questions in mind:

  ▷ How is their financial position similar to or different from your organization's?

  ▷ Are there significant differences in cost structure?

▷ Where are they investing?

▷ Considering their financial condition, are they likely to take competitive actions such as price cutting, easing or tightening credit terms, or entering new geographic markets?

▸ Analyze annual reports for major customers and suppliers:

▷ What are their most pressing financial needs?

▷ What implications do these needs have for our organization?

▷ What do their investment strategies say about future directions and plans?

Draw accurate conclusions from financial and other quantitative information

▼

Depending on their perspective, people interpret reports and analyses in several ways. To draw accurate conclusions, consider the following suggestions:

▸ Talk with your manager to understand how your decision making could be improved if you incorporated more financial analysis. Pay particular attention to the areas in which your manager indicated you could add to your analysis and those in which you drew inaccurate conclusions.

▸ Observe your manager's presentations or read his or her reports and documents to see how financial analyses are used. Note what the financial analysis adds to the presentations or documents.

Together, review sample financial information and discuss areas in which the data could be interpreted differently.

▸ Talk with your manager or a financial person to learn which financial metrics are needed to support investment and expenses. Include this quantitative information in your presentations, documents, and discussions.

▸ Observe your peers, especially those who are particularly successful at getting approval for their ideas. Compare the financial analyses they present with your analyses.

▸ When you listen to and review proposals from your team, go beyond ensuring that the ideas are good. Investigate the financial consequences and effects.

Use reporting formats that track key metrics and financial indicators

▼

Both financial and performance reports should provide accurate information that you and others in the organization need in order to manage effectively. To create useful reporting formats:

▸ Determine what you need to know in order to understand the performance of the work unit, specific projects, people, and other issues. Then set up reporting systems and reports to gather that information. For example, if the availability of parts is important, track availability over time so that you know whether there has been improvement. Ask people who are responsible for the work to determine the necessary information and reports.

Remind people that metrics must be aligned with the organization's business strategy for the results to be meaningful.

▸ Ensure that you measure financial and performance data in a manner that is consistent with the business strategy or project objectives. Some managers find themselves with measurement systems that do not measure what is critical to the business. Identify at least one measure for each goal.

▸ To determine what should be measured, focus on the results you need and the business process outcomes that are necessary to accomplish those results.

▸ Develop a standard format for performance reviews, whether the reviews are for financial performance, project performance, business process performance, or people performance. Standardization will ensure that people consistently focus on what is important. Reviews should provide information that helps people make better decisions or perform better.

▸ After each review, get agreement about the improvements that will be made or the next steps in the process. A financial performance review without next steps does not take full advantage of the review.

Communicate financial information so that others understand it

▼

Managers who excel at using financial information to create vivid images of expectations and outcomes know that it can be a powerful force in motivating and improving performance. Consider the following suggestions:

Use Financial Data

Listen to people explain the financial situation to direct reports, and assess whether the messages are accurate, clear, and understandable.

▶ In your presentations, use financial data to tell the story about what is happening in your business. This will help you concentrate less on the data and more on what you want to communicate.

▶ Listen to presentations or read reports that you find helpful and understandable. One of the most effective ways to improve your use of financial data is to learn from others.

▶ Consider what your employees and others need to know about the work unit's performance or a project's performance. Gather this information and present the data visually instead of reciting numbers. It is easier to make sense of visual displays than a list of numbers.

▶ When you are constructing reports, list the key messages found in the data. Highlight interrelationships between items. Describe what happened, and also show *why* it happened. Strive to "make the numbers talk" in both oral and written communication.

▶ Make effective use of charts and graphs in your PowerPoint or online presentations. Determine the visual format that best supports your key messages. Look for templates that will help you illustrate your information. Keep in mind, for example, that pie charts illustrate relative proportions, line graphs show changes over time, and bar charts compare targets or historical data.

▶ If you do not know how to format data in a way that is interesting, engaging, and memorable, find a skilled colleague who can help you. Use reports that you found helpful as a template for your reports.

▶ Review your reports before you share them with others. Consider whether they could be strengthened by the addition of financial information. Used correctly, numerical data can provide influential support for your recommendations or reports.

▶ Provide the essential data that will make your point. Avoid giving too much detail or unnecessary information, which can cause readers or listeners to become confused or lose interest. Share details as needed and as requested.

▶ When financial information is discussed at a meeting, study how others present, assess, challenge, and gain an understanding of the information. Incorporate their most effective strategies into your own presentations.

Create accurate forecasts

▼

Forecasts are important to all businesses. A forecast is a prediction of future results based on logic and the best available information. Forecasts allow people to plan for the future, allocate resources, anticipate risks, and make investments. An organization typically has its own methods or processes for forecasting, but some elements are common to all. Consider the following suggestions:

▶ Look to your manager and your finance department for formats, components, and expectations regarding forecasting for your work unit. Expect to see sales revenues, cash flow, operating income, supplier expenses, and other categories. Typically, managers are asked to predict results on the basis of planned costs. Organizations usually provide guidelines for cost increases or decreases. Many provide guidelines on results as well.

▶ Review and learn from past forecasts. Understand how they were prepared and how accurate they were. Also look at historical trends. Who contributed to the forecasts? What models did they use? What were the sources of data? If the forecasts were inaccurate, locate the source of the inaccuracy so that you can determine whether there is a risk of being wrong again.

▶ Determine the components of the forecast, many of which will be identified by your manager and the finance department. Also consider the components of the business processes in your work unit, the changes you intend to make, and the business challenges for which you have to determine the costs and results.

Help people revisit their last forecast to determine how accurate it was and to identify areas that could be improved.

▶ Select a forecasting method that takes into account the nature of your business and what is being forecast. Items that have significant downstream impact, such as sales volumes and product mix, probably require more sophisticated forecasting models. Work with your manager, team, and financial support person to determine the variables that should be included in the model. Develop the model and test it thoroughly before you rely on it.

▶ Learn which forecasts can be done simply. For some items, you can add an estimated growth percentage or apply the required reduction in expenses to historical results.

- To create accurate forecasts, look at your work unit's financial reports and identify the major drivers of each revenue and expense line. Look at historical data and other supporting data to understand the interrelationships (for example, commission rates are X percent of sales). Document interrelationships and use them to create forecasts. Constantly check actual performance against your forecast so you can improve your accuracy.

- Consult with others on your team to identify all the costs and risks. They may be closer to a particular project than you are and have more accurate information.

- Involve others, including cross-functional or cross-business unit teams, in forecasting elements for which they are responsible. This will result in a higher level of commitment to managing the budget. It will also teach others the skill of forecasting, help them understand the business better, and give you more accurate information.

Understand your company's investment policies and practices

Discuss the organization's investment policies to ensure that the person understands how and why initiatives are funded.

One of the main functions of a manager is to allocate resources to achieve the work unit's goals. Most organizations have well-defined processes and tools for capital budgeting and investment analysis in order to increase the odds that the organization will allocate its resources to the projects and initiatives that will create the greatest value.

Learning how to use these processes and tools enhances your ability to build a compelling business case for investing in your proposed initiatives, and it gives you an edge in the competition for scarce resources. Consider the following suggestions:

- Meet with a controller or financial analyst to review the company's policies and practices for analyzing both capital and noncapital investments.

- Learn what methods your company uses to analyze projects and allocate resources. If you are unfamiliar with these methods, ask a colleague to walk you through an example.

- Review recent capital appropriation requests submitted by your department. Which were not approved and why not? Ask your controller what might have increased the chances of your project being approved.

▶ Find out the company's "hurdle rate" (the minimum required rate of return) for various types of investments so you can demonstrate that your proposals will generate an acceptable return.

For example, one company imposes a 15 percent hurdle rate for laborsaving devices and other investments to increase efficiency, 50 percent for new products, and 20 percent for everything else (packaging changes, for example). Another company has no minimum return for investments that replace existing assets or are otherwise considered to be an operating necessity, but uses 15 percent for most other investments.

Evaluate the viability of proposed investments before making recommendations or taking action

▼

As a manager, you are responsible for evaluating projects, investments, and expenditures within prescribed limits. Additionally, you have a role in recommending projects or investments to management. To make the process work smoothly and to make smart decisions, consider the following suggestions:

▶ Organizations typically require different amounts of documentation, depending on the size of the investment. Find out the expectations for documenting assumptions, analyzing projects, planning, and so on.

Review people's investment criteria to ensure that they are consistent with the expectations of the organization.

▶ Ask your manager about his or her requirements for decision making. Ensure that you understand the parameters of your authority for investment decisions, which information your manager wants to see, and what he or she needs in order to get higher-level approval.

▶ Identify your criteria for decision making, communicate your expectations in regard to these criteria, and review proposed investments using these criteria. Also recognize that your processes for making decisions need to be consistent with those of the organization.

▶ When you are reviewing investments, carefully consider the assumptions on which the analysis is based. If the assumptions are flawed, the analysis will be worthless.

▷ Explicitly identify the key assumptions of each analysis.

▷ Ask which assumptions are standard within your organization (cost of capital, tax rate) and which are specific to this particular analysis (sales volumes, development costs).

▷ Evaluate the plausibility of each assumption. Is it logically sound? Are any assumptions inconsistent with one another?

▷ Look for errors of omission in the assumptions and calculations. Ask your financial specialist if steps have been taken to ensure that the analysis is accurate.

Strive to maintain the highest quality while managing costs

▼

Measuring the quality of your work against costs is essential as you strive to maintain a balance between high quality and cost control. *What* you measure is determined by your quality criteria or standards. *How* you measure it is determined by the technique that will give you practical, useful information. Consider the following suggestions:

▶ Learn about several cost measurement techniques. Train people to use these techniques.

▶ Select measurement strategies that are user-friendly and appropriate for the process.

Ensure that people know how to cut costs when necessary. Arrange for people to learn from others who have been through cost-cutting efforts.

▶ Be sure to measure the right criteria in the right way—make sure that the criteria and measures are customer focused.

▶ Measure frequently.

▶ Make the results visible. Post weekly or monthly scorecards to communicate results.

▶ Discuss the results with your team. What worked best? What could be tweaked or changed?

Make prudent decisions regarding significant expenditures

▼

Many companies have well-defined processes and tools—timing, level, allocation—for making decisions about expenditures. Follow these guidelines and develop your own within your limits of authority. In addition, you need to communicate expectations about expenditures to your employees. Consider the following suggestions:

▶ Every organization (and even each work unit within an organization) has its own set of standards and norms for what is appropriate and prudent. Review past expenditures and ask your manager what is considered prudent and what is not. Also ask your manager for documents regarding spending policies or guidelines.

Ask the person to tell you about the process he or she used to weigh whether or not to make a large expenditure. Discuss how well it worked.

▶ Before you make decisions about expenditures, develop criteria—including effective sourcing strategies, competitive bidding, analysis of the impact of spending or not spending, and adherence to company policies—for the decisions.

▶ Include people in decisions about expenditures in which they are involved or for which they are responsible. Ask them to prepare information that will help you make a decision on the expenditure. Look at the purpose, anticipated results, the logic of the rationale, trade-offs with other needs, available alternatives, and the cost of not investing. Ensure that total costs are determined.

▶ Establish processes for gathering sufficient information about expenditures. For example, investigate options, understand total life cycle costs, and understand the impact of not making the decision.

▶ Learn how your organization defines "prudent." A prudent decision in one situation may seem imprudent in another. Find out the company's hurdle rate for various types of investments.

▶ Know your own spending tendencies so that you can develop processes that will complement your tendencies and provide the proper controls and supports to enable you to make prudent expenditures. If your answer to most problems is to spend, involve someone on your team whom you respect who has the opposite approach.

▸ Monitor the overall financial health of your organization. You may have money in your budget, but consider the expenditure in light of the overall situation. Always consider current conditions. If your business situation has changed since you created your budget, adjust your spending accordingly.

▸ In evaluating a solution, use realistic cost and benefit estimates. Avoid justifying huge costs by predicting an overly optimistic benefit. On the other hand, dropping a solution because it appears too costly in the short term may be the wrong decision in the long run.

▸ For each potential solution, evaluate the financial costs and benefits based on a range of assumptions. For example, if your figures are based on an assumed 20 percent participation rate, also compute your costs and benefits with a 10 percent or 30 percent participation rate. This will provide information on the financial implications of your assumptions.

▸ Test your assumptions about the expenditure by discussing them with colleagues who made similar purchases.

▸ Communicate expectations to your direct reports. Discuss the rationale for spending policies. Review expenditures as they are incurred and discuss them with your direct reports.

▸ Follow up on the accuracy of your cost/benefit conclusions. Use this information to fine-tune your assumptions and calculations on subsequent projects.

Identify and document decision-making criteria up front

▼

Have the person document must-have and nice-to-have criteria for the situation.

Agreeing on criteria before a decision needs to be made makes it easier to decide on a course of action or make a choice. Disagreement often occurs because people have different decision-making criteria. Consider the following suggestions:

▸ Include the following financial factors in deciding on your criteria:

▷ *Return:* Most publicly traded companies have established a minimum required rate of return on investment that all capital projects must meet. This hurdle rate expedites the process of allocating capital resources to the most worthy projects. Work with your financial specialists to determine the appropriate hurdle rates for the types of investments your work unit makes.

▷ *Risk:* Determine an acceptable level of variability in the expected returns for proposed projects. Also consider which alternatives may be forfeited and which options will remain open if you invest in the proposed project.

▷ *Strategic fit:* Identify the essential elements of your organization's strategy. How closely must proposed projects fit within them?

▸ Financial considerations are only part of the criteria for most decisions. Identify other criteria, such as the reliability of the process or a vendor, experience, impact on employees, and amount of training needed.

Review assumptions underlying financial analyses

Carefully consider the assumptions on which you base your analyses. If assumptions are flawed, analyses will be worthless. Consider the following suggestions:

▸ Explicitly identify the key assumptions of each analysis.

Pair the person with a financial expert for informal consulting.

▸ Ask which assumptions are standard within your organization (cost of capital, tax rate) and which are specific to this particular analysis (sales volumes, development costs).

▸ Consider which assumptions should be included in the sensitivity or "what-if" analysis.

▸ Evaluate the plausibility of each assumption. Is it logically sound? Are any of the assumptions inconsistent with one another?

▸ Look for errors of omission in the assumptions and calculations. Ask your financial specialist if steps have been taken to ensure that the analysis is accurate.

▸ Perform a post-audit on previous projects to uncover factors that may have been overlooked.

Employ appropriate analytical techniques

▼

When you analyze proposals for projects and investments, use the appropriate technique to yield the type of results you need. Choose from the following techniques:

- *Cost-volume-profit analysis* (also referred to as *break-even analysis*): This may be the best analytical tool to use when all of the following conditions are met:
  - ▷ Costs can be reasonably separated into fixed and variable components.

Encourage people to invite someone from finance to speak to their team about analytical techniques and how they are used.

  - ▷ All cost-volume-profit relationships are linear.
  - ▷ The selling price will not vary with changes in volume.

  Use cost-volume-profit analysis for:
  - ▷ New product decisions: Determine the sales volume needed to break even, given expected selling price and expected costs.
  - ▷ Pricing decisions: Determine the increase in volume needed to justify a specific price decrease.
  - ▷ Modernization or automation decisions: Analyze whether to substitute fixed costs (such as equipment) for variable costs (usually direct labor).

- *Payback-period analysis:* Payback period is the time it is expected to take for the cash inflow of the investment to equal the initial cash outflow. It is best used for short-term projects of less than a year, since it does not take into account the "time value of money" (a dollar available today is more valuable than a dollar available at some future date).

  Although discussions about payback periods are common in many organizations, avoid using the payback-period method to the exclusion of other analytical methods. Doing so can give others the impression that you are simplistic in money matters.

- *Net Present Value* (NPV): Use NPV for projects that will last longer than one year, since it takes the "time value of money" into account. In general, NPV is the preferred method for making capital investment decisions. To use the NPV:

▷ "Discount" future cash flows by an appropriate interest rate to calculate their present value.

▷ Subtract the initial cash outlay to arrive at the net present value. If the NPV is a positive number, the project should be accepted according to this criterion.

▶ *Internal Rate of Return* (IRR): IRR also considers the time value of money. The IRR is the interest rate that will yield a net present value of zero, given the expected initial investment and expected future cash flows.

▶ For more information, check out Web sites that provide small-business tools (capital budgeting tools and processes, for example), small-business blogs, case studies, and interpretations of financial news stories.

Perform a sensitivity or "what-if" analysis

▼

All investment analyses require you to make assumptions. In some cases (investing in a proven laborsaving device, for example), the assumptions involve little guesswork or estimation. In other cases (new products, new technologies), the assumptions are softer and call for best guesses that are highly subjective or based on limited data.

A base-case scenario should involve the set of assumptions that you consider most likely. Supplement the base case with several "what-if" analyses to help you see how the outcome may vary if one or more of the assumptions is significantly off.

When people present ideas for financial changes, determine if they have looked at unintended consequences. If not, provide feedback.

To conduct a "what-if" analysis for an investment, take the following steps:

▶ Explicitly identify the assumptions that underlie the analysis. Ask which assumptions and estimates are "solid" and which are "soft." For each soft item, consider how much the actual results could differ from your estimates.

▶ Perform a sensitivity analysis by altering the assumptions you consider uncertain, one assumption at a time. Determine the impact that changing those factors would have. For example, what if sales volumes were 10 percent lower than your best estimate? What if they were 30 percent higher? Work through some best- and worst-case scenarios.

- Determine the factors that most influence the analysis. A thoughtfully designed spreadsheet will help you identify the most critical variables.

- Identify items that are most prone to estimating errors. If necessary, find ways to reduce the risk of estimation error. You may want to use alternative estimation methods, such as consensus estimates from experts or trend analysis.

Conduct post-audits of previous decisions

▼

Continuously improve your decision-making process by conducting post-audits according to a predetermined schedule. Post-audits are particularly valuable for recurring projects.

- Meet with the individuals involved in the original decision and answer the following questions:

  ▷ How much did actual results differ from expected results?

  ▷ Which factors most influenced the outcome?

  ▷ Were the most important factors considered in the financial analysis?

  ▷ Which factors that initially were thought to be significant had little impact on the outcome?

Ask people to review discrepancies over the past year between what they expected and what actually happened.

- Document key findings to facilitate continuous improvement. Share best practices with other divisions and functions.

Develop contingency plans

▼

Contingency planning is an effective way to manage risk while setting a financial course for your work unit. As the pace of change accelerates, the ability to quickly recognize and respond to changes is vital. Consider the following suggestions:

Encourage people to include individuals who raise questions and concerns in contingency-planning meetings. Their point of view can be very useful.

- With your team, review the list of assumptions on which your plan is based.

- Scan the external environment for signals of change. List changes that are likely to occur and could have a significant impact on your business.

- ▸ List the most likely implications of the probable changes.

- ▸ Brainstorm possible responses to each change and come to consensus on the best responses.

- ▸ Develop a high-level plan for responding to change and explicitly identify which events will trigger these responses.

Identify ways to manage risks in making financial decisions

All decisions involve some type of risk. In many cases, risks can be mitigated—for a price. To understand what the risks are and determine what you will do about them, consider the following suggestions:

- ▸ With your team, identify all of the possible risks to a project or a plan. Next, determine the significance of each potential risk using criteria appropriate for the situation. For example, use a scale of 1 to 5 with 5 representing a fatal risk for the project. Next assign a probability of each risk occurring. This process will make the degree of risk in a project more concrete.

When people must take a financial risk, ask about their plans to manage the risk. Ensure that solid risk management is in place.

- ▸ One chief source of risk is assumptions made about the project. It is not uncommon for a project team to unwittingly make some assumptions without a careful analysis. Ask for a list of assumptions upon which a project is based. Talk with your team about the basis of each assumption. Ensure that the assumptions are logical and sound, are supported by documentation, and are agreed to by those involved. Pay careful attention to those on your team who disagree. Make sure you thoroughly understand their point of view.

- ▸ Perform "what-if" analyses to determine how changes in the assumptions would affect the decision. Consider how much the actual results could differ from your estimates. For example, the team may have concluded that customers want a new, improved product. What is the basis for the assumption? Ask what would happen if the assumption were not true.

- ▸ Know your own and your team's track record for making optimistic assumptions. Some people consistently underestimate how long it will take to introduce a new product or make a change. When you are looking at plans, take this track record into account.

▸ Plan for contingencies. Assume that something will change.

Create a budget

▼

A budget represents both the organization's commitment of resources to your work unit and a set of boundaries on your actions. A poorly executed budgeting process can have long-lasting consequences, making it difficult to attract and retain talent, maintain a high level of customer satisfaction, and achieve business goals.

Share information you have about the organization's budgeting process. Ensure that people receive the details they need.

▸ To prevent your budgeting efforts from becoming overly time consuming and chaotic, and to get the resources you need, follow this process:

1. Before beginning the budgeting process, review your strategic plan, set goals and objectives, and determine the resources you need to achieve those objectives.

2. Carefully assess the resources you have and the additional resources you will need during the budget period.

3. Review budgets and actual results for the year to date and the prior year. Look for significant variations and determine whether you should take them into account as you prepare the new budget.

4. Meet with the controller or a finance contact to gain a better understanding of how your work unit's budget fits into the organization's budgeting process as a whole.

   ▷ Discuss the time line and make note of deadlines.

   ▷ Ask about any general guidelines or assumptions (average salary increases, expected changes in raw material prices) you should use.

   ▷ Ask if there are special reports or historical financial information that could aid in the budgeting process.

5. Develop contingency plans for slower growth or business contraction. Ask yourself and your employees, "If business conditions become unfavorable, what can we give up, stop doing, or defer?"

6. Assign responsibility for the preparation of team or area budgets to the people responsible for particular projects or budget areas. Provide adequate instructions to people preparing their portion of the budget.

7. Compile all team or group budgets and reconcile differences. At the same time, watch for errors of omission, especially behind-the-scenes items such as office equipment and supplies.

▸ Establish a schedule for periodic budget reviews. Compare your budget to actual numbers and, if necessary, make midcourse corrections in order to meet the budget.

Readily identify soft spots in budgets and profit plans

It's important for you to examine budgets and profit plans for potential soft spots and to mitigate risk by addressing them appropriately. Budgets and profit plans are based on fundamental assumptions. By challenging these assumptions and considering that the assumptions could be wrong, you gain a better handle on the risk involved and can adjust or create plans accordingly.

▸ Look closely for assumptions. They are often broad and ingrained. Examples are "Our large customers will continue to buy from us" and "The new product will be rapidly adopted."

▸ Perform a sensitivity analysis by selecting key data and altering them. What impact would changing these factors have? For example, what if sales volumes were 10, 20, or 50 percent less than your best estimate? What are the best- and worst-case scenarios?

Ensure that people are challenging their team to identify the assumptions they're using to plan their budgets.

▸ Ensure that your spreadsheet is thoughtfully designed so that it allows you to identify the most critical variables quickly.

▸ What are the items most prone to estimating errors? Look for ways to reduce the risk of estimation error. Examine the data the estimates are based on and, again, question the assumptions.

Get your budget approved

▼

A well-thought-out budget is of little value if management fails to approve it. While it is rare for a budget to be approved without adjustments, you can increase the odds that your budget will survive the intense scrutiny of higher-level management, controllers, and those who are in direct competition for scarce resources. Consider the following suggestions:

▸ Find out the written and unwritten rules and norms of budgeting in your organization. These vary from company to company and from work unit to work unit.

▸ Benefit from the experience of others. Ask colleagues about previous budgeting cycles. Emulate what worked for them and try to avoid the pitfalls.

▸ Communicate frequently with your manager and financial support person to avoid unpleasant surprises at approval time.

Challenge people to predict key questions that senior management might ask about their budget and how they plan to respond.

▸ As you prepare your budget, consider what you will need to defend it.

▸ Be aware of your assumptions and be prepared to back them up with sound logic supported by facts and data.

▸ Be sure you have used the best available sources of data.

▸ Before submitting your budget, consider how others will perceive it. While some managers believe they should pad their initial budget submission so the essentials will survive the red pen, unrealistic requests can permanently damage your credibility.

▸ Pay appropriate attention to factors outside your department. For example, initiatives requiring a large cash investment are less likely to be approved if the company's financial position is poor or if another initiative is consuming large amounts of resources.

▸ Coordinate your budgeting efforts with those who might otherwise compete with your work unit for resources. Discuss resources that you could share, consolidate, or coordinate more efficiently. This benefits each participating work unit as well as the organization as a whole and demonstrates your ability to work as a team.

Assess the relative profitability of products and product lines

▼

Some organizations routinely report profitability at the product level. If your organization does not, ask your finance department to help you gather the information you need to assess product-line profitability. Consider the following suggestions:

- ▶ Compare all your products and services in terms of sales volumes, revenues, and margins.

Have the person compare profitability across your company's top three products. Discuss the level of profitability and the reasons for it.

- ▶ If any items are below an acceptable level of profit, take corrective action. Possible actions could include changing prices, finding cheaper ways to produce the product, instituting minimum order quantities, or deleting the item.

- ▶ Before cutting any products, consider any nonmonetary value that the product line provides. In some cases, it may make sense to retain offerings that appear to be unprofitable. For example, if you reduce a product offering from five items to the two items that represent 95 percent of sales, customers may become dissatisfied by the perceived lack of choice. In other cases, discontinuing one item may result in a decline in sales of a highly profitable complementary item.

- ▶ Periodically repeat this review to judge the success of corrective actions and seek additional opportunities for improvement.

Work with a knowledgeable financial adviser as your mentor

▼

Working with a financial adviser is one of the best ways to learn more about your work unit's role in the organization's performance and how you can improve it. Consider the following suggestions:

Help people find appropriate mentors and financial coaches.

- ▶ Seek out an adviser who is familiar with the reports you receive and the typical financial decisions you make in your job. An adviser may be a member of your internal finance team or a respected peer. When you select an adviser, consider whether he or she can tailor explanations to your level of financial acumen and the types of decisions you make.

- ▶ Involve your adviser in the assessment of your strengths and development needs, and in the creation of your development plan as it relates to financial acumen.

- ▶ Ask your adviser to help you review the financial reports you regularly receive. Check your understanding of each report's purpose and contents. Ask your adviser to explain unfamiliar terminology and to point out subtle interrelationships between items.

- ▶ After you have mastered reading the reports, take time to interpret the statements on your own. Check your interpretations with your financial adviser.

6
Manage Globally

All business today takes place in a global environment. Whether your organization has global offices, customers, partners, vendors, suppliers, or talent, it is essential for you as a manager to realize that you are operating within a global system of business. "Global" is no longer defined as *where* you do business, but as *how* you do business.

Effective managers understand that working successfully within the global business environment and global economy requires a global mind-set that incorporates humility, curiosity, sensitivity, respect for others, a nonjudgmental attitude, and willingness to learn new ways, new cultures, and new ideas and perspectives.

By developing a global mind-set, you will relate better to how your organization does business and will become a key player in creating better communication, relationships, and understanding among colleagues, customers, and world partners.

In this chapter, we will cover the following areas:

▼

- ▸ Stay abreast of worldwide business developments and trends

- ▸ Understand the impact of global events and trends on the organization's plans

- ▸ Convey understanding of the organization's global market position, opportunities, capabilities, and competitive threats

- ▸ Look at issues and problems within the context of the broader global business, not just the needs of your own country

- ▸ Develop a global mind-set

- ▸ Help others develop a global mind-set

- ▸ Learn the business practices of other cultures

- ▸ Develop cultural awareness and sensitivity

- ▸ Demonstrate responsiveness to the needs of the business from both local and global viewpoints

- ▸ Apply understanding of the unique business dynamics (market needs, marketing practices, labor practices, legal issues) when you're working across geographic areas and cultures

- ▸ Adapt to major cultural differences and social norms in doing business across geographic areas and cultures

- ▸ Demonstrate sensitivity to the local and global communities in which you conduct business

- ▸ Consider global market needs and deployment capabilities in formulating and implementing initiatives

- ▸ Identify how capabilities, resources, and infrastructure need to be modified for particular regions or countries

- ▸ Coordinate relevant activities with other countries and regions

- ▸ Manage and develop effective working relationships with people in and from other countries

Stay abreast of worldwide business developments and trends

▼

Encourage people to learn how others view their country and its role in the world and global economy.

Whether you like it or not, your organization operates within a global business environment. No business is immune from the impact of globalization, whether it comes from market growth outside of your home country, outsourcing, or new, unexpected competitors. Consider the following suggestions:

▶ Ensure that people in all areas of your responsibility are paying attention to business development and trends outside the organization's home country.

▷ When you read or listen to environmental scans, best- practices presentations, and market-positioning analyses, ensure that information about organizations and practices outside the organization's home country is included.

▷ Ask people to describe the business trends they have observed around the globe and their implications for regions such as North and South America, Asia Pacific, Europe, Africa, the Middle East, India, and so on.

▶ Be able to identify the most significant business trends in the countries in which you operate or plan to operate.

▶ Meet regularly with leaders from other functional areas to discuss global business trends, issues, and opportunities. Talk about the implications.

▶ Use social and demographic information to identify important trends that will affect business in several countries and regions. For example, what is the impact of a multigenerational workforce, health crises, and an increase or decrease in educational levels? How will these changes affect your organization, markets, and workforce?

▶ Regularly read global business development and trends research, blogs, e-zines, magazines, white papers, Web sites, and newsletters. These are published by industry groups, trade associations, governments, universities, and consulting groups.

▶ Challenge yourself and your colleagues to think about potential business changes that could have a significant impact on your business in the global regions where you operate.

▶ Pay attention to advances in technology in other parts of the world.
People have been caught off guard when they learned that they were
not the leaders they thought they were in a technology or service.

▶ Listen carefully to what people in your organization in other regions
of the world are saying. An organization that has a global presence
usually has an enormous untapped information source about global
business developments and trends. Encourage people who work
outside your region to provide you with information and their point
of view. Make certain that you comprehend what they are saying, and
then show that you are using the information.

▶ Talk to returning expatriates about their experiences. What trends do
they see? How did being in another country affect their ability to spot
trends?

Understand the impact of global events and trends on the organization's plans

▼

The more you understand how world events affect your business, the
better prepared you will be to minimize negative effects and capitalize on
positive ones. To further your understanding, consider these suggestions:

▶ Read and listen to globally focused and country-specific news media,
videos, Web sites, and podcasts. Pay attention to how trends, events,
and news are reported and interpreted, and take note of perceptions
about your organization's home country and its actions.

*Ask people to identify the
top three global trends that
affect the organization.*

▶ Discuss world events with your colleagues in other regions of the
world. Learn about their perceptions of the events and how they will
affect the organization, your business or industry, and your customers.

▶ When you talk to people from other cultures and countries, discuss
both business and social topics with them. Aim to see things from
their perspective. Deliberately look for differences in the way they
handle and interpret issues and situations.

▶ Ensure that the organization does not rely on only one source of
government information or build relationships with only one group
within a country. This is especially important in volatile or highly
politicized countries.

Convey understanding of the organization's global market position, opportunities, capabilities, and competitive threats

▼

In a global organization, leaders need to understand the organization's competitive market position from a global and local standpoint, know its capabilities across and within geographic areas, and understand its current and future plans for competing and operating globally. Consider the following suggestions:

- ▶ Recognize that you first need to understand the current and future impact that being global has on the business, and then understand the implications for you and your part of the organization. If this is new to you, talk to other managers who have experience in this arena. Also do research on what your organization has done up to this point, what it is planning, and how other organizations have responded to similar issues.

- ▶ Understand the ways in which your organization is currently global.

  - ▷ In your organization, does *global* refer to where you do business, where your customers are, where you are located, or how you do business? Organizations typically move through phases of being global. They start by selling to customers in different locations, continue by locating all or parts of the value chain in different regions (referred to as depth of presence), and ultimately operate globally, leveraging global resources to create and support the organization's strategic advantage.

  - ▷ Determine how your organization operates globally. Does it just have sales offices in different regions or countries, or does it also have manufacturing, distribution, and service centers in other regions?

  - ▷ What percentage of the value chain lies outside the company's home country? Where are those parts of the value chain? What is the impact? How is this anticipated to change? For example, outsourcing will change the location of parts of the value chain.

  - ▷ How does the organization leverage its global presence? Has it decided how best to structure and manage the value chain to create the most value to customers?

  - ▷ How is the organization structured? Are all major decisions still made by corporate headquarters and implemented in the different regions, or are the regions a part of the decision-making process? Are the organization's leaders from one country, or do they come from all the countries in which the organization operates?

▷ What percentage of your organization's revenue and profits are derived from markets outside the home country? How is this expected to change in the next five years? What will be the impact of this change?

▷ What is the mix of competitors? Are they global companies? Regional or national companies within particular countries? How do you anticipate this will change in the next five years?

▷ Who are your customers? Are they global companies? A variety of national companies? Are your consumers from one or many countries? How is this expected to change in the next five years?

▸ Understand your organization's sustainable competitive advantages and discuss the role that being global has on these advantages. For example, the competitive advantage may be linked to global scalability or to low-cost manufacturing in a particular region of the world. How does this affect your group now, and how will it affect your group in the future?

▸ Understand your organization's current and future market position. If you do not know this or need more information, talk with your boss or someone in strategic planning in your organization. Here are two examples:

▷ An organization targets other global companies as its customers and plans to deliver similar products and services to these customers around the world. In this case, scalability and consistency are differentiators.

▷ An organization that has a regional rather than a global or country-specific target customer puts a priority on regional needs and adaptations.

▸ Figure out what this all means to you and your part of the organization. It may mean that you and your people need to understand new markets better, that you will be sourcing materials from different countries than you do now, that you will need to work with new people, or that you will work with people differently than you do now.

> ▷ Meet with your leadership team and discuss the implications of where your organization is headed globally.
>
> ▷ Ask your boss for his or her insights.

Ask people to analyze and anticipate what their top two global competitors are going to do in the next six months.

▸ Look at your customers to understand how your organization or part of the organization needs to operate globally.

> ▷ Where is your current customer base located?
>
> ▷ To what degree are these local customers?
>
> ▷ To what degree can they be described as global customers? For example, do they need solutions that will work around the globe, and similar services in all locations that can respond to a range of needs?
>
> ▷ Will these customers continue to generate enough growth for your organization?
>
> ▷ How will the mix between local and global customers change?
>
> ▷ How are you managing the mix between local and global responsiveness?

▸ Considering your organization's global position and strategic plan, identify what you and your people need to do differently to implement the organization's plan.

▸ Discuss with your team the places and practices where you are vulnerable. For example, you may have quality problems in a recent start-up with newly trained employees, or a team in one region may not be working well with another team with whom they need to coordinate.

▸ Examine the global capabilities and experience of your workforce. Use an assessment process that gathers information and perceptions from people from different cultures. Identify opportunities for improvement.

▸ Learn from your competitors.

> ▷ What are your competitors doing?
>
> ▷ What has worked successfully for them?
>
> ▷ If they have competitive advantage in a market, how did they achieve it?

▷ What do you anticipate their next strategic move will be?

▷ What are their greatest successes? How did they achieve them?

▷ What were their greatest failures? If they recovered, how did they do it?

▷ What can you learn from their failures? Can you avoid repeating their mistakes?

▷ Have they gone into markets you did not even consider?

▸ Examine your competitors' business practices in markets that you chose not to enter. Consider what did or did not work for them. Are they doing things that your organization decided not to do? If so, how is it working?

Look at issues and problems within the context of the broader global business, not just the needs of your own country

▼

Whether you work for a global company or a company that does business in the global marketplace, you need to pay attention to local needs and issues while being aware of and attending to broader global business issues. Consider the following suggestions:

▸ Recognize that your decisions affect other parts of the business and other countries. Think about the impact your decisions have on others. For example, if you offer a local customer a lower price for a product, how will that affect your colleagues in other countries? If you and your team set particular expectations for responsiveness to customer needs worldwide, what impact will that have on people in other countries? Whenever possible, involve people in decisions that will affect them.

▸ Think about and do what is best for the whole organization, not just what is best for your part of it.

▸ Identify organizational barriers that prevent people from doing what is best for the overall organization. Work to remove these barriers or at least raise the issues with those responsible.

▶ Make it a regular practice in the decision-making process to look at unintended consequences. How might others be affected by this decision? What might happen as a result of this decision?

▶ Observe how your country's customers differ from customers in other parts of the world. This will help you anticipate how doing business locally might be different from doing business globally.

▶ Consider who, besides people in your own country, needs to be aware of issues, actions, policies, and decisions. For example, if a major service disruption or product recall has dramatically affected how your customers or the public feel about the organization, communicate about the problem, what has been done to correct it, and what you are doing to ensure that it does not happen again. Also communicate your recovery strategy for the customer and the public, and your recommendations for other parts of the business.

▶ Be aware of the fact that what one country or region does affects people in others. For example, vacation time varies from country to country. Some countries permit incentive pay, while others do not. Some countries may have a reputation for awarding business based on bribes. When people hear about differences in business practices, policies, or benefits and are concerned about them, talk through the issues. If you do not have the necessary information, find someone in the organization who can help you understand the issues and the rationale, and help you work through the issues.

Discuss how people in several regions view the same issue. Compare and contrast the views.

▶ Help people deal with the effects of decisions. Hiring contract workers for a job previously done by company employees may make good business sense, but the relationships between your employees whose friends and colleagues were laid off and the contract workers may be strained at first. Help the two groups work though the issues so that the contract workers do not receive the brunt of the anger.

▶ When someone presents an analysis or plan and the global implications are not mentioned, ask how people from different regions were involved in the process and how the regional or country differences are being addressed.

▶ Involve people outside the region in analysis and planning at the beginning of projects, instead of asking for their reactions later.

Develop a global mind-set

No matter how involved you are in international business, whether you manage a foreign subsidiary or simply need to be aware of how world events could affect your industry, the first step is to expand your own understanding of what it means to think globally. Consider the following suggestions:

Have people explain their understanding of how the organization operates globally.

▸ First, understand that unless you have been raised as a global citizen, you probably have a country- or region-specific mind-set. This is natural when you have spent most of your life in one part of the world.

  ▷ Ask colleagues from others parts of the world for their perceptions of how your mind-set or approach has been shaped by your region. Learn how it influences how you see and interpret things.

  ▷ Challenge yourself to think about how your mind-set affects you. For example, do you believe that people can be successful if they work hard enough? This is a region-specific mind-set.

▸ Recognize that a global mind-set really means moving from a geographic concept of "where you do business" to a concept of "how you do business." Fundamentally, it is a different way of thinking about and doing business.

▸ If you operate in a global company with personnel in several countries, you will probably hear complaints that the organization doesn't truly operate globally. Talk to individuals who hold this view to learn what they mean.

▸ Understand that countries have different ideals for a global organization. When you encounter difficulty in becoming a global organization, recognize that part of the problem is that people are striving for a different ideal.

▸ Keep an open mind. Before making a judgment, look at other points of view and consider their merits. Ask, "How else might this be seen or interpreted?" This will help you broaden your perspective.

▸ Remember that understanding another point of view does not require agreement or approval. Expect to find customs and viewpoints that you disagree with, though you still need to understand them.

▶ Examine how other cultures differ from and are similar to your own. Choose one country a month and learn all you can about that country, comparing and contrasting it with your own. Objectively study both its social and its cultural norms.

Help others develop a global mind-set

▼

Emphasizing a global perspective in your team will help your team members prepare themselves for the future and make them more effective in a global business. To help others develop a global mind-set, consider the following suggestions:

▶ Help the team understand the global nature of the organization and how it affects them. Wrestle with the difficult issues of how to handle differing business practices, cultural norms, and values.

▶ Ask your team to figure out how to leverage the resources of the global organization. For example, can you get work done faster by working continuous shifts around the world, or address staffing shortages in one part of the world by doing the work in another part of the world?

▶ Set clear expectations about the global awareness and involvement you expect from each team member. For example, software design teams might be expected to work with worldwide teams around the clock. Other groups might be expected to have strong global representation on their planning teams.

▶ Encourage discussion of global business developments and trends within your team. One way to do this is to ask two team members to monitor the news each week for political, economic, and other developments in regions where you do business. Put them on the agenda at update meetings. Rotate this assignment each month.

Ask people to describe how their mind-sets have been shaped by and reflect their culture.

▶ Challenge your team's culturally based assumptions. When you hear somebody make a statement with a home-culture bias, point out that the assumption might not hold true in other cultural contexts.

▶ Gather information about missteps in global business—an advertising campaign that offended local consumers, for example. Share the information with your team and brainstorm ways the company might have avoided such mistakes.

▸ Ask people in your organization who have recently returned from global assignments to talk about challenges they faced in developing a global perspective and how they met those challenges.

▸ Use a buddy system to link people from your team with individuals in other locations. Have each member pick someone from an office in another city or country and encourage them to develop an informal relationship, sharing information about differences in culture and in business practices.

▸ Pay attention to disparaging comments about how people do things differently. It is critical that you be a role model for valuing people in different countries and circumstances. Hold frank discussions with team members who seem frustrated by working across boundaries.

Learn the business practices of other cultures

▾

Business practices, as an extension of culture, vary widely throughout the world. To effectively conduct business globally, it's essential to understand the key differences between another country's business practices and those of your home country. Consider the following suggestions:

▸ Observe the business practices in different places where your organization does business. Pay particular attention to those with whom you work now or expect to work with in the future.

▹ Are there differences in business planning?

▹ How does each location handle people issues?

▹ How do government regulations affect business?

▹ Are there differences in how people conduct meetings or give presentations?

▹ Are decisions made on the basis of objective criteria only, or do subjective criteria (how long they have done business together, whether the head of the organization is from the same ethnic group, whether people are friends from business school) weigh in?

▷ Is the value of the currency stable? If it is not, how does that affect business practices?

▶ Ask about business practices in another country and the history and rationale for them. For example, learn why some countries restrict who can work in the country and some require work councils to approve management actions. Also find out why it makes sense in some countries to award work only to partners who have special relationships with a company.

▶ Ask people from other countries what business practices of your country they have found to be most different from theirs. Also find out what they have found the most difficult to adjust to.

Arrange opportunities for people to listen to expatriates talk about their experiences and to meet colleagues visiting from other countries.

▶ Learn about best practices of other global companies in your industry or in your customers' industries. Identify similarities and differences among the practices and determine the reasons for them. Compare these practices with your organization's values and practices.

▶ Help employees taking assignments outside their home countries to learn about the business and cultural practices of the new country and region. Expect to do business and cultural training twice: before the people and/or family move and about three to six months after they have been in the country.

▶ Talk to colleagues who have had assignments in other countries.
  ▷ What were the biggest surprises?
  ▷ What were their greatest successes?
  ▷ What would they do differently?
  ▷ What should others know before they take a similar assignment?
  ▷ What did they learn about themselves, their culture, and the culture of others?
  ▷ What were their frustrations?

▶ Take an expatriate assignment. Whether the assignment is short- or long-term, it will dramatically change your awareness of global issues and realities.

▶ Join an organizational task force or project team dealing with global issues. Reflect on and record what you are learning about the business practices of others as you work on the assignment.

Develop cultural awareness and sensitivity

▼

Getting a firm grasp on the variables that affect business in other countries includes knowing how cultures vary. To succeed in a global organization, you need to know about your own culture plus the cultures of people with whom you work or plan to work. It is essential to learn the key cultural customs and practices that will allow you to work together successfully. Consider the following suggestions:

▶ Avoid generalizing from one individual to an entire culture. Imagine how you would feel if someone from another culture believed all people from your country behaved and thought like one person he or she met or saw on television.

▶ Know some of the levels of culture that influence people. Typically these include a national culture; a regional, ethnic, or religious culture; gender; generational level; social class; and organizational or corporate culture. The impact of these levels of culture vary among individuals, but it is important to recognize that a corporate culture often is the newest and may be the most superficial of the cultures.

▶ Know some of the key differences in organizational cultures. The following differences were identified in a study by the Institute for Research on Intercultural Cooperation (IRIC):

▷ Process oriented versus results oriented: how something is done is more important than what is accomplished.

▷ Employee oriented versus job oriented: work is organized around people rather than common job roles.

▷ Parochial versus professional: locally or individually adapted standards take precedence over common professional standards.

▷ Open system versus closed system: a system is flexible, adaptable, and open to input and involvement rather than planned and scheduled.

▷ Loose control versus tight control: decision making is decentralized rather than centralized.

▷ Normative versus pragmatic: what is right or expected is more important than what works.

▶ Think about how the differences listed by the IRIC might affect you and your team. For example, if you are working with a team that is accustomed to tight control of a process, you can expect that a more adaptable, looser method of guiding the process will be unacceptable to them and make them uneasy.

▶ Identify the cultural elements that most affect you and your team. For example, look at how the manager and employees work together, how people determine who is right, and whom people perceive is responsible. Be prepared to talk through the differences.

Examine how language is or is not a barrier in working with global customers and colleagues.

▶ Understand differing points of view and help people work through cultural differences. For example, people who are not accustomed to women in authority positions may have problems reporting to a female manager. In turn, the manager may need help understanding and working through her employees' resentment, which is realistic from their point of view.

▶ Do not assume that people from different cultures view things as you do. Ask people to describe their views and what they think about issues.

▶ Learn the language of the country in which you work, and encourage your colleagues to do the same.

▶ When you don't get the reaction you expect from someone, focus on understanding his or her culture. For example, in some cultures problems are something to be endured, not solved. In other cultures, employees might be uncomfortable when a boss asks for their opinions, because in their culture it is a sign of weakness.

▶ Recognize that businesspeople within a country may not be the same as other people from that culture. Businesspeople become accustomed to other cultures as they work with multinational companies.

▶ Understand that people are products of their culture. Expect to see the impact of growing up in a particular culture on how people behave in business settings. For example, people who were the first generation in their family to be college-educated see education differently than those whose families have attended college for generations. Some people are thrilled to have their jobs and are more than willing to work long hours, while others focus on how much time they can have off for other activities.

▸ Take time to pick up the similarities and differences within different countries and regions of the world. Several unique cultures can coexist within a country or region.

▸ Visit the country or countries on which you are focusing in your work so you can get a firsthand understanding of the local and business culture. Talk with people. Learn the proper etiquette in that country. Become familiar with social structures and norms.

Demonstrate responsiveness to the needs of the business from both local and global viewpoints

▾

To succeed in a global organization, leaders need to balance the needs of the overall global business with the needs of their location. They need to recognize inherent tensions and be willing to work with leaders in all locations to find workable solutions. Consider the following suggestions:

▸ Understand that global and local tensions are normal and that the role of leaders is to work through issues and find the best solutions.

▸ Talk to your counterparts in other locations to learn more about their issues and concerns about working within the larger global business. You may find that you have similar concerns and can work together to sponsor useful changes.

▸ Advocate for organizational processes and structures that encourage collaboration between locations.

▸ Understand your target customers, your strategy for meeting their needs, and the structure and business processes your organization is using to execute this strategy. This will inform and guide your balancing of global and local needs. For example, if the strategy is to provide global solutions to global companies, then the balance will be skewed in the direction of common global practices. On the other hand, if the strategy is to provide local solutions to global clients, then the balance will tilt toward local needs.

▸ As you work with your team, communicate your understanding of the local/global strategy and its implications. Discuss the implications of the strategy so that they understand that the direction of the balance is based on the business strategy rather than on geopolitical alliances, an autocratic corporate headquarters, ethnocentric field locations, or personalities.

▸ Help others in the organization understand the local realities to which the local organizations have to respond. For example, human resource practices differ among cultures. Some countries restrict the number of hours per week an employee can work. Decide how to handle these issues on a country-by-country basis.

▸ Talk to people who have worked in your organization's offices in other countries. Learn about the perspectives they developed by being in another location.

▸ Ensure that product and service information is in the language of the end users.

▸ Use translation resources in the country in which the materials will be used. Have translations reviewed for content as well as cultural meaning and appropriateness.

▸ Use shared terminology within your team and educate groups in other locations so you understand one another. Unclear language can block communication and cause confusion.

Talk about how to balance local and global needs for major customers.

▸ Watch for "us versus them" thinking and discussions. Check yourself and caution others when they talk in those terms.

▸ Openly discuss the obstacles that people face as they work with teams across the organization.

▸ Challenge people to think of the big picture when they negotiate for resources. Encourage them to discuss how they can contribute to the success of the organization by working together instead of merely trying to increase resources allocated to their own areas.

▸ Ensure that communication systems around the globe work with one another and find out what is the preferred method for communicating; e-mail or Skype™ may be preferred over cell phones.

▸ Invite your team to share success stories about balancing local and global needs as they work through challenging issues. Also ask them to exchange their ideas and best practices with other groups.

▸ Study the approaches taken to common business problems in other cultures. Consider whether you could try these approaches at your location.

▸ When you write or interpret policies, identify the desired outcome and the intention of the policy. Expect each location to fine-tune procedures for carrying out the policy. This will prevent situations in which specific policies and procedures don't match the local work environment and thus are disregarded. It will also encourage the involvement and buy-in of the local staff.

Apply understanding of the unique business dynamics (market needs, marketing practices, labor practices, legal issues) when you're working across geographic areas and cultures

▼

Business practices differ for many reasons, including local cultures, customs, economic issues, and governments. As you expand your global reach, you need to determine when to modify practices in order to be most effective. Consider the following suggestions:

▸ Learn about national and local laws that relate to your business. For example, become familiar with certification and licensing laws, requirements for hiring local citizens, antipollution laws, and tax laws.

▸ Talk with human resources professionals in the countries where you operate. What are the differences between the practices in their country and in yours? What practices need to be consistent and which ones can be customized to fit the local culture?

▸ Determine which business processes need to be common across the organization. Ask teams from around the globe to analyze the issue. Also ask your customers, especially those who have operations in more than one country.

▸ Ask people to discuss how a business process is typically done in their culture before you revise it or create a new one. This will help you understand why things are done a certain way and will help you choose options that have the best chance of being adopted.

Ask people if they consult with people in the target country regarding cultural and linguistic issues. Discuss why it is important to do so.

▸ Acquire basic knowledge about the economic systems and business laws of other countries. Business practices that are common in one country may not work or may be illegal in other countries.

▸ Discuss and come to agreement on ethical business practices. Discuss how the organization will deal with business practices that are seen as unethical in some countries. When an organization is global, its actions in one country are assessed and judged by people in other countries.

▸ Identify the best way to introduce a product, service, or new marketing campaign to a country. For example, one organization set up symposia and invited key customers from each country in which products were being introduced. An expert from headquarters was brought in to introduce the new product or campaign, which lent credibility and helped gain customer support.

▸ Determine whether your organization can and should operate in a country that has a very different political philosophy. You may be charged with exporting ideology, unfairly extracting natural resources, or using unethical practices.

Adapt to major cultural differences and social norms in doing business across geographic areas and cultures

▼

Business practices and interpersonal styles vary widely throughout the world. Recognizing and handling those differences can be the deciding factor in a successful international business effort. Consider the following suggestions:

▸ Before you work with people from another country, learn all you can about the cultural norms and customs of doing business in that country. For example, what is the cultural norm about arriving at appointments on time? Where and when are decisions made—at the meeting at which they are discussed or at dinner afterward?

▸ Take into account regional differences within the country. Just as your own country has regional variations, so do all other countries. Regional differences can become pivotal when they affect business practices.

▸ Study the business practices of successful multinational businesses. Identify similarities and differences among the practices, and determine the reasons for them. Compare these practices with your organization's values and practices.

▸ Talk to expatriates about their experiences. What have they learned about themselves, their culture, and other cultures? What are their frustrations? What are their greatest successes? What do they do differently? What do they wish others knew?

Let people know if you see them treating individuals from other countries differently.

▸ Be flexible in how you pursue your goals. The culture and business practices of the country may require you to use a plan different from the one you expected to use.

▸ Recognize that it can take a great deal more effort and time to build a trusting business relationship when you work with people and businesses from another culture.

▸ When you select people to work internationally, choose individuals who are curious, adaptable, and respectful of other cultures and customs. Give them cultural training and ongoing support.

Demonstrate sensitivity to the local and global communities in which you conduct business

▼

As you work in several global regions, you learn how vital it is to understand the subtleties of cultures and communities in which the organization conducts business. Consider the following suggestions to help you demonstrate sensitivity to both local and global communities:

▸ Avoid generalizing from one individual to an entire culture. There is variation within cultures. Get to know several individuals within the community and do research on the culture and history of the area.

▸ Whenever possible, visit the country or countries in which you do business. Talk with people. Learn the proper etiquette in that country.

Learn about its social structures and norms. Seek to understand the local and business culture.

Arrange opportunities for people to work more closely with salespeople to gain understanding of global customers.

▸ Help your team develop a higher level of sensitivity to other cultures and communities. Rotate staff whenever possible so that people can work in other locations. Require people in key roles to develop proficiency in more than one language.

▸ Invite colleagues from other cultures to give their perspective on your culture's approach to doing business. Find out what aspects of your culture make it a difficult working environment for people from other cultures. Encourage candid evaluations.

▸ When you face a challenge, ask members of your team who come from or have experience with other cultures to report on how those cultures would approach the issue.

▸ Ask friends or colleagues who have worked abroad to describe how they learned to work in local communities. Extract ideas that you could use with your group.

▸ Assess the extent to which cultural differences get in the way of achieving your group's goals. People sometimes attribute a problem to culture when the problem lies elsewhere.

Consider global market needs and deployment capabilities in formulating and implementing initiatives

A global organization needs a global business strategy and implementation plan that leverages the global assets of the firm and provides sustainable competitive advantage. It needs to address both global and local issues, particularly in regard to execution. Consider the following suggestions:

▸ Thoroughly understand the business you are in and your customers. Analyze the needs of your current customers and future target markets. Your analysis should include a careful examination of customer needs and how they may vary in different parts of the world.

▸ Understand the value you provide to your customers and whether your value and competitive differentiators vary in different regions. Here are two examples:

Challenge people to learn which business practices are considered unusual in other countries. Discuss any surprises.

▷ In one region, an organization's value to customers was the ongoing service and maintenance they provided. In another part of the world, the same added service was seen as a negative because customers believed that if a product was built well, it would not need service.

▷ In the retail world, large economy size packaging is valued in some parts of the world, but people in other regions have little room for storage.

▶ When you customize products, ensure that they will have value in each local market. You may need more than just options A and B; you may need to customize option A further for each market.

▶ Challenge others in your organization to define your products and services in terms of the core needs they fill for current customers. Do you see similar needs in other countries and markets? Which countries or regions may provide growth opportunities?

▶ As you consider new markets, identify—and then challenge—your assumptions about a new market. In a well-established organization, bring in people from outside the organization to challenge your thinking. It is very easy for an organization to get caught in groupthink.

▶ Look at where your competitors are doing business. If they are not working in a certain location, determine why. If you decide to move into that area, be certain that your strategy addresses the factors that prevented other companies from entering or being successful in that market.

▶ Devise a set of questions to use in assessing a new initiative: What specific global market need does the initiative fulfill? How do you know this need exists in more than one market? What data do you have to back it up? Do you currently have the capability to carry out this initiative? Are people from several regions involved?

▶ Learn from other global companies that have already done what you are considering.

▷ What was the original plan?

▷ How did it change? Why?

▷ What were the biggest surprises?

▷ What were the greatest challenges?

▷ What advice do they have for you?

▸ When you are formulating plans, identify the business processes and practices that need to be in place to execute your plans. For example, the organization may have plans to build a new manufacturing facility but has not yet addressed how to get the product out of the country or how to cover higher transportation costs to distribution centers.

▸ Ensure that resources are available where you need them. For example, if the organization has decided to work in a new region, are employees with the right experience and training available?

▸ Identify when it makes sense to have a common global process and when it is appropriate to have local ones. For example, if you have a product development team composed of people throughout the world working on the same product, you will want to have a common product development process.

Identify how capabilities, resources, and infrastructure need to be modified for particular regions or countries

Have people find out how home-country policies are carried out in other regions.

Adaptability is often a key factor in making global companies successful. As a leader, you are responsible for understanding which elements need to be modified and working with the necessary teams and individuals to make it happen. Consider the following suggestions:

▸ When you change the business or part of the value chain, involve people from other locations and different parts of the value chain to assess the implications for processes and practices. For example, if the next step in a process is no longer going to be done by the people down the hall, what impact will that have on your group when they hand off work to the new team? Figure out the best method for communicating and working effectively across time zones.

▸ Anticipate any broader effects of changes at your organization. For example, if your organization began to do more highly skilled work in a facility, you might need to recruit people with advanced skills or re-train your current workforce.

- When you are making plans to modify existing processes or infrastructure, ask end users how they will be affected by the changes. Don't rely only on people who *think* they know.

- Use standard procedure for examining what might need to be modified so that people don't spend time arguing or discussing process. Most likely your process improvement function already has developed a common practice for the organization.

- Consider the effects of trade laws, taxes and duties, labor laws, exchange rates, currency fluctuations, border issues, intellectual property laws, environmental concerns, and human rights issues.

- Learn from others' experiences. Find someone in the organization who has done something similar to what you are doing. What did he or she learn and do differently as a result?

- Do a constraint analysis to learn the greatest obstacles to the success of a project. Address each constraint.

Coordinate relevant activities with other countries and regions

▼

If people get frustrated as they work across cultures, talk about what they can learn and how they can translate learning into positive action.

Coordinating business activities on a large scale is always a daunting task, especially when it involves issues such as multi-country customers, marketing initiatives, or supply chains. A clear sense of who the players are and what roles they play can help. Consider the following suggestions:

- Recognize that the primary advantage of a global company is leveraging scale, scope, geography, and resources. Challenge your team to identify how to leverage global resources.

- Always use cross-functional and cross-geography teams in analyzing, planning, and executing. Even if geography is not a current factor with a customer, include that factor if you anticipate a market need.

- Use common analysis and planning tools across groups so people can easily communicate with one another and update plans. Assign responsibility for coordination rather than just assume it will get done.

▶ Identify and understand the capabilities you need to carry out your global strategy. Then determine the strengths and limitations of your current capabilities. What do you need to do to close the gap?

▶ If your customers are global organizations, manage them globally with either a single global account manager or a global account team.

▶ Talk with your customers about how their organizations are internally structured and how they work. This will help you to decide how to work best with them. It is invaluable to know whether there is one buyer of your services or products, or one per region, country, or business. Even if you know that organizations are generally centralized or decentralized, how they are structured will vary.

▶ Develop a theme or phrase that quickly and simply states your focus for competing globally: "local and global" or "out-local the locals and out-global the global." Use this theme as a shortcut reminder in discussions: Does this meet our local and global criteria?

▶ Always remain open to making changes based on your own or other team members' increased understanding.

Manage and develop effective working relationships with people in and from other countries

▼

With the growth of global companies, more people find themselves managing people either in or from other countries. If you are in this situation, consider the following suggestions:

▶ Help a global team member who is living outside of his or her own country adjust and develop relationships with peers.

▶ Learn all you can about the culture and country in which you and your employees are working or interacting, including its social and business customs.

▶ Recognize that your employees are influenced by you and the organization, but also have their own goals and are influenced by their own culture. Take time to get to know your employees and understand what is important to them, their concerns, their goals, and any issues related to working for a global company.

▶ Do what you can to ensure clear communication. Use summarizing statements as a way to check what was said and what was heard.

▶ When you work with people in another country, learn a few phrases of their language. This demonstrates respect and an attempt to communicate.

Find out how people leverage their relationships with colleagues in other regions of the world.

▶ If people in a group speak more than one language, use both written and oral communication, since people may be more fluent in one than another. Talk more slowly unless people are very fluent.

▶ When you write or interpret policies, identify the desired outcome and the intention of a policy. Allowing the local team members to fine-tune specific procedures for carrying it out will prevent situations in which policies and procedures don't match the local work environment and thus are disregarded. It will also encourage the local team members' involvement and buy-in.

▶ Pay attention to differences in time zones. Alternate meeting times so that you don't always put the same group at a disadvantage.

▶ Remember that people in remote locations often feel isolated and left out. Be sensitive to relationship issues that your group takes for granted (camaraderie, access to resources) and champion ways to provide more interaction and access.

▶ Ask the local HR manager for assistance in understanding the culture.

▶ Observe whether team members work well with team members from other countries. Monitor whether some people are being sidelined, ignored, or underestimated.

▶ Consider cross-cultural relationship competence training to help people understand different worldviews. When you have a team composed of people who have very different worldviews, it is sometimes necessary to help them understand one another and help them figure out how to work together regardless of their differences.

▶ Ask for feedback from global employees—and recognize that you might not receive it. Providing feedback to the boss may not be done in their culture, or you might not have established enough trust in your relationship yet.

- Learn about your organization's track record and reputation for how it treats employees. Ensure that employees are treated consistently with the organization's values. If the organization does not value its employees highly, work with organization leaders to help them understand how critical people are to the success of the business and to change the organization's approach to valuing and respecting employees.

- Support expatriates and repatriates. Often, they need extra time for moving to a new country and getting acclimated, especially when they have families who must adjust as well.

7

Meet Customer Needs

Customers are the lifeblood of an organization, and it's often the little things that make the biggest difference in creating loyal customer relationships or losing customers to a competitor. How well your organization meets and exceeds customers' needs and expectations can determine whether your organization sustains leadership in the marketplace. Understanding and anticipating customer needs, dealing effectively with customer feedback and metrics, and implementing employee training programs that create exceptional customer service values all contribute to creating a customer experience that fosters loyalty, trust, and referrals.

Happy, loyal customers are worth the investment in time and resources it takes to create a dynamic, responsive customer-oriented culture within your organization. Engaging your key customers and developing a deep understanding of who your customers are positions you to anticipate their needs and sustain strong customer relationships.

In this chapter, we will cover the following areas:

▼

- ▶ Understand who your customers are
- ▶ Identify and anticipate customer requirements, expectations, and needs
- ▶ Develop and promote a clear understanding of the customer's business
- ▶ Provide customers with a variety of options for offering feedback
- ▶ Respond to customer feedback
- ▶ Continually search for ways to improve customer/client service
- ▶ Ensure a level of customer service that differentiates your organization from the competition
- ▶ Provide value to customers beyond their expectations
- ▶ Ensure that customer issues are resolved
- ▶ Meet commitments to customers/clients
- ▶ Hire the right people to meet customer needs
- ▶ Train for customer focus
- ▶ Set high standards for customer service
- ▶ Measure customer focus performance
- ▶ Motivate and reward excellence in customer focus
- ▶ Develop and provide a unified approach to serving the customer
- ▶ Facilitate multiple connections between the company and customer organizations
- ▶ Find ways to involve coworkers who don't normally have contact with customers
- ▶ Develop and provide flexible options to enable employees to meet customer needs
- ▶ Create systems and processes that make it easy for customers to do business with your company
- ▶ Understand and address the customer implications of process changes
- ▶ Remove barriers so you can provide exceptional customer service

Understand who your customers are

▼

Ask people to list their customers. If necessary, add to the list. People often miss internal customers.

Creating committed customers is the goal of successful organizations. Loyal customers fuel success and growth. They are one of the best measures of corporate performance because loyalty can be achieved only by creating superior value. In order to create customer value, you must first know who your customers are. Consider the following suggestions to help you define your customer base:

- Recognize whether your customers are individuals, businesses, or other types of organizations.

- Talk with your marketing group to learn what they know about your customers. It is likely that they have already identified customer groups or segments and can give you information about each one.

  ▷ What are the customer segments?

  ▷ Who are your best customers? Why?

  ▷ What level of penetration do you have within each customer? Within each customer segment?

  ▷ How are your customers changing?

  ▷ What are new customer targets or emerging customer segments?

- Conduct a survey to learn who your most loyal customers are and why. Then investigate to what degree the customer value chain operates in ways that support your value proposition. Make appropriate changes to ensure continued customer loyalty.

- Understand how your customers differ from one another and the implications for you and your teams. For example, you may need to offer a greater variety of product features, different kinds of customer services, or different kinds of customer support.

- If your marketing department has not already done so, separate your customers into relevant groups: age, ethnicity, mobility, geography, buying patterns. This will help you adjust your value proposition to each customer group. For example, health club customers who come in the early morning are usually different from those who come midday. Members who are recovering from surgery or health problems have different needs than those who are into competitive athletics.

- Consider whether a key account program makes sense for your organization. Identify potential key accounts—those customers who are strategically important to your organization. You may identify an account as strategic because it:

  ▷ Represents a large proportion of your revenue or profit.

  ▷ Remains a customer year after year.

  ▷ Has growth potential.

  ▷ Is a key player in the industry.

  ▷ Has the potential to be in a future alliance or partnership.

- Look at how you support key accounts. Many organizations assign an account team to be responsible for a specific account.

- Identify the individuals you serve in each customer organization. These are the relationships you must manage to create customer loyalty.

Identify and anticipate customer requirements, expectations, and needs

Without a clear understanding of customer requirements, expectations, and needs, you and your organization cannot fulfill your customers' needs and ultimately could lose their business. Because customers' needs change, it is equally important to anticipate changes and determine how your organization will respond. Consider the following suggestions:

- If you sell to other businesses or organizations, understand how your product or service is used. If it becomes part of a product or service they sell, understand their customers and their value proposition. This will help you anticipate your own customers' needs.

- Identify the requirements, expectations, and needs of your major customers. Assess whether or not your group is adequately meeting those needs or if you need to change your approach in some way.

- If you are not clear about the needs of a particular customer, get information directly from the source. Set up a phone call or a face-to-face meeting with a key customer contact and learn about what his or her organization is looking for.

▸ Spend time with customers. This will help you know, firsthand, what they want and what will delight them.

Ask people to explain customer requirements and why they are important. Listen for understanding of the customers' businesses.

▸ Recognize the benefits of having a clear understanding of customer requirements and expectations. Look back at a successful project and determine how your understanding of customer needs led to a positive outcome.

▸ Notice when customer satisfaction changes. Perhaps you used to get letters of commendation and thank yous, but no longer receive them or receive fewer.

▸ Study the consequences of not having a clear understanding of customer requirements and expectations. For example, analyze a project that was not entirely successful. How could your team have improved the outcome?

▸ When you or someone on your team is starting a new project, spend some time investigating and outlining key customer needs. Use this information as the framework for the project.

▸ Ensure that you know the influences in the buying process and the criteria for satisfaction. Carefully determine who the buyer is, and also understand who else needs to be satisfied.

▸ Talk with someone who is known for an ability to uncover customer needs. Find out what questions this person asks, how he or she gathers information, and how you can use some of the same tactics.

▸ Set aside an hour a week to scan trade and business journals, annual reports, online sources, newspapers, and market research reports to keep yourself up to date on your customers' businesses.

Develop and promote a clear understanding of the customer's business

▼

When you have a clear understanding of your customers and their businesses, you can make better decisions about the products and services you offer. This will also help you build stronger partnerships with customers. Consider the following suggestions:

▸ Spend time with customers at their site. See your products and services in use. Talk to people who work with the services and products about their experiences, their likes and dislikes about the service or product, what is easy or difficult about working with it, and so on.

▸ Talk with new customers to find out about their businesses. Ask them questions such as:

  ▷ What do I need to know about your business?

  ▷ How does your company position itself in the marketplace?

  ▷ What changes do you anticipate in the business environment in the near future?

  ▷ What key challenges are you facing?

  ▷ What are your current opportunities?

▸ Sign up for RSS feeds to receive automatic updates about your customers.

Find out what people know about how your product or service is used by customers. If they have not seen it in use, encourage them to do so.

▸ Periodically update your information on existing customers. Talk to customers about their business and do a media search on the Internet. Then analyze the information you have collected. Are there any trends?

▸ Think about things from a customer's perspective. What do you wish your business partners knew about you and your business or marketplace? Make sure you know those things about your customers.

▸ Invite customers to speak to your employees and customer teams about their companies.

▸ Make use of internal resources. Ask people who are knowledgeable about different customers and their businesses to share their knowledge with your team.

▸ Stay up to date on major business news. Read at least one local and one national business publication—for example, a regional business journal and *The Wall Street Journal*—regularly. Watch for news on your customers and their businesses, and share your findings with your team.

Provide customers with a variety of options for offering feedback

People who strive to create a customer-centered organization view feedback as an essential tool. They seek feedback to learn what their customers need and want, and to show their interest in their customers. As you seek feedback from your customers, consider the following suggestions:

▸ Ask customers how they would like to provide feedback to your organization. Have they been able to find avenues for offering feedback?

▸ Teach your people how to ask for, listen to, and accept feedback in a constructive way. Set a clear expectation that customer feedback is critical to the success of the business.

▸ Design feedback systems tailored to each customer segment. For example:

  ▷ *Strategic accounts:* use a structured, in-depth interviewing process to deepen your understanding of their business needs.

  ▷ *Smaller accounts:* have your frontline customer service or sales team use a telephone or electronic feedback process.

  ▷ *Consumers:* provide an easily accessible vehicle such as a response section on your Web site.

▸ Personally spend time with customers. There is no substitute for hearing directly from the customer.

▸ Take notes on the feedback you receive. Review your notes every month and keep track of trends, such as the number of customer complaints about a particular product.

Encourage people to ask customers how easy it is for them to provide feedback.

▸ In addition to talking with customers directly, use third parties to provide objective feedback and information from customers. Customers may tell third parties something they wouldn't tell you.

▸ Act on the feedback you receive and let customers know what you have done. Close the feedback loop so that customers know their feedback is valued and used.

Respond to customer feedback

An executive once said, "Talking to customers tends to counteract the most self-destructive habit of great corporations—that of talking to themselves." Businesses have two choices when it comes to seeking feedback from customers: they can choose to know what's on customers' minds or choose not to know. To encourage and be more receptive to customer feedback, consider these suggestions:

Review recent customer feedback. Check to see if people are acting on the feedback. If not, ask why.

- ▶ Treat customers' perceptions as reality, because they *are* reality for your customers. Take their comments seriously. Ask clarifying questions to make sure you understand the message.

- ▶ Listen for information beyond specific product needs. This has been shown to be the greatest skill difference between the most successful and least successful salespeople. Listen for:
  - ▷ Their requirements.
  - ▷ Expectations of you and your organization.
  - ▷ What would exceed their expectations.
  - ▷ Frustrations and concerns.
  - ▷ What keeps your customers awake at night.
  - ▷ Hints of dissatisfaction.
  - ▷ The underlying need, not just the solution.
  - ▷ Their feelings about you and their relationship with you.

- ▶ Welcome critical comments. Most lost customers leave without complaining, which gives you no opportunity to serve them better.

- ▶ Summarize customer comments and develop an action plan. Review the plan with key customers to ensure that it addresses their most critical needs.

- ▶ Commit yourself to responding to the concerns you hear. Dissatisfied customers may tell as many as 20 people that they are unhappy with the way you do business.

- ▶ Determine who needs to know about customer feedback, and plan when and how to tell them.

- Consider an annual or quarterly meeting with long-term customers to discuss changing needs, solve problems, and generate ideas for improvements. Include all key stakeholders from both your organization and your customer's organization.

- Notice how customer feedback is received in your organization. Is it taken seriously, or do you hear sarcastic or belittling comments about customer feedback?

- If your organization does not respect customer feedback, take action. Talk directly to people who do not take customers seriously and drive home the point that you are in business because of customers. Each employee's job is to add value to customers.

Continually search for ways to improve customer/client service

Excellent customer service begins with a discovery process. As you learn about your customers, you can tailor your actions to meet their specific needs. In return, they will view you and your organization as being responsive and dedicated to their satisfaction. Consider the following suggestions:

- Gather all the key people who work with a customer. Evaluate the current state of customer service. Identify what you know and don't know about the customer's satisfaction. Discuss how you can create seamless service among groups. Use specific examples to highlight what works and what needs to be improved.

Have the person ask customer-facing employees what the organization could do differently to serve customers better.

- Ask people in your area to describe the obstacles that prevent them from delivering top-notch customer service. For example:
  - ▷ Individuals lack the authority to make quick decisions.
  - ▷ Flawed processes delay production or delivery of a product or service.
  - ▷ Employees aren't rewarded for helping customers.

- Ask clients to describe any frustrations they have experienced in working with your organization. Look for themes or patterns.

- Check frequently to see if your clients' requirements and expectations have changed. Use information from interviews, surveys, focus groups, hotlines, and help desks.

- Measure customer service activities by whether they truly add value to the customer's experience. Check to see if you're measuring success by whether people are busy or whether customers are satisfied.

- When clients begin by telling you what solution they want, take a moment to learn more about the problem. A more suitable solution— one that the customer is not aware of—may be available.

- Reflect on customer service you have received. What delighted you as a customer and what disappointed you? Apply this awareness to your own organization.

- Work with experienced colleagues who have a reputation for stellar customer service. Learn how they approach the issue of customer service and emulate their techniques.

Ensure a level of customer service that differentiates your organization from the competition

▼

Customers expect excellent service. Organizations whose value proposition is that they know their customers well and that they meet customers' needs better than their competitors must provide a level of service that differentiates them from their competitors. Orchestrating the experience of the customer is perhaps the most vital step of building relationships and providing high-quality customer service. Consider the following suggestions to help your customers have an exceptional experience working with your organization:

Find out what the person knows about how your competitors work with customers.

- Stay attuned to your customer's experience with all parts of your organization. This will help you identify negative or unexpected outcomes, so you can rectify them quickly.

- Understand your competitors and their strengths. Talk with your competitors' customers to learn about their service.

- Guard against becoming out of touch. When an organization has been strong in an area, it is sometimes difficult to maintain that strength or to notice that it is not as strong as it used to be.

▷ Listen to feedback from new customers as well as established ones. Sometimes your new customers have information that you need to hear.

▷ Ask new employees for feedback about their perceptions of the strengths and weaknesses of the organization and of your customer service. They are less likely to be tainted by the past and may see things that you don't.

▸ Before you change a standard process to respond to a customer need, think about the impact the change will have on the customer.

▸ Use as many channels for communicating with customers as possible to increase the likelihood that customers will receive your message.

▸ Create customized solutions for your key accounts. With your largest accounts, it is a good investment for you and your team to tailor interactions to fit customers' unique needs, based on what you know about their expectations.

▸ Identify any systemic or organizational barriers that may prevent your employees from creating exceptional experiences for your customers. Brainstorm ways to remove the barriers. Examples of barriers include lack of authority to make quick decisions, lack of knowledge for understanding problems, and flawed processes that delay production or delivery.

Provide value to customers beyond their expectations

▼

When you understand your customers' requirements and expectations, you can create effective solutions that meet, and even exceed, their expectations, requirements, and needs. Consider the following suggestions:

▸ Make a concerted effort to look at customers' stated and unstated needs. Talk with them in depth, so that you understand their current needs and the forces driving those needs, and can anticipate future needs. Also ask for their "must haves" and "nice to haves." Inquire about what would really delight them.

Discuss what your organization could do to delight customers and go beyond their expectations.

▸ Summarize customer needs and map them against what you are currently providing. Identify new opportunities.

▸ With customer teams, list problems and opportunities for which you currently see no solution or change in circumstance. Then challenge the team by stating that somewhere a competitor or future competitor is figuring out how to solve these problems. For example, patient compliance with medication is a big issue in health care. This is currently seen as a big problem with no solution. Whoever solves this problem will have a big advance on competitors, especially if the solution can't be duplicated easily.

▸ Probe to understand a customer's problem. This will help you design a solution that meets the customer's underlying need.

▸ Clarify your customers' definition of long-term value. If you assume you know what's best or what they consider important, you could be mistaken.

▸ Examine everything you do against these criteria: Does this contribute to meeting our customers' needs? Does it add value?

▸ Define and use a structured process to involve customers when you make product enhancements and develop new products. Also invite customers, suppliers, and distributors to develop effective work processes with you.

▸ Examine the flexibility and adaptability of your service systems to see if they are capable of meeting unique customer needs. Value-added service offerings can differentiate you from your competitors.

▸ Ask what barriers or processes prohibit frontline employees from delivering exceptional, above-and-beyond levels of service. For example, are there too many steps involved in handling a customer complaint? Do employees have the authority to provide solutions on the spot? Policies that enable a fast, courteous, and exceptional response to customers will give your frontline employees a lasting positive impression on customers.

Ensure that customer issues are resolved

▼

Customers judge your organization in two ways: how well you deliver on your commitments and how well you handle problems. Consider the following suggestions:

▸ When a customer issue arises, develop a clear understanding of the issue. You may assume you know the problem, but you may know only your organization's version of it. Ask the classic questions: who, what, where, when, why.

▸ Find out how the customer would like to resolve the issue. You need to fully understand what the customer expects. You might have a different idea of what a satisfactory resolution looks like.

▸ Recognize that you probably cannot resolve the issue by yourself. Involve all necessary people, particularly those who deliver the product or service.

▸ After you resolve the issue, establish processes to ensure that the issue will not arise again.

▸ Provide employees who work closely with customers the knowledge, skills, and authority to handle as many issues as they can as quickly as possible.

Talk about customer issues that people do not believe they are able to resolve well enough or quickly enough.

▸ Have clear escalation procedures so that people know when and why issues should be raised to higher levels in the organization. People should understand that the procedures are based on providing good solutions to customers, giving people information, and taking needed action. Escalation procedures are not and should not be designed to get people in trouble.

▸ Learn from your mistakes. Once you have solved a problem, meet with your team to explore how it happened and what you can do to prevent it from happening again.

▸ Keep metrics on issues and their resolutions. Use your team to identify themes and patterns so that you can resolve systemic issues.

▸ Mistakes made with internal customers may not seem important, but they are. Create the expectation that all mistakes, whether with internal or external customers, should be taken seriously. Create processes for dealing with internal mistakes similar to those you have for external errors.

Meet commitments to customers/clients

▼

Listen to what people say in casual conversation about customers or clients. Provide feedback if customers or clients are not consistently respected.

Customers/clients want and deserve quick action. They want to deal with someone who has all of the information, expertise, and tools to help them quickly and competently. They also expect and deserve efficient follow-through, with no exceptions, on the commitments you have made to them. Consider the following suggestions:

▶ Know your customer's requirements. Fully understand the commitments you have made. Be sure you know when, what, how, where, how many, to whom.

▶ Communicate the commitments to your team. Provide not only detailed information, but also a context for those who may not deal directly with the customer. Why does the customer need it this way? What are the consequences for the customer if your organization fails to meet its commitments?

▶ Ensure that there is a realistic plan to meet the requirements and that it is being implemented. Intervene to get a plan back on track if you need to.

▶ If time has passed since the commitments were made and discussed, double-check to be sure nothing has changed.

▶ Always deliver by the agreed-upon date.

▶ Champion the client's cause inside your organization. Identify other champions with whom you can team up to ensure the organization's response.

▶ If it appears that you have overcommitted, talk with the customer immediately. Understand the situation fully. Can you meet the customer's need in another way?

▶ Follow up to be sure the commitment was met. Just because the product left your organization on time doesn't necessarily mean the client received it as expected. Build this follow-up into your process.

▸ Measure your performance by establishing a tracking system. If you missed the mark, determine where the process got tied up and why. If the problem recurs, find ways to remove roadblocks and inefficiencies.

▸ Give your service people the resources they need to do their job, including quick access to up-to-date information on all customer transactions.

▸ Reduce the number of situations in which people need to obtain supervisor approval. Define the parameters within which your people work, and then give them the latitude to be flexible to meet each customer's needs.

▸ Recognize and reward individuals and teams who consistently meet delivery dates.

Hire the right people to meet customer needs

▼

Successful managers begin their efforts to meet customer needs by hiring the right people. Who the "right" people are is determined by your customer value proposition. To focus efforts, understand your customer value proposition and the talent needed to execute on it. Then use the requirements and expectations for each role and target your interview questions to identify these attributes. Consider the following suggestions:

▸ After identifying your customer value proposition, determine the critical roles necessary to achieve it. For example, if you promise to have the most advanced products in your industry, then a pivotal talent pool for you will be product design. If you promise quick, personal service, you need well-trained frontline customer service employees.

Ask people who are skilled at understanding customer needs to work with those who are less knowledgeable.

▸ Once you know the pivotal roles needed to meet customer needs, identify the skills, knowledge, experience, and attributes needed for those roles. Develop selection processes aimed at identifying and differentiating candidates based on these dimensions.

▸ Select for customer relationship management skills. Recognize the characteristics for good customer relationship management, including:

  ▷ Strong oral communication skills.

    ▷ Cooperation and teamwork.

    ▷ An even-tempered disposition.

    ▷ Sensitivity to and concern for others.

    ▷ Problem-solving and decision-making skills.

    ▷ Commitment to excellence.

    ▷ Enthusiasm and energy.

    ▷ Flexibility and adaptability.

- Use behavioral interviewing techniques to predict how a candidate will behave on the job.

- Consider involving key customers in the selection of new employees who will serve their account.

- Consider using testing or assessments to identify strong candidates. For example, use a reliable test for customer service.

Train for customer focus

▼

Encourage people to ask their direct reports what they need to learn and understand about customer service to enhance their ability to relate to customers.

Once you have hired the best people and know your standards, get off to the right start with a strong orientation and comprehensive training. The benefits of this approach include higher levels of productivity, enhanced customer relationships, and more loyal employees. Consider the following suggestions:

- Give people a brief overview of your customer vision and strategies. Outline your standards and expectations for managing customer relationships.

- Provide opportunities for people to see individuals interacting with customers in the way you want it done. It is very helpful to see what is expected.

- Design and present a fast-paced, energetic program that meets your specific, desired objective.

- Provide orientation to each part of your business so employees understand how to meet customer requirements at every step. Create appreciation for how all work groups come together to serve the customer.

▸ Have fun at the orientation. People who enjoy their training are more likely to enjoy the job and will treat customers better.

▸ Discuss how you build a prospect into a loyal customer. Ask your customer-focus stars to describe the roles they play in reaching that goal.

▸ Demonstrate options for handling customers' requests and objections. Model techniques for dealing with tough cases.

▸ Build your new employees' confidence. Show them the effort you made to hire the best people. Describe the results that the group can achieve together. Invite customers to talk about how your team contributes to their success.

▸ Provide on-the-job training. Training does not have take place in a classroom. Look for opportunities for people to train and practice on the job.

▸ Follow up on the training. Create an environment in which people can apply what they have learned. Provide appropriate feedback and coaching as they continue to develop their skills.

Set high standards for customer service

A team that has common standards for providing superior service is more likely to deliver high levels of customer service. Communicating your standards to every level of your organization will help all teams focus on the same expectations for customer service. Consider the following suggestions:

▸ Show how each job is a link in the chain of exceeding customer expectations. Consider using Michael Porter's legendary value-chain assessment to demonstrate this point. Communicate the message that no matter what the job is, it is valued and important.

▸ Help employees understand how your customers use your services and products and why they have specific requirements. For example, it is helpful to describe the effect on customers when you do not provide quick answers to their questions.

▸ Invite end users to talk with your team about their use of the service or product.

▸ Stress the benefits of the team's efforts for the entire organization and for each individual.

Provide examples of what you consider outstanding customer service. This will help people understand what the organization expects.

▸ Continually update what you know about customers. Share this information with everyone, especially people who have frequent customer contact.

▸ Demonstrate customer focus throughout the organization. Make it a priority for each work group to set customer-focused objectives. Incorporate these objectives into the performance-development process for each work group.

▸ Recognize and reward people who demonstrate high customer-service standards. This will encourage others to change their behavior accordingly.

Measure customer focus performance

▼

What gets measured gets managed. This adage certainly applies to creating a customer-focused organization. Organizations that are serious about improving their service to customers measure their performance in this area. In doing so, they communicate their resolve to all stakeholders: If customer loyalty is a priority, we will measure it, and we will manage our relationships to achieve it. You have many choices about establishing a measurement plan. Consider the following suggestions:

▸ Ensure that there are clear expectations for customer focus. Involve both your employees and your customers in establishing expectations for and measures of outstanding performance.

▸ Be clear about your objectives. For example, you may intend to:
  ▷ Establish a baseline measure.
  ▷ Stay current on research and track trends.
  ▷ Enhance relationships.
  ▷ Evaluate individual performance.
  ▷ Establish priorities for improvement.

▷ Create loyalty.

▷ Determine compensation.

▶ Be clear about what you are measuring:

▷ Overall satisfaction.

▷ Customer commitment.

▷ Transactional excellence.

▷ Service quality.

▷ Product performance.

▷ Competitor analysis.

▷ Market penetration.

▶ In measuring organizational performance, consider all stakeholders: customers, distributors, employees, internal customers, suppliers, alliance partners, investors, prospects.

▶ Look at measures of both outcome and process. In other words, examine the end results and measure how you achieved them. This will help you improve processes, which will lead to improved results.

▶ Determine whether the measurement process will be an ongoing, one-time, or periodic.

▶ Choose your method—survey (paper and pencil, electronic, telephone), face-to-face interview, or focus group—carefully. Success depends on selecting the method that is consistent with the objectives you have established.

Check to see how you are using customer focus in the performance management process. It should be highly important.

▶ Select measurement tools to fit your objectives: Customer Value Analysis, Balanced Scorecard, Quality Function Deployment (QFD), and so forth.

▶ Involve internal stakeholders before launching a new measurement process. Many well-intentioned processes have failed because the right people weren't included in the planning phase.

▶ Shape the message you want to convey through your measurement process. Good measurement tools are designed to communicate a message as well as gather information. For example, a customer measurement process should convey "We are committed to enhancing our relationship with you," not "This is the easiest way for us to get your feedback."

▸ Make good use of the data you've gathered and make sure your customers know that you are using it. From their perspective, it's better to not ask their opinions at all than to ignore or not use the valuable feedback they provide in interviews, focus groups, and surveys.

▸ Analyze the data, identify the necessary actions or improvements to make, and communicate your plan or intention back to your customers.

▸ Periodically assess the systems and processes you establish to meet customer requirements. Discuss what worked well and what needs to be done differently. Periodic reviews are also a good way to catch problems before they become serious.

Motivate and reward excellence in customer focus

All employees want to know that their customer focus efforts are recognized and appreciated. Consider the following suggestions for motivating and rewarding your team members:

▸ Provide incentives for exceeding customer expectations and rewards for people who demonstrate superior performance.

▸ Recognize small wins and accomplishments as well as major ones.

Discuss ways for customers to name team members who provide excellent service. Make sure people share this recognition with the individuals.

▸ Gather recognition from many sources: customers, senior management, managers, peers, and suppliers. Make people's accomplishments widely known.

▸ Recognize that the value your employees create for customers is one of the most effective motivators. It taps their strong inner desire to provide excellent service to their customers.

▸ Realize that positive reinforcement often works best when it is linked to specific rewards. Different things, however, motivate people so tailor your rewards to the individual.

▸ Obtain feedback from people in the know—your customers. One way to get this valuable information is to provide evaluation cards. For example, in a consumer environment, place these cards near the service desk or have service employees hand them to your customers. This feedback can be used for rewarding good service.

▸ Reflect your customers' requirements and expectations in your performance appraisal factors. This will reinforce their importance and allow you to recognize people for meeting and exceeding the standards.

▸ If you have employees from diverse cultures, learn about recognition preferences online, through books and articles, by checking with experts, or by asking individuals. Remember that in some cultures, being publicly recognized is considered embarrassing and inappropriate.

▸ Create avenues for recognizing excellent performers. Establish ongoing programs and modify them frequently. Make sure some of your rewards are instant, immediately reinforcing excellent service.

▸ Celebrate when you achieve goals. Acknowledge the contributions of less-visible employees as well as those who have direct customer contact. Behind-the-scenes contributors seldom get the recognition they deserve.

▸ Recognize attempts to go beyond what the customer expects. Acknowledge and encourage these efforts.

▸ Reward people who overcome difficult obstacles to achieve results.

Develop and provide a unified approach to serving the customer

Everyone in your organization can provide feedback on how to improve, which will help create more loyal customer relationships. This includes people who work directly with customers (account managers, customer service representatives, receptionists, salespeople, service technicians) and people who rarely see a customer (engineering, operations, finance). To tap this resource, consider the following suggestions:

▸ Communicate customer requirements and expectations to everyone in your organization whose work reaches the customer. Explain the reasons for the customer's requirements and expectations, and how meeting these standards will help customers achieve their goals.

► Assess whether the teams in your organization work together seamlessly. This will help you avoid situations in which customers receive five different calls from five different departments, all asking for the same information.

Have the person identify top priorities for customer service across departments. Discuss how the approaches can be aligned.

► Give your customers contact names and numbers within your organization. Make sure your team has access to updated customer information, is ready to answer questions, and is eager to solve problems.

► Set up a communication team for each customer. This team will be responsible for collecting information about the customer and updating people throughout the organization.

► Hold regular interdepartmental meetings to get a broader perspective on customer issues. This will help people understand how their work intersects with that of other departments and whether a solution from one group causes unnecessary headaches for another group.

► Recognize that competing priorities of different groups or departments—design and manufacturing, for example, or sales and operations—could affect the product or service you provide to your customer. Identify ways to gain commitment to total customer focus from all groups.

► Look for areas in which your group or organization is not using a unified approach. Meet with your peers and employees from all levels and functions to come up with concrete steps to rectify the situation.

Facilitate multiple connections between the company and customer organizations

▼

Your customers may be other businesses, but their representatives are real people in those organizations. Developing multiple relationships in your customer organizations builds deeper relationships and provides more connections between you and them. This is important for many reasons, including when turnover occurs in your or your customers' organizations. Consider the following suggestions:

► Identify all the relationships you currently have within your customer organizations.

- Identify additional relationships you should have within the organizations. Review organizational charts to learn about their business structures. Identify key people at various levels and functions with whom you would like to build relationships.

- Create trust and openness with your key customers. Demonstrate interest in them as individuals and understanding of the strategic issues they face.

- Research your customers and become well versed in their organizations and industries. Check their Web sites frequently and look for press releases and earnings reports.

- Build relationships with people over time, paying attention to their needs and providing assistance.

- Build relationships by conducting in-depth interviews with each contact. This discovery process will uncover opportunities to work together in new ways.

- Make a professional connection:
  ▷ Listen to customer problems intently.
  ▷ As you talk to customers, use language that reflects your knowledge of their businesses.
  ▷ Ask informed questions about their role or their business.
  ▷ Share appropriate information about your business or your job.

Discuss ways that people can facilitate multiple connections between their company and customer organizations.

- Make personal connections in ways appropriate to your culture and your customer's culture. For example, in the United States:
  ▷ Make direct eye contact.
  ▷ Smile warmly.
  ▷ Make small talk about weekend plans, vacations, and so on.
  ▷ Have lunch or dinner, and attend events together.

- Talk to your customers about the future direction of your company. This is likely to lead to a dialogue about their direction. Look for fit and congruency.

- Introduce your colleagues into customer organizations. Build a web of relationships that is strong enough to withstand transitions of people and roles.

Find ways to involve coworkers who don't normally have contact with customers

▼

Coworkers who don't have direct contact with customers are untapped resources. They can teach you about how your products or services are created and delivered, they can see things you miss, and they can get satisfaction for their work that creates delighted customers. Consider the following suggestions:

▶ Ask people to indicate whether they would like to be more directly involved in customer work. Discuss options for making this happen. This might be a great development opportunity for people who want to expand their skills or use existing skills in new ways.

▶ When customers visit your organization, introduce them to your team, including those who work behind the scenes. Describe the contributions each person makes and stress that the whole team contributes to the customer experience.

▶ Use cross-functional teams to address customer needs. Invite new team members to work on recurring problems. New people who have not tried to solve a problem before can introduce fresh thinking into the equation.

Discuss which issues generate an us-them response between customer-facing and behind-the-scenes employees.

▶ Learn about your coworkers' interests, talents, and abilities. As you work on customer issues, look for ways to tap into those talents and abilities.

▶ Create an environment in which all employees feel comfortable offering ideas and suggestions, even in areas outside their current role or field of expertise.

▶ Reinforce the concept that everyone, regardless of his or her job, has an impact on customers. Help people make the connection between their work and customers.

▶ Don't assume that everyone wants to work directly with customers. Some people prefer to work behind the scenes, so don't try to push them too far out of their comfort zones. The work they're doing is vital to the organization's success.

Develop and provide flexible options to enable employees to meet customer needs

▼

Discuss how the person's direct reports work with customers. When necessary, discuss better ways to handle a situation.

To successfully meet customer needs, employees need to have a variety of options to choose from, as well as the flexibility and latitude to make decisions without having to get permission from management at every turn. Consider the following suggestions for enabling employees to meet customer needs:

▶ Work with your team to come up with several different options for meeting key customer needs. Use these options as guidelines for dealing with customers. This information will be especially helpful to new employees.

▶ Make sure people know what is and is not negotiable as they try to meet customer needs. Within those boundaries, give them the latitude to make decisions.

▶ Reinforce the importance of being flexible in dealing with customers. As a group, talk about the consequences of being inflexible or too focused on procedures.

▶ Share success stories with your team. Talk about how being flexible helps your organization meet customer needs and solidify relationships with customers.

▶ If people feel uncertain about how to deal with unusual customer needs and requests, encourage them to come to you with questions. Work together to come up with creative solutions.

▶ Don't punish people who have made an honest mistake in an attempt to meet customer needs. Recognize the effort and initiative, and help determine a more effective way to handle similar situations in the future.

Create systems and processes that make it easy for customers to do business with your company

▼

Systems and processes can make or break customer relationships. If a customer is handled differently every time he or she interacts with someone from your organization, it will be frustrating and confusing. It will also cause customers to lose confidence in your company's abilities. Consider the following suggestions:

▶ Communicate customer requirements and expectations to everyone in your organization whose work reaches the customer. Explain the reasons for the customer's requirements and expectations so that people understand the reasons for any variations from your standard processes.

Challenge people to identify the process that gets the most complaints from customers. Discuss how it could be redesigned and how they would measure the change.

▶ Make sure that new people quickly learn systems and processes for working with customers. Also orient them to each part of your business so they understand how each step affects customers.

▶ Set up customer teams in which each person can handle issues and problems for that customer. Make sure each person on the team stays up to date on the latest customer information and has the authority to solve problems.

▶ Ensure that systems and processes are designed with the customer in mind. Sometimes organizations create systems that are convenient for them, but actually make things more difficult or confusing for their customers.

▶ Before you implement a new system or process, analyze it and be sure there is a payoff in customer experience for each action you take.

▶ Work with your colleagues across the organization to compile a list of best practices. Share the information broadly, put it on the intranet, and build the recommendations into your existing systems and procedures.

Understand and address the customer implications of process changes

▼

Very few processes are perfect; most could use a tweak or two, and some obviously need a major overhaul. As you improve and streamline processes at your organization, think about how it will affect your customers. The last thing you want to do is make their lives more difficult. Consider the following suggestions:

▶ Make sure you understand the entire chain of events, from salespeople talking to customers to the customer receiving your product or service. Then you will know who to consult about changing a process.

▶ Assemble a task force to improve a process that affects customers.

▷ Review the purpose of each step in the process.

▷ Reconfigure ineffective steps.

▷ Eliminate unnecessary steps.

▷ Examine the ripple effect of any changes.

▷ Implement the new process.

▷ Follow up to determine if the new process is more effective and more efficient.

▶ Do a beta test with select customers before you implement a new process. Give them something for their trouble.

Ensure that people are communicating process changes to customers, including the reasons why the change is happening.

▶ When you propose changes to a process, be able to state tangible benefits to the customer. Don't change something just for the sake of change. You should be able to quantify the difference.

▶ Determine how long it will take to make the change and how difficult it will be to train people on the new procedures. Also consider how you will minimize the impact on customers during the transition.

▶ People may not want to consider how a change will affect the customer because it makes things more complicated. They may be under a time crunch or have a mandate to make a change. As a leader, you need to make sure that they consider all the implications.

Remove barriers so you can provide exceptional customer service

Even people who are committed to providing exceptional customer service may be blocked by organizational or departmental constraints that prohibit them from going the extra mile. Make every attempt to remove the barriers that get in the way of giving your customers top-notch service.

Common barriers and possible solutions include:

▶ *Frontline employees perceive that they lack the authority to make decisions to satisfy unhappy customers.* Give frontline employees the authority to do what's right for the customer. If necessary, change or make exceptions to your current policies.

▶ *People are satisfied with the status quo.* Raise your standards. Know and communicate what your competitors are doing. Underscore the role that loyal customers play in your success.

▶ *People in your organization believe that you have a corner on the marketplace.* Recognize that today's marketplace is dynamic and competitive. Determine what you can do to go beyond what the competition is doing.

Encourage people to obtain regular feedback from frontline employees to learn how they would improve customer service.

▶ *Frontline workers are stressed from a heavy workload and constantly putting out fires.* Examine processes that may need improvement. Aggressively work with management to eliminate the source of problems—the quality issues. Let your front line know that their efforts are valued and respected.

▶ *Frontline employees and customers face excess paperwork and red tape.* Streamline your complaint-resolution process. Whenever possible, handle necessary paperwork after the customer leaves or ends the phone call.

▶ *Employees are concerned that customers will take advantage of lenient customer service policies or pursue legal recourse for poor performance.* Determine the parameters of a legitimate customer complaint. Teach your employees how to identify and handle legally sensitive issues.

8
Manage Execution

Getting things done. Without effective execution, planning and strategy are meaningless. As a manager, you are responsible for making sure that you and your work group are effective at executing strategy and accomplishing goals in a timely, efficient, and resource-wise manner.

Accomplishing goals takes a manager who knows how, when, and how much to delegate to others and how to evaluate processes for blocks and barriers, and has the ability and insight to solve problems, keep projects and people on track, and make sure that time spent in meetings is productive.

In this chapter, we will cover the following areas:

▼

- ▸ Increase your impact by driving execution of strategy through and with others
- ▸ Develop thorough operational plans that achieve business goals
- ▸ Coordinate work with other groups
- ▸ Know when you or your part of the organization is stuck and find ways to get moving again
- ▸ Remove obstacles in order to move the work forward and/or get efforts back on track
- ▸ Evaluate your delegation skills
- ▸ Increase your willingness to delegate
- ▸ Use a specific delegation process to ensure quality of results
- ▸ Increase the amount and scope of the work you delegate
- ▸ Delegate responsibility to the appropriate individuals
- ▸ Convey clear expectations for assignments
- ▸ Give people the latitude to manage their responsibilities
- ▸ Hold people accountable for achieving their goals
- ▸ Be accessible to provide assistance and support
- ▸ Monitor progress of others and redirect efforts when goals are not being met
- ▸ Plan and facilitate meetings effectively to ensure that objectives are met
- ▸ Ensure that clear agendas and desired outcomes are established for meetings
- ▸ Ensure that meeting structures and processes fit with desired outcomes
- ▸ Perform process checks during meetings and redirect discussion as appropriate

- ▶ Drive the achievement of meaningful results in meetings without overemphasizing processes
- ▶ Identify and address unproductive debate in meetings in order to move issues ahead
- ▶ Follow up after meetings

Increase your impact by driving execution of strategy through and with others

▼

Discuss the fact that strategy is useless until it is executed well. Provide examples of well-executed strategies.

Strategy without execution is useless. Competitive advantage does not come from a vision or stated strategy; it comes from the *execution* of strategy day after day. Consider the following suggestions:

▶ Change the definition of your work from that of an individual contributor to that of a manager. Think about or list what you do. Which activities should you be doing as a manager and what is individual contributor work?

▶ When you first become a manager, you will discover that you continue to do a considerable amount of individual contributor work. While this is normal, look at how you can get more leverage by having others do the individual contributor work.

▶ Catch yourself when you wish you had time for "real work." Often managers are looking for time in which they are not talking with their direct reports, in meetings, handling problems, coaching others, coordinating with other groups, or looking for improvement opportunities. This *is* the work of a manager; *this is what you should be doing.*

▶ Successful managers know that they multiply their impact by working with and through others. Work with your team to develop plans for implementing work-unit strategy and initiatives that will support the strategy.

Develop thorough operational plans that achieve business goals

▼

Effective leaders develop operational plans that spell out what needs to be done to achieve goals and to improve processes. The direction and focus of their plans—which come from the vision and strategy for the group—successfully balance quality, cost, human capital, and other resources. Consider the following suggestions:

▶ Use a standard project or business planning process so that your plans will be thorough and you will not waste time figuring out a planning process. If you do not have a standard project planning process, talk with a peer who is responsible for many projects. Save time—don't invent your own process.

▸ Start with the deliverables and work backward. What needs to happen so you can deliver what is expected? Use a team process to develop plans so that you do not overlook important elements.

▸ Establish performance goals and measures for each project or business you lead. Ensure that goals and measures are aligned with the strategy. Two examples:

▹ Do not invest in a Customer Relationship Management package unless it fits with strategy, you are ready to implement it, and your team is ready to do what's necessary to benefit from it.

▹ While others may be out meeting with people to find alliance partners, if it is not part of the strategy, do not waste your time doing this.

▸ Identify the roles and people you need. Work with HR to develop clear descriptions of the roles, knowledge, skills, experience, and attributes needed for success.

▸ In estimating staffing needs, consider the ability levels of individuals who might work on your project. Adjust time frames and costs accordingly, and keep in mind possible quality implications. Identify cross-functional opportunities for using individuals from other departments.

Review people's plans to ensure that they are linked to work unit goals and priorities. When necessary, suggest revisions or fine-tuning.

▸ Make a list of all resources and supplies that will be required. Specify when each resource will be needed, how it can be obtained, what acceptable substitutes exist, and the impact that each resource has on cost and quality.

▸ Anticipate areas of vulnerability and plan tactics you could use to address each potential problem.

▸ Establish a way to track the productivity, quality, and cost of each category of resources. This will enable you to more accurately estimate your resource needs on future projects and identify constraints that could derail success.

- Stress the importance of accurate estimates of time and resources. Missed deadlines and cost overruns make people unproductive and frustrated. They also have a ripple effect, causing other groups in the organization to miss their targets.

- Ask your teams to use process flow charts to help determine constraints and contingencies on time frames for projects. Encourage teams to share best practices so the entire group can learn from each team's experiences. This will help everyone fine-tune project plans and proposals.

- Establish the expectation that you want to hear about constraints. When you are told about a problem, concentrate on how the team can handle it together. Do not shoot the messenger.

- Avoid quick fixes. A response that addresses only immediate barriers will not be sufficient to handle long-term repercussions.

- Deal with underlying problems. Work with your peers to understand the organization's shortcomings and take corrective measures. If a constraint is related to a failing of a particular individual or work unit, deal with it in a respectful, straightforward way.

Coordinate work with other groups

▼

Have the person identify which kinds of work need to be coordinated with other groups. Discuss the issues and develop an action plan.

Most work in organizations affects more than one group or individual. Whether you are part of the value chain providing the service or product to the customer or part of the support structure, your work affects others. Consider the following suggestions:

- Develop relationships with the leaders of the groups that are upstream and downstream from you in the value chain and ask your team members to develop relationships with their counterparts in the value chain.

- Meet periodically to evaluate how things are going between groups. Do this frequently enough to establish a working relationship. It is difficult to maintain a good relationship if your only contact is to solve a problem.

- In planning, look for contingencies. Involve people who will be affected in the planning process.

Know when you or your part of the organization is stuck and find ways to get moving again

▼

All people and all work units get stuck. Effective leaders recognize when their team is stuck and either figure out what to do to get it unstuck or get help from others to do so. Although it may be hard to admit that you need help, it is a fact of corporate life. Many times, the longer you are with an organization or the longer you are in a role, the more vulnerable you are to getting stuck. Unfortunately, you are also vulnerable to not knowing you are stuck.

Common places that people and teams get stuck

Values or purpose

▸ *Neglect of values.* People work hard because they care—about the mission, about the work they are doing, about one another. If you spend all of your time simply driving execution without getting emotional buy-in and commitment, you'll get stuck.

▸ *Lack of values alignment.* If your team doesn't agree on what to value or believe, or how to work together, it often causes difficulty and nonproductive conflict.

Strategy

▸ *Unclear goals or unclear strategy.* If team members do not know the goals and understand the strategy, they are unlikely to deliver.

▸ *Preoccupation with strategy.* Some organizations spend all their time on strategy and little time on execution. They also get stuck in not achieving the competitive differentiation they want.

Structure

▸ *Wrong structure.* Some organizations are not structured in a way that is consistent with their strategy or work processes. The result is often that it takes an enormously long time to get anything done.

▸ *Unclear structure.* In these days of movement toward and away from centralization, decentralization and working in complex matrixes, it is sometimes difficult to figure out how to get something done and who is responsible.

Processes

▸ *Unclear, inadequate, poorly designed processes.* To ensure execution, clear business processes are needed. Otherwise, people will go off in different directions, honestly believing they are contributing value. The organization will just spin its wheels—people will be busy but won't accomplish anything.

▸ *Too much time spent on processes.* Some organizations spend so much time on internal processes that they do not deliver what they are supposed to deliver.

Systems

▸ *Poorly designed or inadequate systems.* Systems may not link to the overall goals or strategy, they may cause work to be overly complex, or they may rely on individual autonomous behavior, which rarely produces consistency.

▸ *Overreliance on systems or rigidity in the systems.* People might spend too much time fine-tuning their internal systems and processes. Conversely, leaders might spend too little time on details to ensure that the process or system accomplishes what it should.

People and relationships

▸ *Not enough people.* People can only do so much in light of downsizings, unstable economic situations, and organizations trying to get by with less. There is a point at which things get stuck because people simply cannot do anything more.

▸ *Not the right people.* Having the right people in the right roles is critical.

▸ *Dysfunctional relationships.* Over time, people may fall into dysfunctional relationships. The result usually is either too much conflict or too little contact.

When you realize you are stuck, consider the following suggestions:

▸ Try to identify what is getting you stuck. If you can't do this by yourself, ask others, especially those who have knowledge of the work unit and the people but are not involved in the process themselves. Ask for suggestions about what you can do to improve the situation. Listen carefully rather than explain why suggestions will not work.

Talk about the ways people get stuck in the person's group. Share ideas that you have seen other leaders use to get their groups moving again.

▶ When you are stuck in nonproductive behavior patterns with someone, talk with the person. Say that you believe the two of you are stuck in a nonproductive pattern and ask what the other person thinks the two of you can do to get unstuck. Expect that the first thing the person suggests may be what *you* can do differently. Continue to talk until you arrive at a plan that will work for both of you.

▶ Meet with new people after they have been in the organization for about a month. Ask for their observations and questions about the organization. Preface your request by saying that you value new people because they see things that others who have been in the organization for a long time no longer see.

Remove obstacles in order to move the work forward and/or get efforts back on track

▼

Roadblocks and problems crop up in all types of work, from complex, cross-functional projects to routine processes. Whether they stem from external circumstances or from habits, obstacles interfere with productivity. Consider the following suggestions:

▶ As a team, identify the top five top obstacles in your area or with a project. This should be relatively easy, since you probably deal with them every day.

▶ Choose the issue that interferes most with your highest- priority work. Quantify the extent to which it affects your work; this will motivate you to change it.

Discuss the practices and policies that get in the way of performance, of both individuals and the organization. Talk about specific actions the person can take to influence and modify them.

▶ Imagine how a process would work if you could instantly remove its biggest constraint. Then think of five ways to begin removing that constraint.

▶ When you can't think of ways to remove obstacles or solve problems, involve others to get a fresh perspective and to learn from people who have dealt with similar issues.

▶ Discuss the givens under which your team operates. Examine each one to see if it is truly immutable.

▶ Identify two processes that your group will improve in the next six months. For each process, form a team to oversee the change initiative.

- Assemble a task force to reduce the time involved in a work process.
  - ▷ Review the purpose of each step in the process.
  - ▷ Reconfigure ineffective steps.
  - ▷ Eliminate unnecessary steps.
  - ▷ Implement the new process.
  - ▷ Follow up to determine if the new process is more effective and efficient.
- Invite internal or external customers to provide feedback on obstacles they encounter in working with your organization. Ask them to suggest changes and to help you test their proposed changes.

Discuss ways that the person can get feedback from direct reports on delegation—too much, too little, right kind, and so on.

Evaluate your delegation skills

The following checklist provides a quick way to evaluate your current delegation skills. Answer yes or no to each question. No answers may signal areas for improvement.

Evaluation checklist	Yes	No
I delegate an appropriate amount of work—neither too much nor too little.		
I have a good understanding of my direct reports' capabilities.		
I match people's capabilities and career goals with assignments as much as possible.		
I convey clear goals and expectations of the assignment.		
I allow people to use their own style of getting their work done.		
I give my direct reports the appropriate amount of authority for the responsibility assigned.		
I am available to assist and support people.		
I effectively monitor progress.		
I coach people rather than take back a delegated task or responsibility.		
I provide training, mentoring, and other help.		
I hold people accountable for achieving their goals.		
I seek feedback from others on how I can improve my delegation skills.		

Increase your willingness to delegate

▼

It's not uncommon for managers to resist delegating the work they once did themselves. After all, people are often promoted because they were effective individual contributors. However, to be a successful manager, the key to success is to multiply what you can do by delegating to others. Your work is no longer the "technical work"; your work is management. To increase your willingness to delegate, first determine the reasons for your resistance, and then find ways to overcome them. Common reasons for reluctance to delegate include:

▸ *It's easier to do it myself.* Some people believe it is easier to do the work themselves than to explain what needs to be done. While this is sometimes an acceptable reason for short-term projects, more often it is not. The time you spend teaching others will save you time and effort in the long run, and it will also help your team develop new skills and capabilities.

▸ *My direct reports are stretched too much already.* Some managers are reluctant to assign work to already busy people. This prevents your direct reports from learning how to manage more and balance priorities. Protecting people in this way limits their chances to develop problem-solving skills. Furthermore, it results in your doing too much individual contributor work, risking personal burnout, and *not* doing your management work.

Check with people to see if they use delegation as a way to help direct reports acquire new skills.

▸ *I have to do it myself.* Thinking that you are the only person who can do certain work well enough is a danger sign. It's unlikely that you are the only person who can do the work, even though others will probably not work precisely the same way that you do. If you worry that if mistakes are made, the consequences will be disastrous, identify the significant risks and request contingency plans. Begin by delegating parts of responsibilities and coaching people to help them perform to expectations.

▸ *I want to do it.* You may tend to reserve work that you enjoy or receive recognition for doing for yourself. It is difficult to give up work you really like. Learn to achieve satisfaction from coaching others, doing strategic work, and other parts of your job.

▸ *I'll just have to do it anyway.* Some managers expect their employees to fail so they skip the step of delegating because they'll just have to do the work themselves in the end. Ultimately, though, you need to be willing to take responsibility for your employees' mistakes on delegated tasks so that they can grow and develop.

▶ Evaluate how much of your own work you delegate to others. Frequently assess whether a task is something only you can do, or whether someone else could do it. If someone else could do it with instruction and coaching, it will be worth your time to develop the necessary skills in your employee. Letting go of work that others can do frees you to focus on responsibilities that need your attention.

Use a specific delegation process to ensure quality of results

▼

Review with people why delegating is a practical way to increase work production.

Using a common delegation model can help ensure that you are providing people with what they need to be successful in their work. PDI's SOS model helps you delegate and supports the development of your employees' skills at the same time. The three key elements of delegating are selecting, observing, and supporting:

▶ *Select* an individual to do the work. It is the process of appropriately matching individuals to assignments.

▶ *Observe* people, including giving them latitude, monitoring their progress, and coaching them when necessary. Your level of involvement depends on people's experience and motivation, and on the importance of the delegated assignment.

▶ *Support* people by taking action to ensure that they have what they need to complete their assignments. An effective manager finds the appropriate level of support—neither too much nor too little. The skills, interest level, and motivation of individuals and the specifics of delegated tasks determine the support you need to provide.

Increase the amount and scope of the work you delegate

▼

While a team's work is typically allocated according to the roles of its members, you may find yourself overloaded and want to delegate more. Also, people might need development opportunities, or they might ask for increased challenges. Consider the following suggestions:

▶ If others have told you that you do not delegate enough, ask what they believe you should delegate.

Help people identify what to delegate. They may have a limited view of what can or should be delegated.

▶ If you wonder whether the amount you delegate is appropriate, ask others for feedback. Sometimes it is not the *amount* you delegate, but *what* you delegate.

▶ Listen carefully if you receive feedback that you delegate too much. This may indicate that someone thinks either that you do not work hard enough or long enough, or that you delegate responsibilities that should be yours.

▶ Use this process to determine which work to delegate:

1. List all the work for which you are currently responsible. Then classify it using these categories:

   M: manager work that you must do yourself

   S: work you can share with others

   D: work others can do

2. Examine the work you categorized as M. Are you unnecessarily holding on to anything? Could you further develop your team by passing along some of this work?

3. The work you can delegate is limitless. To expand your range, review your list to see if you are retaining any of the following types of work, which are often good candidates for delegation.

   ▷ Routine decisions.

   ▷ Individual contributor work.

   ▷ Less complex tasks that may not be the best use of a manager's time.

   ▷ Work that requires knowledge or skills that you want people in your group to develop. Delegating this work will increase the number of people who know about a certain area or have critical skills related to your operation.

   ▷ Any of the phases needed to solve problems, including identification, analysis, issues and alternatives, stakeholder opinions and feelings, and solution options. These phases could be individually assigned, or one person could be responsible for the entire effort.

   ▷ Elements of a complex, multistage project.

▶ Use this tool to assist you in delegating effectively:

PROJECT: _____   **DELEGATION MATRIX**

Project Team Members	Deadline	Elements/Tasks of Project Delegated	
		1.	**How will I observe progress?**
		2.	
		3.	**What support do I need to provide?**
		4.	
		1.	**How will I observe progress?**
		2.	
		3.	**What support do I need to provide?**
		4.	
		1.	**How will I observe progress?**
		2.	
		3.	**What support do I need to provide?**
		4.	

Delegate responsibility to the appropriate individuals

▼

It's easy to assign too much work to experienced workers and too little to those who require more assistance. To improve your ability to strike a balance, consider the following suggestions:

▶ To choose the appropriate person, do the following:

1. Consider any employee who:

▷ Currently has the requisite knowledge or skills to do the work.

▷ Has a high level of interest in the area or has asked to do similar work.

▷ Has a need to further develop skills in this particular area.

▷ Has the time to do it.

2. Narrow your list of candidates by considering the dynamics of the work:

▷ Visibility and importance of the work.

▷ Amount of interaction with other projects, people, and resources.

▷ Complexity of the work.

▷ Amount of teaching and coaching time you or others have available.

▶ For a high-profile or highly complex project or responsibility when you have little time to provide support, assign someone you know can do the work independently. On the other hand, if you or others have time to provide support or it is a less complex or less visible project, you might want to take more risks.

▶ Consider motivation as well as experience. A less experienced person who is excited about a project may be more successful than an experienced person who disagrees with the project's purpose or desired outcome.

Discuss who is on the person's team, their skill sets, and who could take on specific responsibilities.

▶ Involve key individuals in planning the distribution of work on large projects. Use a planning meeting as an efficient means of clarifying roles and responsibilities, identifying what materials are needed, working out details, and distributing work.

▶ Refrain from assigning too much work to people who have a proven track record. You will overload key individuals and miss opportunities to develop the skills of the rest of your team.

▶ Assign whole jobs instead of bits and pieces. People feel a greater sense of responsibility when they handle an entire job.

▶ Periodically evaluate how effectively you are distributing work among your team.

▷ What is working well?

▷ What problems or inefficiencies (missed deadlines, inadequate skill levels) exist?

▷ What could be done differently in the future?

▶ Effective managers delegate assignments to the lowest possible level. As you think about delegation, start at the lowest level and work your way up until you think of someone who seems appropriate. Once you have made an assignment, be supportive but give advice and make changes in others' work wisely and sparingly—too much advice prevents people from learning to think on their own and does not allow them to learn from their mistakes.

Convey clear expectations for assignments

▼

Regularly acknowledge people who convey clear expectations. Ensure that they model this skill for others.

You and your employees need to understand what is expected for assignments. Even experienced employees can waste time if they don't have clear direction; in the worst cases, they may produce results that bear little or no resemblance to the desired outcome. To clarify expectations, consider the following suggestions:

▶ Determine how much involvement people will have in deciding the specifics of the assignment. The more experienced the employee, the more involved he or she should be in determining goals, expectations, timing, methods, amount of help, and so forth.

▶ Involve people in defining and clarifying expectations. Come to a mutual understanding about the:

▷ Goal and scope of the project.

▷ Success criteria. ("This project will be successful if . . .")

▷ Completion date.

▷ Specific instructions or guidelines, such as who can provide background information or administrative support.

▷ Level of authority the person has in doing the work. For example:

– Makes decisions and does the work; lets you know the outcome.

– Makes decisions; tells you before acting.

– Makes recommendations; the two of you decide on the course of action.

- Comes to you with recommendations and you make the final decision.

- Carries out the project after you tell him or her exactly what to do.

▷ Areas of high risk or visibility.

▷ Required progress reports.

▷ Required final reports.

▶ Discuss the assignment and answer any questions.

▶ At the end of the discussion, ask people to describe their assignments in their own words. This will help you determine whether you have mutual agreement about the assignment. Don't end the discussion until you're certain that they fully understand your expectations.

▶ During the course of a project, keep track of any instances of unclear or inadequate direction. Note the cause of each misunderstanding so that you can improve your direction on future assignments. You may wish to ask your employees for feedback on your direction and guidance.

Give people the latitude to manage their responsibilities

▼

Giving people sufficient latitude goes hand in hand with delegating. Managers who retain too much responsibility are often seen as controlling and lacking in respect for others. Consider the following suggestions for giving people enough breathing room to manage their own responsibilities:

▶ When you establish goals with your employees, ask how much involvement they want from you and what you can do to be most helpful. Then follow through on their requests whenever possible.

Give people with strong execution skills additional responsibility to increase the scope and complexity of what they manage.

▶ Look for projects where you can assign complete authority. This will save you the most time in the long run, and the project is likely to be more fulfilling for the person.

▶ When people update you on projects, encourage them to recommend solutions or options to solve problems.

▶ In determining the amount of latitude to give an individual, consider experience and motivation. Give more latitude to a person who is highly skilled and motivated. Conversely, individuals learning new skills are likely to benefit from closer guidance.

▸ Let people go forward with their ideas unless you have a major problem with their plans. Keep in mind that learning from mistakes is one of the most effective ways for people to develop their skills.

▸ It is important for people to be able to critique themselves and to recognize when they have done something well. Rather than providing feedback yourself, ask people to provide their own critique or recommend that they ask their customers for feedback.

▸ Periodically discuss with individuals the amount of latitude you give them. Do you tend to give too much direction on some assignments and too little support on others? In which situations do you give the appropriate amount of latitude? Make corrections based on their input.

▸ Evaluate how much authority you can and should give others for their assignments. People need to know they have the authority to accomplish their objectives without needing your approval for every step. Create a checklist of levels of authority and select the appropriate one for each assignment (for instance: 1. Proceed without approval 2. Proceed, but inform me of your actions 3. Obtain approval before proceeding). Then make sure that you follow that level during the assignment.

Hold people accountable for achieving their goals

At times, it may seem easier to do a job yourself than to hold others accountable for doing it. If you find that this is the case for you, consider the following suggestions:

▸ Make sure people understand the goals they are accountable for achieving. Establish measurable outcomes for each objective and discuss acceptable and unacceptable levels of performance.

▸ If you hesitate to hold people accountable, remember that you are ultimately responsible for your group's results. You can't afford to have a team that doesn't perform.

▸ Learn the difference between holding people accountable and micromanaging. Focus on results, not on whether they are achieved in exactly the same way you would achieve them.

▸ Beware of the boomerang effect: an individual, with your explicit or implicit acceptance, gives back a task you delegated to him or her.

When people are having trouble with their direct reports delivering, ask them to describe what they have done in terms of accountability.

▸ Rely on regular progress reports to help you and your employee ensure that goals are met. If deadlines are being missed, ask for an assessment of why, and of how he or she plans to correct the situation.

▸ If an individual is not meeting his or her goals, try the following:

▹ If the discrepancy is minor, alert the person and ask him or her to find ways to get back on track.

▹ If the discrepancy is major, invite the person to discuss the situation with you and to work out a plan to get back on track. Rather than taking the entire task back or assigning it to someone else, get a commitment for at least part of it. You may need to make recommendations for restructuring the work or obtaining additional resources.

▸ Recognize work that is done well. Spend as much (or more) time recognizing good work as you spend discussing problems.

Be accessible to provide assistance and support

▼

Even though you are busy, one of your primary management responsibilities is to be available to answer questions and address concerns. Consider the following suggestions:

▸ Walk around and talk with people. Ask how things are going. This provides an opening for people to bring up issues.

▸ Periodically ask what you can do to be helpful to your direct reports. Especially do this when you notice that they are very busy.

▸ Update your calendar regularly. Give your team access to it so they can arrange time to meet with you.

Discuss what kind of support is needed in the person's group. Identify where cross-training might be an option.

▸ If you are often away from the office, set up times to check in at the office, either by phone or in person, and let people know that your assistant has this information.

▸ Set up regular meetings (weekly, biweekly, monthly) to answer employees' questions and get information to stay up to date on their assignments.

▶ Find ways to be available to people in other locations. For example, be willing to schedule off-hour phone calls with people in different time zones.

▶ Take time to contact employees periodically, particularly those you do not see daily. Taking time to talk informally conveys a message of support. Also, your employees will be less likely to view you as an absentee manager.

Monitor progress of others and redirect efforts when goals are not being met

▼

An important part of delegation is checking on progress. Monitoring does not mean interfering or micromanaging. It means checking in periodically to ensure that people are proceeding without difficulty. Consider the following guidelines:

▶ Take advantage of natural opportunities (casual conversations, meetings) to check on progress.

Ensure that people do not mistake activity for results. While it is fine to appreciate others' efforts, they might need to be redirected in order to meet goals.

▶ Periodically conduct more formal reviews of plans and progress. Schedule them so people will have time to prepare updates and questions.

▶ Ask individuals to write action plans and provide progress reports. Depending on the person's experience level, you may want to be involved in determining what the progress report should include to ensure that all the important components are addressed.

▶ Establish the expectation that you want to hear about problems before they mushroom. When you are told about a problem, concentrate on how the person plans to handle it. Do not become the problem solver.

▶ Keep in mind that individuals require different levels of your attention and involvement, depending on their experience. Be prepared to spend more time with people who require personal attention.

Feedback is essential for keeping an individual or a team on track. It helps people correct mistakes that could become serious problems, reinforces positive behaviors, and encourages the development of desirable work habits. Consider the following suggestions:

▸ Check in frequently. Ask people to evaluate their progress, their work, and their performance.

▸ Find opportunities to observe people in action. Also talk with others in the organization and read updates and reports. Provide feedback on what you hear and see.

▸ Give timely feedback. Don't wait until you have several things to discuss—you might wait so long that it won't be relevant or helpful. Also, people might wish that you had told them sooner so they could have changed their behavior earlier.

▸ Focus on providing relevant information that will promote successful completion of the assignment.

▸ See everything, overlook a lot, and correct what counts.

▸ Communicate the fact that you are willing to provide feedback. This will encourage people to consult with you.

▸ When someone is off target, initiate a discussion and learn how the person views the situation. Until the two of you agree that the person is off target, he or she will not do anything differently.

▸ Ask the person who is off target what she or he plans to do to correct or change the situation. As much as possible, draw the ideas out of the person, rather than telling him or her what to do. Get a commitment on a course of action and agree on a time to check to see if the change is working.

Plan and facilitate meetings effectively to ensure that objectives are met

▾

To prepare for and facilitate effective meetings, consider the following suggestions:

▸ *Choose the setting.*

▹ *Meeting date and time.* Choose a time when people will be available and a date by which you will have all the necessary information. Also select a time that will allow the meeting to end at a logical time, such as just before lunch. When people are in different time zones, be as considerate as possible. Do not always ask people from another part of the world to accommodate people in your time zone.

▷ *Location.* Select a room that is accessible to everyone. Let everyone know where the meeting will be held and if videoconferencing will be used.

▷ *Room size.* Select a room that is neither so large that participants are far away from the action and from each other nor so small that they feel cramped and don't have room to write or sit comfortably.

▷ *Ventilation and temperature.* Ensure that the room is not stuffy, drafty, hot, or cold.

▷ *Equipment.* Be sure that all necessary equipment is on hand and set up. Don't waste meeting time looking for a flip chart or a TV monitor. Test all equipment before the meeting. Ensure that technical help is available.

▷ *Furniture arrangement.* Set up the room to maximize group attention and participation. If the group is small, use a semicircular seating arrangement that exactly accommodates the number of people involved. If you must use rows, use several short rows rather than a few long rows so that people will be near each other and can easily see who is speaking.

▷ *Seating.* Encourage participants to sit near each other rather than spreading out across the room. This will promote equal participation. On videoconference calls, plan the seating so all participants can be seen.

Attend meetings led by people you're coaching. Afterward, discuss what was effective and what they would like to improve next time.

▶ *Organize the meeting.*

▷ Limit the number of participants. Invite only those who are needed for decision making or who require the information that will be presented.

▷ Prepare an agenda and distribute it well in advance so participants can gather materials and prepare their assignments.

▷ Prepare any presentation materials, handouts, and/or flip-chart materials.

▷ If people will be joining the meeting by teleconference or videoconference, e-mail them necessary information and materials ahead of time.

▷ If you are using a laptop projector, ensure that the screen is in focus and legible from the back of the room.

▷ Determine whether you need to translate materials for the discussion. Even though the company may have an established language for business, it may be helpful to translate highly important materials.

▶ *Facilitate the meeting.*

▷ Start the meeting on time. When people expect meetings to start late, they arrive late. If they walk in after a meeting has started, they are more likely to arrive at the next meeting on time.

▷ Begin by reminding people of the time allotted for the meeting and assure them that the meeting will end on time.

▷ Establish ground rules. For example, ask each person on a conference call to say his or her name before speaking.

▷ Review the agenda and the amount of time allotted to each item.

▷ Appoint a recorder to take minutes and monitor the time. Have this person keep track of action steps, responsibilities, and follow-up dates.

▷ Focus your energy on listening to people. Also ask questions. Questions are excellent tools for monitoring and facilitating discussions.

▷ Encourage everyone to participate, including people who are usually quiet. Find out what they know, think, or feel about the topic under discussion. People who contribute to a group's decisions and plans feel more committed to carrying them out.

▷ Invite participation from people on the conference phone or video. Pay attention to technical issues that affect how easily or how frequently someone can get into the conversation.

▷ Integrate contributions. Link points of view and identify areas of understanding, agreement, and disagreement.

▷ Summarize key ideas and major points to keep the group focused and on track with the agenda.

▷ Express your concern if the meeting is straying from the agenda or if specific items are taking longer than originally planned. As a group, decide whether and how the group should monitor itself to keep the discussion focused.

> ▷ Intervene when someone takes too much time. Calmly interrupt and say something like, "John, thanks for that observation. Now, I'd like to find out what Jane's views are."

▶ Plan and conduct meetings in an orderly fashion to make effective use of time and to facilitate a clear exchange of ideas, information, discussion, and decision making.

Ensure that clear agendas and desired outcomes are established for meetings

▼

Before an important meeting, have the person take you through the agenda and objectives to see if they are clear and on target.

Meetings can be productive and worthwhile, or they can be a waste of time. Agendas are essential for conducting efficient meetings. They allow group members to prepare for meetings and ensure that desired outcomes are understood.

▶ In preparing an agenda, use the following steps:

1. Put the name of the meeting at the top of the agenda. Add the date, time, location, duration, and participants and their roles.

2. List agenda items in the order in which you will address them. Put the highest-priority items first so that group members will focus on them. Consider asking other team members to help you plan the agenda.

3. Specify who will be responsible for each agenda item and what type of action you want to take on each. For example, you may have "information only," "discussion only," and "decision required" items. This helps people prepare for the meeting and clarifies the reason for addressing each item.

4. Establish time limits—an approximate amount of time for each agenda item. Enforce time limits on "information only" and "discussion only" items. On a "decision required" item, acknowledge when the time limit has been reached, then ask the group to decide whether and how to continue with the item.

The following example illustrates one way to structure an agenda:

Goal-Setting Kickoff Meeting

September 15, 10:00AM – 11:30AM

Desired Outcome: Communicate and establish criteria for next year's goals

Item	Process/Action	Time
1. New goal-setting guidelines	Presentation	10:00 – 10:15
2. Next year's corporate goals	Presentation	10:15 – 10:25
3. Next year's division goals	Discussion: assign responsibility to department heads	10:25 – 10:45
4. Next year's individual goals	Discussion: set dates for completion	10:45 – 11:10
5. Process for completion/review	Discussion: consensus	11:10 – 11:30
6. Adjourn		11:30

Ensure that meeting structures and processes fit with desired outcomes

An effective meeting involves far more than getting a group of people in a room or on a conference call to talk about an issue. Proven meeting structures and processes can help you achieve more consistent results. Consider the following suggestions:

- Establish common meeting protocol and rules, such as:
  - ▷ Send pre-meeting work and agendas ahead of time.
  - ▷ Start and stop meetings on time.

▷ During brainstorming, don't criticize or evaluate ideas.

▷ Establish a clear purpose for each agenda item.

▷ Distribute notes from the meeting, including decisions, assignments, and deadlines.

▸ Clearly identify the facilitator of the meeting and the facilitator's responsibilities, including keeping the team on task. (As the leader, you might facilitate the meeting yourself, use a meeting facilitator, or rotate facilitating among team members.)

▸ Determine what is needed to achieve the outcome for each agenda item. This is how you match process and outcome. For example, if a decision needs to be made, determine the information that is needed and the discussion that should occur for a decision to be made. How can you get that to happen? Get ideas from others about how to get people the information they need, provide for the involvement they want, and arrive at a mutually acceptable decision. If plans need to be coordinated, determine the process you will use.

Connect people with skilled meeting facilitators to learn about the structures and processes they use.

▸ Be aware that there is always more than one way to achieve an outcome. If you can think of only one way to address an issue, ask others for their ideas.

▸ Realize that each agenda item may require a different meeting process and that you may need to adjust the process based on how the meeting is progressing. For example, if participants are resistant to what you are saying, you may need to shift from a formal presentation to a more facilitative process.

▸ Determine your role and the different roles required of the meeting participants. For example, your role might include one or all of the following, depending upon what you hope to accomplish in your meeting:

▷ Kick off the meeting and facilitate introductions, then assume the role of a participant.

▷ Facilitate discussions and draw out as many ideas from as many people as possible.

▷ Share key information that others need to have.

▸ Determine what process you will use to communicate the outcome of the meeting and to ensure that people follow through on their commitments.

▸ Use the last five minutes of a meeting to debrief. Ask "What went well with this meeting?" and "How could we improve the next meeting?" Make notes to review later. Getting into this routine and taking action on recommendations will make your meetings more productive.

▸ When you need to generate new ideas, hold a brainstorming session to generate free association between ideas as well as open new avenues of thought. Brainstorming gives you many different ideas in a short period of time. Use the following process:

1. Identify the issue.

2. Ask the group to share ideas as they think of them. Use the following ground rules during this phase of the brainstorming process:

   ▷ Focus on quantity, not quality.

   ▷ Expect and encourage wild and zany ideas.

   ▷ Prohibit criticism and evaluation of ideas.

   ▷ Build on others' ideas.

3. As the meeting facilitator, follow these guidelines:

   ▷ Ensure that all participants have an opportunity to share their ideas.

   ▷ Acknowledge participants who may not be able to get their ideas out quickly.

   ▷ Record all ideas exactly as stated.

   ▷ Promote a congenial and relaxed atmosphere. Encourage laughter.

Perform process checks during meetings and redirect discussion as appropriate

Meetings can easily get off track and fail to achieve their intended purpose, especially when they are not facilitated effectively. To ensure that your meetings are productive, conduct process checks and redirect the discussion when necessary. Consider the following suggestions:

▸ Make sure that the purpose and desired outcome of the meeting are stated clearly upfront.

▶ Create a norm that all participants are responsible for keeping the meeting on track. While you as facilitator will perform more formal process checks, productivity will be increased if everyone shares responsibility for following the agenda.

▶ Use process checks to keep the meeting on track. For example, 10 minutes before the allotted time on an issue ends, summarize what you have discussed so far and ask the team how they want to spend the final 10 minutes. Another process check might involve saying, "We have just spent 15 minutes arguing about who dropped the ball. Is this how we want to spend our time?" Process checks allow you to comment on what is going on in the group, allow the group to talk about how it is working together, and enable you and the group to make changes so everyone can work together more effectively.

▶ Before the meeting starts, make a mental note of how many process checks you plan to make. For example, if the meeting is only an hour long, you might decide to do one process check halfway through the meeting. Realize that once you begin the meeting, you might need more or fewer process checks than you originally planned.

▶ When people get off the topic, bring them back by making a comment such as "This is an interesting discussion, but I am concerned that we have strayed from the original purpose of our meeting."

▶ Realize that some process checks are informal and subtle. To keep the meeting moving forward, use techniques such as the following:
  ▷ Paraphrase comments that are important or controversial.
  ▷ Summarize what has been decided or accomplished so far.
  ▷ State conflicting viewpoints.

Challenge people to redirect those who take the group off task.

▶ Pay attention to when and how experienced facilitators perform process checks and how they get discussions back on track. Try these same techniques in the next few meetings that you facilitate.

▶ If you hesitate to get a meeting back on track, examine the reasons why. You might feel uncomfortable interrupting people, especially assertive people. You might be interested in the tangent. You might have a difficult decision to make and welcome a reason to postpone it.

Drive the achievement of meaningful results in meetings without overemphasizing processes

Research indicates that managers spend 25 to 75 percent of their working time in meetings. Meetings can be vital communication and decision-making forums, as long as they are efficient and productive. Consider the following suggestions:

▶ Determine if a meeting is necessary. Is there truly a need to gather people to discuss the issue? Are you holding meetings for a reason or out of habit?

Sit in on a few meetings to observe how people facilitate interaction among participants and what outcomes they achieve.

▶ Look at your calendar and identify the different kinds of meetings you have, their frequency, and their length. Can any be eliminated, shortened, or improved?

▶ Be sure your meetings have a clear purpose (to exchange information, gain support, solve a problem, generate new ideas, arrive at a decision, check progress, establish plans) and agenda. You and others need to know the purpose and expected outcomes of each meeting.

▶ Be realistic about what you can accomplish during a meeting. If you limit the scope and the number of topics, you will be more likely to achieve closure on issues. Ask participants to share only relevant information.

▶ Ensure the appropriate people are at the meeting. Include those who can make a contribution and those who need the information that will be covered.

▶ Distribute agendas in advance (whenever possible). It is a courtesy to participants, and it helps them prepare for the topics and discussions. Consider using an agenda that gives a brief description of each topic.

▶ Set clear time parameters. Meetings that are 60 to 90 minutes long tend to stay more focused. Longer meetings are more effective when they are divided into shorter segments with breaks.

▶ Start and end meetings on time. A casual approach to meeting times can interfere with other meetings and activities. If you will be leading a meeting but there is a chance you will be late, ask someone ahead of time to start the meeting for you.

▸ Maintain balance between sticking to the agenda and spending enough time on an issue to make progress. When it is appropriate, use brainstorming and other discussion processes, but make sure the discussion leads to the necessary clarity, decision, or commitment.

▸ Ask questions. Knowing how to ask the right questions can be more important than knowing the answers. Questions will help you draw out ideas, explore all relevant points of view, and balance participation between participants.

▸ Debrief after meetings. What went well? What changes do the participants recommend? Debriefing helps the leader by getting the group or team involved in managing meetings better.

▸ Prepare a written summary within 48 hours to help everyone remember what was discussed and decided. Distribute the summary to all participants and anyone else who needs to be informed about decisions, action steps, and target dates.

Identify and address unproductive debate in meetings in order to move issues ahead

Generally, when meeting participants become disruptive and unproductive, and debate gets the group off track, it may be because (a) the group is not following its own norms or process guidelines, or has not yet established norms for working together or (b) the dialogue has become so intense that everyone gets pulled into emotional camps without realizing it. To get back on track, consider the following suggestions:

▸ Establish group norms for all meetings. At the beginning of a meeting, create a list of norms or rules that all participants can agree upon. Norms are behaviors that will guide the group over the course of its work. Some typical norms are:

▹ Come prepared.

▹ Don't interrupt other participants.

▹ Choose a decision-making method, such as consensus.

▸ Address violations of group norms. This is called norming the group. For example, if a team decides to begin meetings on time, then start them on time and if someone comes late, say, "Good to see you. Join us. Of course, we have already begun." This sends both a welcoming message and a norming message of "Come on time. We won't wait for you." Don't stop the meeting to bring the person up to speed.

▶ If people are interrupting one another and arguing unproductively, call for a time-out or a process check. Say that the group agreed to listen to one another, but that has not been happening for the last 10 minutes. Then be quiet until one of the participants says something. If it is an idea about how to resolve the issues, great. If it is a defensive comment, norm more strongly: "Not listening to one another will get us nowhere." Then turn to the group: "What shall we do differently to get beyond this disagreement?" In this way you are enlisting the help of the team to redirect participants.

▶ Talk with team members offline. Find out what their issues are and what they are going to do to work more productively with other team members. Notice that you are not telling them to behave; you are asking them what they intend to do differently.

▶ If there are frequent disruptions in your meetings, consider using a trained facilitator to help the group get on track. A trained facilitator can:

Introduce people to a skilled meeting facilitator to learn how to conduct process checks and redirect discussion.

  ▷ Point out what is happening in the group at a given moment.
  ▷ Ask participants what they want to do about conflict.
  ▷ Call a time-out if people are disruptive.
  ▷ Remind the group of its norms.
  ▷ Ask a member to summarize the issues.
  ▷ Solicit the perspectives of less vocal members.
  ▷ Deal with disruption by inquiring about people's concerns, asking for their cooperation, or giving them feedback about their impact on the group.
  ▷ Introduce alternative points of view. Remember that groupthink can greatly diminish a team's effectiveness and the quality of its decisions.
  ▷ Ask for a proposal about how to move the group forward when there is an impasse.

Follow up after meetings

▼

Review a sample of a meeting recap to see whether action steps, deadlines, and decisions are clearly documented. Offer feedback where necessary.

Summarizing a meeting at its conclusion and following up later are essential to ensuring the full effectiveness of a meeting. Consider the following suggestions:

▸ At the end of the meeting, take a few moments to discuss what went well, what problems came up, and what you can do about how the group works together.

▸ Distribute copies of meeting minutes and reminders about assignments and deadlines to everyone who attended, plus any others who need the information.

9

Build Realistic Plans

Knowing how to create plans that incorporate realistic expectations and that accurately estimate the resources and time available and the effort involved is part of a manager's responsibility. Without a manager who has a good sense of how to plan, when to plan, and what steps to plan for—and who knows the common pitfalls of failed planning—work groups can end up being chaotic and unproductive.

Effective planning starts with understanding your company's strategic vision and goals, and how your unit relates to accomplishing those goals. By considering the various factors involved in planning and taking the time to make sure you have covered them, you'll be able to keep projects moving smoothly and successfully toward completion. You'll also be able to make sure your direct reports are using successful planning strategies for their projects.

In this chapter, we will cover the following areas:

▼

- ▸ Understand your organization's strategic vision

- ▸ Translate business strategies into clear objectives and tactics

- ▸ Identify action steps needed to accomplish team or work group objectives

- ▸ Identify and obtain resources needed to accomplish team or work group objectives

- ▸ Involve others in planning

- ▸ Integrate planning efforts across work units

- ▸ Establish clear, realistic time lines for accomplishing goals

- ▸ Identify risks and assumptions in plans, anticipate problems, and plan for contingencies

Understand your organization's strategic vision

▼

Ask people to explain the organization's strategic goals. Listen for depth of understanding. Ask what role they and their groups have in accomplishing the goals.

Effective planning requires an understanding of the organization's vision and goals, the strategies chosen to accomplish the goals, and the business processes necessary to achieve the goals. This understanding enables leaders and teams to set work unit goals, strategies, and plans that support the vision. To better understand your organization's strategic vision and link it to your team's work, consider the following steps:

▶ First, articulate your organization's vision and strategic direction.

▷ What are the organization's vision and goals?

▷ What is the organization's sustainable advantage over its competitors?

▷ Which business processes are critical to the success of the strategies and vision?

▷ What role do you play or does your team play in the success of the organization?

▶ Next, if you cannot answer these questions, ask for help from your manager or coach.

▶ Finally, communicate this information to those you supervise so that they understand the organization's direction. They will need this information to set their own goals and guide their teams.

Translate business strategies into clear objectives and tactics

▼

Detailed action plans help you translate business strategies into clear objectives and action plans for your work unit or team. Plans also help you focus department or team output to best serve the organization's needs and help you stay in touch with the big picture when day-to-day details threaten to cloud the larger goals. Consider the following suggestions:

▶ Clarify the role you and your team(s) play in achieving the organization's goals by identifying the business processes for which you are accountable and determining what your part of the organization must do to achieve these goals. Include objectives for how to improve the business processes necessary for success.

▸ Identify the primary constraints or barriers to achieving the goals. Plan what you will do to address them. This is important because this is where you are most vulnerable.

Review a team's operational plan, focusing on the link between the plan and business strategies. Question things that are not linked to business strategies.

▸ Ask individuals and teams to list their objectives and plans. Give them a template to use to ensure that all pertinent components are addressed.

▸ Review these individual and team objectives and plans to ensure that they are compatible with and support the organization's strategy.

▸ Develop objective measures of success that will tell you when you have achieved an objective or goal.

▸ Put all of this information into a format that is clear, accessible, and easy to update.

▸ Be flexible, and be prepared to change your tactics if internal or external factors alter the company's strategic direction.

Identify action steps needed to accomplish team or work group objectives

▼

Ask people to note what their plans depend upon. What action steps need to get done in sequence?

Action steps help you plot the critical path for your projects. If you don't identify specific action steps, you'll get stuck, people will be confused, and your strategies and objectives will fall by the wayside. Consider the following suggestions:

▸ Understand how your work group supports the broader strategy of your organization. Learn why the strategy was chosen and whether there are any guidelines on how people should pursue it.

▸ Set goals and determine strategies and tactics to achieve the goals. Next, put together action plans that detail the steps needed to accomplish the plan and achieve goals.

▸ Ask a series of questions to organize your thoughts:
  ▷ What needs to be accomplished? What is the desired result?
  ▷ What are the main tasks?
  ▷ What specific action steps are required for each main task?
  ▷ Who will be held accountable for each step?

    ▷ How much time will each task take?

    ▷ Which tasks need to be done in sequence? Which tasks can be done out of sequence?

    ▷ Which tasks can be done simultaneously?

    ▷ Which resources will be required? How will you secure the resources?

    ▷ How will you measure success?

- Identify internal and external constraints to carrying out your objectives and tactics.

- Meet with colleagues who are skilled in translating objectives into specific action steps. Ask them to describe the process they use to develop action steps and tactics. Incorporate their techniques into your planning.

Identify and obtain resources needed to accomplish team or work group objectives

When you implement team or work group objectives, you need to have the right people in the right place at the right time. To make realistic estimates of budget, staff, and other resources, consider the following suggestions:

- Thoroughly define the scope of the project. Make sure you identify the budget, goals, objectives, and desired results, along with the processes needed to accomplish them.

- Make a list of all the resources in your area, and those that you have access to in other areas of the organization. Include as many types of resources as you can, from capital equipment and budgets to administrative support and individual or group expertise. This will help you maximize your options.

Identify people who accurately predict needed resources. How do they consistently estimate what it takes to get a job done?

- For each resource, note when it will be needed, the different ways it can be obtained, and what acceptable substitutes exist. If you haven't worked on this type of project before, review the resources that were required on a similar initiative.

- Identify potential resources before you need them. For example, develop contacts with people in your organization. Learn about their areas of expertise, both on and off the job. When you need help, they may be able to help you or refer you to specialists outside your organization.

▸ When you are preparing estimates for staffing needs, consider the skill levels of the individuals who will work on your project and adjust time and cost appropriately. Also look for cross-training opportunities to make use of resources from other areas of the organization.

▸ When you work with a team, challenge them to use resources in the most efficient way possible.

▸ Check with colleagues, mentors, and your manager to see if you requested and obtained the correct resources. Their feedback will help you detect any gaps in your plans or flaws in your approach. It will also reinforce what you are doing well.

▸ Establish a way to track the productivity of various resources. This will enable you to estimate your resource needs more accurately on future projects.

Involve others in planning

▼

Deciding when and how to involve people is a leadership skill that should always be part of the planning process. When you are making plans, involve the people, teams, and constituencies that care about the outcome, the plan, or the process. Consider the following suggestions for involving others in your planning:

Ask people to identify who should be consulted or involved in planning a specific initiative. Verify that they included the appropriate people.

▸ Identify the business processes involved in accomplishing the goal and the process owners for each part of the process. Typically, these people or their representatives should be included in the planning.

▸ Recognize that most planning processes need to include the people and teams who are affected.

▸ Use a team approach to planning in complex situations where results are critical, many people are involved, and it is challenging to construct the plan.

▶ Balance the need for involvement with the need for action and speed. Communicate the need for speed. Set time limits on the planning process.

▶ Train people in team processes so that team planning will go more quickly and smoothly.

▶ Include vendors and suppliers when their commitments are necessary and cannot be assumed—for example, when the project requires that new technology from a sole supplier be ready on time.

Integrate planning efforts across work units

▼

Identify which parts of the plan are dependent on other departments and functions and ask them for input.

Integrating planning efforts across work units is easier said than done, but absolutely essential. It takes a concerted effort to get people together, create a workable plan, and sort through competing priorities. Consider the following suggestions:

▶ Realize that your area is not an island. Make a habit of involving others in your planning efforts. Take into account the people on your team, other teams in the organization, your customers, and your suppliers.

▶ Determine the support and integration you will need from other work groups. Bring these groups into the planning process early to take advantage of their expertise and enlist their cooperation.

▶ Even when you do not see a direct connection between your proposed plan and other work units, review your plan from their perspectives to determine if they might see a relationship. Send a copy of your plans to them; err on the side of communicating too much rather than too little.

▶ For each plan, list the key stakeholders, the business processes involved, and the owner of each process. Determine how each person on the list can be involved. Decide whether each person should:

  ▷ Be an active planner.

  ▷ Serve as an information resource or subject-matter expert.

  ▷ Review the plan.

  ▷ Receive communications and updates.

▶ When one of your direct reports plans a project, ask how the plan affects other work units and what conversations the person has had with his or her coworkers in those areas. These questions will reinforce your expectation regarding integrated efforts.

▶ Bring cross-functional teams together to review plans:

  ▷ Does each group understand its role and responsibilities in the plan?

  ▷ Are handoffs and checkpoints clear?

  ▷ Do you have adequate communication plans?

  ▷ Does everyone feel involved and included?

▶ Designate liaison people to help you effectively plan across work units. For example, product managers or customer representatives could facilitate and coordinate planning efforts for particular products, clients, or projects.

▶ Analyze and address barriers to collaboration. Set a clear expectation that people and teams will work together cooperatively.

▶ Realize that coordinating efforts among locations will require greater effort, especially when you are working in multiple countries and time zones. Talk with people who have more experience in this area about how they made global teams work.

Establish clear, realistic time lines for accomplishing goals

Unrealistic time lines can create more problems than they solve. For example, an impossible schedule set by one work unit can affect the schedules of many other groups, causing inefficient use of resources, delayed products, and a general sense that things are out of control. Consider the following suggestions:

▶ When you're leading a project, estimate the length of time each phase will take. Make a chart that lists the time needed for each phase. This will give you a graphic depiction of the total time required.

▶ Compare your timetable to the time required on similar assignments that are now complete. Is your plan realistic? Where should you build in extra time? Where can you cut time?

> ▶ Look for phases of the project or assignment that are time-dependent on other phases. These areas of interdependence could turn into bottlenecks.

As you look at plans, check for an appropriate balance between involving people in the process and completing a plan in a reasonable amount of time.

> ▶ When you have a proposed time line, ask your team or a trusted peer to challenge your assumptions and identify potential problems with the schedule. Address any issues you overlooked.

> ▶ Review your timetable with people who will be working on the project. With their input, set final deadlines for each action step. Be sure that the due dates are clear and agreed upon.

> ▶ Consider involving your customers and/or suppliers in the planning process. Their input can help you develop realistic time lines. Also, you will be more likely to gain their commitment to the process.

Identify risks and assumptions in plans, anticipate problems, and plan for contingencies

▼

Life doesn't always follow a project plan. If you question assumptions, anticipate risks, and develop contingency plans, you can avoid many problems and mitigate others when they occur. Consider the following suggestions:

> ▶ Identify the assumptions in your plans and test their accuracy. For example, your plan may depend on the assumption that people on your team have the necessary expertise. If that assumption is wrong, the plan will encounter problems, such as missed deadlines and uncertainty over how to handle unexpected issues.

> ▶ After a plan is drafted, brainstorm with your team about what could go wrong. Make a list of the most likely problems and how you will handle them if they occur.

> ▶ To identify risks on your projects, use the following process:

> 1. Determine the critical path of the project. List all the tasks and decision points.

> 2. Analyze each component to detect areas of risk. For example:

> ▷ You might not have enough information to make a decision.

> ▷ It might take extra time for people to learn a new technical procedure.
>
> ▷ A service group that you use might experience staffing problems.
>
> ▷ You might lose a key resource at a critical time.

3. Categorize potential problems into high- and low-risk areas. Consider how likely it is that each problem will occur and how damaging it would be.

Review the person's action plans. Ask about risks in the plans, and add your own thoughts.

4. Prepare several possible approaches for dealing with likely problems.

5. Incorporate safety factors for high-risk areas:

> ▷ Allocate more time and/or funds to these phases.
>
> ▷ Introduce tough control methods.
>
> ▷ Set up a communication process so people hear about problems immediately and can address them promptly.

10
Manage and Improve Processes

How things get done each day determines how effectively goals and objectives are achieved. As organizations grow larger, the importance of standardized processes grows too. The more consistently processes are followed, the better the chance of producing high-quality results. As a manager, you will oversee and review numerous processes for their success rate and their efficiency, and to make sure they produce the best outcomes.

It's also important to understand how people relate to processes, to be able to evaluate and create new ways of doing things, and to make sure that you are incorporating input from all key stakeholders. There are specific ways to review, monitor, and improve processes, and when they are applied, they can create a much smoother workflow for you and your group.

In this chapter, we will cover the following areas:

▼

- ▶ Define and communicate expectations for quality outcomes

- ▶ Develop common process-management tools and methods

- ▶ Designate process owners who are accountable for successful execution

- ▶ Help others understand their work from a process perspective

- ▶ Help others understand the impact of variation and how to manage it

- ▶ Identify and implement the appropriate work structures and processes to accomplish goals

- ▶ Integrate input from stakeholders to prioritize process-improvement efforts

- ▶ Ensure currency of process standards and process documentation

- ▶ Identify ways to streamline and/or improve efficiency of work

- ▶ Manage quality by using data to identify trends and track progress

- ▶ Analyze process breakdowns to ensure that lessons are learned

- ▶ Investigate and adopt best practices and lessons learned from within and outside the organization

Define and communicate expectations for quality outcomes

▼

Ask people how they determine if they are delivering high-quality products and services. Check the connection between quality measures and actual requirements.

Quality standards are driven by current and anticipated customer requirements and the organization's positioning. In addition, teams need to simultaneously improve business processes so that the organization can meet a higher level of customer requirements and drive down costs. Consider the following suggestions:

- ▶ Identify "must have," "nice to have," and "want in the future" requirements. Manage to those levels.

- ▶ Ask customers about their requirements. Also understand how the product or service is used and by whom. Include:
  - ▷ Product specifications.
  - ▷ Service requirements.
  - ▷ Time considerations.
  - ▷ Cost considerations.
  - ▷ Delivery issues.
  - ▷ Previous problems or concerns.
  - ▷ Anticipated future needs.

- ▶ Ensure that everyone involved with the product or service (the value chain) knows and understands the requirements and expectations.

- ▶ Communicate standards and requirements to your vendors and suppliers. To develop quality partnerships with them, consider the following suggestions:
  - ▷ Communicate expectations and quality standards for your products and services with the vendors and suppliers who will be contributing goods or services to the creation of those products.
  - ▷ Select vendors on the basis of both quality and price. Poor quality at a low price is still poor quality, no matter how little it costs. Know the total cost of a sale, including rework and replacement costs.
  - ▷ Develop solid partnerships with your vendors and suppliers so you can count on each other. Let them know that if they deliver quality products and good service, you will give them your business.

> ▷ If you do not have a choice of vendors, determine how to expand your options. Many managers feel stuck because they are getting poor-quality products or service from suppliers or vendors, and they think they have nowhere else to go. Work with your team, the organization, and the industry to develop your options.
>
> ▷ Require that your vendors use process-improvement processes. Consider training or consulting with them to improve quality.

Develop common process-management tools and methods

▼

When you have standardized work processes, you do not have to reinvent the wheel for each new project or situation. Instead, you can modify a standard process to fit each new initiative. Similarly, process-improvement methods can also benefit from standardization. Organizations focused on this area create improvement processes, train specialists to consult with and support process-improvement teams, and train employees on basic techniques and processes. Consider the following suggestions:

▸ Use resources available in your organization (such as individuals' learning and experience, books, online sources, and experts in process improvement) to identify improvement methods, processes, and tools.

▸ If your organization has standard process-improvement procedures, select a team to be trained on these procedures and then have them serve as the work unit's advisers in process improvement.

Share the process management tools that you have found helpful. Provide examples of how and when the tools can be used.

▸ If the organization has many different work processes, such as project-management methodologies, simplify and use one. Communicate the standard work process and process-improvement procedures and tools so that people are aware of them. Also, recognize and celebrate improvement successes.

▸ Some effective tools for standardizing work processes follows:

> ▷ *Flow charts* convey the relationships of one process or person to another through visual descriptions of work cycles. They are treelike diagrams that represent the work flow among process components. Standard symbols such as circles and squares are used to identify tasks, and lines are used to represent relationships. Flow charts are especially effective when there are complex process relationships

and when several tasks occur simultaneously. Using flow charts, you can identify critical paths and track progress.

▷ *Project planning worksheets* provide overall snapshots of projects. A project planning worksheet breaks a project into specific tasks and steps, shows estimates of the time required and the cost involved for each task or step, and identifies the person or group responsible for carrying the task through to completion.

1. MAJOR GOAL/TASK What must we do?   **PROJECT PLANNER**

2. ACTION STEPS What steps are needed to reach the goal or complete the task?	**3. WHEN** Completion Date/Time	**4. WHO** D=Do S=Support	**5. COST** What costs are involved?	**6. TRACKING** How/when will we monitor progress?

7. EVALUATION What went well? What didn't go well? What did we learn? Implications?

▷ *Gantt charts* represent time relationships in a project. A Gantt chart works particularly well for projects that involve simple, repetitive tasks, projects that will not go through many process changes, and projects for which the plan needs to be communicated simply and directly to others. Gantt charts do not work well for highly interdependent steps.

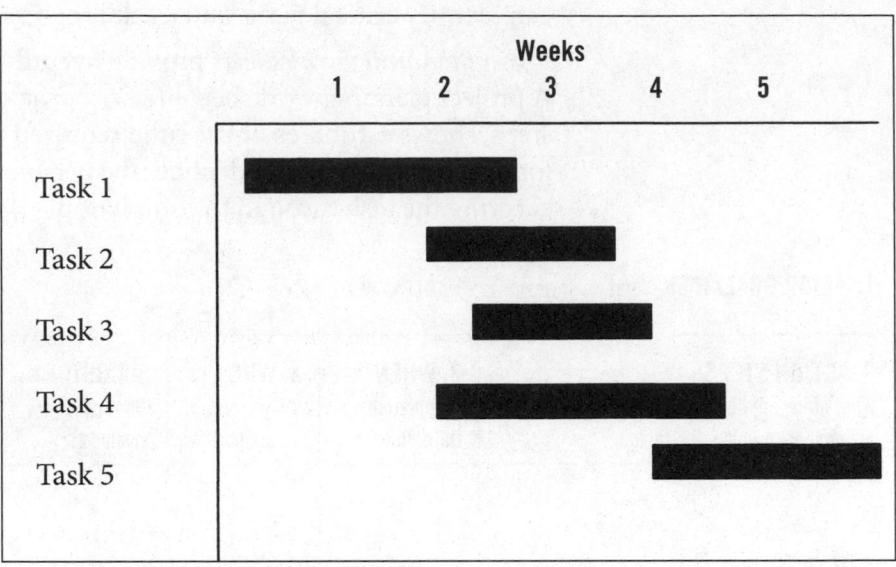

▷ *Control sheets* are simple spreadsheets that list due dates, designate responsibilities, and serve as a communication tool to both manager and employees.

▷ *Error logs* (or process breakdown logs) track information about specific incidences. Reviewing them over time reveals trends that indicate process weaknesses.

▷ *Work plans* are used to assign and prioritize work and to communicate estimated time standards for individuals or work groups on a daily, weekly, or monthly basis. They can also be used to track estimated versus actual time for job completion. Actual times that differ significantly from estimated times might indicate a need for further analysis of the process for completing that job.

▷ *Standard Operating Procedures* (SOPs) spell out the steps for completing a task. SOPs are very useful as a training/cross-training tool if employee turnover is high. They are also useful for activities that are long, complex, or done infrequently.

▷ *Checklists* can be used when documentation is important or when it is crucial that no step be overlooked.

Standard versions of these tools are available in both paper and electronic formats. Many organizations create their own versions for internal use. If you do not know where to locate such resources, consult process-improvement literature, check with your improvement teams or quality-process people, or talk with a manufacturing or customer service group. They typically use these tools regularly.

- In addition to standard tools, use a standard method—a specific way in which something is done. The following are common, useful standard methods:

  ▷ *Cross-functional teams* consist of people who work in different departments. A temporary team might be formed to develop and implement a new process. Permanent teams might form for processes that depend on many different groups working together cohesively.

  ▷ *Meeting management guidelines* provide a standard way to conduct meetings. They usually cover agendas, start and stop times, how to handle conflict, and so on.

  ▷ *Brainstorming protocol* provides guidelines for effective brainstorming in groups.

  ▷ *Project initiation meetings* trigger the start of a project. Participants include project owners from various functions, the customer, and other groups. The meetings are used to clarify requirements, work processes, and how teams will work together.

  ▷ *Vendor meetings* allow you to review vendors' abilities, determine what they need from you, and discuss ways of serving each other better. Vendors often can suggest how to serve customer needs better.

  ▷ *Customer reviews* provide a standardized process for gathering information from customers to improve customer relationships and satisfaction.

Designate process owners who are accountable for successful execution

▼

The manufacturing industry is aware of the importance of process owners who are responsible for the continuous improvement of their processes. Other industries can also benefit from the dramatic improvements and increased productivity that come from process improvement. Responsibilities of process owners may include the following:

- ▶ Create and maintain documentation about the process, including flow charts, SOPs, and checklists.

- ▶ Collect feedback from internal and external customers to monitor potential areas for improvement.

- ▶ Communicate to stakeholders to make them aware of process changes.

Ask people to take responsibility for process improvement. Set specific effectiveness targets for them and challenge them to figure out how to reach those targets.

- ▶ Follow up on process improvements after they are implemented.

- ▶ Suggest where gaps in training may exist.

- ▶ Maintain and report on the measurements relating to the process.

- ▶ Regularly review and update all documentation and measurements that relate to the process.

- ▶ Keep abreast of trends or technology that could improve work flow.

Help others understand their work from a process perspective

▼

People who understand the concept of work processes can see how their work fits into the overall picture and understand its impact on delivering value to customers. This also makes them more knowledgeable when they participate in efforts to improve processes. Consider the following suggestions:

- ▶ Help people understand that the work of the unit is composed of tasks that result in an output. The way these tasks are put together is a process. Each person in the work unit is part of one or more business processes that deliver value.

> ► To understand a process, ask people who are involved in it to map the steps in the process. Ask them to identify the inputs and outputs for each step.

Have people look at a process to see if it is sufficiently linked with other parts of the organization, including with internal customers.

> ► Ask people to specify the inputs necessary for their work, to describe the work they do, and to identify the outputs. Help them understand what is done with their outputs by asking who receives their outputs and what difference the quality makes to the recipients.

> ► Distinguish between core processes and support processes. Core processes deliver value to customers directly, with assistance from support processes. Core processes include customer support, product development, and distribution. Support processes often include HR, legal, and finance.

> ► Suggest that upstream teams interview downstream teams to understand how upstream work affects downstream work. For example, order entry people could interview customer fulfillment people to understand how unclear specifications and lack of customer information affects fulfillment.

Help others understand the impact of variation and how to manage it

▼

The clearer and more standardized the work process is, the more likely that quality will be consistently high. Without clarity and standardization, you are likely to have a higher rate of variation in the work process. Consider the following suggestions to help your group and organization understand the impact of variation:

> ► Create a flow chart of the processes in your area. Then explore with the team what happens when variations—accommodating last-minute requests, not following established communication steps, adjusting for employee absences—are introduced into the process.

Discuss the impact of variation and how to manage it, including when variation is justified as a business need.

> ► Look at specific examples of how clients were affected when people did not follow established processes. Have the team keep track of these types of situations so the group can discuss how to better manage them. Sharing feedback from internal and external customers can be a powerful learning tool.

▶ Explore the value of saying no to requests for variations. Sometimes people don't feel empowered to refuse extreme requests. You may need to coach them on how to address a customer need without significant variations.

▶ Log customer requests for variation so you can recognize new customer needs. It is far better to respond to new customer needs with new processes than to have each request become a variation.

▶ Show that variations are not cost effective in terms of both quantifiable and nonquantifiable costs. Quantifiable costs include rework time, employee overtime, extra equipment maintenance, increased overhead costs, and product profit margins. Nonquantifiable costs include longer work hours and cycle times, increased employee frustration, and lower productivity.

▶ Understand that frequent process variations make training and cross-training more difficult. In fact, training in areas with high variation can be time consuming and can reduce the productivity of both trainer and trainee.

▶ Explore trends in variations that indicate that other work groups may need to improve a process. Do your employees consistently have to change the way things are done to make up for another department's poor planning, unrealistic turnaround times, or miscommunication? Use this information to help other teams improve their efficiency and effectiveness.

Identify and implement the appropriate work structures and processes to accomplish goals

An organization's structure, which includes the roles and relationships among people in the organization, must be dynamic. What once worked well may no longer work due to changes in expectations, people, and so on. Effective managers regularly review and adjust the structure of their part of the organization to meet changing work processes, changing internal and external needs, and the skills of employees. Consider the following suggestions:

▶ Don't focus solely on changing structure. Identify the business processes before you work on structure. Without a clear understanding of the value chain and business processes, you will not get the structure right.

▶ Identify the critical roles needed to perform the business processes of the team. Then look at which roles are linked to one another. This will help you create a structure that makes sense.

Discuss ways to evaluate whether a process or structure is suitable for the situation.

▶ Design your structure with empowerment in mind. Whenever possible, create a structure in which people do the whole job, not just a piece of it.

▶ Ensure that your organization's structure is current, especially if you have just experienced reorganization, downsizing, significant growth, or product or service changes. Reevaluate job descriptions and reporting relationships.

▶ Look at how employees in remote locations, contract workers, and alliance partners fit into the structure. These staffing methods can work effectively as long as the reporting relationships are clear, people know how they connect to the organization and who they connect with, they have access to technical resources, and there is a clear understanding that these individuals are part of the team.

▶ When you are developing a new product or initiating an interdepartmental project, create a cross-functional task force to determine work processes and make recommendations for structure. Include participants at several levels of the organization.

▶ When you are working on recurring problems, staff the team with representatives from groups that were not previously involved in order to get new perspectives. For example, include customer representatives and administrative support people.

Integrate input from stakeholders to prioritize process-improvement efforts

When you have decided which parts of a process to change, make sure you and your team understand how people outside the team will be affected. To help integrate input from stakeholders and prioritize process-improvement efforts, consider the following guidelines:

► Determine which process is most critical and should receive the highest priority. Ask teams, vendors, and customers for their points of view.

When people want to change their work structure, ensure that they are involving people who can help them understand the effect the change will have.

► Describe the most critical process from beginning to end as it is now and define how you want it to look in the future. Use "as is" (current) and "to be" (desired) process flow charts to articulate changes and explain them to others.

► When a process is long or complex, involve people from different functional areas to organize issues related to the change and to keep people informed. Involve stakeholders who have a vested interest in what is happening, including external customers, internal customers, and vendors. Use stakeholder meetings to:

  ▷ Understand broader issues between teams.

  ▷ Discuss how changes will affect various stakeholders.

  ▷ Determine priorities to work on, resources needed, appropriate people, and so on.

  ▷ Identify ways to manage change to minimize negative effects.

  ▷ Agree on how to communicate what is happening during change.

  ▷ Talk about individual or group habits that may need to be addressed.

► When it is necessary to involve a large group, begin with some initial fact-finding in smaller groups or one-on-one meetings. This will help ensure that everyone's time is used effectively.

► To gain the most value from process-improvement meetings, consider these suggestions:

  ▷ Set an agenda for the meeting.

  ▷ At the beginning of the meeting, discuss expectations, parameters for the discussion, and norms for the group.

  ▷ Select a strong facilitator who is respected by the group. Provide training for people who want to become facilitators.

Ensure currency of process standards and process documentation

Standards exist so that business processes work smoothly, and so that you can maximize the probability that customer needs will be met. Process documentation helps you ensure that standards are known, followed, and improved. However, if the documentation is never reviewed, standards could become an administrative burden rather than a management tool. Consider the following guidelines to help you ensure that standards and process documentation are current:

▸ Update documentation as one of the steps in executing a process improvement. When a team completes an improvement project, ask to see the documentation for the new part of the process.

▸ Review situations in which process variation was caused by unclear or inadequate documentation. Use these examples to illustrate the importance of communicating expectations and work process steps throughout the value chain.

▸ Work with process owners to review and update all documents. Team members who are new to the process can help you identify steps that are unclear or inadequate.

Talk about barriers that keep people from updating documentation. Pick one and discuss steps the person could take to address it.

▸ Update documentation when:
  ▹ New technology is employed.
  ▹ Organizational, departmental, or process changes occur.
  ▹ Roles or assignments shift within the team.
  ▹ People are unavailable due to illnesses, sabbaticals, unforeseen departures, or other reasons.
  ▹ Customers' needs change.
  ▹ Certain functions become obsolete.

▸ Choose a central location for storing both paper and electronic documentation. If people can't access documentation, they won't use it, let alone update it.

Identify ways to streamline and/or improve efficiency of work

Challenge people to identify ways to streamline and/or improve the efficiency of their work. Ask what they are going to work on first.

Inefficient work processes lead to wasted time and effort. Often, work can be done in a smarter way if people eliminate or modify inefficient procedures and systems, or create new approaches. Consider the following suggestions:

▶ Gather the people involved in the work process. Map current processes and identify problem areas, bottlenecks, and recurring problems. For example:

▷ Identify duplication of effort.

▷ Note places where the formal process is often circumvented.

▷ Highlight internal and external customer service problems.

▷ Examine the level at which decisions are made.

▷ Include what is working well. Examine why.

▷ Determine if any steps can be eliminated or combined to save time.

▶ Investigate the cost of the constraint or problem areas. Do the problem areas result in customer needs not being met, higher costs, or a longer cycle time? Before deciding on priorities, understand the impact of each bottleneck.

▶ Prioritize areas to address based on customer priorities and internal considerations. For example, if part of the process takes a long time and creates unnecessary conflict among team members, you may want to put this high on the priority list. Eliminating inefficiencies might allow team members to concentrate on meeting other customer needs.

▶ Establish goals and desired outcomes for the process-improvement effort. Team members should not be working on process-improvement projects without clear goals and deliverables.

▶ Once you have decided which part of the process to address, investigate it in detail. What is working and what is not? Generate and review alternate procedures that would meet the same objective. It may be possible to combine the best elements of several alternatives to obtain one outstanding solution.

▶ Arrange for a pilot program to test a new process. Measure the success of the pilot against the criteria established for the new process.

▸ Continually look for ways to improve processes, products, and services and set up a regular schedule to examine how things are working and how they could be improved. Gather data regularly from stakeholders and customers and set up brainstorming sessions with those involved in the process to generate fresh ideas and perspectives.

Manage quality by using data to identify trends and track progress

Measuring your work against defined standards is essential to a high-quality process. *What* you measure is determined by your goals. *How* you measure determines whether you get practical, useful information. Consider the following suggestions:

▸ Observe the process and then develop measures for describing what you observed. Measures may be taken continuously or discretely. When you develop continuous measures, you are able to see patterns faster than when you have to make many discrete measurements.

Ask people what they learned from the trend data. Discuss how they used the data to make decisions.

▸ Select measures based on their usefulness and feasibility. A useful measure is closely linked with high-priority customer requirements, is accurate, is comparable to other data (such as industry data), addresses a potential improvement area, and can be an ongoing measure. Measures are feasible when there is a high probability that you can get the data, the collection methods are relatively easy, people are likely to cooperate, and the measures are not too complex.

▸ Learn about a variety of measurement techniques. Make sure people on your team are trained on several techniques.

▸ Select measurement strategies that are user friendly and appropriate for the process.

▸ Be sure to measure the *right* criteria in the *right* way. Make sure that the criteria and measures are focused on the customer.

▸ Use both qualitative and quantitative data. Qualitative information might include employee morale, attitude, motivation, and level of frustration. Quantitative data might include measures such as time to market, number of customer compliments, and error rates.

▸ Display data in formats that make it easy to see trends and meaning. If people can see the data and understand the meaning and relevance, they will be more likely to cooperate with data gathering and support data-based process improvement.

▸ Develop a measurement baseline before you implement your changes.

Analyze process breakdowns to ensure that lessons are learned

▼

Quality and service are moving targets—what is considered exceptional quality today will probably become routine tomorrow. Because expectations constantly change, continuous improvement is a must. Use process breakdowns and quality problems as opportunities for learning.

▸ The following is an example of a standard process-improvement procedure:

After process breakdowns, ask people to analyze lessons learned and determine what they plan to do differently.

1. When a problem occurs, determine whether it has occurred before and if it is likely to happen again. If the answer is yes or maybe, form a team to examine why it might happen again. Ask the team to focus on three to five levels of "why" to clearly identify the steps in the evolution of the problem. Often, simply asking why will identify causes and suggest options.

2. Ask the team to look at the cause of the problem and ask how it could have happened or, if it is a recurring problem, how it does happen.

3. Ask the team to determine an improvement plan that addresses each possible cause.

▸ Apply the lessons learned from analyzing process breakdowns. Ensure that the necessary changes are implemented.

Investigate and adopt best practices and lessons learned from within and outside the organization

▼

An effective leader of system and process improvement makes a point to learn from others, gather best practices, and share learning with others. To assist you in learning from your organization and others, consider the following suggestions:

▸ Identify areas in which you want the team to improve and organizations that excel in these areas. Invite people from these organizations to talk with you about their work.

Encourage people to identify a lesson learned by another group and describe how they will apply it in their area.

▸ Check with your value chain partners to see if any are willing to train and develop parts of their value chain in process management.

▸ Communicate the results of process-improvement efforts so others can learn from them as well.

▸ Ensure that team members use the lessons they have learned. When you initiate an improvement project, ask what principles or learning from other projects are being applied. Also ask about risks the team identified based on previous lessons learned. Asking these questions will draw attention to the fact that you want people to use what they learned.

INTENDED ACTION: **ACTION ANALYZER**

EXPECTED REWARDS Based on lessons learned	PROBABILITY	POSSIBLE RISKS Based on lessons learned	PROBABILITY

Action taken and result:

- ▸ Attend leadership and management development programs, webinars, and conferences that include people from other organizations so that you can hear about and learn from their experiences.

- ▸ Ensure that teams use best-practices models as a starting place for their work. Then, to gain competitive advantage, improve upon those practices.

- ▸ Use your company's intranet to post and exchange information about process improvements.

- ▸ Read articles, blogs, white papers, and newsletters to keep up with current trends in quality management, particularly those that address issues your company is facing. Use the articles to illustrate effective and ineffective implementation.

11
Champion Change

Change is constant at most organizations today. It is also one of the hardest factors for people at all levels to deal with. Even when there is a clear need for change, resistance, fear, uncertainty, and ambivalence are common reactions.

As a manager, you can make change easier if you understand change, normal reactions to change, and methods to ease stress and help people adjust. Leading through change is a significant responsibility that you can learn to embrace with skill.

The most common initial reaction to change is a feeling of loss of control. By listening actively, helping people examine their feelings and concerns, and determining ways they can be empowered to feel more in control during the change process, you'll make change more acceptable and more effective.

In this chapter, we will cover the following areas:

▼

- ▶ View change as a way of life
- ▶ Understand how individuals react to change
- ▶ Understand how organizations respond to change
- ▶ Understand resistance to change
- ▶ Identify your role in the change process and execute it well
- ▶ Involve others in the change process
- ▶ Leverage the involvement of key stakeholders and opinion leaders
- ▶ Understand different kinds of change
- ▶ Prepare people to understand changes
- ▶ Be specific about the implementation process
- ▶ Champion new initiatives within and beyond the scope of your job
- ▶ Increase awareness of the benefits of the new initiative
- ▶ Encourage others to take appropriate risks
- ▶ Motivate others to welcome change
- ▶ Address resistance to change
- ▶ Clarify new behaviors and practices, and what constitutes successful implementation
- ▶ Create opportunities to learn, practice, and experiment with new behaviors
- ▶ Establish roles to support change
- ▶ Allow opportunities for flexible implementation
- ▶ Set up systems and structures to support changes
- ▶ Manage the change process while maintaining operating effectiveness
- ▶ Establish and use feedback processes to monitor implementation of key events and their impact
- ▶ Reinforce and reward both progress and success

View change as a way of life

▼

Change is part of life. You can fight it or you can decide to embrace it. You can become skilled at adapting to change and, even more important, at leading and managing change in your work life and your personal life. Two concepts are important: change hardiness and being change smart.

Change Hardiness	Being Change Smart
▸ It is the ability and skills to adapt to change.	This refers to a group of skills:
▸ Some people are more change hardy than others.	▸ Know when change is needed.
▸ People find ways to make change their own and take control.	▸ Leading and managing the change process.
▸ People feel confident that they can be successful.	▸ Establishing processes to ensure the success of change.
▸ People develop competence in the skills and behaviors necessary for change.	▸ Signaling when more change is needed.

▸ How change hardy are you? The following questions will help you make that assessment:

▹ Do you typically look at change as:

a. a nuisance

b. an opportunity

▹ Do you find yourself more concerned about:

a. what will be lost as a consequence of change

b. the possibilities of change

▹ Do you seek to:

a. include new initiatives only if they are shown to be truly necessary

b. enthusiastically incorporate new initiatives into your existing plans

▷ Do you think change will make it potentially:

    a. harder to achieve your goals

    b. easier to achieve your goals

▷ Do you get:

    a. frustrated that changes and new initiatives just keep coming

    b. excited about the possibilities for continual improvement

Identify how people can improve in handling change. Some may need to stop generating unnecessary change, while others need to be more flexible.

▶ If you answered B on most of the choices, you have the attitude and approach of someone who is change hardy. If you want to be more change hardy, it is relatively easy to do. First, make the decision to be more change hardy. Next, whenever a change occurs, figure out how you can feel in control, confident, and capable.

▷ *To feel in control*, determine how you can make some choices about the change. You might be able to decide how the change will be implemented, or you might only be able to decide how you will feel about it. No matter what external circumstances may be, people always can choose their perspective and their attitude. Even in the most dire circumstances, people can examine their thoughts and underlying beliefs and choose what they will think and believe. Feelings follow thoughts. Gently remind people that they have power over their thoughts and help them see how they might reframe their thinking to see the change in a more positive manner that is meaningful to their lives, goals, and career objectives.

▷ *To feel confident,* recall all of the changes you have already coped with. Thinking about the changes you have survived and how you have grown from them will help you get in touch with your strength and give you confidence that you will be able to handle the new situation. Change-hardy people do this consistently.

▷ *To be more capable,* assess whether you have the skills, knowledge, and approach you need to cope with the change successfully. Once you ensure that you have what you need in the change situation, you will feel, and be, more capable of handling and thriving in it.

▶ Determine how change smart you are. People who are change smart:

▷ Understand how they and others react to change.

▷ Are able to use this knowledge to help themselves and others manage change better.

▷ Have a model for leading and managing change that enables them to create a compelling vision for change, get others on board, work through implementation issues, and execute change successfully.

▷ Know how to communicate about change to keep others informed and involved, galvanize support, and deal with the many challenges of change.

Understand how individuals react to change

▼

Assess how people react to change. Some welcome it and are the first to get on board. Others are reluctant and tend to accept change only when it is required.

Reactions to change are personal. If it's a change you want, great! If it is one you don't want, you may feel anger, frustration, and resistance. If it is a change you agree with, terrific, but if you think it is a bad idea or unnecessary, then what a waste of time!

It's the same with other people. Each person has a view of the change, which will affect how he or she reacts to it. Consider the following suggestions:

▶ Look at what the change means to others. Does it mean a loss? Does it require them to do something different? Talk with people about how they see the change.

▶ Change is not the same as a transition. Change is situational; it is a new job, new process, new team. Transition is psychological; it is the process people go through to come to terms with a new situation.

Change	Transition
Understood in terms of a beginning or starting something	Understood in terms of endings, letting go, or leaving something or someone behind
Usually happens quite quickly	Takes more time
Experienced externally	Experienced internally

- Transition has three parts: an ending, a neutral zone, and a beginning.
  - ▷ The challenge in ending is letting go of what was. This part of the process usually involves grief.
  - ▷ The challenge in the neutral zone is finding clarity amid confusion.
  - ▷ The challenge in a beginning is managing the ambivalence of starting something new.

- Grief is part of transitions. Signs of grief include anger, denial, anxiety, disorientation, depression, and hope.

- Expect to help people through the transition process and provide support.

Endings	Neutral Zone	Beginnings
Help people see what is and what is not different or over.	Accept that people will be stressed, uncertain.	Recognize that it is not easy to let go.
Help people identify the loss.	Help people move from complaining to problem solving.	Recognize that letting go triggers feelings of other losses.
Mark endings.	Set short-term goals.	Recognize that it will take time.
Expect and accept feelings of grief.	Allow people to get support from others. Don't expect people to be perfect.	Recognize that people need different amounts of time.
Help others see what they might be gaining.	Help others see themselves as competent to meet the change.	Provide training and support.

- Recognize that it is difficult when a change affects a person's status or perception of status. For example, a person who goes from reporting to a vice president to reporting to a director usually feels as if he or she is not valued as highly as before.

▸ In helping others deal with change, address issues of status. Demonstrate that they are valued and respected by asking for their advice and involving them in decisions. If possible, do not diminish signs of status.

▸ When you do need to take signs of status away, do so based on some logic or rationale that others can understand. For example, have all people in particular job groups move to cubes, rather than arbitrarily let some people keep their offices and ask others to take cubes.

▸ Help people move toward something to offset the loss—of habit, of relationships, of predictability—that often comes with change. It is easier to cope with loss when there is something to replace it. For example, if a work process is changed, ensure that people know what the new one is. When relationships are lost, help people get connected to new people with whom they will be working.

▸ Allow people to move through the process of letting go of old ways, learning and adjusting to new ways, and adopting new ways. There is always a transition period. How long the transition lasts often has to do with:

▹ Whether people think the change is a good one.

▹ Whether people have some role in deciding what they will do.

▹ Whether people know what is expected.

▹ Whether people can do what is expected or needed.

▸ Expect that the direction and pace of change will not be linear or even. The change process is messy; people move ahead and move back.

Understand how organizations respond to change

▼

Successful managers understand how their organizations handle change. Organizations, like individuals, respond to change in different ways. It depends on a variety of factors such as the type of change and the change hardiness of the organization. Some organizations are overly cautious or change resistant. Others display a kind of change hardiness, and adapting to rapid change is the norm.

How an organization handles change also depends on whether it is dealing with a transactional change or a transformational change. Transactional change is often easier because it is finite and it involves something specific like a work process or a change in role. Transformational change is much more extensive and open-ended, and it has a greater impact; it involves fundamentally changing something.

Most large organizations engage simultaneously in various types of change. Yet these changes are not necessarily in sync with each other, and they may be limited by people's capacity to adapt to overlapping changes. The challenge may lie in people's ability to sustain their focus, the allocation of limited resources, or competition to determine which initiatives will gain hold and survive over time.

Managers also need to consider whether the team they lead is ready to embrace change. How nimble is your group?

▶ Do people treat change as an event to get past, or as a way of life?

▶ Do people ask "How will we implement change?" rather than "Why should we?"

▶ Do people ask about desired outcomes of change to ensure alignment with the big picture?

▶ Does the organization have clear processes (changes in work processes, for example) for implementing transactional changes?

▶ Does the organization have experience with transformational change?

▶ Are resources (time, support, change-enabling roles, teams) made available to help people learn?

▶ Do teams quickly propose contingency plans? (How to address immediate commitments while preparing for new ones, for example.)

Discuss the organizational norms about change. Just as people have tendencies in how they react to change, so do organizations.

▶ Do people get excited when they're planning how to accomplish new initiatives?

▶ Do people ask not only about the immediate change, but also about subsequent changes that might be necessary?

To build a more agile organization:

▶ Adopt a common change management process.

▶ Teach people the basics of leading and managing change.

- Consider adding "leading and managing change" as a core leadership competency.

- Educate people about the change process.

- Adopt a common framework and process for communicating about change.

- Bring in people who are skilled in transformational change.

Understand resistance to change

Help people understand the need to work with individuals who are resisting change. Dealing with the issue of resistance is key.

Resistance to change is common especially when people think that they have no choice, that the change is a bad idea or will not work, or that the change will result in their losing something that is important to them. Effective managers expect resistance and work with it. They see resistance as a sign that people are involved, not that people are trying to make the change harder to implement. People resist change when they:

- Think it is unnecessary.

- Believe it is wrong.

- Think it will make the situation worse.

- Fear that the change will mean personal loss—of security, money, status, friends, freedom.

- Resent the way the change was introduced.

- Believe they had no input in the decision.

- Believe the change will not be successful.

- Lack confidence that they will be able to perform new practices effectively.

- Are satisfied with the status quo. (They subscribe to the belief that "if it's not broken, don't fix it.")

- Believe the timing is poor.

- Believe that prior initiatives were not properly implemented.

- Lack faith in those driving the change.

Identify your role in the change process and execute it well

▼

It is important that you identify your role in the change process, since your responsibilities will depend on your role. For example, you might be the initiator of the change, the sponsor of the change, the implementer, or the recipient.

Initiators of change identify the need for change and create the vision for it. As an initiator:

- Create a compelling vision of the change that ignites the energy and commitment of others.

- Remember that the biggest enemy of change is complacency. You may need to work hard to build the case for urgency.

- Be out front communicating the vision and building support for the change.

- Recognize that with transformational change, leadership of the vision for change and the change process is critical because the change process will be long and will itself include many changes.

- Identify the leadership team for the change or transformation. Ensure that you find experienced change leaders for the team.

- Involve others in designing and implementing the change process.

- Do not (and do not expect to) work out all of the answers and the whole plan before you involve others. Instead, involve people as a way to gain buy-in.

- Communicate internally and externally about the change.

- Prepare outside stakeholders, such as the market and large customers, for the change.

- Provide tangible support to those implementing the change. Be a role model for what is needed, and communicate progress and confidence.

- Show that you care that individuals will be affected by the change. Be ready to provide resources to make the change successful.

Sponsors of change use their position and influence to support change. Sponsorship is especially important when a staff person wants to implement a change.

▸ If you are the sponsor of change, your role is similar to that of an initiator, other than the fact that it may not be your idea.

Example: An organization's communications group develops a plan to address a negative view of the company and a drop in brand awareness. Now they need the support of line management in order to execute the change. They're looking to you the sponsor to create buy-in and support for the change.

▸ You and your leadership team need to be out front, supporting the change.

▸ When you are talking about the change, refer to your change implementation team to give them credibility to execute the change.

▸ Continue to be available to lend your support for the change.

Implementers of change translate strategy into a workable plan and guide execution of that plan.

▸ Identify what the vision or change means for your group or for your level in the organization.

▸ Create a clear picture of the importance and relevance of the change for your part of the organization.

▸ Recruit your change leadership team.

Ensure that the person is a role model for new behaviors or processes.

▸ Ensure that the team has knowledge and skills in change leadership and implementation. Agree on common processes to speed up implementation.

▸ Involve those who will be affected by the change to determine what needs to be done differently and how it will happen.

▸ If you are dealing with a transformational change, break it into pieces and processes.

▸ Set up action plans and change management plans for the change, or for specific parts of the change.

▸ Alert others to the problems and unexpected consequences that may occur in the change process. Work with the change management team to deal with each problem or unintended consequence.

- ▶ Find quick wins to build confidence that new processes or behaviors will work and will lead to success.

- ▶ Develop criteria to let people know what success looks like.

- ▶ Celebrate successes.

- ▶ Communicate, communicate, and communicate.

Recipients of change are those to whom change happens. Sometimes change happens to you. For example, you may learn that you have to decrease expenses by 20 percent, you have to change vendors in China, or you need to become part of an enterprise system. In these situations, you are expected to get on board and adapt to the change. Consider the following suggestions:

- ▶ Ensure that you understand the vision, rationale, and need for change, and the consequences of not changing. This will often help you to get on board.

- ▶ Understand the plan and what is needed to address and execute change.

- ▶ Be involved in as many decisions as you can about what should be done and how it should be done.

- ▶ Ensure that work continues and that you continue to focus on customer satisfaction during the change.

- ▶ Identify potential problems and solutions.

- ▶ Develop criteria to measure the success of the change in your area.

- ▶ Provide ongoing feedback and improvement ideas.

Involve others in the change process

To maximize buy-in, minimize resistance, and make change work, involve others in the process. When people feel that they are valued participants in planning and implementing change, they are more likely to be motivated to make the change successful. Even if they have no choice about whether to implement the new initiative, they can still have an impact on how it is accomplished. To ensure that others are involved, consider the following suggestions:

Observe whom people involve in the change process. Ensure that they involve the right people by asking: Who else should be involved?

▸ Involve people early in the change process.

▸ Whenever you can, let people make decisions about changes. Provide information so they can make good decisions. For example:

▷ Rather than deciding yourself that a new schedule is needed in a call center, present the employees with the data that indicate this need. Let them decide what the data tell them and suggest options to address the situation.

▷ During large-scale, transformational change, involve people in various parts of the change processes. Enable people to plan as much as they can and to be as prepared as they can be for unexpected occurrences.

▸ Be clear regarding what people can and cannot have a choice about doing.

▸ When someone makes a decision, involve the people who will be affected in deciding how to implement the change.

▸ Make a list of all individuals who should be involved in shaping the initiative, and who should be involved in determining the best timing and process for implementing it. Recognize that who is involved will shift as you move through stages of the process.

▸ Solicit and use input from your team, peers, and manager when you are planning your change effort. When you request input from a large and diverse group of people, it is not usually possible to follow all of their suggestions. Therefore, indicate up front that you cannot guarantee that every suggestion will be implemented, but say that you will genuinely try to include as many as possible.

▸ Ask employees from the areas affected by the change to serve as experts in determining the steps needed for the change.

▸ Test changes. For example, pilot new work processes or ask for volunteers to test the change. Solicit feedback on what is working well, where the problems are, and how to work out any difficulties.

Leverage the involvement of key stakeholders and opinion leaders

▼

Ask people whom they need to get on board to support a specific change. Have them articulate why each person is needed.

Some change is so positive and so welcome that people embrace it easily. Other changes require lots of work to build understanding and gain buy-in. Sometimes people take change seriously or buy into it only because of who communicates the need to change. Other people take their cues by watching what their leaders do, not just what they say. Consider the following suggestions for using involvement to support change efforts:

- ▸ Involve informal leaders early in the decision-making process. Informal leaders can have a tremendous impact on the success or failure of change efforts.

- ▸ Involve informal leaders in transformational change. They will be invaluable to the change process.

- ▸ Ask the most appropriate senior manager or executive to help communicate the need for change.

- ▸ Analyze carefully whose support is needed in order to get the people you need on board to make the change work. While everyone is needed for change, the reality is that you need certain people to support the change in order for others to feel comfortable about supporting it.

- ▸ If the change has been carried out in another division or company, seek to involve people who participated in that change. Create an opportunity for them to describe what happened and what the benefits were. Ask them to present a preview of the change process.

- ▸ Ask key leaders, both formal and informal, to participate in relevant kickoff and training sessions.

- ▸ Involve key leaders in reviewing feedback on the change, providing ongoing messages to employees, rewarding people who help move the change process along, and working on the next part of the change process.

- ▸ Whenever it's appropriate, ask change leaders to model the new behavior. For example, if people are being asked to use a new Customer Relationship Management (CRM) system, ask area managers to use the system and build it into their review process with their direct reports.

Understand different kinds of change

▼

Change varies. It may be a simple change in process, or it may be as widespread as implementing a new performance management process, adopting Six Sigma, or making a series of changes as part of a major industry transformation. Consider the following suggestions:

▶ *Identify* the kind of change you and the team or organization are going through so that you can anticipate what to expect and what will be most helpful.

  ▷ *Top down, leader-led change.* There is a clear vision, a clear change process, and clear outcomes expected from the change. (This is, of course, when the change leader or visionary is doing it "right.")

  ▷ *Leader initiated, emergent process for the participants.* The leader has the vision and communicates it, and provides tools and assistance for the participants to decide how to implement it.

  ▷ *Leader framed problem, but not a vision for the future state.* Participants are integral to defining the future state, developing the change process, and defining the desirable outcomes. Participants are in charge of implementation.

  ▷ *Emergent vision.* Participants identify problems or opportunities and find solutions. This kind of change is common in businesses in which the competitive landscape changes, and when participants see that many different things need to change almost simultaneously. It is characterized by multiple stakeholders and overlapping changes that continue over time. There may not be a clear vision for the end state as such; the vision may be to continually respond to the competitive environment.

Ask people to post an FAQ page on the intranet where employees can learn more details about the change and find progress updates.

▶ Recognize what kind of change is taking place and your role in it. If it is a leader-led change, it is your responsibility to have a strong and compelling vision and to build a coalition that can lead the change. If you are in a participant role, your role is still important because you need to decide whether and how to implement the change, or even define the opportunity.

▶ Based on the kind of change, anticipate the extent to which people will buy into it.

Prepare people to understand changes

▼

Communication is key to preparing others for change. First and foremost, you need to clarify exactly what change or changes need to occur. Is it a major transformation of work processes or an adaptation to existing practices? Does it affect a single division or will it cut across functions and operating units? Who is involved and who is not? Will customers be affected, and in what way? The clearer you are about the change and the expected behavior, the more likely it is that people will respond.

To ensure that people are prepared to understand a change, consider the following suggestions:

▶ Create urgency for change. Without a sense of urgency, it is unlikely that a change will occur; it is far easier for people to continue doing things the same way.

▶ Explain clearly the importance of the change to the organization and the rationale for the change. Be prepared to answer questions about its importance.

▶ Communicate the consequences for the organization or team if the change is not made.

▶ Communicate the vision and objectives frequently. People need to hear the new direction and the reasons for it repeatedly throughout the change process.

▶ Publicize who is on the change leadership team. Involve both formal and informal leaders as part of this team.

Ask for and review change plans to ensure that all bases are covered. Look for a solid communication plan as part of the overall plan.

▶ Recognize that people may begin to understand the implications of change only when they are midway through the transition. Encourage leaders to be available to talk with people about their reactions throughout the process.

▶ Communicate in person about the change. In today's online world, people still need the human touch. Do not expect to manage a large-scale change only through e-mail.

▶ Prepare regular updates so people know what is going on. Track the success of the change process so people see that they're making progress and can feel a sense of accomplishment.

- Provide ways to check rumors. The more you communicate honestly and directly, the fewer rumors there will be.

- Communicate even when you do not have all of the answers. It is okay to tell people that you do not know something.

- Be straight with people. Talk about problems and what is being done about them.

- Do not expect that you can keep secrets.

- Ask people who have issues about the change to describe their feelings. Instead of constantly trying to defend or sell the change, let them work through how they feel and how they can handle the situation. Sometimes people just need to talk and have someone listen.

- Recognize that initial reactions to change may reflect personal style. Some people prefer to talk, while others need to read and think about the change. Some people are comfortable knowing the big picture and trust that there will be opportunities for adapting the plan as it is implemented. Others prefer to see a clear schedule of events. Be sensitive to the diversity of preferences as you communicate the plan for change.

Be specific about the implementation process

▼

Many times it is the *process* of change, not the change itself, which evokes strong reactions. When people do not know how a decision was made or who made it or who developed the plan of action, they become concerned and behave in ways that look like resistance. To ensure that your communication is as specific as it can be, consider the following suggestions:

- Tell people about the decision-making process that resulted in the change and the implementation process.

- Ensure that people have adequate information to know why a transformational change makes sense.

- Outline the steps of the implementation process from beginning to end, and share your outline with stakeholders.

Ensure that leaders of a change initiative clear their schedules for the first day of implementation so they can be available to answer questions.

▸ Help people understand the plan for dealing with normal work during the change.

▸ Determine whether service to customers will be disrupted. If so, let customers know in advance and work with them to minimize disruption.

▸ Let people know if it will be necessary for different units to go through the same process at different times and, if possible, when and how this will occur. This will allow people to plan.

▸ If work processes need to stop temporarily during the change, indicate when and for how long.

▸ Consider communicating some things that will not be affected by change, or practices that will not be interrupted. It is often helpful for people to know what will remain the same.

▸ Help all stakeholders understand what they will need to do and when.

▸ Tell people when they will begin to see the results of the change process and what to look for.

To better implement change in the midst of constant or overlapping changes, consider the following guidelines:

▸ Identify the perspectives of all those involved in the change. How does it affect the various groups involved? What is the likely level of acceptance in each group? Why?

▸ Identify other changes affecting the people and teams involved in this change. Talk with people about their confidence to handle more change. Ask what they need in order to feel greater confidence of success.

▸ Find ways to combine initiatives so that people are not overwhelmed with the amount of change.

▸ Carefully gauge when to position the changes you want as big changes or small changes. Some people are energized and excited about change, but others are not. At some point, most organizations and their people simply get tired of hearing that they need to get behind a big, revolutionary change because it is necessary to deal with competitive threats. It may be helpful at times to position a change as a necessary one, not a big deal, or as an incremental change.

▸ Establish temporary transition teams for large changes. Leading large changes might be a full-time job.

Champion new initiatives within and beyond the scope of your job

Successful managers do not just manage change and implement new initiatives—they actually champion initiatives, both within and beyond the scope of their job. They spot when it is needed, recognize good ideas, and drive the acceptance and implementation of change. Consider the following suggestions:

▸ Plan to champion ideas and initiatives that address key constraints on or opportunities for the organization, work unit, or customer satisfaction. This will focus your efforts on what is important.

▸ Champion initiatives as you would develop, manage, and support projects. Just as you would never think of implementing a project without a plan, don't consider starting a change effort without a change management plan.

▸ Communicate, communicate, communicate. Answer these questions: What? Why? For what benefit? When? Who? With whom? Where?

Ask people to identify new initiatives they think should occur within their area of influence. Ask what they plan to do. Provide feedback.

▸ If you're trying to decide when to support an idea or initiative, use this quick test: Does it address critical priorities? Are you comfortable that the right people thoroughly analyzed the information and selected the solution?

▸ When you are supporting a change effort, expect to be challenged. People might wonder why you're supporting something that takes up resources that could be used on other projects (their projects, for example). Be able to explain why you're supporting the new initiative and how you expect the organization to benefit. Don't sow doubts about your support.

▸ Be available to support people. Run interference when necessary. Provide ongoing encouragement and guidance throughout the project.

- Get yourself into the loop so you have access to creative, speculative, and even wild ideas. Listening is a simple but important way to walk your talk about innovation.

- Provide a soft landing for failure. Some experiments will not work out. Do not let that derail people's careers. If they fear that failure on a risky project will result in serious damage to their careers, they will understandably avoid risk.

- Help the team stay focused. There are times during an initiative when they may be tempted to follow other (equally interesting) ideas and lose their focus. Keep your team on track.

Increase awareness of the benefits of the new initiative

The logic of a change may seem intuitive or obvious to those who identified the need for change. Those charged with implementation may accept the change without much questioning or may question the wisdom of or necessity for the change. Those who are expected to carry out the new initiative must have a sufficient reason to change, particularly if they are satisfied with current practices. Consider the following suggestions:

- Communicate the limitations of current practices. What are the long-term consequences of maintaining the status quo? What aspects of current practices are difficult, unpleasant, or unsafe, or limit organizational performance? How might current practices be inconsistent with other goals that matter to the intended recipients of change?

- Provide access to the information that led to the decision to make the change. Respect the fact that people will want thorough information.

Talk with people about their before and after pictures of the change. This will help them clarify what they are trying to accomplish.

- Determine the tangible benefits of the new initiative or new ways of working. Provide measurable benefits or display expected benefits with pictures and graphs.

- Anticipate how to answer these questions: Why us? Why now? Do we have a choice about whether we do this?

> ▸ Indicate who else in the organization is behind the initiative. It helps people to know which individuals and constituencies—key senior executives, bargaining groups, customers—support the change.

Encourage others to take appropriate risks

▼

When people are evaluating whether to take a risk, have them brainstorm a worst-case scenario and how they would handle each issue.

Change does not occur without risk. If you are afraid to rock the boat, you will have a difficult time leading change and encouraging your employees to champion new ideas and initiatives or to lead change. On the other hand, taking unneeded or large risks is not wise. Therefore, it is important to strike a balance between wise risk taking and foolhardy behavior. Consider the following suggestions when encouraging others to take appropriate risks:

> ▸ When considering a change, think of it as a risk that needs to be assessed and planned for. As with any risk, assess the reasons for doing it and not doing it.
>
> Example: Changing the selling model used by your account managers might be a risk because they do not know the new model well, it may require new skills, and it might call for a different incentive structure. On the other hand, the current model of selling might have led to decreased sales over the past three quarters, the loss of key accounts, and the loss of key sales managers.

> ▸ Identify the potential negative consequences of the change. Whenever possible, determine what can be done so these consequences are no longer risks, or plan what would need to be done if the negative consequences occurred.

> ▸ Tell your team that you prefer wise risk taking to maintaining the status quo. If you are trying to move a conservative group, say that you prefer action and mistakes to maintaining the status quo.

> ▸ In assessing risk, look at how skilled the person or team is at recovering from mistakes. Some teams can take greater risks because they are superb at recovery.

- Use force-field analysis or risk-management analysis strategies to help others assess risk. The risk-management area of your organization can show you the techniques they use to manage risk.

- When mistakes are made, focus on learning from them. Use debriefing sessions; ask what went well and what people learned.

- Capture learning and use it the next time. For example, when the team begins a new project, ask what they learned about this kind of project the last time. Ask a person who led a similar project that failed to consult with the group members to help them avoid the same mistakes. This will enable people to save face by becoming experts from their learning experiences.

- Encourage others to make changes and improvements by following up with them on progress, noticing small improvements, helping them understand the reasons behind the necessity for change, and making progress visible and celebrated.

Motivate others to welcome change

Change is occurring more frequently every day. Organizations often need to move quickly to take advantage of opportunities. Employees who expect and welcome change will be a step ahead. Consider the following suggestions to prepare your team to expect change and learn to adapt quickly:

- Review the information at the beginning of this chapter about being change hardy and change smart and how to prepare your organization and your people to expect change.

- Demonstrate your own enthusiasm and commitment to change. When your commitment is obvious to your employees, their motivation and involvement in the success of the change effort are likely to increase.

When people hear others claim that something won't work, encourage them to challenge others to think of how it could work.

- Teach people to remember their successes with change as a way to build up their resilience.

- Coach your team on what they need to do to make the change work. Knowing these strategies will give them resources for dealing with future changes.

▸ Celebrate and communicate successes—even small ones!

▸ In presenting change, emphasize its benefits. When you're approaching individuals, support the change based on what you know is important to them. Don't be manipulative, but let them know how the change will help them.

Address resistance to change

People vary in their reactions to change. Some naturally welcome change and its promised benefits while others fear change and resist letting go of the status quo. Ambivalence is also common; people can both welcome and resist the same change. Resistance is to be expected. A realistic assessment of resistance will help you design an implementation plan more likely to succeed. Consider the following suggestions:

Ask people to explain others' concerns regarding a change; explaining others' point of view will increase their own ability to deal with the change.

▸ Treat resistance as a problem to be solved, not as a pathological condition.

▸ Remember that those who are resisting change are sometimes right. It might not be a good idea, it might be poorly planned, or it might not give the intended results. Therefore, listen to concerns as a way to improve your plan, clarify your thinking, or rethink what you want to do.

▸ View resistance as an indicator of how much people care, not as an indicator of how difficult they are.

▸ Work with resistance rather than fight it.

To change resistance into support:

▸ Help people figure out how they will benefit from the change.

▸ Involve people in the decision-making and planning processes as early as possible.

▸ Develop an attitude that resistance is neither good nor bad. In fact, signs of resistance can signal opportunities to improve the change effort or implementation process.

▸ Encourage people to openly express their thoughts and feelings about the change.

▶ When resistance occurs, listen carefully and try to understand it. People who are feeling resistant don't want to hear why the change is necessary. Instead, explore their concerns and take their feelings and concerns seriously.

▶ Recognize that it takes time to work through resistance to change.

▶ Reduce personal loss as much as possible.

▶ Provide ways for people to be successful.

▶ Involve people whom others respect as part of the change management team.

▶ Help people see the vision behind the drive for change. When they believe the change makes sense, they will be more supportive.

▶ Help people understand the timing of the change and the consequences of waiting.

▶ Align incentive systems with the change.

Clarify new behaviors and practices, and what constitutes successful implementation

Ask people to explain their understanding of changes and help them clarify what steps they need to take to implement the changes.

Sometimes the vision behind a new initiative is so obvious that everyone can support it. Yet even in these cases, how to put ideas into practice may seem ambiguous and elusive. The more specific you can be in communicating the actions necessary for carrying out change, and the more you can contrast new and old behaviors, the more successful others are likely to be in carrying out those actions. Consider the following suggestions:

▶ Make new work behaviors clear. Describe new expectations clearly.

▶ Determine when new work processes are needed.

▶ Compare how the work was done in the past to how you want it to be done now.

Use a two-column chart. Lay out the two versions of each work process so people can easily see the difference between them.

Old Process	New Process

- ▶ Be specific about which behaviors and practices need to be learned, modified, and discontinued.

- ▶ If new initiatives require different types of decisions, identify the types of situations that are likely to require those decisions.

- ▶ If training is needed, consider demonstrating the new behaviors. This can be based on how practices are done elsewhere, or it can be a simulation of realistic situations and the new behaviors. Invite those present to describe the differences they see between old and new behaviors.

- ▶ In leadership or employee training programs, ask one group to handle a situation in the old way and another to handle it in the new way. Talk about the differences.

- ▶ When people begin to practice the new behavior, talk about how it worked, what people thought, what worked well, and where problems occurred.

- ▶ Identify the measurements that will indicate progress toward successful implementation. Use both group and organizational measures.

Create opportunities to learn, practice, and experiment with new behaviors

It takes time to learn and develop new skills and practices. Even when people support the ideas behind a new initiative, resistance may surface if people don't believe they can successfully carry out the specific behaviors. To support people in learning and practicing new behaviors, consider the following suggestions:

- Communicate the need to learn new behaviors. Create time and opportunities for people to learn and practice. Use technical experts if you need to.

- Obtain the active support of managers whose employees must learn the new behaviors. Work with these managers to determine the best time for people to attend training.

- Create opportunities for people to learn together, to experiment with different ways of accomplishing tasks using new practices, and to describe what they discover to be best practices.

When new processes are implemented, be sure project leaders build in time for team members to learn the new processes.

- Provide access to experts who can assist people as they try out new practices: set up a toll-free telephone number, establish a telephone hotline, designate an e-mail address for questions, set up a Wiki or blog to allow people to communicate their questions and experiences, and assign floorwalkers to offer on-the-spot assistance.

- Provide positive reinforcement for practicing new behaviors, learning key behaviors, and carrying out full sequences of complex changes.

- Reinforce people's confidence in their ability to successfully carry out new behaviors. Publicize best practices, the processes by which some groups experiment with change, and how other groups worked through initial difficulties and failures to accomplish desired changes.

- To help employees feel like they have the time to learn and practice new behaviors, obtain temporary support for the work group during the training period or just afterward, when people are experimenting with new practices.

Establish roles to support change

New behaviors and processes often require support in the form of technical expertise, advice on interpreting guidelines, or help in managing the details of implementation. Consider the following suggestions to help you create roles to more effectively support a change:

- Determine the leadership roles needed for successful change. This might be a change champion or it might be a full change management team.

Ask people to identify who needs to be included in their team's support network.

▸ Identify the skills and experience needed for the various change leadership roles. Carefully select the right person or people. Assign the roles to people who can accept additional responsibility. Clarify the roles: championing the change, getting people on board, communicating the purpose of the change, ensuring that necessary support is available, reporting progress.

▸ Create a communication network for change champions so that they can exchange best practices, have their own questions answered in a timely way, and know that they are part of a group that is making the change real.

▸ When a temporary team is created to manage large-scale changes throughout the organization, provide any additional training and support that the team may need. Consider the following suggestions:

  ▷ Ask that the team participate in team development to fully understand its purpose, to develop internal practices and participation, and to create its own role structure and rules for guiding implementation of change.

  ▷ Provide opportunities for the team to communicate regularly with key executives who initiated the overall change. This will let them raise issues that surface during implementation and ask for resources or guidance. It also helps ensure that the change remains a top priority over time.

  ▷ Publicize the team's role and describe ways that people can work with the team.

Allow opportunities for flexible implementation

People do not like being told what to do. Nor is there usually just one way to do something. When you plan or implement change, allow for individual choice and flexibility. Consider the following suggestions:

▸ As you study the new initiative, look at the goal for the change. Then think of a variety of ways in which the goal may be accomplished.

▸ Whenever possible, allow people to have some choice about what they will do. You might be able to leave the choice completely open as long as it accomplishes the goals, or you might decide to have people choose among options.

▶ Consider whether there is only one right way to carry out the new practice or if a variety of practices are possible as long as the same basic outcome is achieved. If you cannot think of more than one way to do something, check with others.

Encourage people to schedule forums where employees can discuss their concerns about implementation of change.

▶ Decide whether the situation requires that everyone use one method. If so, ask those involved to look at the options, decide on criteria for making the best choice, and choose the best solution, process, or behavior.

▶ Encourage people to experiment as they implement new practices. Communicate variations in implementation through several media, such as meetings, regular e-mails, or a Wiki or blog where people can learn about different ways to implement the change.

▶ Identify internal and external resources—designated change leaders, members of the transition team, human resource development consultants, technical experts—to help managers and teams with flexible implementation.

▶ If people seem stuck or resistant to change, ask what modifications might make the change work better.

▶ Find out about existing processes, commitments, or customer demands that might make change difficult to accomplish at this time.

▶ Help the group determine how it can both accomplish its other objectives and make changes. Recognize that it may be necessary to delay a particular group's participation in new initiatives until other commitments are satisfied or renegotiated.

Set up systems and structures to support changes

▼

For change to happen efficiently in both the short term and the long term, supporting structures and systems are needed. Consider the following approaches the next time you embark on a change effort:

▶ Recognize that change is not just change in individual behavior. It often involves change in the organization's structure, systems, and work processes.

▸ Assess your current structure, systems, and processes:

  ▷ Which ones are currently aligned with the change?

  ▷ Which ones need to be more closely aligned?

  ▷ What factors might block the change or make it more difficult?

▸ Use a team approach to identify supporting and blocking factors. Do not expect that your change management team can spot all of the factors. This is a time to make use of the people who are resistant to change. They are often skilled at spotting potential problems.

Ensure that people examine which systems and processes currently support a change and which ones need to be modified.

▸ Identify the informal cultural factors that might make it challenging to carry out the change. For example, let's say you are asking people to start solving problems at the customer site. They might be hesitant to do this because previously they had to ask for permission or solicit ideas from others before they could address a customer problem.

▸ Many people might welcome the change and view it as positive. Other people might not believe they have the necessary information to make decisions and solve problems. Identify what structure needs to be in place for the change to work.

▸ Try a zero-based approach, which essentially asks this question: If we did not have any structure, processes, and systems in place, what would we create to support the new vision or change initiative? This approach requires you to look at the vision or goal of the change effort and build structure, systems, and work processes from the ground up.

Manage the change process while maintaining operating effectiveness

▼

One of the many challenges of change is that it needs to occur while you are doing your regular work. Achieving balance between maintaining operating effectiveness and leading change is an ongoing challenge. Consider the following suggestions:

▸ When you develop a plan for change, figure out how routine work will still get done.

  ▷ Identify the regular work you and others need to do.

  ▷ List potential disruptions to current operations and figure out how to deal with them.

▷ Involve others in identifying ways to minimize disruptions.

▷ Communicate ahead of time about possible disruptions.

▷ Develop temporary solutions to disruptions.

▷ Meet with customers to plan together how to deal with disruption in normal operations.

▷ Assign a team to be responsible for maintaining normal operations.

Identify others who lead and manage change well. Find opportunities for people to learn from them.

▸ Change causes uncertainty and makes people uncomfortable, so communicate often. Frequent updates help people cope more effectively with change.

▸ Help people understand the need for change. Understanding why a change is necessary helps people deal with the disruptions, inconvenience, and extra work.

▸ Make positive results visible. Communicate early and often about all wins, even small ones.

▸ Communicate about progress, so people know that the disruption will not last forever and that they are actually making progress.

Establish and use feedback processes to monitor implementation of key events and their impact

▼

The only thing worse than bad news is no news at a time of uncertainty. A steady flow of feedback about progress is important. Frequent feedback lets you modify your approach, obtain additional resources, and learn about progress. Consider the following suggestions:

▸ Develop a step-by-step implementation plan with key milestones and time lines. This is particularly helpful with transformational change, because it helps people understand what they can expect.

▸ Create templates for communicating about progress, including report formats and graphics. Ask all change agents and leaders to use these templates. It will be easier for people to track and understand the change and its progress if they don't have to decipher a new format for each person or group's report.

▸ Set clear expectations about what each level of leaders should be communicating about the change.

Make sure there are good measures to evaluate the success of a change. Then ask people what they learned as they worked through the change.

▸ Establish clear measures of success. For example, if a change should decrease costs, evaluate whether costs are decreasing. Beware of changes for which it is impossible to develop tangible measures. They are likely to be more difficult to implement because they may be perceived as unnecessary or as a preference of the leader that does not make a significant difference.

▸ Ensure that people involved in the change participate in the evaluation process. Ask a variety of stakeholders about the success of the initiative.

▸ Recognize that original plans usually have to be modified, because nothing goes exactly as planned. Make the appropriate changes to the plan and the evaluation process.

▸ Invite people to describe their successes, disappointments, and surprises during and after implementation. This will help them capture learning for future change efforts.

▸ Encourage people to make suggestions on how to improve implementation. This promotes organizational learning about successful change management.

▸ Publicize the results of periodic surveys about the change. Use this opportunity to discuss honestly what is working well and what is not.

Reinforce and reward both progress and success

▾

Change needs to be reinforced and rewarded. In some changes, people see immediate benefits. In other changes or steps toward change, it is necessary to build recognition into the change process. Consider the following suggestions:

▸ Ensure that people know what benefits the change should bring. Keep track of whether the benefits are occurring.

▸ Work with others to identify indicators of whether the change is working, then ask them to track those indicators. Progress is easier to see when people know what to look for and are deliberately looking for it. If the change requires new behavior, let people know that you see their efforts.

▸ Recognize that people's behavior does not change quickly or consistently. Therefore, expect that it will take time for people to adopt new behavior.

▸ Identify specific accomplishments related to the new initiative that should be rewarded. Consider rewarding the first individuals or groups to accomplish the change. This reinforces and celebrates efficiency at accomplishing change.

Suggest that teams brainstorm and list the benefits of a change and the consequences of not following through with it.

▸ Also consider rewarding all employees after the entire group has accomplished a change. This reinforces collaboration and a sense of collective success.

▸ Identify any current rewards that need to change. For example, organizations going toward a team-based approach often need to change their individual-based reward systems.

▸ Look for opportunities to use nonmonetary rewards—letters of appreciation, small celebrations, congratulatory calls and messages from leaders—to reinforce achievements. Be careful not to overdo the use of coffee mugs, T-shirts, or buttons, especially if large monetary rewards are being given to others for carrying out the change.

▸ Allow managers to distribute "spot bonuses" as a way for them to show active support for the change and reinforce their employees' behaviors.

12
Show Drive and Initiative

Your commitment and dedication to your organization are critical to achieving goals. By showing strong drive, taking initiative, staying productive, and not being afraid to take on new challenges that stretch your abilities, you will achieve higher results and open the door to future opportunities.

As a leader, you set the standard for performance. You also must set the standard for balance while keeping projects on track, developing new ideas, and making sure people have the resources they need to meet those objectives.

Your direction and leadership in setting priorities, being enthusiastic, and having a can-do attitude influence the people you work with. Success follows intention—and being clear on what you want and need to achieve is the first step.

In this chapter, we will cover the following areas:

▼

- ▶ Commit to your organization
- ▶ Aggressively pursue organizational success
- ▶ Establish aggressive goals and drive for results
- ▶ Convey a sense of urgency when it is appropriate
- ▶ Tackle problems head-on and work to resolve them without delay
- ▶ Bring issues to closure
- ▶ Set high personal standards of performance
- ▶ Seek out new work challenges
- ▶ Take on additional responsibility when you're asked to
- ▶ Maintain a consistent, high level of productivity
- ▶ Put in extra effort and work to accomplish critical or difficult tasks
- ▶ Persist in the face of obstacles
- ▶ Overcome procrastination
- ▶ Handle multiple demands and competing priorities; make efficient use of your time
- ▶ Process documents efficiently

Commit to your organization

▼

Be a role model. Show your commitment to your team and your organization. Show that you care about individuals beyond the contributions they make.

Being committed to your work and your organization is essential for your success on the job, and it results in higher job satisfaction. It also improves work relationships, because relationships are strained when people are in jobs or at organizations they do not like. Consider the following suggestions:

▶ If you do not find satisfaction in the work you do or with your coworkers, figure out what changes you need to make. Many organizations are open to job changes.

▶ Decide whether you are committed to your organization. Start with the reasons you decided to work there, what you hoped and expected to accomplish, and what you have accomplished. Look at what you like and dislike about your work and the organization. Consider future opportunities and directions within your organization.

Aggressively pursue organizational success

▼

Success rarely just happens. People prepare for it, plan for it, work for it. Even if they just happen to be in the right place at the right time, they know enough to take advantage of the situation. To pursue organizational success, consider the following suggestions:

▶ Focus on performance and execution. Link performance goals to business goals so people understand how their efforts affect organizational success.

▶ Devote yourself to critical projects that directly affect the organization's success. Use these opportunities to stretch your leadership skills. For example, volunteer to launch a new product or implement an organization-wide process change.

▶ Constantly look for opportunities to grow the business. Study market changes, competitor moves, customer needs, and emerging opportunities. Discuss these issues with your manager and peers, and come up with ideas on how your organization could respond. Together, take action on your ideas.

> ▶ Talk with people in other organizations to get a realistic idea of other organizations. It helps to get a fresh perspective.

> ▶ Pay attention to how you pursue initiatives. Don't sacrifice your integrity or that of your company to reach your goals. Aggressive is one thing; illegal or unethical is another.

People want to trust their organization and have confidence in it. Listen to their perceptions of and concerns about the organization.

> ▶ Discuss with long-term employees why they have stayed at the organization.

> ▶ Talk with people who understand where the organization is headed and what the future looks like so you can visualize possibilities for yourself.

> ▶ Look at the match or mismatch between your values and the organization's values. It is difficult to stay at an organization whose values you do not respect.

Establish aggressive goals and drive for results

As a leader, you are not measured on your intentions; you're measured on results. People are counting on you and your area to achieve your goals so that you can make a strong, positive contribution to the organization. Consider the following suggestions:

> ▶ Clarify the results you need to achieve. Make sure your expectations match those of your manager and senior leaders. You don't want to spend time and effort going in the wrong direction.

> ▶ Set aggressive, measurable goals and objectives with your team. The more specific and detailed your goals are, the more meaningful and attainable they will seem to others. People with a clear understanding of goals are more likely to achieve results.

> ▶ Emphasize the need for results, not just activities or long hours. Find out if people try to look busy by spending a lot of time on low-priority issues. When you talk about project updates, focus on driving results, not a long list of activities.

> ▶ Develop accurate and responsive measures to monitor your area's performance. You need data that not only help you monitor your area

and make adjustments, but also allow you to demonstrate the impact your area has on the organization.

▶ Align your reward systems with the results you want to achieve. Sometimes reward systems unknowingly or unintentionally reward the wrong results or behavior. Make sure your employees and teams understand what they need to do to achieve meaningful results.

▶ Seek feedback from others on your ability to balance process with getting results. If you tend to be overly focused on how things get done, others may see you as not focused enough on achieving results.

Set clear goals with people, so that you both know what is needed and what will be delivered.

▶ Show your employees how their efforts contribute to the bottom line and to organizational success. Make results meaningful and understandable for others by explaining them clearly and showing the impact they have on the entire organization.

▶ Celebrate accomplishments and use them to motivate and drive more progress. Without minimizing your accomplishments, challenge yourself and others to keep improving.

▶ Focus on results, not activities. Make sure your team has measurable goals that can be tracked. Discuss with your people how their results contribute to the bottom line and to organizational success. Discuss what you and your team are or are not doing to affect the organization's results.

Convey a sense of urgency when it is appropriate

▼

Urgency is a double-edged sword. If you fail to convey a sense of urgency, people may miss deadlines. If you give the impression that everything is urgent, people may not prioritize their work appropriately. Either approach is problematic. To convey an appropriate amount of urgency, consider the following suggestions:

▶ Prioritize your group's projects so you can calculate how much urgency you need to express on each one. This will enable you and others to focus appropriately.

▶ Determine how often and how well you convey urgency. Communicating the same amount of urgency and importance on every initiative can create unnecessary stress and resentment. Here are some questions to get you started:

▷ Do you convey urgency on the right projects?

▷ Do you convey urgency on too many projects?

▷ Do you convey urgency only on your own projects?

▸ Seek feedback from your team about how you communicate urgency. Solicit specific information about when you display appropriate urgency, when you show inappropriate urgency, and any patterns you seem to follow.

Talk with your team about increasing its pace when necessary. When the organization needs to operate faster, you should set that expectation.

▸ When you introduce a new initiative, clarify its importance and give specific deadlines. Once people clearly understand what must be done and the urgency behind it, they will be more motivated to achieve results.

▸ Share the responsibility for communicating urgency with others. People may respond best to messages from other stakeholders, process owners, or leaders. Identify situations in which you should step back and allow someone else to convey the message.

▸ Make sure your reward systems motivate your employees and teams to get results. Consider creating informal rewards for individuals. For example, a good-natured contest to quickly bring an issue to closure can keep people focused on urgent work.

Tackle problems head-on and work to resolve them without delay

Issues and problems are guaranteed in business. In most cases, the sooner you tackle them, the better. Confronting problems early keeps them from getting out of hand and conveys the message that you are willing and able to resolve tough issues and problems. Consider the following suggestions:

▸ When you learn of an issue that could or will affect your group, assess the seriousness of the situation. Do you need to respond personally, or can you ask someone on your team to look into it? If you delegate responsibility, be clear about how quickly you expect the issue to be resolved.

- Set a time frame for solving a problem. For example, set deadlines for investigating the problem and implementing a solution. Record these dates on your calendar and follow them closely.

If people are unable to solve problems themselves, it often signals an organizational issue. Explore this possibility.

- If people tell you about a problem, clarify what they expect you to do. Are they simply informing you, or do they expect you to solve it? If you agree to get involved, tell them how you plan to proceed. If you don't respond, people may conclude that you are unconcerned or reluctant to address the problem.

- Deal with personnel problems when they occur. Leaders lose the respect of their peers and employees when they are not willing to deal with people who negatively affect the team's effectiveness or morale.

- If you are reluctant to move quickly on an issue, determine why. You might lack information or time to process it, be unsure of what action to take, or fear negative consequences. Once you have identified the obstacles, determine how you can address your reluctance and move forward.

- If a problem recurs, you probably have not addressed the root source. Take some time to determine why solutions did not work in the past and what would solve the issue permanently.

Bring issues to closure

▼

Ask people about any unresolved issues and how they are going to bring each to closure.

Unresolved issues vary in the disturbances they cause, but they all have one thing in common: they take up time and energy. To resolve issues in your area, consider the following suggestions:

- Communicate the urgency and importance of resolving the issue. Explain how it affects performance, productivity, morale, and so on. Then challenge others to help you resolve it.

- Take time to investigate the issue and identify the real cause. Avoid quick fixes. A solution that addresses only immediate, visible symptoms will not be sufficient to handle long-term repercussions.

- Create a plan, with specific dates, to deal with the issue and bring it to closure.

- ▶ Follow through until you resolve the issue. Persistence sends a strong message that you take the issue seriously and are willing to do what is necessary to resolve it.

- ▶ If the issue exists within a team, gather everyone involved and set the expectation that a resolution must be found. Give all parties a chance to share their views through discussion, e-mail, or an online forum. Identify areas of agreement and then facilitate a discussion to resolve areas of disagreement. If necessary, seek a neutral third party to intervene and negotiate or arbitrate a solution.

Set high personal standards of performance

▼

Let people know what is expected of them. Recognize accomplishment and appreciate effort. Encourage people to go beyond what they think they can do.

Organizations look for individuals who are committed to excellence and willing to invest themselves in their work. Achieving and maintaining high personal standards can be satisfying for you and beneficial to your organization. Consider the following suggestions:

- ▶ Determine what is most important to you. What do you value? What do you want to accomplish? Write a personal statement of goals and standards to which you are committed. These are the goals in which you're going to invest your time and energy.

- ▶ Guard against underestimating your potential when you set performance standards. People often don't realize their own abilities, or they feel that setting high standards will set them up for failure. Be bold: set standards that you find challenging.

- ▶ Review the goals and results that the organization deems important. Determine how you can set performance standards that fulfill both your priorities and the organization's.

- ▶ Meet with the individuals on your team to discuss goals and your expectations for their performance. This will give each person a chance to share his or her perspective and bring your attention to any information that affects your expectations.

- ▶ Ask each individual on your team to identify stretch objectives that exceed the job requirements and are challenging yet attainable. The more input people have in setting performance expectations, the more energy they will put toward achieving them.

▶ Take time to congratulate yourself and others who accomplish a goal or meet a higher standard. Hold a team party to celebrate team accomplishments.

Seek out new work challenges

▼

Who should seek out new work challenges? Anyone who wants to enrich his or her job, learn new skills, gain visibility, meet new people, and become excited again about coming to work. Consider the following suggestions:

▶ Talk with your manager about your willingness to take on challenging assignments and your desire to expand your career. Indicate your interests and ideas, and discuss possible action steps.

▶ View your career in terms of the type of work you'd like to do, not just in terms of specific roles that you know currently exist. Instead of following a familiar path, you may be able to create a new path that takes advantage of your unique skills and interests.

▶ Find a mentor who can help you locate opportunities for increased responsibility and handle them successfully. A mentor's guidance and objectivity are invaluable.

▶ Watch for opportunities to work in other functions, such as special projects or task forces. This will broaden your skills, increase your cross-functional knowledge, and help you learn about further opportunities.

▶ When you identify an assignment that you would like, talk to people who are currently in that role. Learn about the knowledge and skills that you would need to be successful in it.

Let people know when you want them to take initiative—especially if your organization has a history of avoiding risks.

▶ Be realistic about your commitments. You may become so enthusiastic about a new challenge that you take on more than you can handle. As you take on additional assignments, make sure that you still manage your current job responsibilities capably.

▶ Consider being a coach. Preparing to teach others and help them work through issues will enrich your skills.

▸ Take the initiative regarding activities and responsibilities. This will demonstrate your commitment to the organization and increase the variety and challenge of your job. Talk with your manager about your desire to broaden your range of responsibilities. Indicate your interests and discuss possible action steps. Adopt the view that your responsibilities include identifying and seizing opportunities beyond your specific job accountabilities.

Take on additional responsibility when you're asked to

▼

Ask people about new opportunities and challenges they would like to have in their work. Discuss how they can prepare for new responsibilities.

There may be times when you are asked to take on work that falls outside your job description. Even though it may not fit your plans, it can be an opportunity to enrich your current role and learn skills for a position you would like in the future. Consider the following suggestions:

▸ When you are asked to take on new responsibility, consider the request carefully. It is likely that you were asked because there is an immediate need and people believe you will do a good job. Your response may affect not only your current role, but also whether you will receive future opportunities.

▸ If the additional work is unusually thorny or unpleasant, focus on what needs to get done. View it as a temporary assignment and do your best work despite the circumstances. People will remember your attitude in a difficult situation.

▸ Look at what you can learn from the additional responsibility. Talk with your manager about whether he or she views this as a good opportunity for you, and whether it is work that needs to be done.

▸ Understand how your answer, whether it is yes or no, will affect how people view you.

Maintain a consistent, high level of productivity

▼

Being productive often isn't as difficult as being consistent. Both are possible if you plan well, stay flexible, and monitor your progress. Consider the following suggestions:

- Get feedback from your manager and colleagues about your productivity level. Do you display a high energy level and accomplish a lot of work? How does your productivity affect your team and other employees? How does it affect your area's reputation?

- Monitor your personal productivity. At the beginning of each day, create a detailed plan of the work you expect to complete that day. List the tasks according to priority and estimate the amount of time you expect each to take. At the end of the day, determine how much of the work you accomplished and how long it took.

- If you find it difficult to maintain high energy on the job, you may want to assess your fitness level. A balanced diet, regular exercise, adequate sleep, and periodic breaks during the day are integral to sustaining energy on the job.

- Determine which activities you spend most of your time on. Do you focus on things that are important, that are most easily done, or that appear to be most urgent? Consistently focus on the most important activities first.

- Identify distractions and recurring problems that affect your area's productivity. For example, an inefficient process may be causing you to use more resources than necessary. Work with your team to brainstorm ways to reduce or eliminate these problems.

If people are not satisfied with their team's results, challenge them to resist making excuses and to take responsibility for improving results.

- Track your area's accomplishments. Evaluate how productive the week, month, or quarter has been. Keep a continuing record of your progress and that of your employees.

- Create backup plans to maintain productivity during crises or problems. For example, figure out how your area can accomplish its responsibilities if you lose key personnel. Maintaining consistent productivity is often a matter of planning and readiness.

- Become savvy about process. Work with a process specialist to review your work processes to ensure that they are as efficient and productive as possible.

Put in extra effort and work to accomplish critical or difficult tasks

▼

When it takes extra time and effort to complete a critical project or solve a difficult problem, persist and demonstrate your commitment to getting results. Consider the following suggestions:

▸ Estimate how much time and effort it will take to achieve a goal and plan accordingly. An accurate estimate can help you pace yourself and stay on track, especially on lengthy projects.

Evaluate whether people regularly work less than others and determine whether they need to make more of an effort.

▸ Readily put in extra time to deal with a crisis or meet a tight deadline. Critical goals require a serious commitment from organizational leaders. When you cannot work longer hours, find other resources to meet the need.

▸ Putting in extra effort does not necessarily equal putting in extra time. Your contribution can also be in resources or expertise. Identify alternative ways to maximize your contribution.

▸ Don't ask your people to work long hours or put in extra time if you are not willing to do so yourself. But also guard against expecting others to consistently work long hours even if that is what you choose to do.

▸ Be candid with yourself, your team, and your family and friends about the time and effort it will take to accomplish a goal. Explain why the goals are important and why they require so much time and effort. A shared understanding will help you neutralize negative reactions.

▸ If there are questions about how much time and effort you're putting in, prepare a summary of your accomplishments. This may help people focus on your results instead of on the number of hours you worked.

▸ Focus on the benefits of reaching your goals, especially when the going gets rough or the hours get long. There is often a phase during a long project when things seem bleak. Keep your eye on the goal and keep working. Even if it seems like you're inching along, you're making progress.

▸ Develop strategies to maintain your motivation and energy. For example, develop a network of supportive colleagues and friends who can encourage you, and take time to exercise and eat healthy foods.

▸ Celebrate when you reach your goal. It is important to acknowledge what you accomplished.

Persist in the face of obstacles

▼

You can count on obstacles appearing as you pursue initiatives. How you handle them depends on your persistence and your attitude. If you have a positive attitude, you will be more likely to keep trying and to believe that there is a solution. If you have a negative attitude, you'll be more likely to become cynical and give up. Consider the following suggestions:

▸ When you run into an obstacle, assess the situation. What is the problem? What is causing the problem? How is the obstacle affecting your ability to get results? Develop a solid understanding of the obstacle to get a better idea of how to address it.

▸ Think positively. Instead of telling yourself that overcoming the obstacle is impossible, tell yourself that a solution exists and will eventually come to you.

▸ Remember that there are multiple ways to approach problems. Your method is not necessarily the only way. Ask others to help you analyze the issue. Invite input from people you don't usually ask, such as vendors, customers, or friends.

Monitor how people speak about a problem. Do they refer to it as a challenge and an opportunity, or as a problem and a headache?

▸ Talk to supportive peers about the obstacle. They can give you additional perspectives, tell you how they handled similar obstacles, and help you brainstorm possible solutions. They can also help you keep your spirits up.

▸ Maintain a strong network with people within and outside your area. Removing obstacles can be difficult, especially if removing an obstacle in one area creates an obstacle in another area. If you have strong relationships, you can work collaboratively to identify potential solutions and likely consequences.

▸ Encourage employees to think of new or innovative ways to address obstacles. Because they are closer to the work, they often have the best ideas for removing obstacles.

▶ Realize that some obstacles are not going to be overcome quickly. You may need to develop an interim solution and revisit the issue later.

Overcome procrastination

▼

Discuss how to have a candid discussion about the effects of procrastination. Many procrastinators do not realize the havoc they create for others.

People procrastinate in different ways, to different degrees, and for different reasons. In each case, the consequence is the same: stress. Consider the following suggestions:

▶ Determine why you procrastinate. For example, you may lack confidence or skills. You might think routine reports are a waste of time. Interpersonal conflicts might make you uncomfortable. You might be stymied by ambiguity.

▶ Reframe undesirable work. Instead of focusing on what you dislike, focus on the sense of accomplishment you'll feel after you finish it.

▶ If you put off projects that seem difficult or overwhelming, make a list of the small steps involved in the project and do them first. Build momentum that can carry you through more difficult work.

▶ Tell yourself you'll work on a project for half an hour to see how it goes. By the end of the half-hour, you may have found that the work isn't as difficult as you thought.

▶ Reward yourself along the way—a coffee break after writing the introduction to a report, or a short walk after a meeting.

▶ Ask your team how your procrastination affects them. Make a note and keep it in sight as a reminder that your delays and/or lack of action have consequences for other people.

Handle multiple demands and competing priorities; make efficient use of your time

▼

Do you often reach the end of the day feeling as if you've worked hard but accomplished little? People frequently spend time on things that reduce the tensions of the moment instead of things that relate directly to achieving goals. To determine whether you are using your time wisely, consider the following suggestions:

▶ Identify your A (most critical); B (important); and C (least critical) priorities. Ask the following questions:

Recommend time management programs and resources to help people who have difficulty managing their time.

▷ Which tasks will most benefit my organization?

▷ Which tasks support organizational or departmental priorities?

▷ Which tasks does my manager consider most important?

▶ For the next week, keep a detailed record of how you spend your time. Each day, write down what you do and for how long. Analyze your results to determine whether you are devoting the bulk of your time to your high-priority work.

▶ Divide your workload into phases to make it more manageable. Determine what should be done tomorrow, next week, and next month, then plan accordingly.

▶ Schedule time for essential work. Block out time on your calendar so it won't get filled with other appointments and meetings.

▶ Delegate less important tasks to others, or let them go undone.

▶ Ask yourself, "If I ran this organization, would I pay someone my salary to work on what I am working on right now?"

Process documents efficiently

At times, documents seem to take over your life. Every day they fill up your e-mail, arrive in the mail, and spill over the sides of your desk. People copy you on memos just in case you're interested. You print or save documents and convince yourself that you'll read them. How can you deal with all of this information? Consider the following suggestions:

▶ Identify the information that will help you accomplish your most important objectives and responsibilities.

▷ Glance through each piece quickly to get an initial understanding of its contents and impact on your work.

▷ Sort the documents in order of importance.

▷ Read carefully, highlighting key points.

> ▷ Make notes to yourself or others. Cross-reference other documents that relate to this piece.

> ▷ Take action, or delegate or redirect the material.

Recommend that people find others on the team who are good at organizing documents and pick up some tips.

▶ If follow-up is necessary, add a reminder to your calendar and save the document where it will be easier to find.

▶ Every six months, spend a few hours deleting unnecessary electronic files and recycling paper files that you no longer need. You can generally eliminate files older than six months.

▶ To reduce your e-mail load, remove your name from distribution lists that are no longer useful or relevant.

13

Lead Courageously

As a leader, you will face situations that require courage—either to say yes or no, or to deal with difficult issues that involve disagreement or tension among people. If you live by your values, send clear messages through your actions, and learn how to be assertive without being aggressive, you'll gain people's respect and they will see you as a trustworthy colleague.

Facing difficult situations with courage takes a deep commitment to values, outcomes, or both. Being courageous doesn't mean you won't feel fear, doubt yourself, or question your decisions. It does mean that your actions will consistently align with what matters and with what you value. You will also be called upon to help others find their courage—and your example and encouragement will be invaluable.

In this chapter, we will cover the following areas:

▼

- ▶ Clarify what is important to you
- ▶ Demonstrate the courage to do what is right despite personal risk or discomfort
- ▶ Be assertive
- ▶ Say no when necessary
- ▶ Drive hard on the right issues
- ▶ Take a stand and resolve important issues
- ▶ Lead others to follow through on difficult actions or initiatives
- ▶ Be willing to make bold yet well-reasoned moves in the marketplace
- ▶ Demonstrate inspiring leadership and courage such that others want to follow you

Clarify what is important to you

▼

Provide opportunities for people to clarify their values. Values inventories and career development programs are two options.

All great leaders have clear values that serve as the bedrock from which they lead. Having a solid understanding of your foundational values and beliefs will guide you during challenging times. To clarify what is important to you, consider the following suggestions:

▸ List leaders and others you admire and your reasons for admiring them. Then look over your list and identify recurring themes and values. Identify which of these values you find important for your life.

▸ Reflect on what you value most in your life. Write down your answers to the following questions and keep them in a place where you can review and update them regularly.

　▷ What do I value most?

　▷ What do I feel passionate about?

　▷ What is worth fighting for or standing up for?

▸ It may be difficult to identify personal beliefs or values because they are so ingrained. Ask a close colleague, a friend, or your direct reports about the values they see you demonstrating. You might ask "Having known me for three years, what do you see me valuing most?" or "How would you describe my leadership style and values?"

▸ Think about the legacy you want to leave your team and your organization. What do you want to be remembered for? Evaluate what you are currently doing and make necessary changes.

▸ Develop a leadership message or vision that describes how you want to lead. Periodically review how well your behavior matches this vision.

▸ Ask yourself how you want your direct reports to think about you. If they were to describe you to someone else, what would they say about how you lead and what you value?

Demonstrate the courage to do what is right despite personal risk or discomfort

Leaders face situations in which the most appropriate action might be risky and result in negative reactions, concerns, complaints, and problems. They need managerial courage to take the right action. Consider the following suggestions:

▶ Thoroughly assess the situation: options, risks, contingency plans, recovery strategies. Involve others in the assessment so that you are confident you have the best minds and best people working on the issue. Decide what you will do based on both short- and long-term consequences and the fact that things change.

▶ Develop contingency plans and alternatives.

When necessary, provide cover for people who are taking risks. You may need to endorse the initiative in order for your peers to accept it.

▶ When you want to approach something in a way that differs from what others believe should be done, develop a thorough understanding of their thinking and rationale before you make a final decision.

▶ Seek advice and counsel from others. They may see the situation in another way, suggest more options, or provide important insight.

▶ When a decision entails risk, assess the risk carefully. Ask others to assist with this assessment so you have a broader base of knowledge and experience to draw from.

▶ When you are facing a tough decision, such as trimming the budget or downsizing, carefully analyze various alternatives, get other people's input, and settle on the course of action that meets the criteria you deem important. Then, when you communicate your decision, you will have the background and data to support your actions.

▶ Don't overlook the people aspect of making tough decisions. Be prepared to deal with other people's reactions and to direct people to resources that will help them deal with the impact of the decision.

▶ Identify one risk you are afraid to take. Carefully analyze its potential benefits and negative consequences. Figure out what you would do if the worst-case scenario occurred. Then decide whether you can take the risk.

Be assertive

▼

Some people try so hard not to be aggressive that they end up being passive. Others strive to change their passive behavior and then come on so strong that they are seen as aggressive. There's another option: assertiveness. Assertive people recognize that their views have value, and they're willing to express them in a respectful way. Being assertive is not about getting what you want or getting people to agree with you. It is about respecting yourself and others: valuing your views and ideas, asking for what you want, saying what you want, expecting that your views will be respected and considered. Assertive behavior is about you, not about the other person. The purpose of being assertive is not to get someone else to behave differently, but to get you to behave differently. To be more assertive, consider the following suggestions:

▸ If you have not been assertive in the past, you might be hesitant to speak up or might not know how to do it well. Find a coach or role model to help you get started. Study how people start discussions, deal with interruptions, express their views, share ideas in groups, and respond to criticism.

▸ Clarify in your own mind the difference between assertive and aggressive behavior. Observe people whom you believe fall into each category. Notice how assertive people share their views but don't force them on others. Typically, assertive people look for ways both people can "win." They listen as much as (or more than) they talk. And they consistently show respect for others, even when they disagree.

▸ If you are not sure how to construct and deliver your message so that you will be perceived as assertive, not aggressive, use the following techniques to frame a strong, direct message:

Notice when people seem to have more to say but hold back. Discuss what types of situations require a straightforward approach.

  ▹ State your observations first. Observations are facts, things that can be seen, heard, or taken in through your senses. For example, "You were 15 minutes late for our meeting" is a fact. "You were inconsiderate in coming in late" is an opinion. Facts are objective, cannot be argued, and help the other person understand what you are saying.

▷ After you state your observations, express your thoughts and feelings in statements prefaced with "I." For example, "I was frustrated when you were late because it resulted in 15 minutes of unproductive time for the group."

▷ Finally, state what you want the other person to do. Make statements about your needs, rather than solutions. Stating needs opens the door to generating many alternative solutions, while stating solutions can close the door.

For example, "I would like you to be on time for meetings" is a statement about your needs. A solution is "I will call you five minutes before meetings start to make sure you will be on time." The first statement naturally leads to a discussion of options on how to meet the need, while the second statement closes off discussion of other options and places the responsibility for solving the problem on you.

▸ Listen to the other person's response to your message. He or she may not be pleased with what you have to say, and it is important for you to hear the person out.

▸ Practice stating assertive messages before delivering them to others. Role-play them in your mind, practice saying them to a trusted colleague, or rehearse in front of a mirror. Sometimes just getting the words out once makes it easier to say them later in the actual situation.

▸ Expect that others might be surprised if you become more assertive. People become accustomed to how others behave and it is disconcerting when someone changes. You can expect that others might not be as pleased with your new behavior as you are. A little humor—"Yes, you're right, I did decide to stick up for myself" or "I decided I had stayed quiet long enough"—often helps people get over the awkwardness.

▸ To continue to motivate yourself when you find it hard to be assertive, pay attention to how you feel when you ask for what you want or behave assertively. Look at your career goals. Even if you don't have a current need to be assertive, increased job responsibility and promotions may require that you develop this skill. If you are a parent, think about the lessons you can demonstrate for your child or children.

Say no when necessary

▼

Successful managers know how to say no. People working together don't expect agreement every time they have an idea or a proposal—there can be different points of view and competing agendas. Saying no is an important way to stay focused, show consistent values, and demonstrate your commitment and follow-through. Consider the following suggestions:

▶ Say no when you need to. Don't procrastinate or soften the blow by being tentative, but do explain your rationale. If you can, link your rationale to organizational goals.

▶ When you stand up to others, assume that they mean well and acknowledge their good intentions: "I appreciate that you want the project to be successful. I have another way to look at what we need to do."

▶ Be willing to confront hard issues. In the long run, no one will benefit if people ignore issues that must be addressed and resolved.

▶ As you deal with difficult issues, take into account the people or relationship aspect of your actions. Do this to help you implement the decision, not to change it.

Coach people on how to say no in a way that will be accepted. Recommend that they be clear about why they are saying no.

▶ When you say no, monitor your nonverbal actions. People believe what you do more than what you say. If you appear to be uncertain, they will keep trying to change your mind. If you appear to be confident, they will be more convinced that you will hold firm.

▶ Recognize that even though people may respect your view, they might feel compelled to try to modify it, especially if they disagree with you.

▶ When you encounter resistance, find out why the person or group objects to your position. Set up a meeting where you can learn more about opposing views. Focus more on understanding those views than on explaining yours.

▶ After you have done all you can to understand opposing viewpoints, hold firm when you believe that:
  ▷ You have all the essential facts or input needed to make a decision.
  ▷ The decision is fair to all the stakeholders involved.

  ▷ The decision is consistent with policy decisions made in the past.

  ▷ Acquiescing would result in action that is unethical, unsafe, illegal, or entirely inappropriate in the workplace.

  ▷ Any other decision would be harmful to the organization, your team, your customers, or the quality of your product.

- Do not leave others with the impression that you are still open to further discussion if you are not. Send a clear message that your decision is final. You can lose respect if you claim that this is your final decision, and then keep changing your mind.

- Don't be a "yes person" to upper management. Most upper-level managers are more impressed by people who stand up for what they believe is important.

Drive hard on the right issues

▼

Discuss the degree to which people should drive an issue, especially issues core to the organization's strategy.

As a leader, you need to choose your battles carefully. It is especially critical that you address the issues that affect your most important goals either positively or negatively. To ensure that you drive hard on these issues, consider the following suggestions:

- Choose which issues merit your attention.

  ▷ Does this issue have a direct impact on business performance?

  ▷ Who is affected by the issue?

  ▷ Who wants or needs the issue to be resolved?

  ▷ Could this issue damage important relationships?

  ▷ Is this issue an obstacle to achieving your goals?

  ▷ Will this issue be important in the near future?

  ▷ What would happen if you didn't address the issue?

- Check your priorities with your manager to make sure you agree on the critical issues in your area.

- Understand the critical paths for strategic priorities in your area. Address issues and problems that could block or hinder the success of those initiatives.

- Identify processes, projects, or groups that detract from business performance and make it a priority to turn these areas around. Unclear goals or lack of direction may be the problem; clarification could give these areas the boost they need.

- When you identify the issues you're going to champion, develop a clear message about what you're going to do and why. Realize that you will need to repeat your message many times before people start to pay attention to it.

- Address issues with your team. Assign responsibilities, making sure you clarify roles, deadlines, and expected deliverables. Ensure that people understand the importance of the issues and why you need to address them now, in this way.

Take a stand and resolve important issues

You owe it to yourself, your colleagues, and your leadership to consider important issues carefully and make well-reasoned decisions or develop well-reasoned positions. Consider the following suggestions:

- Identify important issues in your area and across the organization. Talk with executive leaders to learn what they are concerned about and the direction in which they are taking the organization. Also pay attention to the priorities people discuss during planning and problem-solving meetings.

- Understand how quickly you need to develop your position on an issue. People may need you to weigh in at a meeting within a few days, or you may have several weeks.

Discuss why people might be reluctant to take a stand and what would happen if the situation remained unresolved.

- Look at issues from a number of perspectives. If you receive conflicting information, ask probing questions to evaluate the accuracy, underlying assumptions, and reliability of each source and set of information.

- When possible, ask a team to look at an issue and bring you an analysis and their recommendations. This is a great learning opportunity for them.

▶ Find out how people in other teams, businesses, or locations view the issue. An issue is defined by, and depends on, the values, attitudes, business culture, and expectations of the people involved in and affected by it.

▶ As you solidify your position on an issue, think about or write down your reasons for your viewpoint. List your conclusions and the data that led you in that direction. This will help you explain your rationale.

▶ When people ask you to be their advocate or to take a stand on a particular issue, listen carefully. Decide what you will do, and then get back to the person with your decision. If you cannot give your support, explain why.

Lead others to follow through on difficult actions or initiatives

▼

As individuals take on responsibility, they encounter situations in which they must make tough choices. Sometimes they turn to their manager to make these decisions for them. To help your employees develop confidence in their ability to follow through on difficult actions or initiatives, consider the following suggestions:

▶ Talk about the actions people are contemplating. Ask them to outline the pros and cons, and the interpersonal issues that they anticipate. This will help them anticipate scenarios and plan for contingencies.

Observe whether people are taking action on someone's behalf instead of providing support. Offer feedback.

▶ Empathize about the difficulty of the issue or decision. Express confidence in the people's judgment and experience when you are comfortable that they will handle the situation well. If you do not have confidence, talk through the issues. Have them take the lead in the conversation and tell you how they see the issues and courses of action. This will give you an opportunity to hear how and what they are thinking so that you can decide whether they need more guidance.

▶ The amount of guidance you give will depend on individuals' expertise and experience. Gauge your coaching appropriately: provide more for less-experienced people, and less for those who have been on the job longer.

▸ Resist taking responsibility for your employees' decisions. In areas that are clearly their domain, lend your expertise but stop short of making decisions for them. When you take on problems that employees should be handing, you might unintentionally undermine their confidence, and you will definitely limit their learning. By coaching people to take responsibility, you will build their skills and make them less reliant on you.

▸ Ask individuals how confident they are in their ability to handle a situation or in the decision they made. Then ask how they could increase their confidence.

▸ Model risk taking. Talk about tough choices you have made. Discuss the risks involved and the issues you considered.

▸ Recognize your employees' initiative. Even when they make a mistake, take time to applaud their resourcefulness. Then talk through what went wrong and suggest ways to do it differently in the future.

Be willing to make bold yet well-reasoned moves in the marketplace

▼

Reward people who show initiative, who experiment, and who pursue innovation in the marketplace.

Leaders need to anticipate and make bold choices or they will never leap ahead of their competition. Consider the following suggestions:

▸ Know what your competitors are doing. Anticipate their moves. Anticipate that at least one competitor will be so bold or so desperate that it will do something disruptive (wildly unexpected or unusual) in the marketplace.

▸ Develop a differentiated and sustainable strategy. Then take action to support and implement it.

▸ Determine how your competitors will attack or compete with your strategy.

▸ Figure out how well your competitors know you. Have they raided your firm and hired employees who know your strategy? Do you have evidence that they use you as a benchmark? Anticipate what your competitors think you will do, and then do something different.

▸ Conduct a thorough risk analysis so that you know what level of risk you are taking on. Understand the assumptions upon which your strategy or analysis is based. Then systematically ask what would happen if each assumption were wrong.

▸ When you are considering a bold move, look at the worst-case scenario and figure out how you would deal with it.

Demonstrate inspiring leadership and courage such that others want to follow you

▼

A leader cannot lead without people who want to follow or be involved. People are inspired by individuals who have a vision, who are passionate about it, and who want to enlist others in the quest. Consider these suggestions:

▸ Ask yourself what you dedicate yourself to do or to accomplish because you care so deeply about it. Authentic and genuine commitment to a vision that goes beyond oneself is inspiring.

▸ Create a compelling picture of what is and what could be, and link it to what you and your people value. For example, instead of creating a product that merely meets customer requirements, create a product that also thoroughly impresses your customers because of its impact on their customers.

▸ Formally and informally share your thinking with your people. Some will be won over by hearing about thought processes and rationale, others by strong emotion.

Ask people to describe a situation in which they were inspired by a leader. Draw out lessons they could apply with their teams.

▸ Show how important an issue is to you. Have the courage to show your personal commitment and be willing to put yourself on the line.

▸ Take necessary risks to support your vision. People are watching how hard you will fight, what you will do, and whether you are able to attract others to your vision.

14

Influence Others

As a manager, you will be required to influence others to accept or support new proposals, ideas, changes, and initiatives. This takes skill, patience, and a commitment to understanding what motivates people and what they value.

To successfully influence people, you must first take the time to build support. You can do this by creating and maintaining relationships with others who can assist you in achieving your objectives or from whom you may want to gain buy-in later. Keep in mind that people enjoy and trust relationships when they feel appreciated and heard, and when they believe that their own interests matter to you.

In this chapter, we will cover the following areas:

▼

- ▶ Exercise good judgment and timing
- ▶ Readily command attention and respect in groups
- ▶ Know which battles are worth fighting
- ▶ Identify the agendas, concerns, and motivations of others
- ▶ Anticipate the positions and reactions of others accurately
- ▶ Generate enthusiasm for ideas by tapping into shared values
- ▶ Know whom to involve and when; build coalitions or alliances
- ▶ Give compelling reasons for ideas
- ▶ Ensure that your positions address others' needs and priorities
- ▶ Prepare appropriate influence strategies
- ▶ Promote or assert your own positions and ideas with confidence and enthusiasm
- ▶ Hold firm to your own position when necessary
- ▶ Negotiate persuasively
- ▶ Win support from others; get them to take action
- ▶ Influence and shape the decisions of upper management

Exercise good judgment and timing

Remind people to choose a moment when others have time to listen attentively before they launch into an important topic.

Requesting resources during budget cuts, criticizing the work of someone who stayed up all night to finish it, and pointing out that you warned of a consequence that just occurred are all examples of poor judgment and poor timing. Some people are so concerned with demonstrating that they were right, or so sure they know the best way, or so oblivious to what others think and feel that they harm themselves with their poor judgment and poor timing. These people are often seen as abrasive or insensitive. To avoid this fate, consider the following suggestions:

- Recognize that timing is important. Your message may be the right one, but it won't be received well if it is delivered at the wrong time.

- Before delivering your message, ask yourself: How will others feel if I say that? or What will others think of me if I say this?

- View your comments or requests in the context of the situation. Here are some examples of poor judgment and poor timing:
  - Telling the leader of the organization's quality effort that the quality program is just a new fad.
  - Commenting that the organization is not truly committed to diversity at a meeting announcing a new diversity program.
  - Disagreeing with an idea just to generate discussion or analysis when the decision has already been made and no amount of discussion will change it.

- Realize that it is better to praise people publicly and criticize them in private. If you criticize someone in a large meeting, it will become an ego issue. A private conversation allows people to modify their positions.

- Pay attention to the cultural aspects of positive and negative feedback. In some cultures, it is considered rude to compliment others in public.

Readily command attention and respect in groups

If you express yourself well, you can capture people's attention. If you follow through on your commitments, you can earn their respect. Consider the following suggestions:

▸ Determine your typical behavior in group settings. What kind of contributions do you make? Do you simply agree with people, or do you make suggestions and ask questions?

Recommend that people practice giving persuasive presentations in front of others in order to get useful feedback.

▸ In addition to speaking up more often, demonstrate enthusiasm and confidence when you state your opinions. Don't hesitate to voice your thoughts or to label them as your own. Find ways to ensure that other group members take your contributions seriously and consider them when making decisions.

▸ Use effective eye contact and speak to all individuals in the group.

▸ Prepare for meetings. Knowing the points you want to make and how to state them will make you more confident and persuasive.

▸ Look for opportunities to lead groups. Volunteer to lead a task force or project group, and try some new techniques to increase your impact. To get a feel for how effective your techniques are, ask people in the group for feedback.

Know which battles are worth fighting

Managers who have to win every issue, even at the expense of other people, reduce their overall effectiveness and diminish their credibility in the organization. Because they are so busy advocating their own agendas, they are not sufficiently aware of the needs or concerns of others. Consider the following suggestions:

Ask people to keep a log of the conflicts they engage in and rate the seriousness of each. Remind them to let go of small problems.

▸ Ask others about any conflicts in which they believe you are unwisely invested. Talk with your peers about the price you are paying for this involvement.

▸ Solicit feedback about whether you frequently get into conflicts that others believe are unimportant or costly to you, your team, or your relationships with others.

- Learn to catch yourself before you get locked into a conflict. Here are some signs that you are emotionally involved in a conflict:
  - ▷ Your voice gets louder.
  - ▷ You feel angry or hurt.
  - ▷ You talk a long time or explain your point of view over and over again.
  - ▷ You feel challenged or judged.
  - ▷ You feel frustrated, irritated, or fed up.
  - ▷ You say hurtful or judgmental things, such as "I'm sorry that you seem incapable of understanding this situation."

- Look for a role model—someone who chooses the right battles. Observe what the person does that you could emulate.

Identify the agendas, concerns, and motivations of others

Before you can influence people and bring them together, you need to know what drives them. As you build relationships, you learn more about what people want to accomplish and what motivates them. Consider the following suggestions:

- Identify your stakeholder groups: customers, shareholders, employees, suppliers and vendors, strategic partners, the community at large, and other groups.

- Periodically review and update your knowledge of each group. For example, learn what their goals are for the year, what business they're trying to bring in, obstacles they face, and recent successes. Compare the needs, preferences, and expectations of each group to see where they overlap and where they conflict.

Ask people to identify what would influence an individual you both know. Compare this with your own understanding of that individual.

- Look for common expectations across stakeholder groups. For example, some groups may expect products and services to be of the highest quality. Others may expect the organization to have sound management and planned growth.

- Develop strong relationships with representatives from each stakeholder group. Meet frequently with them to keep up to date on their issues and concerns.

▸ Try to understand a situation from each group's point of view. Even if you think you have a thorough understanding of what motivates them, confirm your assumptions by talking to them. This will help you uncover details that you might not have known and develop a better understanding of the nuances of the situation.

The following ideas will help you dig beneath the surface to discover what motivates people's behavior.

Ask tactful yet direct questions.

▸ What is the personal impact if we proceed on this?

▸ What is the worst that could happen to you in this?

If you listen without judging, they may share one or two sensitive issues. Remain silent and wait for an answer to show your interest is sincere.

Offer tentative hypotheses.

▸ I imagine that if we go that route, your team will take some heat.

▸ When we've done this in the past, it hasn't always reflected well on those who had to make the call. Let's see what we can do to avoid any collateral damage to your area.

▸ If I were in your shoes, I know I'd be concerned about what's going to happen to me.

By floating some potential issues and showing interest, you make it safer for them to acknowledge their concerns and perhaps offer more.

Observe them carefully and reflect on their reactions.

Because you always have to assume that there is more than what they are saying, watch carefully to see what type of ideas they support or reject. Consider what they stand to lose or gain.

▶ Communicate with people throughout the organization. Take a break from e-mail-only communication. Take the time to walk through the halls and stop to chat with your direct reports and others. Ask them how their work is going, what their concerns are, and what changes and improvements they would like to see.

Anticipate the positions and reactions of others accurately

▼

Anticipating accurately how people are likely to react to your proposal or idea is often key to influencing them successfully. You won't be caught off guard or ill prepared, and you will have a better chance of making your case despite reluctance or resistance. For example, if you know that your manager feels strongly about a particular topic, you can present ideas in a way that shows recognition of and alignment with your manager's position. Consider the following suggestions:

▶ Regularly discuss work-related topics with your colleagues. Take time to invite them to lunch or for coffee so you can talk in an informal environment.

▶ Keep notes on what you learn so you will remember where others stand on particular issues and what their needs, goals, and agendas are.

▶ Before presenting a new idea or action plan, determine whose support you absolutely need to have. Talk with individuals who work with those people or review your past experience with them to determine what you need to do to win them over.

Ask people whom they consulted to learn how an individual might be influenced. Discuss why this is helpful.

▶ Meet with peers or higher-level managers who seem knowledgeable about others' positions to learn more about how they "read" people and gather useful information.

▶ To track how people view your proposal, use the chart below. Fill in the name of a person or group, and a short note about why support your proposal, are neutral about it, or want to block it.

Support	Neutral	Block

Generate enthusiasm for ideas by tapping into shared values

▼

People want to do more than go through the motions—they want to do work that matters. When you appeal to deeply held values and goals, your words and ideas resonate with people. They intrinsically understand that your proposal not only will help the organization, but also will help them live out their values and pursue their goals. Consider the following suggestions:

▸ Convey your enthusiasm—it will inspire and motivate others.

▸ Learn about the values of the individuals on your team. As a group, come to a consensus on your shared values. Note where individual values are aligned and where there are differences.

▸ Create an environment in which people can live out their values. Make it a place where people identify and discuss values, feel comfortable talking about values in group situations, and have a process for working out issues in a way that recognizes and honors values.

Ask people to make a list of what key individuals value. Review the list and offer feedback.

▸ When you present your ideas to an audience, refer specifically to your shared values. Make the connection clear. For example, your proposal might address the fact that:

▷ People feel strongly about developing state-of-the-art expertise in their area.

> ▷ People want to deliver superior products that create high customer satisfaction and loyalty.

> ▷ People want to serve a segment of the local community.

> ▷ People want to create products in an environmentally friendly way.

- ▶ People are encouraged by stories of other people's successes. Tell stories about people who created a value-centered workplace. Describe how people clearly defined their values and focused on what mattered to them.

Know whom to involve and when; build coalitions or alliances

▼

Arrange for people to work with others who influence in ways different from their own. Challenge them to try new influence behaviors.

At times, you need to band together with other leaders to generate sufficient support for your ideas. Proactively meeting with people to explain your ideas and initiatives can help you win support at the beginning of an initiative instead of trying to change opinions after the fact. Consider the following suggestions:

- ▶ Identify whom you would like to include in a coalition or alliance. Look beyond your immediate work environment to the larger system. For example, consider involving people who contribute to the same core business processes you do, internal and external customers, vendors and suppliers, and people from sales and marketing.

- ▶ Be clear about why you want to form a coalition or alliance. Have a specific purpose and goal. Know why it makes more sense to approach the issue as a group than as individuals.

- ▶ Work together to decide the role of each group within the coalition or alliance. You should know what is expected of each group and what they will contribute to the effort.

- ▶ As each new group joins the coalition or alliance, ask them if they know of other groups that might be interested so you can invite them as well.

- ▶ Leverage the strengths of the coalition or alliance. Use diverse perspectives to generate stronger ideas and refine them. Extend your reach by asking each group within the coalition or alliance to contact everyone within its sphere of influence.

▶ Work out disagreements in the group before you communicate your ideas broadly. It will be better if you present a united front. This doesn't mean that you won't have a range of perspectives, but everyone should agree on the basic message and purpose.

▶ As a group, decide who will take the lead in communicating the message. You may choose to present as a group or to send representatives from each group in the coalition or alliance.

▶ Meet periodically with the broader coalition or alliance to discuss your efforts and progress. Determine whether you need to alter your plans or activities. Also, renew your commitment to achieving your stated goals.

Give compelling reasons for ideas

▼

Some people are impressed by a strong, logical argument, while others are swayed by a vigorous, impassioned personal appeal. To be most compelling, adapt your message and your style to suit the audience and the situation. Consider the following suggestions:

Remind people that logical persuasion is only one method of influencing.

▶ Before presenting your ideas, study your audience.

▷ What is important to your audience? What are their main concerns about your message?

▷ How will your message benefit them?

▶ Conduct informal discussions with members of your target audience to explore their understanding of the issue. Use what you learn to tailor your message to meet their needs and concerns.

▶ Make sure you're prepared before you talk to people. Identify your key messages and the supporting material for each message. Be sure to address any concerns you uncovered during your discussions.

▶ Put your ideas in a logical order that is easy for people to follow. In general, the simpler you can make the message, the better. You can add more detail as people ask questions.

▶ Give a brief introduction before you present your ideas. For example, "I've asked everyone to meet today to talk about next year's marketing strategy. I have three ideas I want to share, and then I would be interested in getting your input."

▸ When you deliver your ideas, pay attention to the reaction of your audience. Do they appear engaged? Are they asking questions? Look for signs that they are interested in what you are saying and want to know more.

Ensure that your positions address others' needs and priorities

Situations do not have to turn into zero-sum games. If you pay close attention to the needs and priorities of individuals and groups within the organization, you can find ways to tie your positions to theirs and create win-win results. Consider the following suggestions:

▸ List all the people your proposal would affect. Begin with the most obvious groups and individuals, and then move outward to the larger system in which your group works.

▸ Meet with people from each group on your list to talk about your idea, request, or proposal. Learn more about their needs, interests, and concerns. What is important to them? What are their main concerns? How would they like to work with you and your team?

▸ If your idea or proposal will cause problems for others, ask these questions:

  ▹ Why is it a problem? What could be done to alleviate the problem?

  ▹ What would make the extra trouble worth it to them?

Ask people to explain the point of view of someone they want to influence. This will help them come up with ideas the other person will support.

▸ Influence gained by exchange is cooperative rather than adversarial. Once you have assessed other people's interests and needs, find something you can offer them. Determine the value of what you are asking them to do and offer something that is (at least) of equal value to them. If they accept your offer, everyone will win.

▸ Compile a thorough inventory of what you can legitimately offer to others at your level, and at other levels in the organization. List your offerings in several categories, including power, recognition, money, fame, opportunities, learning, and inclusion. Examples of what you might offer are:

▷ The use of equipment or personnel to help with a particular project.

▷ Access to information.

▷ Active support for an idea or request.

▷ Public praise.

▷ Genuine appreciation.

▷ A promise to return the favor in the future.

Prepare appropriate influence strategies

▼

Building a broad base of support within and across work groups, functional areas, and organizations is beneficial and often necessary to obtain the level of influence you need for a particular proposal. Consider the following suggestions:

▶ Raise your visibility within the organization. Identify five to ten key people who are necessary for your success and invest time building rapport with each person. Influence is often as much a function of who knows you as of whom you know.

▶ Build positive relationships with your colleagues. Don't wait until you need something from them to show an interest in their ideas, goals, and concerns. Take a genuine interest in them now.

Discuss people's strategies to influence others in order to get approval on a solution. Talk through their rationale and approach.

▶ Understand what is important to the people you're trying to influence. You need to know what motivates them, what concerns them, what they're trying to accomplish, and what persuades them.

▶ Approach people who share your viewpoints and suggest that you join forces to advocate for your position. Brainstorm ways you could work together and support each other.

▶ Recognize that influencing techniques do not work instantaneously; you probably won't change people's minds during a single meeting or conversation. Instead, progressively move people toward accepting your idea.

- Use a range of influencing styles, including:
  - ▷ *Networking.* Identify people who can support you, especially opinion leaders, and build relationships with them. Include people from inside and outside your organization.
  - ▷ *Pie making.* Increase the scope and value of solutions so all parties will benefit. Find solutions that exceed the expectations of all parties.
  - ▷ *Brokering.* Facilitate win-win exchanges of goods and services.
  - ▷ *Banking.* Keep track of your assets and the holdings of people around you as you influence and negotiate.
  - ▷ *Leveraging power and resources.* Use status, information, services, and scarce goods to gain greater influence.
  - ▷ *Inspiring.* Appeal to people's values, interests, and concerns.

Promote or assert your own positions and ideas with confidence and enthusiasm

▼

Provide feedback about verbal or nonverbal behavior that diminishes people's influence when they're delivering a message.

If you want to engage, motivate, inspire, captivate, energize, or convince people, you need to present your ideas with confidence and enthusiasm. Your ideas deserve the best delivery you can give them. Consider the following suggestions:

- Increase your confidence by becoming well versed in your topic. Be ready to talk about it both broadly and in detail, and to answer a wide range of questions.

- Clarify your purpose for sharing your ideas. People need an overall sense of what you're talking about and why they should listen to you. If you don't have a clear purpose, people may understand your points but fail to understand why you're making them.

- Show your confidence by talking about how people will benefit from your idea. Talk about how it connects to other initiatives, both present and future. Tie your idea or solution to an already acknowledged problem.

- If you do not show enthusiasm naturally or easily, choose words that will emphasize your message. Use words that are more dramatic and powerful than you would generally use to express your excitement about the idea.

- Study how several leaders present their ideas and positions, how they respond to challenges and tough questions, and how they show boldness and confidence. Practice using some of their methods.

- If you don't feel confident or enthusiastic about your idea, determine why and resolve the issue. Otherwise people will pick up on the contradiction between your words and your attitude.

- Use nonverbal actions that show your enthusiasm. Project your voice, smile more, and use broader gestures.

- Don't lose momentum and energy in your argument by getting bogged down in details. Give people the overall picture, and get into more detail as you answer questions.

Hold firm to your own position when necessary

As a leader in your organization, you are probably an advocate for individuals, groups, ideas, initiatives, programs, and issues. When you face opposition, your people count on you to hold firm. Consider the following suggestions:

- When you defend your position, monitor your nonverbal actions. People will believe what you do more than what you say. If you appear to be uncertain, they will keep trying to change your mind. If you appear to be confident, they will be more convinced that you will hold firm.

- Recognize that even though people may respect your view, they will feel compelled to try to modify it, especially if they disagree with you.

- When you encounter resistance, find out why the person or group objects to your position. Set up a meeting to learn more about their views. Focus more on understanding their views than on explaining yours.

When you see people being too forceful in an attempt to get their own way, let them know this is causing others to resist them.

▸ After you have done all you can to understand opposing viewpoints, hold firm when:

▹ You feel that you have all the essential facts or input needed to make a decision.

▹ You believe that the decision is fair to all the stakeholders involved.

▹ You believe it is consistent with other policy decisions.

▹ You believe that acquiescing would result in an action that is unethical, unsafe, illegal, or entirely inappropriate in the workplace.

▹ You are convinced that any other decision would be harmful to the organization, your team, your customers, or the quality of your product.

▸ If you are the decision maker, send a clear message that this is your final decision on the matter. Do not leave others with the impression that you are open to further discussion. You can harm your integrity if you claim that this is your final decision and then back down later.

Negotiate persuasively

▼

Effective negotiation depends on a number of factors, including preparation, knowledge of the other person's position and needs, and creativity in coming up with alternative solutions. The following techniques can help you improve your negotiation skills:

▸ Before presenting your point of view, think about and investigate others' positions and needs. What is important to them? What are their goals? What can you do for them? The answers to these questions will give you the information you need to frame your argument during the discussion.

Listen to a person who is trying to influence others. Would you be influenced? Why or why not? Discuss your perceptions.

▸ Take the time to examine the pros and cons of both sides. Too often in the attempt to persuade, people argue the advantages of their own position and the disadvantages of the alternative. They inevitably get nowhere because they are simply not communicating. Be willing and prepared to discuss and accept both the pros of others' arguments and the cons of yours. Use the chart below to assist you in assessing all positions:

	Pros	Cons
Position A		
Position B		
Position C		
Etc.		

▶ Talk with others who have dealt with the people with whom you will be negotiating. Find out what tactics have and have not worked in the past.

▶ Know what you want from three perspectives: what is absolutely necessary, what is ideal, and what you would be willing to give up.

▶ Be prepared to bargain, barter, and trade to find an agreeable exchange. Think about the resources you have to offer that would be of value to each person or group you want to persuade.

▶ Go into a negotiation with the perspective that the other side is your ally rather than your enemy. Thinking about dealing with an ally can help you look for solutions that benefit both of you.

▶ In negotiation meetings, listen carefully to what others are saying. Try to discern the needs behind their requests. If you successfully identify their needs, you can better generate alternatives from which you both can benefit.

▶ Refrain from getting into a win-lose discussion in which the only alternatives are for one of you to benefit and one of you to lose out. If the discussion reaches that point, note this fact and communicate your desire for both or all of you to get something out of the agreement you reach.

▶ Be careful not to burn your bridges. If you succeed at the expense of others, don't be surprised when future attempts to influence these people fail, or when they take advantage of an opportunity to benefit at your expense.

▶ Draw out information by using open-ended questions (questions that call for more than yes and no answers) to facilitate dialogue.

▶ If you are presented with new facts, continue the discussion until you have a clear understanding of this information or, if appropriate, postpone the meeting and take time to get up to speed before you meet again.

▶ Avoid becoming emotional or defensive.

▶ Prepare for the possibility that no decision will be reached. Create a list of actions you could take if you fail to reach agreement.

▶ Don't be too committed to reaching an agreement quickly. Some alternatives may not yet be readily apparent.

▶ Be willing to modify your position if your needs can be met through an alternative solution that will better meet others' needs as well.

Win support from others; get them to take action

▼

In a role play, challenge people's positions to see how they respond and how they incorporate your opinions.

Gaining support from others is a skill that can take time and practice to hone. Good ideas are often not enough to get others to accept your point of view. If you find that you don't get support for your ideas as often as you'd like, consider the following suggestions:

▶ Ask someone you trust in your organization for input on your ability to win support. Have this person watch you in situations in which you are attempting to gain others' support. Get feedback on how you came across and what you could have done differently.

▶ If you feel comfortable, ask for feedback from the people who did not support you. What were their concerns? What could you have done that would have swayed them?

▶ Observe people in your organization who seem particularly skilled at getting others to take action. What techniques do they use? What do they do when they run into roadblocks? How do they state their arguments? What appeals to you when you listen to them?

▶ Incorporate some of the most effective techniques you've observed into your influencing efforts and see how they work for you. Take care not to choose a technique so far out of character for you that you won't be able to use it effectively. Not all techniques work for all people.

▶ Before presenting your idea, explain it to a few trusted colleagues. Get their input on its feasibility, and encourage them to challenge you on the various aspects of the idea. Use this information to analyze aspects you might have overlooked.

▶ Be aware that your speaking style directly affects how convincing you can be. Record yourself as you practice presenting your idea and ask yourself the following questions:

▷ Are my tone of voice and inflection consistent with the meaning of my words and the intention of my message?

▷ Does the pace of my speech facilitate understanding?

▷ Are my enthusiasm and liveliness appropriate for the topic and setting?

▷ Are my words clear enough for others to understand easily?

▶ If you want others to support your efforts, reciprocate by supporting their ideas and objectives whenever possible.

▶ Take the time to get to know higher-level managers and people in different functions. Volunteer for a cross-functional committee or project so that other managers can get to know your ideas and experience your enthusiasm firsthand. Find ways to stay in touch with these people after the committee has disbanded or the project is over and build relationships that benefit both parties.

Influence and shape the decisions of upper management

One of the most important areas in which to focus influencing efforts is upper management. The ability to win the interest and support of your manager and his or her peers is a critical skill to have. To develop your skill, consider the following suggestions:

- When you propose an idea or action to upper management, be clear about how it will benefit the organization—how it will help solve a problem, cut costs, increase return on investment, decrease turnover.

- When you see that a decision from higher-level management might have a negative impact on your area, let your manager know and cite tangible consequences.

Enable people to attend meetings with upper management so they can see issues, interactions, and influence strategies at work.

- Watch what is important to upper management. Look for ways to spot opportunities important to the company. Strategize with your manager.

- Meet with your manager periodically to let him or her know what you are doing, and to hear about issues that concern upper management.

- Use time wisely. When you meet with busy higher-level managers, keep your explanations brief and focused. Don't burden them with details they do not need, decisions you can make, or problems you can solve. Instead, provide your manager periodic, condensed updates on your work groups' activities.

- Find a mentor higher up in the organization who can help you learn to influence those with more authority than you. Mentors may have insights about norms or general techniques, suggest tactics specific to certain individuals you will encounter, or connect you to networks that would otherwise be closed to you.

- Be willing to make appropriate concessions. People's trust in you will grow when your initiatives benefit the entire organization, not just your own area. Your manager will be more willing to give you what you want if he or she sees that you have a balanced perspective about what is best for your area and what is best for the company.

15

Motivate Others

One of the joys of being a leader is the opportunity to motivate and inspire people to achieve their best, reach for their dreams, and pursue goals that will enable them to grow in both their professional and their personal lives.

By creating an inspiring work environment, you can help people see beyond what they perceive as their limitations and aspire for more, and you can bring out excellence in them. People respond to leaders who encourage, praise, appreciate, and create an honest approach to opportunities and possibilities. Work becomes more enjoyable and more meaningful, and both the organization and its employees benefit.

In this chapter, we will cover the following areas:

▼

- ▸ Create an environment in which people do their best work
- ▸ Create an environment that makes work enjoyable
- ▸ Inspire people to excel
- ▸ Foster a sense of energy, ownership, and personal commitment to the work
- ▸ Encourage others to define new opportunities and continuously improve the organization
- ▸ Adapt your approach to motivate each individual
- ▸ Convey trust in people's competence to do their jobs
- ▸ Inspire action without relying solely on authority
- ▸ Celebrate and reward significant achievements of others
- ▸ Positively address work environment and life balance issues

Create an environment in which people do their best work

▼

Discuss how people within a team can engage and inspire each other, and not just depend on the manager to do it.

Leaders can create an environment of enthusiasm and excellence by communicating high expectations, fostering optimistic, positive attitudes about people and their work, and ensuring that people feel appreciated and valued for their achievements and efforts. To create a climate in which all stretch beyond what they thought they could do, consider the following suggestions:

▸ Meet with the individuals on your team to discuss what is important to them, their goals, and your expectations. This will give you an opportunity to talk about expectations and arrive at mutually agreeable goals that people feel good about.

▸ Ensure that people know you are paying attention to their efforts by giving them timely, specific feedback and recognition. Positive words will encourage people, and constructive comments will help them change their tactics and behaviors to be more successful.

▸ Ask each individual on your team to identify "stretch objectives"— challenging goals that exceed job requirements but are still attainable. The more input people have in setting these objectives, the more likely they will be to pursue them.

▸ When people seem to be experiencing low morale or having difficulty, talk with them to find out what is going on. Sometimes people will not want to say much, but they will appreciate that you noticed and showed concern.

▸ When people do talk with you about their concerns, focus on listening instead of finding a solution right away. Help them figure out what would be most helpful. Sometimes just raising concerns is enough; other times people want to find a solution.

▸ Advocate the view that mistakes are opportunities for further learning, not humiliating experiences that cost people their credibility.

Create an environment that makes work enjoyable

▼

Excellent leaders show passion for the work they do and deliberately cultivate a culture in which people can enjoy their work. This translates into a higher level of success for both individuals and the organization. Consider the following suggestions:

▸ Examine your views toward fun at work. Does it seem like a contradiction in terms? Do you have fun at work? Why or why not?

▸ If you think fun is frivolous, think again. Fun does not automatically lead to lower productivity or lack of focus. It can coexist with hard work; in fact, fun on the job can motivate people to work harder and be more productive.

Invite an expert on employee engagement to talk to people about creating a positive environment.

▸ Realize that you can't force people to enjoy themselves. Your attempts are likely to backfire if you put people into situations in which they feel they must act as if they are having a good time. Instead, give people the freedom to create their own fun, and ask them to contribute ideas for creating a positive work environment.

▸ If people have a vague sense that the environment could be better but they're not sure how, ask them to describe a workplace that they would enjoy. Challenge them to be specific and to bring examples from other workplaces.

▸ As a group, generate several concrete suggestions on how to make the environment more enjoyable. Choose some suggestions to implement immediately. Implement a few at a time so you can measure their effectiveness.

▸ Identify a unit in the organization in which people consistently enjoy their work. Interview the unit leader and some of the employees to learn more about their approach to work and to working together. Ask them to share their approach with your group.

Inspire people to excel

▼

Many people build their expectations on what they think is possible. As a leader, you have the opportunity to help people see what's beyond their current horizons. Consider the following suggestions:

► When you have confidence in people's ability to excel, say so. But say it only when you mean it—not just to make people feel good.

► Find out what people believe is blocking or hindering them from outstanding accomplishments. Work together to remove the barriers.

► When you encounter people whose aspirations are not as high as you think they could be given their skills, experience, and talents, tell them your perceptions. Tell people what you see in them and why you believe they have a lot of potential. Some people have not had support from others to dream or to have high aspirations.

► Learn about the personal hopes and aspirations of your direct reports. Ask each person questions such as:

  ▷ What unique skills and attributes would you like to capitalize on? What skills do you wish to develop further?

  ▷ What do you hope to accomplish at the organization?

  ▷ If you could create your ideal job, what would it look like?

► During career discussions, listen carefully as people describe their career goals. You may find that some people have lower aspirations than others, especially those who have or are perceived to have unique challenges in their way. When it's appropriate, redirect them. For example, people who are not native speakers of English may aspire only to one or two career promotions above where they are, whereas you see much greater potential for them.

Brainstorm ways to support high-performing individuals.

► Meet with your direct reports as a group and talk about the group's hopes and aspirations. Ask questions such as:

  ▷ What aspects of the team's vision and mission inspire you?

  ▷ If we could remove all constraints, what would we like to accomplish? What do you think we can accomplish?

  ▷ What do you think the organization will look like in two years? In five years? How do you see yourselves or the team fitting into that picture?

► Once you know what people think is possible, compare their views to yours. As a leader, you have access to information that not only *allows* you to see the bigger picture, but *requires* you to do so. For example, the organization might be planning to start a new line of business that would expand your group's responsibilities.

▶ Identify the characteristics of a culture in which people can dream big dreams—a place where people encourage questions, feel comfortable talking about options that don't currently exist, refrain from cynical and negative comments, and know how to try out new ideas in a pragmatic way.

▶ People are encouraged by stories of others' successes. Tell stories about individuals and teams who had high goals and were determined to do what it took to achieve them. You will often find that the people weren't any more talented than your group, but they were willing to take a chance.

▶ Help people on the team see themselves as winners. Set goals to be the best and celebrate accomplishments.

▶ If people have low expectations and minimal hopes, learn why. You may be dealing with a history of low expectations, a series of flops, cynicism, a lack of resources, or a perception of impossible odds. These issues will always stand in the way until you address them directly.

Foster a sense of energy, ownership, and personal commitment to the work

▼

When individuals have an opportunity to meet both professional and personal needs within the same environment, they often achieve optimum performance. As a leader, you can help create this environment for each person on your team. Consider the following suggestions:

Discuss why it is important that a team take action on a vision instead of continue to discuss hypothetical situations.

▶ Develop strong relationships with your direct reports. Learn about individuals' personal and professional goals, what work they want to do, and what roles they want to play in helping the team achieve its goals and vision.

▶ Make explicit connections between the team's goals and vision, each person's needs and motives, and personal and professional goals. Watch for opportunities to link people with work, situations, or experiences that will help them to meet their goals.

- Show your excitement as you talk about the team's goals and vision, and indicate how pleased you are that people are willing to pitch in and work together. Your personal commitment to the team will inspire others to strengthen their commitment.

- Capitalize on people's competitive spirit and sense of pride. Provide benchmarking information about your external competitors or other teams within your organization. Also, work with the team to set goals to become the best.

- Understand that with some individuals, recognition can play a positive role in inspiring work commitment. They will perform at a high level so that they get visibility for their contributions. Also, they may put pressure on others to get on board so that the team will be more successful.

Encourage others to define new opportunities and continuously improve the organization

▼

Ask people to identify ways that they improve and contribute to a productive workplace.

Effective leaders challenge their people and teams to ask questions and to look at old problems in new ways. Together, they identify what is working well and what is stalled, and develop ideas that will improve performance. Consider the following suggestions:

- Discuss with team members how the team or organization can improve. Ask people to challenge assumptions, identify root causes of problems rather than symptoms, and think through all the implications of the solutions they propose.

- Ask your direct reports what you can do to be a better leader or a better boss for them. Implement some of their recommendations to show that you take their input seriously.

- Encourage people to think beyond current customer needs. What will be important to your customers tomorrow, next year, and in five years? What is going on with *their* customers? How will that affect what your customers want from you?

- Observe how people on your team react to issues and problems. Your team's ability to generate new ideas and challenge the status quo will depend to some extent on the preferences of your team members.

Some people are curious by nature, while others are more likely to accept things the way they are. Take advantage of the ingenuity of team members who enjoy creating new things and the resourcefulness of people who like to improve things. Both approaches have value.

▶ Ensure that the team's vision is aligned with the organization's. Then people will be confident that they are spending their time and energy on areas that the organization values.

▶ Focus attention on the areas where you'll get the most leverage. Too many changes may make the work environment unstable, and people may find it difficult to focus because they're trying to do too many new things.

Adapt your approach to motivate each individual

Effective leaders realize that the hopes and aspirations of people vary. They learn about their employees and adapt motivational strategies to each individual.

Six broad categories describe what energizes and motivates people. When you want to motivate a team member, review these categories. Consider how specific types of work or assignments could meet an individual's needs or motivators:

▶ *Achievement Motive: Driven to personally accomplish significant goals.* This person takes risks, pushes himself or herself, achieves challenging goals, subjects others to stress, and seeks visible results.

▶ *Balance Motive: Driven to seek work environments that place equal emphasis on nonwork activities.* This person wants flexible hours, enjoys nonwork activities, dislikes overtime, likes time off, and may like to telecommute.

▶ *Autonomy Motive: Driven to act independently and to express creativity.* This person prefers to do his or her own thing, wants independence, takes initiative, contributes to and enjoys the beauty in the world, and develops new ideas, materials, and methods.

▶ *Power/Influence Motive: Driven to seek out opportunities for recognition, prestige, authority, and/or control.* This person seeks success in others' eyes, seeks to lead and set direction for others, prefers tangible recognition, focuses on getting ahead and advancing his or her career, and wants visible signs of prestige.

Examine situations in which attempts to motivate people failed. Discuss why the actions were unsuccessful.

▶ *Security Motive: Driven to seek work environments that provide security and stability.* This person prefers stability, job security, and predictability; seeks comfortable, clean, and safe working conditions; and prefers a regular income.

▶ *Relationship Motive: Driven to seek out opportunities to build strong relationships and/or to be of service to others.* This person seeks to relate to and help others, fosters harmony, provides service to others, emphasizes giving to others, and works with and lives by strong values of religious, racial, social, ethnic, or cultural groups.

Convey trust in people's competence to do their jobs

▼

Smart leaders surround themselves with competent people who can do the work well. They are not afraid to hire people who are more capable than they are in particular areas. Once they've hired people, they trust them to do the work. Consider the following suggestions:

▶ First, hire people you trust to do the work well. Create a clear role description for each position, including the knowledge, skills, abilities, experience, and approaches the person needs. This will help you identify the type of person you would trust in that role.

▶ Work with your human resources people to develop an effective selection process that reliably results in the right people being hired for jobs in your part of the organization.

▶ When you delegate a decision or an assignment, explain the issue and your ultimate goal. Communicate the result needed, but let your people figure out how to get the results.

Discuss how people can rebuild trust in individuals who have made mistakes.

▶ Check in periodically. Make yourself available to answer questions. Talk through issues or decision options, but don't make decisions for people. This will give individuals opportunities to learn how to evaluate the options and deal with the consequences of their decisions, both positive and negative.

▶ Support others' decisions as often as you can. If you second-guess people, they won't approach decisions seriously because they won't feel responsible for them.

▶ Develop an understanding of each person's decision-making process and experience. Structure work so that you delegate what you know a person can do, and work together in areas in which the person needs more experience.

▶ Resist taking over if things go wrong. Instead, coach people on how to correct mistakes. They will learn more and develop greater confidence in their ability to handle problems.

Inspire action without relying solely on authority

▼

Talk about leaders who led their teams to accomplish challenging goals. Have people figure out skills that were used and try them out with their teams.

As a leader, you know that using your authority is not always the best lever to generate action, and often it does not work. Instead, it's better to use an influence strategy that fits the situation. Consider the following suggestions:

▶ Inspire people. Craft messages and approaches that appeal to their values and beliefs. Encourage people by expressing your confidence in their abilities. Convey your trust in people's abilities through your words and actions.

▶ Persuade people to your point of view by appealing to what is important to them. The key to this approach is finding out how to meet their needs and concerns. Sometimes this means only that you need to communicate how your plans will meet their needs. Other times, you may need to modify what you want so that it is more appealing to others.

▶ Persuade people to your point of view by using your expertise. Apply your knowledge, exchange information and ideas, and work cooperatively with people. This approach works best if people share the goal and an understanding of its importance.

▶ Assume that a person or group wants to help you. Discuss the project or initiative in a way that assumes the person wants to be involved and wants to help. (Of course, this approach works best when you have an existing relationship.)

▸ Make a personal appeal. Solicit support and help from friends, colleagues, relatives, and other people with whom you have a reciprocal relationship.

▸ Compromise with others. Make an agreement that allows both parties to meet some of their needs. Even if neither of you gets everything you want, it will keep the project or initiative moving forward—and create some shared history that you can build on later.

Celebrate and reward significant achievements of others

▼

Recognizing people's contributions and rewarding their effort and results will improve their performance. Consider the following suggestions:

▸ Recognize strong performance quickly. Research shows that the sooner a reward is delivered, the more impact it will have.

▸ Be specific. Don't just say "great job"; let people know what you are recognizing in specific, tangible terms. Emphasize the impact—on you, the team, the organization—so that the person can see the positive consequences of his or her performance.

▸ Help people increase their understanding of their strengths and what they do well. This is one of the most helpful things you can do to develop others' skills.

▸ Make your employees' successes visible. Communicate their achievements to the organization, showing pride in and support for them.

▸ Guard against taking people for granted. To assess whether you're overlooking people, think of employees who make your life easier, who support the team with extra effort whenever it's needed. Thank them for their efforts and praise their work.

Talk about the best ways to show appreciation.

▸ Observe the common ways that performance is rewarded within your organization. Talk to your peers to find out what rewards they use for their teams and employees. Also, meet with your human resources representative and discuss ways to reward and recognize performance.

▸ Find out when and how people prefer to receive recognition for their work. For example, some people may appreciate frequent encouragement and recognition throughout a project, while others may prefer to be recognized when the project is complete.

Positively address work environment and life balance issues

▼

Encouraging people in your group to maintain an appropriate balance between work and life will help them achieve consistently positive results. Consider the following suggestions:

▸ Recognize that work/life balance needs differ between individuals. Some like to focus on their careers, while others focus on important activities outside of work. The balance may shift over time as people change their focus.

▸ To assess the current environment for work/life balance, review the norms and expectations for work hours. How do they fit with the needs of the work? With the needs of your employees? How many hours do people put in each week? How do people treat team members who put in more or fewer hours?

Observe people's work/life balance, and suggest ideas for positive adjustments.

▸ What messages do you want to send about work hours? About balance? Consider the messages you send by your behavior. What type of role model are you?

▸ Ask people to evaluate their work/life balance. Balance doesn't mean that things will always be 50/50. Sometimes work requires more time, and sometimes personal life requires more time. It's a matter of understanding the trade-offs and making appropriate decisions.

▸ Work with your team to figure out how to honor the preferences of team members while meeting the needs of the work. If people express frustration with current expectations or excessive workloads, hold group discussions to resolve these issues. Encourage the group to come up with solutions: redistributing work, training additional people, borrowing people from other groups, developing more efficient systems.

16
Build Talent

Ensuring that your group has the right employees is a critical step toward making sure that your organization achieves its goals effectively. By working with HR and taking a strong interest in how people are hired, brought on board, supported, and developed, you can strengthen the quality of your employees and foster your organization's reputation as a great place to work.

Take a strong interest in finding the right people for your organization and in helping new employees achieve their best performance. You can create a friendly, supportive environment and make sure that performance is measured fairly and consistently—which will help attract the best talent and retain key employees.

In this chapter, we will cover the following areas:

▼

- Attract and select high-caliber talent
- Promote the organization externally as an attractive place to work
- Utilize a variety of recruiting resources and strategies to provide needed talent to the organization
- Improve the interviewing process
- Use multiple interviewers
- Increase your interviewing effectiveness
- Avoid common rating errors
- Help new employees be successful
- Apply knowledge of what motivates employees in order to retain key talent
- Develop successors and talent pools
- Address issues and concerns of the current and future workforce
- Make placement and reward decisions based on people's capabilities and performance
- Shape roles and assignments in ways that leverage and develop people's capabilities
- Onboard employees to new roles
- Use performance management to improve performance and develop employees
- Ensure that effective processes are in place to evaluate people's capabilities
- Identify required capabilities and skill gaps within own organizational area
- Provide feedback, coaching, and guidance

- ▶ Ensure that people are learning from customers, contractors, and other external sources

- ▶ Promote sharing of expertise and a free flow of learning across the organization

- ▶ Hold others accountable for developing their people

Attract and select high-caliber talent

▼

Provide people with your view of their team's strength and their ability to attract and select high-caliber talent.

Having the right people is the key to success for leaders of any work unit or team. Successful managers work closely with HR, their colleagues, other employees, and the community to attract and recruit people to the organization, filling positions quickly with people who are right for the jobs. Consider the following suggestions:

▶ Begin by identifying the most critical positions in your group. These are the roles in which it makes a big difference whether the person is average or great.

▶ Put yourself in the shoes of those you want to attract to the organization or to a particular role. Knowing what you know and taking a realistic view, would you be attracted to the organization or the role? If not, what can you do about it?

▶ Remember that interviews are a two-way process. Not only do you choose the candidate, the candidate also chooses your organization and decides whether he or she wants the job.

▶ Think of each interaction with potential employees as an opportunity to recruit them and get them excited about working with you and the team.

▶ Ensure that each interaction shows you and the group in a positive light: return phone calls quickly, put candidates at ease when they arrive, give them time to talk informally with team members, clearly describe the interview process so that they know what to expect.

▶ Talk with employees who recently joined the group to get feedback about the recruiting, interviewing, and entry process. Listen carefully as they describe their experiences and reactions, and look for ways to improve the process.

▶ Ask for feedback from your HR group about what you might be doing unintentionally to discourage candidates. For example, in one company, managers were so busy that candidates took other jobs before the managers had time to interview them.

▶ If you are trying to attract a different kind of candidate than you have in the past, ask your HR group or an action learning team to study what draws the type of candidates you want to attract. The most common way to do this is to interview prospective talent pools and people who recently joined the organization. One firm discovered that the candidates they wanted liked specialty coffees and read particular local magazines.

- ▶ Use your network to let people know what types of candidates you are looking for.

- ▶ Videotape yourself talking about your organization, your vision, and opportunities for people. When you watch the tape, think about whether you would be engaged by the message. Assess your delivery and whether the message is clear. Determine what changes you will make, either by yourself or with a coach, and practice your delivery.

- ▶ Determine whether potential candidates are available in other countries.

- ▶ Review unsolicited résumés. If you get résumés that look good, talk to the people who sent them, even if you have no openings at the present time. If the individuals turn out to be promising, keep in touch.

- ▶ Build relationships with alumni groups and placement officers at colleges and universities that produce high-quality graduates in your field. Realize that some companies begin the recruiting process in high schools.

- ▶ Participate in professional organizations where you can meet talented professionals.

- ▶ Use several recruiting sources to maximize your talent pool. Many employers and hiring managers use only one or two sources (online ads, newspaper ads) to attract potential employees.

Promote the organization externally as an attractive place to work

Organizations compete fiercely for top talent as well as for customers. Having a reputation as an attractive place to work helps them attract and retain people. This reputation can also help them in the marketplace as customers do not want to buy from organizations that are in the news for questionable practices, whether it is poor labor practices or assaults on the environment. Consider the following suggestions:

▶ Talk with people about the organization's reputation. Sometimes the reputation is obvious because of media coverage, either positive or negative. Rather than commission more studies and surveys, find the information that already exists. Many organizations have a long list of reports about how the organization is viewed.

Discuss how the person can promote the organization at professional association meetings and events.

▶ If the organization's reputation is unknown, commission a study. Find out what the reputation is among employees and potential employees, customers and potential customers, and other important constituencies. As part of the study, investigate the impact of the reputation on the constituent groups you are interested in.

▶ Take action when a negative reputation is preventing you from attracting the people you want to hire. Spend your resources on necessary and obvious action.

▶ Communicate internally about the strengths of the organization as an attractive place to work. Use information about why people were attracted to it and why they stay.

▶ Build the organization's reputation by taking part in community service projects. Increase the organization's visibility in the community in areas that will help your reputation.

▶ If there is recognition in your country of a "Top Employer" or "Best Place to Work," or a similar designation, recommend that your company try to achieve that recognition, or that the company pursue practices similar to those of the winners.

▶ Ensure consistency between the organization you are trying to promote externally and the experience of employees, customers, suppliers, and other groups. Listen carefully for feedback that indicates a need for changes within the organization before you work on building its external reputation.

▶ Find out why employees stay. Ask them yourself, or ask your HR manager to get this information.

▶ As you look at issues of reputation and perceptions of the organization, remember that your experience of the organization may be very different from the experience of others. You may also find that different constituencies view the organization quite differently. For example, employees from recently acquired organizations could be a lot more positive or negative than those who were already with the organization.

▶ Ask for recommendations on how to improve the organization's reputation and people's experience with the organization. Prioritize actions; address issues that will make the most difference to the constituencies you are most concerned about.

▶ When you make promises to change, underpromise and overdeliver. Be careful not to set yourself or the organization up for failure. For example, if you and the leadership team are not willing to provide the resources and attention to drive the changes, either do not start or limit expectations of what you can accomplish.

Utilize a variety of recruiting sources and strategies to provide needed talent to the organization

▼

Finding the right talent for your work unit is critically important. Among the connections you can use are employees, colleges and universities, people in the field, and professional organizations. As you look for recruiting sources, consider the following suggestions:

▶ Use several recruiting sources to maximize your talent pool. Expand beyond the one or two sources, such as newspaper ads or postings on your Web site, typically used in your organization. Take advantage of social media networks such as LinkedIn.com and organizational or professional groups on Facebook—many companies find great talent referrals through these networks.

Discuss the importance of using a range of recruiting tools, including social media.

▶ Ask employees to recruit people they know. If you discover that they are not willing to recruit their friends and acquaintances, find out why. This is a significant sign of dissatisfactio n with the organization.

▶ Find out where and how to locate potential candidates and what attracts them to a company. For example, some potential candidates are more likely to use e-recruiting sources than newspaper ads; some are more likely to be attracted to the organization's reputation for flexible benefits than to its customer service awards; college graduates are likely to use job fairs.

- Participate in professional organizations that provide opportunities for you to meet talented professionals.

- Develop relationships with recruiters and recruiting agencies that have a track record of making suitable matches.

- Provide detailed information to recruiters so that they understand the job for which they are recruiting candidates. Also give them information about the company, its values and culture, and your work unit.

- Use your own network within and outside the organization to let people know the roles you're filling and the kind of candidates you're looking for.

Improve the interviewing process

Although the interview is often the primary mechanism for obtaining information about job candidates, many interviewers spend more time describing the job than finding out about the candidate. As a result, many interviewers make hiring decisions that are based more on "gut feeling" than on objective data.

- Use the following process to help you obtain better information during the interviewing process:

  1. Before you interview, determine the specific requirements of the job to be filled, including the knowledge, skills, and other competencies needed to perform the job effectively.

  2. Prepare an interview guide containing questions that you will ask all candidates. Research has shown that using a standard outline improves the reliability and validity of hiring decisions.

  3. Emphasize questions that probe a candidate's past behavior in areas related to the job. The best predictor of future performance is past performance in similar positions. Also, recent and long-standing behavior has much greater validity than old and sporadic behavior. Effective questions include:

     ▷ What is the most difficult decision you made in the past six months?

     ▷ What was your most challenging customer service situation, and how did you handle it?

▷ What is the most successful team accomplishment your management team has had, and what was your role in achieving it?

Avoid asking questions that are based on hypothetical circumstances, that inquire about the candidate's attitude, or that rely too heavily on the candidate's stated goals. These questions often generate hypothetical "textbook" answers that the candidates know you want to hear.

Ask people to conduct a mock interview with you as the candidate and give feedback about their interviewing style and skills.

4. Create a comfortable environment for your candidates. Be on time, spend a few minutes chatting informally to put them at ease, and avoid interruptions.

5. Take notes during interviews to make sure you can evaluate candidates based on facts rather than unclear recall when the time comes to make the hiring decision.

6. Try to get additional information about candidates to confirm your conclusions. Reference checks and the conclusions of other interviewers can substantiate or contradict your own findings. If other interviewers disagree with your conclusions, consult with them and review the data they collected. You may discover that you obtained different information.

▶ Determine areas in your own questioning that could be improved.

Use multiple interviewers

▼

When people need to hire for key roles, participate in the interviewing process. This will allow you to observe their skills.

Using multiple interviewers helps reduce individual biases and neutralize the impact of rating errors. It also makes more efficient use of interviewers' time and permits the collection of in-depth information. Consider the following suggestions to make the multiple-interviewer process more effective:

▶ Assign responsibility for coordinating the process to one individual. Typically, this is someone from the HR department.

▶ Give each interviewer a copy of the job description or a list of necessary knowledge, skills, abilities, and other qualifications.

▶ Assign each interviewer different dimensions of the job so that each can focus on a specific area. For example, one person could obtain information on technical skills, another could assess people skills, and a third could investigate project-management skills. Build in some overlap so there is more than one perspective on each skill area.

▶ Have each interviewer use a standard outline containing questions that focus on the candidate's past behavior and accomplishments in the area being evaluated. Also, decide which interviewer will tell the candidate about various aspects of the job and organization so interviewers don't repeat or contradict one another.

▶ After the interview, have each interviewer rate the candidate on the dimension he or she was assigned.

▶ Compare the independent ratings and look for a consensus. If there is a discrepancy among ratings or if a key position is being filled, have the interviewers get together to discuss the candidate and arrive at a consensus.

Increase your interviewing effectiveness

Interviewing is a skill that improves with practice. Consider the following suggestions to improve your interviewing effectiveness:

▶ Make sure the candidate does 80 percent of the talking.

▶ Learn to differentiate good information from "sizzle." Good information usually contains specific behaviors that the candidate has engaged in; sizzle sounds good but means little and falsely inflates your evaluation of a candidate.

Remind people to ask interview questions based on the types of challenges candidates may face in the new job.

▶ Be comfortable with silence after you have asked a question. This will allow the candidate to think and take initiative.

▶ Display energy and show enthusiasm for the job for which you are interviewing.

▶ Videotape yourself doing a practice interview. Watch the tape by yourself and later with others. Solicit feedback on how you can improve your skills.

- Avoid ineffective types of questions, such as:
  - ▷ *Questions that can be answered with yes or no.* These questions begin with *did, should, would, are, will.* Instead, use open-ended questions that start with *what, how, give me an example, describe.*
  - ▷ *Leading questions.* These questions tell candidates what they should have done and are prone to falsified responses. For example, "You must have had to put in a lot of extra hours to get everything done on time, huh?" is a leading question. To elicit a more meaningful response, change it to "What did you do to handle the situation?"
  - ▷ *Threatening questions.* These questions affix blame and imply that the candidate did the wrong thing. For example, "Why didn't you just put in some overtime?" may be perceived as threatening. Such questions are likely to put candidates on the defensive and may inhibit their responses during the rest of the interview.
  - ▷ *Questions about philosophies, beliefs, and opinions.* Candidates tend to respond to questions like "In your opinion, what qualities are essential to effective leadership?" with "canned" answers designed to tell you just what you want to hear. This information tends to be misleading and may confound your perception and rating of the candidate. Asking the candidates to describe their actions in leadership situations, on the other hand, will tell you more about them.
  - ▷ *Run-on and multiple-choice questions.* These questions tend to give the candidate hints about what to say, and they may be confusing.

Avoid common rating errors

It is human nature to commit the following rating errors in evaluating candidates. Developing awareness of common rating errors is the first step in avoiding them and will result in more accurate selection decisions on your part.

- *First-impression effect.* An interviewer evaluates the candidate during the first four minutes of the interview. The evaluation is based on first impressions (smile, eye contact, handshake) that are weighted too heavily and carry into the entire interview.

> ▸ *Contrast effect.* An interviewer who sees a very weak candidate first, may rate the second (average) candidate higher than is warranted due to the contrast between the first and second candidates.

Review the common rating errors and discuss examples.

> ▸ *Blind-spot effect.* An interviewer may not see certain types of deficits because they are just like his or her own. For example, an interviewer who prefers the big picture may not appreciate a detail-oriented person.

> ▸ *Halo effect.* An interviewer may see a candidate who is strong in one dimension as being strong in all dimensions.

> ▸ *High-potential effect.* An interviewer judges the candidate's credentials rather than his or her past performance, experience, and other behaviors.

> ▸ *Dramatic-incident effect.* An interviewer places too much emphasis on one specific behavior area. One problem may wipe out years of good work in the eyes of the interviewer.

Help new employees be successful

New employees' first few days and weeks are critical. This is the time when long-lasting impressions are made. How you treat people when they first join your group and how you help them be successful in their jobs are critical to their success and your success. Consider the following suggestions:

▸ Before a new employee arrives, involve team members in developing an effective orientation to the job and the team. It is critical that new people know what is expected in terms of both the job and being a member of the team. Determine the "survival information" people need to know about the job and about the team. For example:

  ▷ What are the work hours? When do people come in and when do they leave?

  ▷ What are expectations for team members? Do people typically work together or alone? Do people typically lunch together, separately, or at their desks?

  ▷ How do you know what to do? Is work assigned, does work come to you, or do you plan and organize it yourself?

▷ How are work emergencies handled? Does everyone pitch in?

▷ What information does a person need to have the first week, month, and quarter?

▸ Know what is covered in the organization's orientation program so that you do not repeat things that were already explained.

▸ Take responsibility for ensuring that new employees receive the orientation to their jobs, your department, and the organization. Decide which parts of the orientation you need to do and which parts would be appropriate to delegate to others.

▸ On the first day, introduce or reintroduce the new person to the rest of the team. When you make introductions, talk about how people will work with one another. That will help individuals get to know each other and help them understand who is involved in the work they do.

▸ Arrange for a new person to have lunch with you and others on the team on one of his or her first days.

▸ Talk with new people before and after work during their first several weeks. This will show your interest, make you available to answer questions, and give you opportunities to help out.

▸ Establish clear expectations. Talk with new people about what you expect and ask them what would be helpful to them.

▸ Let people know that it is okay to ask questions.

Ask people to develop onboarding plans for new team members. Ensure that they have included all of the necessary elements.

▸ Tell people how long it takes to learn the job. Some jobs with a long ramp-up time may discourage people unless they know what to expect.

▸ Assign an experienced person to be a "buddy" for a new person. Let the new person know that the experienced person is available to answer questions. This is a great development opportunity for the experienced person, too.

After a few weeks, ask whether the job is like or unlike what the person expected, and how.

▸ Provide a lot of feedback about performance. When people first begin a job they are typically very open to feedback, want to do the job well, and are looking for help. This is the time to talk about the "small things" you notice. Do not assume people will get better on their own. They may not know there is a problem with what they are doing. Unless you say something, they will not know what to change or how to do something differently.

▸ Talk with new people about their observations of the organization and the team. New people provide an opportunity to get feedback about work processes, the culture, how things are done, and so on.

▸ Notice the signals you are sending. Are you making yourself available? Are you interested in and open to others' ideas or do you say "We've tried that before"?

▸ Survey new employees to get suggestions for improving the organization's orientation program. Ask them what they think new people need in order to function comfortably and effectively.

▸ Ask new people to help you evaluate the effectiveness of your orientation program by providing feedback at designated points—two weeks, one month, two months—after they start working for you.

Apply knowledge of what motivates employees in order to retain key talent

▼

Managers need to have a basic understanding of motivation to be able to diagnose motivation in a work unit and make improvements. Review online studies of employee motivation factors. Consider the following suggestions:

▸ Managers cannot affect motivation without understanding people's needs and the importance of those needs. Talk to your employees to discover what motivates them. Ask questions such as:

▹ What do you enjoy most about your job? What do you enjoy least?

▹ What do you wish you could do more of?

▹ What have you done in the past year that you feel best about?

▹ What accomplishments are you most proud of?

▹ What would your ideal job be?

▸ Discuss your employees' goals—both short and long term. How do individuals think their goals might change? Find out how the importance of particular needs changes over time. For example, someone who is raising teenagers might now value staying in the same place until the teenagers are out of high school, but earlier might have valued travel in the job.

▶ Match roles and assignments with people's interests whenever possible.

Ask people about their direct reports' career goals and what motivates them. Discuss whether current retention efforts are working.

▶ Ensure that people have enough components of their jobs that they like. If this is not possible given the work that needs to be done, consider working toward other, more motivating roles for them.

▶ Use these assumptions about people to help you understand motivation:

▷ People want to do a good job. People feel good when they do well and feel bad or discouraged when they do not.

▷ People want control at work. People want to be able to make decisions and influence what happens. Leaders maximize motivation when they maximize the amount of control people have.

▷ People do not want to be held accountable for things that they believe are beyond their control. For example, you don't want others to give work direction to your employees and yet still hold you responsible for their accomplishments.

▷ People want their efforts to be respected and appreciated.

▶ To improve motivation, increase both people's perceptions and the reality that their actions make a difference. Give people the resources they need to align goals and do their jobs. In heavily matrixed organizations, training should be provided in influencing and effective team processing so that people believe they can work successfully in that environment.

▶ Convey trust that people can accomplish their work. When managers signal doubt that their people can make good decisions or can handle something, most people act less capably than before.

▶ Don't micromanage, even new people. Instead, train people, break work down into manageable steps that they can handle successfully, and establish checkpoints.

▶ If work needs to be improved, do not fix it yourself. It is discouraging for people to have someone redo something that is their responsibility. Instead, help them improve it.

▶ Let people make mistakes, and express confidence that they can improve.

▶ Observe people over time to understand what is important to them and what they view as rewarding. Some people like public recognition; others do not.

▶ Make work fun and enjoyable. Express enthusiasm for and interest in the assignments you give people. Show interest in what they are doing. Ask about projects and follow through on their ideas. In general, let people know they can count on you.

▶ Ask people which work unit goals they want to work on. Whenever possible, ask them to set their own goals and standards. Empowerment results in more accountability.

Develop successors and talent pools

▼

Having successors for key positions increases the health and viability of the organization and your work unit. You cannot guarantee that your key people will stay with the organization, and you never know what might happen to an individual. You may want a person to take on a different role, but your options will be limited if you have not prepared a successor for that person. When you do not prepare a successor for yourself, your own career may be more limited too. Many organizations now view the lack of preparation of a successor as a sign of poor leadership. Consider the following suggestions:

▶ Understand your talent pipeline. Who is available in your organization? Who do you have coming up? What are the constraints?

▶ Work with your leadership team and HR manager to identify the key roles in the work unit for which it is most critical to have successors. Also, identify the people you are likely to want to promote and those you believe are most likely to leave.

▶ Use a performance modeling process to determine the most important competencies for the organization or for a particular position or level. This process identifies how the roles and expectations in the organization are changing and the specific knowledge areas, skills, abilities, performance standards, and characteristics you need. Your HR group should be able to help you find performance models for key roles.

▶ Set up processes for assessing talent so that you know your bench strength and possible successors, and can begin the development process. Assess both performance and potential. Typically, you and people within the work unit can assess current performance as long as you have good performance data. Potential is more difficult. Use external or internal consultants who are knowledgeable about measures of potential.

▶ Evaluate potential successors against your performance model. Supplement your judgment with external assessments. This combination will help ensure a complete and correct assessment.

▶ Ensure that each potential successor has a development plan and opportunities to practice new skills, and is held accountable for developing.

Discuss succession planning efforts under way at the organization. Share your challenges and successes in carrying it out.

▶ Conduct regular talent reviews with your leadership team so that all of you know the talent in the organization, know what needs to be done to develop each person, and understand the priority of developing particular talent so you can meet business goals.

▶ Conduct bench strength reviews for key positions. Identify primary and secondary candidates for each key position and determine their readiness for the role.

▶ Help the organization distinguish clearly between succession planning and career planning. Organizations plan succession; individuals plan careers. Recognize the significance of each and use them as complementary tools to ensure your organization's success.

Build Talent

Address issues and concerns of the current and future workforce

▼

Successful managers know what's important to their people and keep an eye on emerging issues such as large numbers of people retiring, employees becoming responsible for elderly parents, and the need for flexibility. Employers are paying more attention to recognizing, respecting, and responding to their employees' interests and concerns. To address these issues, consider the following suggestions:

► Review your organization's flexibility in responding to workforce interests and concerns. Your workforce probably consists of many groups—including nontraditional workers, people in part-time roles, people with disabilities, retirees, and immigrants—whose interests and concerns vary. Be aware of issues such as:

  ▷ A desire for flexible schedules in addition to financial incentives.

  ▷ The need for meaningful work, even in part-time positions.

  ▷ Opportunities for sabbaticals.

  ▷ Health and wellness options.

  ▷ Time to attend to family issues, such as leave for childbirth, child-related emergencies, school-related activities, and elder care.

  ▷ Relocation concerns of dual-career families.

  ▷ Recognition and reward practices that can be tailored to individual preferences.

Discuss how issues—generational expectations, for example—affect your workforce.

► Determine how the organization needs to respond to a diverse employee base.

  ▷ Foster diversity in your workplace. Strive to have people from all geographic areas and cultures represented at all levels of the organization.

  ▷ Use communication techniques—important documents in multiple languages, pictures, diagrams—to assist people who are not fluent in the company's official language.

  ▷ Provide remedial education for people who do not have some of the necessary skills.

▷ Consider designing entry-level jobs and using technology so that a command of the company language is not critical. Use pictures and symbols.

▷ Establish rewards that are valued by different cultural groups and be flexible about holidays, time off, and leaves. For example, give people time off to celebrate their religious holidays.

▷ Create partnerships between managers and employees to discuss appropriate accommodations to their work and to resolve workplace issues.

▷ Create career-development programs to match people with jobs that fit their skills, wants, needs, and values.

▷ Support community education systems and increase training efforts in basic education.

Make placement and reward decisions based on people's capabilities and performance

▼

Decisions about hiring, placement, promotion, and rewards should be made with a clear understanding of the expectations of the role, the results needed, and the methods used to achieve the results. Leaders need to set clear expectations about how they will make decisions and consistently follow through on those processes. Consider the following suggestions:

▸ Use a performance modeling process to determine the most important competencies for a particular position or level. A performance modeling process should identify the business challenges for the role; the responsibilities, tasks, and business processes in the job; the competencies, abilities, and knowledge needed; and the level of performance expected in these areas. For example, a performance model would describe the current challenges for a customer service representative, the responsibilities of the job, the skills needed to perform in the job, the level of performance needed in dealing with customers, and the capabilities needed to work on a customer service team.

▶ Determine criteria for hiring. Typically these include skills and comparable experience, interest, level of competence, and match with the culture.

▶ Carefully evaluate potential candidates against your performance model. Determine the measures that will be used to evaluate candidates, such as track records, testing, experience, indicators of potential, customer feedback, and references. Decide what level of competence is needed in each key area.

▶ Supplement internal judgments with external, objective assessments for key jobs. A combination of internal and external expertise will help ensure a thorough and accurate assessment.

As you review how people reward and promote others, ask about their view of performance and how they assess others' potential.

▶ Draft a performance plan with current employees at the beginning of the year that identifies the work unit goals that each person is responsible for. Set tangible measures of results. For example, if the person is expected to be responsive to internal customers, determine indicators for this. For maximum buy-in, ask employees to take the lead in developing plans and goals. Reserve the right to modify the goals if you believe there is not enough stretch.

▶ Provide ongoing feedback: Ask people to take the lead in reviewing their progress each month, identifying what they plan to do next or differently, and critiquing what they have done. This enables them to learn and develop. It also usually results in less defensive behavior.

▶ Create transparent data collection systems so that people know what data are being collected about their performance, can have input into the data that are collected, and are able to give their interpretation of the data.

▶ Work with the HR and finance groups to develop rewards for a job well done. Ensure that people know about rewards and incentives ahead of time. Involve employee task forces in providing feedback on rewards and incentive systems that are relevant to them.

▶ Before you implement a new incentive system, create a model or anticipate unintended consequences. New systems always have unanticipated effects.

Shape roles and assignments in ways that leverage and develop people's capabilities

▼

Make sure people clearly explain to their employees the development reasoning behind their decision to assign a project.

Many experts agree that the most powerful development happens on the job. As a leader, you can develop people both by being creative about the assignments you give them and by shaping their roles. Consider the following suggestions:

▸ Use job assignments and projects to help people develop or use new skills.

▸ Work with your employees to craft development plans in which their goals match the current and future needs of the organization.

▸ Determine the basic requirements for each role in the work unit; these are the capabilities that a candidate must have in order to take on the role. Next, identify the requirements that can be developed on the job. Place people in jobs in which there is a match for at least the basic requirements.

▸ When you place people in roles in which they do not have some of the capabilities they need, develop a plan with them to develop the skills. Ensure that they understand that this capability increase is necessary for the performance of the job, and is not just "nice to have."

▸ Provide the support people need to be successful. Regularly talk with them about how their work is going, what help they need, and what they are learning.

▸ Give employees temporary lateral assignments that will help them see the business from other perspectives or give them opportunities to develop new skills.

▸ Rotate responsibilities among team members to broaden each person's experience.

Onboard employees to new roles

▼

Whenever a person takes on a new role, he or she will be able to perform in the role faster when you do "onboarding." Onboarding is a process through which a person begins a new role and joins a group. Even if a person is already part of the group, it is still important for you to onboard that person in the new role. Consider the following suggestions:

▸ Review job expectations with the person.

▸ Discuss with whom the person needs to have relationships in order to do the job well. Help the person develop the relationships. Provide introductions, tell people about the new person and his or her capabilities, provide linkages to people, and lend your credibility to help the person be seen in high regard by others.

Discuss elements of onboarding that go beyond responsibilities, such as determining who should be in a person's internal and external network.

▸ Tell people why you hired this person so they understand what you see in the person and become acquainted with his or her strengths.

▸ Ask the person to talk with team members and people in the business process about their view of the role and their expectations. For example, a new market researcher should talk with people in the marketing function and in other functions that use market research to learn what is going well, how they believe the process could be improved, and their expectations for the person in the role.

▸ After the person knows your expectations, has talked with internal and external customers, and develops a picture of how he or she intends to do the job, ask the person to meet with others to talk about his or her vision for the role and what can be expected from him or her.

▸ Suggest that the person talk with others to hear concerns and answer questions. This may seem scary, but it is the most effective way to find out if the person is carrying baggage from other roles. For example, the person may have been in a role in which there was little room for creativity. In the new position, the team members want someone who will do things differently. They might be concerned because they did not see evidence of creativity in the person's previous role.

▸ Establish a support network. Introduce employees who are new to their role to more experienced people who can provide support and assistance at times you are not available. Inform experienced employees of their responsibilities in this area.

Use performance management to improve performance and develop employees

Although performance management is sometimes seen as an ineffective administrative exercise, successful managers use it to set goals and clarify expectations, improve performance, and develop employees. Consider the following suggestions:

▶ Work with employees to set goals that flow directly from the goals of the work unit. Set specific expectations for both the *what* and the *how* of the job. For example, stating that you want "communication skills" is not specific enough; stating that changes should be communicated to customers within eight hours is a clear standard. Also include goals for development.

▶ Ask that your direct reports set their own goals. Coach them so that the goals are appropriate.

▶ Talk with your employees regularly about performance and progress on developmental objectives. Provide ongoing feedback and coaching. Ask them to take the lead in both setting goals and the review process. This will create more buy-in of the goals and the process.

▶ Treat developmental objectives as seriously as results objectives. Ensure that development goals are focused on areas that are important to current or future performance.

▶ Ask people what you can do to help them. Follow through on agreements to provide help.

Have frequent discussions with people about their performance and the performance of their direct reports. Catch people doing things well.

▶ In conversations about the results of an assessment or performance review, talk about the person's goals and the requirements of the job *before* you talk about the person's perception of his or her capabilities and others' perceptions of the person's capabilities. This allows the assessment to be based on what is needed, not on arbitrary opinions.

▶ Evaluate performance with internal and external customers. Seek feedback from customers using structured interview processes, surveys, customer comment lines, and so on.

Use evaluation processes conducted by others when you need an objective viewpoint and when others have a better vantage point or different point of view than you do. When you want to look at a person's potential, consider using outside assessment processes. Managers are best at evaluating current performance, not potential.

- ▶ Choose an assessment process based on several criteria, including how you're going to use the data, the importance of objectivity, and the degree to which people can evaluate particular attributes, competencies, knowledge, or cultural fit.

- ▶ Assess results, capabilities, and process measures. Use the following guidelines:

  - ▷ *Manager appraisal* is useful when you want a quick assessment, you believe you have the most accurate view of the person's strengths and needs, and you have a clear understanding of current and future requirements.

  - ▷ *Self-assessment* is important for identifying people's preset view of themselves. People usually are willing to work on needs that they have personally identified. However, self-perceptions can be inaccurate. Self-assessment does not work well when future needs are substantially different from current requirements.

  - ▷ *Multirater feedback or 360-degree feedback* is most useful when the perceptions of others are needed—for example, when other people are more familiar with the person than the manager is. Multirater feedback is helpful for development but does not provide accurate comparative data unless it is specifically created to distinguish between people.

  - ▷ *Collaborative assessment,* in which both the manager and the direct report rate competency on a set of skills, is an effective way to combine the judgments of the manager and the individual. It is less effective if either party does not have an accurate understanding of the competencies needed.

  - ▷ *Objective assessment* from an external source is valuable when the competencies are new, they are not easily measured by observation alone, a measure of potential is needed, or you need and want an outside perspective. For example, if ratings on your performance management system do not differentiate people, question whether internal ratings alone are an effective assessment of capabilities.

Ensure that effective processes are in place to evaluate people's capabilities

▼

As a manager, you need to know your employees' capabilities, readiness for new roles, and potential for growth. Effective and fair measurement of capabilities is needed. Consider the following suggestions:

- Understand what you want to know about capabilities:
  - ▷ How much *potential* does a person have? How much responsibility and complexity can he or she manage?
  - ▷ Is a person *ready* for a particular job? Does he or she have the knowledge, skills, and abilities to do the job?
  - ▷ Is the person a good *fit* for the role?

Ensure that people are determining their direct reports' potential for growth.

- Once you know what you need to measure, ensure that you use accurate methods:
  - ▷ *Measures of current performance* tell you whether a person is likely to be successful in a similar role.
  - ▷ *Performance data* give you some information about performance in a new and different role, but not enough. Use an objective assessment that measures necessary future competencies.
  - ▷ *Potential* is best measured through testing. Talk with your HR department about resources for testing.

Identify required capabilities and skill gaps within own organizational area

▼

As a leader, you need to have the right people in the right place at the right time. It's important to know the gaps between the capabilities you need for the work unit's current roles and what you will need in the future. Additionally, you need to develop a plan to fill these gaps, either through development of your current employees or by hiring people with the necessary capabilities. Consider the following suggestions:

- Examine the roles or jobs needed to accomplish the work of the group and the capabilities that people in those roles need. Identify specific critical behaviors that make a significant difference between adequate and excellent performance.

Ask people to identify the gaps between the current capabilities of those in key roles and the needed capabilities.

▸ Identify the differences between people in the role who perform well and those who do not. Talk with people, observe people in action, or use action-learning teams of high-potential employees to determine these differentiators.

▸ Ensure that you have the necessary bench strength for key roles. Typically, you should have at least two back-ups for roles that are pivotal to success.

▸ Decide how you will fill critical talent gaps. There are two primary methods to close a talent gap: either hire people with the necessary capabilities and experience, or develop current talent.

Provide feedback, coaching, and guidance

▼

Development is a partnership between the employee, his or her manager, and the organization. Managers play a key role by equipping people with the tools, knowledge, and opportunities they need to develop themselves. Consider the following suggestions:

▸ Find out what is important to people. Ask about their goals, what motivates them, what interests them about their jobs, what they have done that makes them proud. This information will help you understand them better.

▸ Provide opportunities for people to assess their capabilities relative to the needs of the organization and relative to their own goals and priorities. People will find it helpful to compare their own assessment, your point of view, and the point of view of coworkers. Help people understand any differences in perceptions.

▸ Help employees put together development plans that align their goals and interests with those of the organization. Focus on what they need to develop for success in their current jobs first, then for future jobs.

▸ Provide feedback, both positive and critical. Remember that feedback is information and it is a dialogue. The purpose is to be helpful, not to vent frustration or anger.

▸ When you provide feedback, first discuss the other person's intentions and view of the situation. What had the person intended or planned?

How did it work? Would the person do the same thing next time? Let the person provide his or her own feedback whenever possible. It is far better that the person recognize what went well and what should change than for you to tell him or her.

▶ Find out what people learned from feedback experiences. Ask questions like these: What did you learn from this? What had an impact on you? What was the most valuable insight?

Frequently ask people what they have learned from a particular situation or experience. Ensure that they ask the same question of their direct reports.

▶ Help people solve problems and learn by asking questions. People learn more through self-discovery than by simply being told something.

▶ Help people learn skills they can use to develop themselves: getting and using feedback; finding role models, peer coaches, and mentors; learning from experience; finding effective training programs; using online development resources.

▶ Be a role model for development. Pursuing your own development tells others that you value development. Ask others to help you by providing feedback, giving you information and ideas, and noticing whether you are changing.

Ensure that people are learning from customers, contractors, and other external sources

People who pay attention have hundreds of opportunities to learn each year. Your customers may excel at improving business processes and anticipating their own customer needs; your suppliers may be skilled in just-in-time inventory. Encourage people to take advantage of all their opportunities to learn from external sources. Consider the following suggestions:

▶ Set the expectation that you want people to look for opportunities to learn, to take opportunities to learn from others, and to share their learning with others. Model this behavior by talking about what you have learned from others.

▶ To support and reinforce these expectations, regularly check to see what people have learned from others. Reinforce the idea of looking for opportunities to learn by asking what a customer organization is good at and what your organization can learn from it.

Pay attention to awards or recognition received by your customers, suppliers, or other external partners. For example, a customer may have been recognized as "Best Place to Work," or a contact may be teaching a continuing education course in supply chain management. These are clues about what you can learn from them.

Ask people what they have learned from customers and vendors in the past six months.

▸ Emphasize the importance of sharing what you learn. People waste time reinventing things. For example, one group may develop an effective planning process with a customer. Make sure this learning is shared with others.

▸ Recognize signals that you have problems. Stories about one salesperson not knowing that another salesperson called on the same customer are not funny. Your competitors are figuring out how to avoid these mistakes.

▸ Note barriers to sharing learning across boundaries. For example, businesses within an organization sometimes spend more time and energy competing against each other than against external competitors. Stop this wasteful competition. Ensure that you focus on external competition. Remove the barriers to sharing.

▸ Encourage people to build relationships with others in the organization from whom they can learn. Then support their efforts: ask what they are learning, how they are applying that learning, and what difference it has made.

Promote sharing of expertise and a free flow of learning across the organization

▼

Imagine that the people in your group learned an invaluable lesson that saved them thousands of dollars, and that lesson was applicable to every group in the organization. Now imagine that no one else in the organization had an opportunity to hear it. What a waste! Organizational silos typically block or hamper people's ability to work together, share information and knowledge, share learning, and use resources of all kinds. This leads to redundancies, inefficiencies, and ineffective use of resources. Consider the following suggestions:

- Set the expectation that you want your people to:
  - ▷ Know people in other parts of the organization.
  - ▷ Know what is going on in other parts of the business.
  - ▷ Share learning with others.
  - ▷ Check to see what is already known at the beginning of a project.
  - ▷ Identify people who might be interested in project results or learning.

- To support and reinforce these expectations, ask what people are learning. This will emphasize that you want people to pay attention to what others are doing and to learn from them. Ask questions such as:
  - ▷ Who has done something like this before?
  - ▷ What can we learn from group X about this?
  - ▷ What have people tried in the past?
  - ▷ What did you learn when you talked with X?

Discuss specific ways that the person can promote knowledge sharing and build it into project plans.

- Build awareness in your team of the importance of capturing and sharing knowledge across the organization. Share stories of past successes. Talk with your team about successes in other parts of the organization.

- Put "checking with others" into the process for doing things in the organization. For example, the first step of a new initiative could be finding out what other people in the organization are doing about the issue.

- Institute debriefing sessions on projects to share learning within the group. Invite others who would benefit.

- Ensure that people who work with the same customer exchange information and learning. Customers are not impressed when they have to tell several people the same thing.

- Identify barriers to sharing across boundaries. Learn whether people compete against each other instead of against external competitors, and why. Work with your peers to focus your groups on more productive targets.

- Make sure you lead by example and willingly share your expertise and experiences with people.

Hold others accountable for developing their people

▼

Since development is such an important part of a manager's job, hold *your* employees accountable for developing *their* direct reports. If individuals sense that it doesn't matter whether or not someone changes, it is less likely that the person will change. Consider the following suggestions:

▶ Set the expectation that managers will hold their employees accountable for developing knowledge and skills. Talk about your expectation, establish processes to ensure that they check on their employees' progress, link development to increased performance, and talk about people who have developed their employees.

Each quarter, have people give an update on their direct reports' development progress.

▶ Request that all employees have development plans based on the current needs of the work unit, their own skills, their future goals and needs, and the future goals and needs of the organization. Use a framework for the plans that mirrors project plans, so that people view their development as they would a work project.

▶ When you create project or business plans, look at the skills and behaviors necessary for the plan to work. Investigate whether team members have the knowledge and skills to execute the plan. If they do not, plan how to develop the necessary knowledge or skills. This approach communicates the importance of development in achieving business results.

▶ Ask about progress reviews when you meet with people. You will find that people pay more attention to development when you pay attention to what they are doing for themselves and with their direct reports.

▶ Provide development resources so that people have access to ideas about how to do things more effectively. Look for books, e-courses, seminars, workshops, webinars, teleseminars, and podcasts that have just-in-time learning components.

▶ Sponsor training programs for managers and employees on current learning, development, and coaching strategies. Do not assume that people know the most effective ways to learn.

▶ Model what you want people to do. Develop your own learning plan, let people know you are working on development needs, ask for feedback, and share what you have learned.

17

Coach and Develop Others

Studies show that the best development results are achieved when a manager or coach is actively involved in the process. As a manager, you have the ability to develop your coaching skills to help your people achieve their development goals. As you take a personal interest in their development, you'll build a relationship of trust, and foster an environment of continual learning.

Most people do not get excited about development unless they understand its importance to their own career goals. When you tie people's individual development to organizational objectives, it creates a win-win situation. Coaching others hinges on trust and requires the ability to give and receive feedback that highlights strengths, potential, expertise, and experiences. Create a strong coaching approach and you'll help people become their best.

In this chapter, we will cover the following areas:

▼

- ▶ Adopt a systematic approach to coaching
- ▶ Assess your coaching skills and style
- ▶ Know what it takes for development to occur
- ▶ Build trusting coaching relationships
- ▶ Avoid common coaching mistakes
- ▶ Understand what's important to people
- ▶ Get people excited about development
- ▶ Accurately identify strengths and development needs
- ▶ Help people assess their skills
- ▶ Help people identify development objectives
- ▶ Use "GAPS" to identify top-priority objectives
- ▶ Help people create effective development plans
- ▶ Create coaching plans
- ▶ Handle underperformance in productive ways
- ▶ Teach people an effective development process
- ▶ Increase people's development skills
- ▶ Create an effective learning environment
- ▶ Be a strong role model for development
- ▶ Tailor coaching to each individual
- ▶ Coach people in different geographic areas
- ▶ Coach people who are different from you
- ▶ Give clear, motivating, and constructive feedback
- ▶ Equip people to get useful feedback
- ▶ Use 360-degree or multirater feedback tools

- ▸ Provide challenging assignments to facilitate individual development
- ▸ Show interest in people's careers
- ▸ Help people stay with development
- ▸ Address performance issues
- ▸ Help people learn from experience and developmental experiences
- ▸ Recommend training programs, readings, and other resources
- ▸ Help team members help each other with development
- ▸ Reinforce the learning process in your area

Adopt a systematic approach to coaching

▼

Discuss the benefits of using a coaching framework, especially for a person who is new to coaching.

While there are many techniques and tools for coaching, it is useful to have an overall approach that unifies what you are doing. PDI's *Leader As Coach* strategies can help:

▸ *Forge a partnership:* Build trust and understanding. Trust allows people to know that you are interested in them. Understanding enables you to be most helpful.

▸ *Inspire commitment:* Build insight and motivation so that people are committed to change and focus their energy on goals that matter to them and to the organization.

▸ *Grow skills:* Help identify effective ways to learn new knowledge and to grow and develop skills and capabilities.

▸ *Promote persistence:* Support people in their development even when they get discouraged or diverted.

▸ *Shape the environment:* Build organizational support to reward learning and remove barriers.

Assess your coaching skills and style

▼

	You:	5	4	3	2	1
Forge a partnership	Show you are interested in the person. Listen more than you talk. Approach resistance and reluctance to change with curiosity. Ask for feedback on how you can strengthen your coaching relationships with others.					
Inspire Commitment	Have an understanding of the goals and values of the people you coach. Share information regarding expectations and success factors for the person's current and future responsibilities. Have an understanding of how the people you coach view their performance and capabilities. Help people understand others' perceptions of their capabilities. Help people identify development goals that are aligned with their personal priorities and the needs of the organization. Help people put together a solid plan for their growth and development.					
Grow Skills	Create a safe and effective learning environment. Help people find the best methods to learn new skills. Help people find readings, training programs, mentors, and other resources. Encourage people to take risks and learn from their mistakes. Help people learn the right lessons from their experiences.					
Promote Persistence	Help people find assignments and other opportunities to practice their skills. Help people to identify daily reminders to stay with their development. Take advantage of "coachable moments" (e.g., times when people experience success, disappointment, or are trying a skill for the first time). Help people stay energized by revisiting their goals and recharging their development efforts. Regularly discuss feedback that is relevant to people's goals.					
Shape the Environment	Know your own strengths and limitations. Act as a role model by sharing your development objectives, seeking feedback, and sharing what you have learned. Show your team that you value development through the rewards and opportunities that you directly influence. Work to align organizational policies and processes with coaching and development.					

5 = Almost always   **4** = To a great extent   **3** = To some extent   **2** = To a little extent   **1** = Not at all

Know what it takes for development to occur

Development is change. We know from field research that people will not change unless certain conditions exist. The necessary and sufficient conditions for development are illustrated in the PDI Development Pipeline®.

The PDI Development Pipeline®

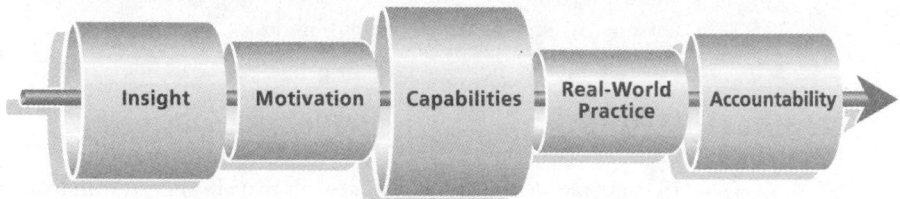

Insight	Do you know what to develop?
Motivation	Are you willing to invest the time and energy it takes to develop yourself?
Capabilities	Do you know how to acquire the skills and knowledge you need?
Real-World Practice	Do you have opportunities to try your new skills at work?
Accountability	Do you internalize your new capabilities to actually improve performance and results?

Discuss the PDI Development Pipeline® and how people can use it with their employees.

In order for people to change, they need to know what is expected and how they match up against expectations. They also must want to change, have access to methods to gain knowledge and develop their skills, and have opportunities to practice their new skills. Finally, they need to be accountable for their development. If these conditions exist, people will develop.

▸ Use the pipeline to figure out where you and your employees are constrained in the development process.

▹ Ask people what they believe they need to develop.

▷ Ask them what motivates them to change their behavior. When you're looking at a development plan, ask what difference it will make to business results if they change a behavior.

▷ Find out if people believe they have access to knowledge, skills, role models, and best practices to help them develop.

▷ Ask whether people see opportunities to practice new behaviors.

▷ Ask what difference it will make to people if they develop new skills. Also find out what difference they believe it will make to you if they address an issue.

▶ Focus time and resources on areas of constraint. Many organizations and people continue to build their course catalogs or implement action learning when the constraint to development is actually accountability or motivation.

▶ Ask yourself what difference it makes whether people develop particular skills.

Build trusting coaching relationships

▼

Ask people what they see as their coaching strengths, how they want to improve, and how they plan to increase their skills.

Trust is the foundation of any effective coaching relationship. In fact, trust (or lack thereof) typically makes or breaks a coaching relationship. Consider the following suggestions to get your coaching relationships started on the right foot:

▶ Demonstrate that you have people's best interests in mind by genuinely promoting a win-win approach, showing compassion, and listening intently to their needs and concerns.

▶ Show consistency between your words and your actions by making realistic commitments and demonstrating follow-through. Do not overpromise. If you state that a change is important, then follow through to see how the person has changed.

▶ Be predictable by letting people know what to expect from you.

▶ Let people know how you are trying to balance individual and organizational interests.

▶ Explain changes and apparent discrepancies in your actions.

▸ Be aware of your own capabilities so that you will know what you can do for the person you are coaching, and when you need to tap the expertise of others.

▸ Be willing to admit when you have made a mistake.

Avoid common coaching mistakes

▼

Coaches, even those with the best intentions, consistently make common mistakes. Being aware of these mistakes will help you catch yourself before you make them and give you a chance to redirect your efforts.

▸ *Explaining or talking instead of listening.* Set your mind on exploring, not fixing. Let go of your desire to help, motivate, or change people, and instead try to understand them. Assume that no two people are exactly alike in their values, goals, motives, and experiences.

Demonstrate that coaching does not need to take large amounts of time by using "coachable moments" yourself.

▸ *Advising before understanding.* Suspend your agenda. Focus on listening and concentrate on learning more about people's goals and what matters to them.

▸ *Problem solving.* Help people solve their own problems instead of solving them yourself. It's like the saying about a fish and fishing: it's more powerful to teach people something than to give them something.

▸ *Repeating your views when you meet resistance.* Seek to see the world through the eyes of the people you are coaching. Ask questions to help them clarify their own thinking. For your coaching to have an impact, people need to believe that you understand them.

Understand what's important to people

▼

A good coach listens to people and finds out what is important to them. Unless you understand them, it is difficult for people to believe that you care about their interests—and it is unlikely that you will be able to tap into what motivates them to change. Find out by asking questions:

▸ What excites them about their work?

▸ What do they find most meaningful and rewarding?

▶ Where do you see their greatest energy and enthusiasm?

▶ What are their goals and why?

Remind people to keep a running list of what is most important to their direct reports.

▶ How do they view themselves?

▶ How do they appraise their skills and abilities?

▶ Do they have a tendency to either inflate or undervalue their abilities?

▶ What are their current challenges?

▶ What do they believe about their ability to develop?

▶ Are they confident they can change?

▶ Are they willing to take risks to change?

▶ Do they think their development will make a difference?

Get people excited about development

How many times have you seen individuals do nothing about development objectives they have set? The reason is simple: people do not get excited about development unless it is important to them. That is why you need to understand people's motivation. Consider the following suggestions:

▶ In addition to *asking* people what motivates them, *observe* what motivates them. Observe which activities they spend their time on.

▶ Notice when people are energized about their work. When people talk about things they care about, they become animated.

Share one of your development goals, why you're excited about it, and how you're pursuing it.

▶ Talk about how an action will help people obtain something that is important to them. For example, when you're giving an assignment, talk about how the assignment will enable them to meet a person they want to know.

▶ Focus development efforts on areas that will help people do something that is important to them. If you expect people to change simply to meet an organizational need, you will be disappointed.

▸ Get excited about your own development. Excitement is contagious. For example, tell people about development events in which you learned useful information or gained new insights or perspectives. Let them share in your excitement of learning something new.

Accurately identify strengths and development needs

▼

Effective leaders know their team members and what they can do. Accurately identifying strengths and development needs is far more than being able to get a good read on people. Effective managers understand the skills and capabilities for the jobs in their areas and assess people in relation to these needs. Consider the following suggestions:

▸ Identify what you believe to be the strengths and development needs of people in your area. Then use an objective assessment to check the accuracy of your understanding. A good assessment process will give you reliable information about people's fit in their current roles, potential for future roles, and readiness for future roles. Make note of where your perceptions were not aligned with the assessment results.

▸ If you do not want to use objective assessment, consider using perceptual assessment with a 360-degree instrument that provides perceptions from the boss, the self, and two or more other perspectives. While a 360-degree instrument does not provide objective data, it tells you whether your view of a person is the same as or different from others'.

Delve into the situation in which the skill will be used. Discuss how a strength in one situation could be a liability in another.

▸ Remember that strengths and development needs are relative. The same level of skill might be a strength in one role and not high enough for another role.

▸ Serve as a coach in an assessment center conducted by a consulting firm that trains managers to use professional assessment technology. Many high-level leaders have found that participating as an assessor and coach in an assessment center has done more for their understanding of what excellence is than anything else they have done.

Help people assess their skills

▼

Many people are successful but have no idea why. It is not false modesty; they really do not know. Unconscious competence is common, but it's a limitation. When people know what they do and how they do it, it makes them much more competent, flexible, and able to learn quickly. This is called conscious competence.

Help people understand their strengths and development needs by providing opportunities for them to assess themselves and others.

Encourage people to give their direct reports opportunities for multirater feedback experiences.

▶ Ask people to assess themselves for their performance review discussion and for a monthly follow-up. Ask them to lead this discussion so that they can practice doing the assessment and plan for next steps.

▶ Use 360-degree feedback instruments so people can assess themselves and learn how others view them.

▶ Ask people to determine the level of skill for a new role in the group. Then discuss their perceptions.

▶ Decide on common performance standards so everyone knows what is expected. Ask people to develop performance standards for some of their responsibilities. Talk with people in HR to get help from experts; it is not as simple as it looks.

Help people identify development objectives

▼

A GAPS grid can help people identify development needs that are important to them and relevant to the organization. The grid allows you to collect information about four key areas and use it to focus development discussions.

Complete a GAPS grid with people to give them firsthand experience in using the tool.

▶ To learn more about people's goals and values, find out what matters to them. *Goals and values* are the internal motives and values that drive behavior. Possible questions to ask are:

▷ What do you value and care about most?

▷ What is important to you in your work and your career?

▷ What are your career interests and aspirations?

▷ What gives you the greatest sense of satisfaction and reward?

▷ What gives you the least amount of satisfaction? Why?

- Ask people to describe their abilities. *Abilities* include their view of their capabilities and performance, especially in relation to what is required of them and what they want to do. Possible questions to ask are:
  - ▷ How do you view your performance and capabilities?
  - ▷ What skills are your strengths? In what areas are you most likely to offer your expertise to others?
  - ▷ Where do you need to improve? In what areas do you turn to others for assistance?

- Ask people how others perceive them. *Perceptions* include how others view people's capabilities and performance, including interpretations and assumptions about what they observe. Information you might share (and encourage a person to gather):
  - ▷ Personal observations.
  - ▷ Feedback from others about the person's capabilities.
  - ▷ The person's reputation among people at different levels in the organization.
  - ▷ How the person performs in areas critical to success in current and future roles.

- Share your expectations and the organization's standards or expectations for current and future roles. *Success factors* comprise the expectations regarding performance and behavior relative to current and future roles and responsibilities, organizational and team objectives, and market and business challenges. Information you might share (and encourage a person to gather):
  - ▷ Clear expectations of performance for the person's current and possible future roles, including skill requirements, required experiences, and additional educational needs.
  - ▷ The mission and strategic plans of your organization.
  - ▷ Pressing issues and goals that face your organization, including internal and external perspectives about industry trends and competition.
  - ▷ Capabilities in greatest demand in your organization, and which of them are expected of this person, now and in the future.

GAPS Grid: Critical Information for Development

Where the Person Is	Where the Person Is Going	
Abilities: *How the person sees him- or herself*	**Goals & Values:** *What matters to the person*	**The Person's View**
Perceptions: *How others see the person*	**Success Factors:** *What matters to others*	**Others' Views**

Use "GAPS" to identify top-priority objectives

▼

People make development a priority when it is linked to their goals and existing motivations. When people recognize gaps between their GAPS (*Goals, Abilities, Perceptions,* and *Success factors*), they are usually energized to do something to resolve the differences.

▸ Once a person's GAPS have been identified, jointly work through the following process to identify the one or two most critical development objectives:

1. Identify the person's top personal priorities. People cannot work on everything at once, so ask them what matters most to them at work, considering both short-term and long-term objectives.

Ensure that people are working with direct reports to create development goals that are consistent with organizational priorities.

2. Match priorities with organizational incentives. Consider aspects of the person's performance that are most important to the organization now and in the future.

3. Look for alignment between personal priorities and organizational interests. Consider creative ways for both the person and the organization to get what they want. Mutual commitment is achieved when people's goals and organizational standards are aligned.

4. Maximize return on investment (ROI) by choosing development objectives that will yield the greatest payback for a given amount of effort.

5. Pick one or two development goals that make the most sense to begin working on now.

▸ Because GAPS change over time, revisit this process periodically.

Help people create effective development plans

▾

One of the best ways to plan for development is to base action steps on how people really develop, as described in *Development FIRST: Strategies for Self-Development* (Personnel Decisions International, 1995). The strategies outlined in this book add up to a self-development process that works:

▸ Talk about the benefit of using an effective process for development. Ask for an example of the last time people developed a new skill. Some people will readily give you an example, while others will struggle to think of something. Ask about the process they went through to develop the skill.

▸ Relate an individual's development process to the Development FIRST® model, which outlines the following strategies:

Focus on priorities: Identify critical issues and goals.

Implement something every day: Stretch your comfort zone.

Reflect on what happens: Extract maximum learning from your experiences.

Seek feedback and support: Learn from other people's ideas and perspectives.

Transfer learning to next steps: Adapt and plan for continued learning.

▸ Ask your people to create a plan to develop a skill or behavior. Sample forms, including a development plan and a learning plan, can be found in the appendix of this handbook.

Review employee development plans to ensure that they are useful, meaningful, and based on solid development best practices. Check for the following components:

▸ *A limited number of development priorities.* For best results, people should not tackle more than one or two objectives at a time.

▶ *Opportunities to incorporate daily action.* Successful development is evolutionary, not revolutionary. Smaller daily activities will yield better results than one big burst of activity. An effective development plan specifies situations, time, and people that will trigger development action.

▶ *Focus on job development activities.* Training and development programs are useful, but people also need on-the-job practice.

Have people give you a high-level overview of their group's development goals and plans. Discuss patterns and potential adjustments.

▶ *How and when the person plans to reflect on new learning.* Research shows that it is not enough to practice new skills: people need time to think about what they have learned. They need to talk about, write down, and think about what they did, what happened, and what they learned.

▶ *Ways to get ongoing feedback and to track and sustain progress.* People need to get accurate, current information on progress to persist toward their goals. An effective plan identifies:

  ▷ Sources and processes for getting relevant feedback.

  ▷ People who can provide encouragement and support.

  ▷ How the person will measure progress toward his or her goals.

▶ *When and how people will review their plans and transfer them into next steps.* Plans often need to be adapted as circumstances change and people get more skilled.

Create coaching plans

▼

Research shows that development planning is more successful when the person's manager or coach is involved. A coaching plan provides a vehicle for organizing what you need to do to help your people. The coaching and development processes work together. Just as your employees need to know when and how they can rely on you for guidance, you need to understand the specifics of their development plans. A dialogue enables the two of you to finalize your learning and coaching plans. You can find a coaching plan template in the appendix of this handbook. Consider the following suggestions for creating a coaching plan:

- Once a person's learning objective has been determined, decide how you need to be involved in the developmental process. You might be involved in the following ways:
  - ▷ Identify role models or be a role model.
  - ▷ Observe the person.
  - ▷ Debrief about the person's activities and learnings.
  - ▷ Link the person with someone else in the organization for assistance.
  - ▷ Approve attendance at a development program.
  - ▷ Provide feedback.
  - ▷ Arrange for an assignment.
  - ▷ Provide ideas for options.

Explore different types of coaching plans and discuss what would work best for this person.

- Investigate what learning style works best for the person. Does he or she learn best by seeing something done, by doing, or by listening or reading?

- Determine your strategies for working one-on-one with the person, orchestrating resources and learning opportunities, and enhancing self-reliance.

- Suggest reading, training programs, and online resources to supplement the person's development. Also think of ways you can help him or her apply learning to the job.

- Find ways to help the person overcome typical obstacles he or she is likely to encounter during the development process.

Handle underperformance in productive ways

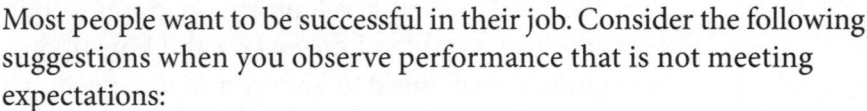

Most people want to be successful in their job. Consider the following suggestions when you observe performance that is not meeting expectations:

- Make sure you and the individual have the same goals and expectations. Mutual understanding of performance objectives and expectations is a critical, integral aspect of performance management. In fact, effective performance is defined through this mutual understanding.

▷ Schedule a conversation with the person. Choose a time when you will not be rushed.

▷ Begin by ensuring that you have an up-to-date mutual understanding of specific performance objectives and expectations.

– Find out what the person is trying to do and how he or she views the performance.

– Share your expectations and perceptions.

▷ Listen thoughtfully to the person's view of the situation. Paraphrase what you heard to ensure that you understand it.

▷ Discuss discrepancies. Seek to understand underlying reasons for them.

▷ Analyze external factors—systemic problems, lack of resources— that influence the person's performance.

– If ineffective performance is a function of poor communication, you should clarify goals, objectives, and expectations. Be specific about instances in which expectations were not met.

– If ineffective performance is due to misaligned goals, listen to the person's ideas and perspectives. Determine if there is a way to realign his or her goals.

– If ineffective performance is due to lack of skill, knowledge, or experience, provide coaching and development opportunities. Give more direction when the person is working in areas in which his or her experience is limited.

– If organizational rewards or goal-setting policies are contributing to ineffective performance, identify areas in which competing objectives encourage good performance in one area and poor performance in another.

– If the person believes he or she cannot be successful because of factors beyond his or her control, figure out what can be done to remove the obstacles. For example, the person may need to ask others for help, or you may need to solicit ideas from a peer in another function.

▷ Once you have a shared understanding of the situation, solicit from the person ideas and solutions for closing the gap between

Encourage people to talk to their direct reports about what they perceive to be barriers to optimal performance.

expectations and results. Agree on steps to be taken and a time frame for each step.

▷ Keep the conversation focused on the future rather than the past.

▸ Follow up on the person's performance. Be sure to recognize and reinforce any improvements in behavior—especially in the beginning—until the new behaviors are incorporated into his or her routine.

Teach people an effective development process

▾

You can help people learn by helping them set up a process. While learning is natural, it can be made much more effective and efficient by applying Development FIRST® strategies:

▸ *Focus* on only one or two learning priorities at a time. For example, narrow a learning objective from "increase listening skills" to "ask open-ended questions." Have the person work on this behavior until it becomes routine and then move on to the next listening behavior. While this may sound simplistic, it is much more effective than trying to learn five or six behaviors at a time.

▸ *Implement* something every day. A new behavior or skill needs to become a daily habit. When people are working on a skill, have them specify where and how they will work on it each day. It might be as simple as reflecting on ideas during their evening commute or using a new behavior at a morning meeting.

Ask people if they are helping others reflect on and learn from their successes and failures.

▸ *Reflect* on what happens. Ask people to talk with a colleague, write in a journal, or set aside time for concentrated thinking. Questions for reflection might include:

▷ What did I do?

▷ How did it work? As I expected? If not, what was different?

▷ Was it an improvement? Why or why not?

▷ What were the consequences for me, for others, and for the work?

▷ What did I learn?

▷ What do I wish I had done differently?

▷ What will I do next time?

- *Seek* feedback and support. Feedback is critical to change. Recommend that people find several feedback sources to tell them whether they are on track and whether their actions are making a difference.

- *Transfer* learning to next steps. Once people attain a particular level of skill, they should look at what they need to do next. They may decide that additional skill is necessary in the same area, or it might be time to move on to developing the next skill.

Increase people's development skills

Ask people what they are doing to connect others with role models and mentors.

Responsibility for development belongs to the person you are coaching. Therefore, a substantial part of your job as coach involves helping others help themselves. Consider the following suggestions:

- Recommend that people read *Development FIRST.* The book discusses ways to learn and is a helpful resource for people who want to become more effective and efficient in their development.

- Encourage people to scan their daily schedules to find the best situations in which to learn or to practice something new. For example, a meeting might provide an opportunity to observe facilitation skills.

- Suggest that people get learning tips from coworkers who have recently faced similar learning challenges.

- When people directly ask you to solve their problems, hold your comments in check. Determine how to use the opportunity to help them find their own solutions.

- Help people take advantage of existing opportunities to stretch themselves. Tell people about opportunities, let them know why the opportunities would be beneficial, and encourage people to take them.

- Encourage employees to network to find others who have the skills or knowledge they wish to learn. Discuss strategies for finding mentors and role models. Help individuals get access to people from whom they want help. Let people know about less well known individuals who can help them.

- Help people find additional coaches. Remind them that one person rarely can provide everything they need for their development. Have them find people to play the following roles in their development process:
  - ▷ Sounding board for new ideas.
  - ▷ Supportive presence who celebrates success and provides encouragement.
  - ▷ Accountability partner.
  - ▷ Feedback partner.
  - ▷ Their confidant.

Create an effective learning environment

People learn more quickly in the right environment. Consider the following suggestions for creating an environment that is conducive to learning and development:

- Model your commitment to development by sharing your development objectives and asking for regular feedback. In particular, ask others to give you feedback on your coaching efforts.

- Tailor your coaching and support to each person's individual learning style.

- Be genuine. Let your personality, insights, observations, and self-disclosures add depth and richness to your coaching efforts.

- Emphasize small, reasonable steps. Because people learn in small steps, expecting too much too soon can discourage progress.

Discuss with people the kind of learning environment they want to create and ask how they plan to foster it.

- Promote active experimentation. When people try new things in different ways, they solidify their understanding of what really works and prepare themselves to use the skills effectively in a variety of circumstances.

- Give people permission to make mistakes as long as they learn from them. Focus on what they learned rather than on how they performed.

- Encourage people to talk to each other about what they learned from their mistakes. Back up your words with willingness to talk openly about your own mistakes.

- Remember that your position as a manager may make some people especially sensitive to what you say or do. Avoid offhand remarks and irrelevant criticisms.

Be a strong role model for development

▼

Commitment to your own development demonstrates just how much you really care about development. If you invest in your own growth, others are more likely to believe that you mean business. To increase your personal impact as a role model for development:

Encourage people to pursue learning and discuss their progress.

- Regularly talk about your development with others. Let them know what you are working on.

- Get a coach for yourself and let people know that you have one. This sends a powerful signal about the priority you put on development.

- Invite feedback and coaching from others. Make it easy for them to talk with you about how you are doing.

- Share what you learned from both your successes and your mistakes.

- Push yourself out of your comfort zone by taking risks and experimenting with new approaches.

Tailor coaching to each individual

▼

Individuals are unique. Consequently, you need to tailor your coaching process to each person. People learn differently, and they need different kinds of coaching. Consider the following suggestions:

- Talk with people about how you can best help them. Also ask them to describe the best coach they have worked with, and reflect on what you can learn from their descriptions.

- Recognize differences among people. For example, some people like to try things first and then consult with others. Others like to practice before they use a skill in a real situation. Some like to learn best practices; others like to discover them.

Talk about ways that people can tailor coaching. Share some of your experiences.

▶ Work with people's preferences in learning and developing whenever possible, and as long as the methods are working for them. When they are not working, recommend a change. For example, people may read books about making presentations and believe that will improve their skills. It may help, but unless they practice and give presentations, it is unlikely there will be much change.

▶ Discuss your coaching with people and ask for feedback regularly. Express your interest in knowing how you can help them, be a better coach, and learn from them.

▶ Respect the fact that an individual might want coaching from someone other than you. You should not be the only person your employees look to for help and guidance.

▶ Be sensitive to the varying levels of supervision and coaching support people may need. Ask them what they feel comfortable with and remind them that you are always open to more or less involvement.

Coach people in different geographic areas

▼

Coaching from a distance is becoming common in today's work environment. The need for a strong bond of trust and candor is especially critical because you often need to use indirect sources to coach. Consider the following suggestions:

▶ Let people know that you are a resource for their development and that you intend to help them even though you are not in the same location.

▶ Set expectations for development, including having a development plan and reviewing progress, just like you do with people who are in your location.

▶ Be accessible. Leave a phone number where you can be reached, give your assistant a phone number where you can always be reached, and check your e-mail often.

▶ Try to meet with the people you're coaching at least once or twice a year, and preferably more often.

▸ Use videoconferencing as a way that the two of you can see each other.

▸ When you talk on the phone, do not do other things at the same time. Research has shown that people can tell when others are multitasking. If you think it's not a big deal, remember how you feel when you are trying to talk with your boss and he or she continues to look at e-mail or take phone calls.

Ask what people are doing to coach and develop direct reports who are in different geographic areas.

▸ When you're visiting in other geographic areas, take time to build relationships. For example, ask your employees to take you around their areas. Ask questions about what you see and pay attention to what they talk about. Most likely they want to show you things about which they are proud. Take time to let them do this. Do not insist on going directly to difficult issues. Consider arriving the evening before so you can have dinner together.

▸ Adjust your work schedule to overlap working hours in your remote employees' time zones.

▸ Create an electronic forum to keep the communication flow going.

▸ Link peers with one another so that people have a variety of connections to the organization. This will give them opportunities to share feedback, tips, and ideas.

Coach people who are different from you

▼

Discuss some of the inherent challenges in coaching, especially when there are contrasting styles and expectations.

Most managers have employees who are different from them in some ways. In fact, if you are a smart manager, you make a point of hiring people who are different from you so that you have a diverse mix of skills, capabilities, and personalities on the team. An effective manager does not treat all people the same; he or she treats people as they want to be treated. Some people want lots of support and guidance; others prefer to be left alone—they'll call you when they need help. Consider the following suggestions:

▸ Ask people how you can be most helpful to them. Ask for examples of when you and others have been effective or helpful as coaches. Also find out what they do not like in a coach.

▸ Pay attention to when people are most open to discussion and how they like to structure it. Some people tend to be more open to conversations in the morning, others later in the day. Some people prefer informal conversations; others like to prepare.

▸ Determine whether it is working well to follow an individual's coaching preferences. There may be times when you need to change your approach. For example, people might say they will come to you when they need help, but they don't and they continue to have problems. This is an example of when you should intervene rather than wait for a request for help.

▸ If you are coaching people from different cultures, talk about that fact and what it means to each of you. Reach out to people from different cultures to let them know that you want to help them be successful.

▸ Recognize that coaching is viewed differently across cultures. In some cultures, people expect managers to take care of them and look out for them; in other cultures, people do not believe that it is safe to let others know about their development needs; and in some cultures, people expect that their manager will ensure that they have good development opportunities and coaching.

Give clear, motivating, and constructive feedback

▼

Feedback is essential to development. It not only helps people correct mistakes, it also reinforces positive behaviors and helps people achieve their goals. Consider the following suggestions:

▸ View feedback as a process of discovery, not delivery. The goal of feedback is to help people get specific information.

▸ Think of constructive feedback as an opportunity for mutual understanding, not persuasion. Try to understand first: ask what people intended to do and what feedback they would give themselves. Look for links between your perspective and the other person's. That way, the feedback will be more clear and understandable.

▸ Make feedback adaptive, not formulaic. Feedback is most effective when it is sensitive to the person and the situation rather than following a standard recipe. Effective feedback givers individualize their approach and adapt it to different circumstances.

▶ Provide nonjudgmental information rather than "positive" or "negative" feedback. Judgments about a person are likely to elicit defensiveness.

Have people practice making feedback more descriptive and less evaluative.

▶ Discuss feedback regularly so that it becomes a process, not an event. Feedback is most effective and motivating when it is part of a regular process of inquiry rather than a single conversation.

▶ Engage in a dialogue and avoid the tendency to lecture. Help people understand the difference between their intentions and other people's perceptions of their behavior.

▶ Let go of the need to convince people that you are right. If they become defensive or stop listening to you, check to see if you are pushing too hard on your point of view.

▶ Allow periods of silence in which people can absorb what you are saying and respond to it.

▶ Don't dilute your message with unnecessary qualifiers like "maybe," "perhaps," and "a little."

▶ Avoid overwhelming people with too much feedback at one time. Focus on relevant and significant observations instead of covering every detail. Relevance is more important than comprehensiveness.

▶ Read people's nonverbal cues to get an indication of whether you need to elaborate, provide support, or allow them to process their feelings and reactions.

Equip people to get useful feedback

▼

Ensure that people are teaching others how to request and respond to feedback.

As a coach, you engage others in feedback discussions. A more important coaching responsibility involves equipping others to embark on their own search for feedback. With this approach, individuals own the responsibility for obtaining feedback, and they develop the ability to obtain it. Consider the following suggestions:

▶ Determine what information people need in order to develop, and what information they want to get.

▶ Help people find good sources of feedback. Suggest that they consider a cross section of people who have an opportunity to observe their behavior, and who will be direct and honest with them. This group might include peers, managers, customers, team members, and friends.

▶ Educate people on how to prepare their feedback givers so they can provide helpful information. For example, people who are working to improve their public speaking might ask feedback givers to pay particular attention to their use of visual aids.

▶ Coach individuals on how to create an environment in which it is safe for people to discuss candid feedback. Teach them how to ask direct, specific questions, probe for additional information, avoid defensiveness, and show appreciation for feedback.

▷ Suggest that, when people feel defensive, they summarize feedback rather than respond with explanations or their point of view.

▷ Encourage people to show appreciation by thanking others for the feedback and mentioning how they plan to use it.

▷ Have people guess at an example of the behavior the feedback giver is talking about in order to solicit additional feedback. This provides an opening for the feedback giver to confirm or clarify what he or she meant.

▶ Suggest that individuals identify one or two people they can rely on regularly for mutual feedback and support.

Use 360-degree or multirater feedback tools

Multirater feedback can be an effective tool for jump-starting the feedback process. The anonymity and confidentiality of multirater instruments often result in more candid feedback than face-to-face methods and can help people gain a clearer sense of their abilities and others' perceptions.

Remind people that 360-degree feedback is for gaining a clearer picture of development needs, not material for criticism.

▶ Check whether your multirater feedback process has the following characteristics:

▷ The objectives of the process are clearly defined.

▷ The roles and expectations of the participant, manager, and coach are clear.

▷ The competency model and instrumentation are well researched, reliable, and valid.

> ▷ Feedback reports and collateral materials are user-friendly.

> ▷ Clarification of the feedback results is built into the process.

> ▷ Development is the key emphasis of the process. The feedback is linked to development tools and processes.

▸ Personnel Decisions International provides state-of-the-art multirater feedback instruments and processes that meet all of these criteria.

Provide challenging assignments to facilitate individual development

▼

Many experts agree that the most powerful individual development happens on the job. As a coach, you can provide challenging on-the-job opportunities both by being creative about the assignments you give others and by providing opportunities for people to work with other people and in other functions. Consider the following suggestions:

▸ Identify assignments in which you can optimize the level of challenge for your employees.

▸ Put people in charge of a cross-functional task force to give them exposure to other functions and an understanding of interrelationships.

▸ Have people represent you at meetings, presentations, and conferences.

Help people identify which assignments they can delegate to increase others' authority or span of control.

▸ Put people in situations in which they have to perform a "fix-it" function to get experience managing change, analyzing business problems, and tackling tough assignments.

▸ Give people temporary lateral assignments that force them to see the business from alternative perspectives.

▸ Assign projects that involve interaction with your manager to provide exposure and experience working with higher-level managers.

▸ Delegate complete responsibility for managing a complex project from start to finish.

▸ Assign people to mentor new or inexperienced employees. This will require them to learn how to coach, to explain things, and to support people.

- ► Challenge yourself to find ways for people to gain access to other people and functions. Periodically ask yourself the following questions:
  - ▷ What people can I help them network with?
  - ▷ Are there new places where they can practice and learn?
  - ▷ Who are the best people to learn from (role models, other coaches, experts), and how can I link my employees to them?
  - ▷ What are the best places to see this skill in action? How can I help them gain access to these opportunities?
  - ▷ What are the best available resources (software, readings, e-courses, webinars, teleseminars, podcasts), and how can I help people gain access to them?

- ► Find ways for people to learn from external sources such as customers, suppliers, and contractors.

Show interest in people's careers

▼

Encourage people to talk to direct reports about career paths at your organization.

Successful managers are honestly interested in their employees as people. They care about them as individuals, not as a means to an end. One of the best ways to demonstrate this interest is to be concerned about the careers of your employees. Consider the following suggestions:

- ► Have regular discussions about people's career interests and goals. Check that they are aiming high enough. Some people do not have goals that are consistent with their level of capability.

- ► When people's career goals are higher than or different from what you thought, provide information about what is required for the roles they want. This will help them calibrate their goals accurately.

- ► Develop plans to help people move toward their career objectives. When you want someone to take on a new role, think about how it will be helpful to his or her career goals.

- ► Support people as they plan their careers. HR departments often have career centers or career planning programs. Also, look at the career plan template in the appendix of this handbook.

▸ Recommend that people talk with others about how they were able to get to where they are in the organization. Many people do not have a specific job they want; instead, they stay open to new assignments and opportunities.

Help people stay with development

▼

It's easy for people's development efforts to get derailed. You can help by reenergizing and refocusing them on their objectives and their reasons for pursuing them. Consider the following suggestions:

▸ Regularly check on people's progress toward their goals. This will help you recognize when they have slowed or stopped their development efforts.

▸ Talk with people about their development priorities and the reasons behind them. Most of the time people get derailed because they lose focus on the importance of the change. Ask them to reexamine their motives for developing.

▸ Learn why people slow their development efforts. They might be discouraged because they think nobody has noticed their efforts or how much they have changed. They also might believe that changing their behavior doesn't seem to matter to others.

▸ Find opportunities for people to practice their skills as often as they can in as many settings as they can.

Ask people about their development progress. What's working? Where do they need more effort and focus?

▸ To prevent discouragement, set reasonable intermediate goals. A series of small wins keeps people motivated.

▸ Help people see cues that signal when they are slipping into old habits. For example:

▷ Emotional reactions that send people back to familiar habits.

▷ Noting an opportunity to apply a new skill but not taking advantage of it.

Address performance issues

▼

Most people want to be successful in their jobs. Ineffective performance is often a sign that the coaching and development process needs to be adjusted.

▶ Consider the following process when you observe performance that is not meeting expectations:

1. Make sure you and the employee have adequately discussed his or her GAPS (*Goals and Values, Abilities, Perceptions of others,* and *Standards/Success Factors* for goal achievement). A mutual understanding of a person's GAPS plays an important part in the performance-management process. Find a time for the conversation when you will not be rushed. Discuss how you both view the performance.

   ▷ Ask what people are trying to do (their *Goals and Values*) and how they see their own performance (their *Abilities*).

   ▷ Share your expectations *(Standards and Success Factors)* and *Perceptions.*

2. Discuss the discrepancies. Probe to understand the underlying reasons for discrepancies.

3. Listen thoughtfully to the person's view of the situation. Paraphrase what you heard to ensure understanding.

4. Come to an agreement on what the person will do differently. Ask for his or her ideas on how to close the gaps between what is being done and what is needed. Mutually agree on the steps to be taken and the time frames for each step.

Challenge people to address performance issues. Discuss likely consequences if poor performance continues.

▶ Follow up on the person's performance. When you are monitoring the employee's actions, be sure to recognize and reinforce improvements in behavior—especially in the beginning—until the employee has incorporated these new behaviors into his or her routine.

Help people learn from experience and developmental experiences

▼

Unless people reflect on what they learn, they run the risk of completing a string of disconnected activities. To help people solidify their learning, consider the following suggestions:

▸ Before the event or assignment, jointly plan what people hope to learn or practice. Tell them what you believe they can learn from the experience and why it is important to them.

Encourage people to talk with team members about recent development experiences and what they learned from them.

▸ Discuss how often you will talk about what they are learning. Decide on practical things like who will contact whom, who will take the lead in the discussion, and what you expect from one another.

▸ When you're debriefing, focus on both ends of the spectrum—what went well and what didn't.

▸ Make sure the debriefing session encourages open communication. During the session, synthesize what was learned; do not pass judgment.

▸ Use effective, open-ended questions to help people fully realize what they learned from an experience.

▸ Discuss what people learned and the next steps in their development process. Use the session to reflect on what happened and to translate that learning into new situations or opportunities.

Recommend training programs, readings, and other resources

▼

Although the most powerful development opportunities occur on the job, people may need to supplement their learning with other ideas and information. They could attend training programs; read books, articles, or blogs; take interactive online courses; listen to podcasts; attend webinars or teleseminars; or watch DVDs. Consider the following suggestions:

▸ Discuss specific learning objectives and intended results before people invest their time in learning through external resources. With this preparation, they can focus on what they need to learn and obtain the necessary information.

▶ Identify resources that are current and timely. Check the recommended readings and suggested seminars listed in the back of this handbook, and get recommendations from colleagues and HR professionals.

Encourage people to look beyond the classic book or training course and consider new resources like user communities and interactive games.

▶ After selecting the appropriate resource, consider the optimum time for people to participate in the learning experience or absorb the material. Time the learning so that it occurs just before they need to apply the skill on the job. This usually yields the greatest transfer of skills or knowledge to the job.

▶ When people have completed the learning resource, take time to discuss what they learned and how they will apply the knowledge and skills.

Help team members help each other with development

▼

Team members can be a tremendous source of help to one another. You can play a role in creating the environment where this becomes the norm. Consider the following suggestions:

▶ Establish ground rules with the team that promote candor and openness.

▶ Match team members who have specific skills with those who need to develop those skills.

▶ Create learning loops. Make it routine for team members to bring what they learn back to the team.

▶ Encourage team members to create opportunities for people to practice new skills (for example, have people practice presentations skills during a team meeting). Then have people debrief with the team after they try new skills.

Find out what people do to link direct reports with others for informal coaching. This is one of the most important things a manager can do.

▶ Make it routine for individuals to make their development goals public. Then establish a system for extending support and holding each other accountable for achieving development goals.

▶ Focus more on *how* than on *what*. Encourage people to describe new things they tried, their struggles, and what they learned, rather than just the final results.

▸ Use project milestones, quarterly planning sessions, and other natural junctures to reflect on group learning.

▸ Spend two or three minutes at the end of each meeting evaluating what worked well and what didn't.

Reinforce the learning process in your area

Change is easier and longer lasting when the environment reinforces the learning process. Periodically audit your environment to identify ways to further enhance learning and development. Consider the following questions:

▸ How can you further integrate development into your department's business-planning and performance-management practices?

▸ What can you do to make development activities, including sharing information and taking risks, safer for everyone in the group?

Ensure that people emphasize development in their business-planning and performance-management practices.

▸ What additional resources (including people's time, money, and new opportunities) can you deploy to support development?

▸ How will you continue to reinforce the importance of development for everyone?

▸ How can you publicly recognize and reward employees who develop themselves and others?

▸ What processes can you establish that will promote learning from other people, both within and across departments?

▸ What are the development barriers that people mention most frequently? How can you help remove those barriers?

▸ In what ways can you be a champion or spokesperson for development throughout the organization?

▸ How can you form a coalition of those who share your focus on development to influence organizational policies and practices?

▸ How will you hold other managers accountable for developing their employees?

18
Promote Teamwork

Knowing how to build, lead, and work effectively in teams is crucial to accomplishing your organization's goals. Today many teams cross geographical and cultural boundaries. A team leader's ability to understand how successful teams work, what they need, and how they evolve over time plays an important role in fostering team spirit.

Teams are not just groups of people; they must share a common mission and vision, established operating practices, and have excellent communication skills. It takes great people skills as well as organization and cooperation for teams to succeed. By learning how teams work and how to keep them on track, you'll make teamwork smoother for everyone.

In this chapter, we will cover the following areas:

▼

- ▶ Link the team's mission to that of the broader organization
- ▶ Foster the development of a common vision
- ▶ Make the team's mission and strategies clear to others
- ▶ Build collaboration by establishing, communicating, and reinforcing shared values and norms
- ▶ Promote teamwork among groups; discourage "us versus them" thinking
- ▶ Facilitate the development of teams through the stages of team growth and maturity
- ▶ Provide clear direction and define priorities for the team
- ▶ Clarify roles and responsibilities with team members
- ▶ Use a team approach to solve problems when it is appropriate
- ▶ Involve others in shaping plans and decisions that affect them
- ▶ Invite and build upon the ideas and input of others
- ▶ Value the contributions of all team members
- ▶ Credit others for their contributions and accomplishments
- ▶ Acknowledge and celebrate team accomplishments

Link the team's mission to that of the broader organization

Talk about the organization's vision and mission. Fill in any missing information and correct any misunderstandings.

Effective leaders thoroughly understand their organization's vision, goals, and business strategy, and also understand how to link their team's mission to the overall vision and strategies of the organization. They translate broad, overarching concepts into tangible, concrete actions and goals. Consider the following suggestions:

▸ Set up a time to discuss your organization's vision, goals, and strategy with your team. Ensure that your team knows and understands them. Spend time discussing the logic behind the direction and why the choices were made.

▸ If you are not well versed about the process and logic used to develop the vision and goals and identify strategic differentiators, invite someone to join your team for this discussion.

▸ Carefully identify and understand the critical business processes necessary for the success of the organization. Determine the role your team plays in achieving the organization's goals.

▸ Whenever you talk about your team, consistently link its goals and role to that of the broader organization. The clearer you are about the role your team plays in achieving the goals of the business, the more targeted you can be about the goals and priorities of the group, the people you need to execute those priorities, and the business processes for which you are responsible.

▸ Understand what the organization expects from your team. In particular, understand your team's goals and how progress toward those goals will be measured. This is the baseline information you need to set the direction for your team.

▸ Look for synergies between your team and other groups. There may be areas in which your combined efforts could better serve the organization. Take the initiative to talk to your peers in other groups to explore options.

Foster the development of a common vision

Working from a shared set of values and a common vision gives leaders and team members a sense of direction, purpose, and security. Consider the following suggestions:

▶ Begin by discussing the organization's values, vision, and goals with team members so they understand the bigger picture. If this is a new area for you, consider partnering with a more experienced colleague to lead the discussion. This will give you more confidence that you will present the information accurately.

▶ Work with your team to develop a vision that defines its purpose and goals, and the team's role in achieving the success of the business. Include the following sections:

  ▷ A clear statement about the team's role and work in the organization.

  ▷ The goals of the team and how success will be measured.

  ▷ Team members' preferred approach to working with one another and others in the organization.

▶ Ensure that each employee has a clear set of objectives and expectations that tie in to the team's goals. Ask individuals to set some preliminary goals. Then meet with each person to review the goals and modify them if necessary.

▶ A few weeks after you introduce the vision, invite team members to describe the impact it has had on their actions. Are people having a hard time making the vision real? As a team, confirm that individual goals and priorities are aligned with the vision.

Invite people to watch an experienced leader facilitate a visioning session.

▶ Watch for cynicism about the vision. People may have seen visions come and go without having an impact on the organization, and they may be cynical about a vision's ability to move people. As a team, determine how you can make it different this time.

▶ Determine whether you could expand or alter the role your team plays within the organization. You may have a talented group that could take on a broader role, move into new areas, or accomplish more challenging goals.

Make the team's mission and strategies clear to others

Teams and people work together better when they know what to expect. As a team leader, you are responsible for ensuring that your team has the necessary amount of visibility in the organization and that other groups and individuals understand your team's mission and strategies. Consider the following suggestions:

▶ Identify the teams and people whose support you need, and those with whom you and your team need to interact well.

Challenge people to list their team's top three strategies in 60 seconds.

▶ Sit down with the leaders of these groups to talk about your team, its goals, the role it plays in the organization, and so on. Talk about the support you need from one another and about mutual expectations.

▶ Use real-life examples to communicate your team's mission and strategies. If you use a lot of buzzwords or jargon, people will just nod and wait for the meeting to be over. Make the strategies real so that people will start to understand exactly what your team is trying to accomplish.

▶ Use shared terminology within your team, and educate outside groups so that they understand you. Unclear language or jargon can hinder communication and cause confusion.

▶ Create an "elevator speech" that describes what you and your teams do. In addition, prepare a short presentation (one to three minutes) describing your team's mission and strategies. You never know when you'll need to advocate for your team, justify your work, or lobby for resources. When you have an opportunity, don't waste it by rambling.

▶ Anticipate questions that people may ask about your team. Think of a full range of questions, from basic to challenging, friendly to hostile. Prepare answers to each and practice them so you'll always be ready to respond.

Build collaboration by establishing, communicating, and reinforcing shared values and norms

Behaviors that build trust, openness, and a sense of give-and-take are critical to a team's success. While you can't control how team members feel about each other, you can help them establish values and norms that guide how they behave toward one another. Consider the following suggestions:

Caution against overdoing team-building exercises. Team members continue to build relationships as they work together.

▸ Set aside time for team members to talk about how they want to work together and what they want as guiding values and team norms. Discuss and agree on a set of behaviors that guides how people will interact with each other, make decisions, and accomplish the team's goals.

▸ Ensure that team members have a shared understanding of what the values and norms mean. Occasionally revisit established values and norms to give the team a chance to modify or add to them. Also discuss them each time new people join the team.

▸ Keep team members focused on their shared purpose and their accountabilities to one another. If people don't live up to values and expectations, talk about it. Team members need to realize that their actions have consequences and impact.

▸ When the team faces a challenging situation, discuss responses that are consistent with the team's values and that will build trust and openness within the group.

▸ Set norms for conflict management. Conflict is inevitable for high-performing teams. Discuss how to address tough issues in productive ways.

▸ Foster a spirit of teamwork within the team—don't allow people to focus only on individual gain or contribution. Make it a priority to remind people why they are working as a team and help them see how cooperation helps them achieve goals faster and more effectively.

Promote teamwork among groups; discourage "us versus them" thinking

▼

Many initiatives require the cooperation and combined effort of teams across the organization. Leaders need to address obstacles before they become serious impediments. Consider the following suggestions:

▸ Promote teamwork among different groups by showing respect for other functions and professions. Avoid labels, stereotypes, and disparaging remarks about other groups or units.

▸ With other team leaders, discuss how to help your teams work together effectively. If you decide to bring teams together to discuss expectations and how to work together, involve the leaders of all teams.

▸ Meet periodically with other team leaders to discuss ongoing issues, and plan together. Effective teamwork requires interaction. If you are in several locations, use communication technology such as videoconferencing to enable people to see each other.

▸ Watch for "us versus them" thinking and discussions. Check yourself and caution others when they talk in those terms.

Talk about the effect that speaking negatively about other groups can have on a team.

▸ Make sure that teams who need to work together have shared expectations. For example, have teams involved in a project meet to discuss their part of the work or the value chain. Discuss what each team needs from the other to be successful. Your goals for this meeting are to ensure that the teams understand each other's worlds, that they know what others need from them, and that they agree about what each team will do.

▸ Periodically meet with teams that need to work together to discuss what is working and what could be improved. Put together improvement plans so that you are continually making progress.

▸ Encourage people to focus on mutual goals.

▸ Openly discuss the obstacles that people face as they work with teams across the organization. Are the obstacles systemic, interpersonal, or situational? Form a task force to analyze the issues and make recommendations. Hold yourself and other leaders accountable for making meaningful changes.

▶ Create "ambassadors" who serve on more than one team. Because they will be familiar with issues and challenges in several areas, they can provide a broader perspective and break down barriers between teams.

▶ Invite your team to exchange ideas and best practices with other groups. Guarding against the "not invented here" trap will help all groups improve their effectiveness.

▶ Challenge people to think of the big picture when they negotiate for resources. Encourage them to discuss how they can optimize the success of the organization by working together instead of merely trying to increase resources for their own areas.

Facilitate the development of teams through the stages of team growth and maturity

▼

A group of people is not the same thing as a team. Teams are created, and there are regular stages in their development. Leaders play an important role in growing and supporting teams through each stage of growth. If you know which stage your team is in, you can manage expectations about its performance and deepen your understanding of people's behavior. Consider the following suggestions:

Forming the team

In this phase, a group of individuals comes together. They may begin to see themselves as a team if the individuals recognize that they are dependent upon one another for the success of a goal or project. Your role is to:

▶ Ensure that the team has a clear charter that outlines its purpose, scope of responsibilities, goals, and boundaries of authority.

▶ Assist the team in selecting its members and assigning roles and responsibilities.

▶ Ensure that team members believe that they need to work together to achieve a particular goal. Unless team members are mutually dependent, there will be little incentive to work as a team.

▶ Create opportunities for team members to get better acquainted and build rapport.

Establishing norms and operating practices

In this phase, a team typically goes through a period of conflict and disagreement. This is not an indicator that the team is in trouble. Instead, it is the normal clarification of roles, learning what can and cannot be expected from one another, adapting to the needs of the team, and clarifying acceptable team behavior. For example, a team member may have committed to a certain amount of work for the team but has discovered, along with the team, that he or she is not able to follow through on that commitment. This person is not a bad team member; he or she is a person with a priority-balancing problem that needs to be addressed before the team can be successful.

During this stage, the team sorts out issues that keep it from coming together as a coherent, high-performing unit. In this phase, you can help the team in several ways:

▸ Further clarify roles and responsibilities.

▸ Provide time for team members to work out differences in perspectives and approaches.

Discuss the type of support a team needs at different stages of development.

▸ Recognize that this stage is normal and help team members to work through differences without judging people. Solve the problems; don't make people the problem.

▸ Identify conflicts and facilitate discussions to reach productive solutions.

▸ Manage the tendency of subgroups to form coalitions and compete against each other.

▸ Provide opportunities for team members to have fun together and build camaraderie.

Focusing on productive team performance

In this stage, the team works well together. It meets regularly, demonstrates progress, and makes decisions together. Team members are optimistic about the team's success and are comfortable with one another.

In this phase, you can build on the team's success in the following ways:

▸ Help people see how well the team is working together.

▸ Point out how people are working through issues so that they learn which behaviors are making them successful as a team.

▸ Foster creativity, innovation, and new ways of thinking.

▸ Seek new ways to raise the bar of team performance.

▸ Convey appreciation for each member's contributions.

▸ Recognize positive outcomes and progress on goals, and reward team spirit.

Renewing the team

In this phase, some aspect of the team changes, requiring the team to reconfigure and rebuild. For example, new people might join the team, the leadership might change, or the team might have a new goal. When this happens, the team needs to spend time together to revisit goals, roles, responsibilities, and plans. Many of the activities you did in the forming stage can also be helpful in this stage.

Your role may include:

▸ Clarifying the team's mission and goals, or redefining the team's mission.

▸ Facilitating team members' interactions as they reestablish goals and agreements regarding team behavior, especially when team membership has changed significantly.

▸ Encouraging the mutual support and involvement of all members in renewing the team and exploring alternatives.

Provide clear direction and define priorities for the team

▼

Team members can waste valuable time if they don't have clear direction for their work. In the worst cases, they may produce results that bear little or no resemblance to the desired outcome. To provide clear direction and define priorities, consider these suggestions:

- Work with the team to define the project or work. Include the following:
  - ▷ Purpose and goal of the project.
  - ▷ Deadlines and deliverables that have already been determined.
  - ▷ Instructions and guidelines, as appropriate.
  - ▷ Who will make decisions, how they will be made, and the level of authority for the decision makers.
  - ▷ Required reports and communication.

Find opportunities to observe people's facilitation skills.

- Discuss the project with the team and invite people to ask questions. Don't end the discussion until you're certain that the team fully understands the scope of the project and your expectations.

- Check in with the team during the project to show support, troubleshoot, answer questions, and run interference. People need to know that you're involved and interested in their progress.

- Keep track of areas in which you gave unclear or inadequate direction. Figure out where and why misunderstanding took place so that you can be clearer next time.

Clarify roles and responsibilities with team members

Team members work best when they know what is expected of them and they know what they can expect from others. Lack of role clarity is one of the chief barriers to effective teamwork. Often "personality conflicts" are simply a lack of clarity in roles.

- Ensure that each employee has a clear set of objectives and expectations that clarify the role he or she plays in achieving team goals. It usually works best for employees to identify their perceptions of their roles and set their own goals with input from you. You as the leader can then review these; modify or add to them only when necessary.

- Whenever you begin a new team project, meet as a group to discuss roles and expectations with one another.

- During team projects, hold update meetings at which each person talks about what he or she is working on. This will help you clarify or refine roles. Also consider recommending that team members describe what help they need from one another. This could include tangible help, such as producing data for a report, or developmental help, such as ideas about how the person could more effectively influence another team.

- ► Convey your expectation that team members will collaborate with and support one another. Intervene when it is clear that a team member is interested only in his or her personal success. Ensure that the person understands that he or she will not be successful without being collaborative.

- ► When team members disagree about role expectations, ask them to meet with you to work through the issues.
  - ▷ Find uninterrupted time for the team to meet.
  - ▷ Ask an objective person to facilitate the meeting if emotions are heightened or if you believe you cannot be objective.
  - ▷ Have each team member state specific expectations of other team members. If it seems helpful, structure this discussion by having people describe what they would like others to do more or less of.
  - ▷ Use the discussion as a catalyst to clear the air and develop new working agreements.

Connect people with expert role models who regularly form successful teams.

- ► Periodically meet with team members to learn about their perceptions of their roles and their job expectations. Discuss similarities with and differences from your expectations.

- ► Work with your unit to identify voids in responsibilities and find ways to fill them. When consensus is not possible or appropriate, make a decision and let the group know the rationale for your decision.

- ► Clarify each team member's role and how she or he contributes to attaining the goals and mission of the team. Also help team members understand how their efforts and performance affect the overall results of the organization.

- ► Capitalize on opportunities to regularly communicate priorities and responsibilities to the team.

- ► Sometimes teams start to rely more heavily on one or two highly productive team members. Remind everyone (including yourself) to contribute his or her fair share of effort, and periodically ask people if they are feeling overburdened.

Use a team approach to solve problems when it is appropriate

▼

When team members are involved in problem solving and decision making, they are more likely to accept decisions and to feel ownership and shared responsibility for the goal. Consider the following suggestions:

Discuss the types of decisions that should be made by a team and those that should be made by an individual.

▶ Determine when and to what degree to use a team approach for problem solving. In general, the higher the level of commitment and buy-in your team members show, and the more creative, varied, and informative the input and opinions they offer, the more important a team approach for solving problems becomes.

▶ A team approach to problem solving and decision making tends to work best when:

  ▷ Full acceptance of the decision is necessary for effective implementation.

  ▷ Information from more than one person is required to make the decision.

  ▷ A high-quality result is desired.

  ▷ A creative solution or a new approach is needed.

  ▷ The decision does not need to be made quickly.

▶ Make a list of all the decisions you made in the past month. Assess the quality and the acceptance of your decisions. Would your final outcome have benefited from a team approach? Look for trends, such as avoiding team involvement on certain kinds of problems or decisions.

▶ Seek feedback from your team, your manager, and your peers. Ask for their perceptions of when you have effectively used a team approach to solve problems and when you have missed opportunities to do so.

▶ Identify other managers who effectively use a team approach to solve problems. Use them as role models. Observe what they do that makes them effective and ask them for tips on how you might improve your own approach.

Involve others in shaping plans and decisions that affect them

▼

Leaders need to involve the right people at the right time. When you make plans, involve the people, teams, and groups that are needed for success, and those who care about or will be affected by the plan, the process, or the outcome. Consider the following suggestions:

- ▶ Identify all the individuals and groups who have a stake in an issue. Check with your team and colleagues to make sure that you have all the necessary people and teams. At a minimum, involve people within the value chain. While you may choose not to involve all who think they should be involved, you do need to address their perceived need to be involved. For example, make sure a team member personally tells them about the plan and the rationale rather than expecting them to ferret out the information for themselves.

- ▶ Decide how and when to involve specific people and teams. For example, you may want to involve some individuals in the total planning process and ask others to provide input before the planning begins. Meet with people either one-on-one or in a team.

- ▶ When you meet with people, give them the big picture and clarify what you want from them. For example, you may want them to:
  - ▷ Define a problem or opportunity.
  - ▷ Help develop options for addressing a problem.
  - ▷ Choose a course of action.

Remind people that team decisions are often challenging, even with a good process.

- ▶ Conduct the meeting so that you get the input you need and the individuals feel involved in the process. Once people feel invested, your objective will become a shared objective.

- ▶ As a group, decide who should take responsibility for carrying out each element of the proposed plan.

- ▶ Develop a communication plan to keep people informed.

Invite and build upon the ideas and input of others

▼

Because ideas drive business and solve problems, it's important to make it clear that you want input and ideas from all team members. Consider the following suggestions:

▸ Make it clear that you expect people to contribute ideas and help solve problems. Stress that you value all ideas.

▸ Create the expectation that people will build on the ideas of others rather than criticize them. Also communicate that you don't want people to try to one-up each other.

▸ Be clear about your purpose for soliciting ideas. For example, specify whether you are looking for many ideas or whether you want an individual's best recommendation.

Have people practice building on others' ideas.

▸ Agree on ground rules for brainstorming and idea sessions. For example:

▷ Generate as many ideas as possible.

▷ Build on the ideas of others.

▷ Save critiques for later.

▷ Stay within the time limit.

▷ Capture ideas, not a word-by-word transcription.

▷ Ignore implementation constraints for now.

▸ Help people build on ideas by encouraging them to say *and* instead of *but* when they respond to suggestions.

▸ Be a role model for building on the comments of others. Expand on what others say by stating what you heard and then adding your ideas to it. Look for natural, positive connections between your ideas.

▸ Encourage people to share their ideas, even if they are fragments rather than fully thought out plans. A single idea often starts a chain reaction.

▸ When someone evaluates an idea during a brainstorming session, quickly say, "We're just brainstorming now—no critiquing" and move on. Repeat this phrase each time people critique ideas until the team learns this norm.

> ▸ Tell people ahead of time that you will want their ideas about a topic. Creative ideas are not typically produced on demand. People need time to think and let their ideas brew.

Value the contributions of all team members

▼

All team members are important to the success of the organization. As a leader, you can foster an environment where people value each other and recognize the importance of each role on the team. Consider the following suggestions:

> ▸ Examine whether you genuinely value the work of each individual on your team. Some people believe particular roles are more important to business success, and others value work only if it is intellectually complex. Your team will function more smoothly if you demonstrate that you value each person.

> ▸ Listen to all team members' ideas and opinions, and thank them for their input, whether or not you agree with their point of view. Listening will show that you take them seriously and that you value their ideas.

> ▸ People often feel valued when they are included. Include team members at all levels in as much planning, decision making, and problem solving as possible. When direct involvement is not appropriate, make sure you discuss plans and decisions with the team, and give people time to react and plan their next steps.

Give suggestions on how to coach individuals who have a difficult time collaborating.

> ▸ Be a positive role model for valuing others' contributions. Take interest in what people are working on, thank them for their work, and give them specific feedback about their value to your team and the organization.

> ▸ Check whether individuals feel valued by seeking input on the ways that people on your team either value or devalue others' work. You may want to ask people to send you written examples instead of asking them to speak up in a group setting.

▸ Give your staff feedback if you see any of them devaluing members of the team. If you ignore their behavior (hoping it will go away), they will take that as tacit approval of their behavior.

▸ Ask for advice from others. People feel valued when "the boss" asks for their help.

Credit others for their contributions and accomplishments

▼

Remind people who are reluctant to share credit with a team that shared credit doesn't minimize an individual's contributions.

People want to be appreciated and valued for their contributions. As a leader, you are a role model. People are especially interested in whether you give people proper credit for their ideas and accomplishments. As you work with individuals and teams, consider the following suggestions:

▸ Monitor how you talk about successful efforts. For example, consider how often you use the word I instead of we when you're referring to a team effort. Also consider whether you share credit with others when you are recognized for individual success.

▸ When you acknowledge the success of a project, make sure you recognize the efforts of all team members involved, no matter how small their role or contributions.

▸ Solicit feedback on whether you share credit when you talk about team successes. You may find that you are willing to give credit when you're talking to your team but take all the credit when you talk with people outside of your group.

▸ Ask a team that recently completed a successful project or initiative to share its learning and experience with other teams or departments. This is a good way to acknowledge team members' success as well as help others learn from it.

▸ Frequently tell your team members that you appreciate their contributions. Be specific about what they have done well.

Acknowledge and celebrate team accomplishments

▼

Acknowledging and celebrating team accomplishments is a powerful way to reinforce the importance of teams and their contributions, recognize team efforts, and keep motivation and momentum going. Consider the following suggestions:

▸ Recognize and reward team performance, not just individual performance. Set specific team goals and recognize when people achieve them.

Challenge people to find at least three new ways to recognize individuals and teams.

▸ If teamwork and teams are important to getting work accomplished in the organization, include the contribution that individuals make to teams as a part of individual goal-setting and rewards programs. Consider holding back individual rewards unless there is also strong evidence of team cooperation.

▸ Look for opportunities to make team accomplishments or contributions more visible to the organization. For example, talk about them when you speak to other leaders in the organization. Write about successful team projects in the company newsletter or blog. E-mail others in the company when you are celebrating important accomplishments, especially when people throughout the company have been following the team's progress.

▸ Celebrate team accomplishments. Choose milestones that you want to celebrate, put them on your calendar, and schedule an event.

▸ Acknowledge and reward teams immediately when they accomplish an objective or overcome difficult obstacles. Research shows that the sooner the reward is delivered, the more impact it will have.

19
Foster Open Communication

Developing and fostering good communication skills in your organization takes intention, practice, and dedication. The good news is that communication skills can be learned and improved with use.

As a manager, you can build communication skills in your team through your own modeling, by helping others learn new and better ways to communicate, and by making sure that people receive and provide information as it's needed. Good communication begins with an honest and supportive approach to dealing with others. It's a personal as well as a professional skill, and when it is used well, it creates a smooth flow of information and ideas.

In this chapter, we will cover the following areas:

▼

- ▸ Establish effective communication systems and processes
- ▸ Encourage open exchange of information and viewpoints
- ▸ Provide others with open access to information
- ▸ Use communication methods appropriate to the situation
- ▸ Keep people up to date with information
- ▸ Make sure people have no "surprises"
- ▸ Facilitate discussions to ensure that everyone's viewpoint is heard
- ▸ Structure creative ways to obtain input from others
- ▸ Communicate the message that every idea is worthy of consideration
- ▸ Encourage others to express their views, even contrary ones
- ▸ Express reactions and opinions without intimidating others

Establish effective communication systems and processes

▼

Discuss communication issues that are helped or hindered by organizational structure and culture.

Open communication often seems easier to accomplish on a small scale. When it expands across groups or organizations, it becomes exponentially more complex. As a leader, you can play a part in determining communication systems on a broader scale. Consider the following suggestions:

► Make sure your communication strategy supports your organizational strategy and structure. For example, if you have participatory management, information needs to flow easily and quickly to the decision makers.

► Build communication strategies into your business plans. Specify the type of information sharing and feedback you need in order to accomplish your goals. Be detailed in your plan; don't just write "Keep people informed." Write down *how* you will keep people informed.

► Determine if communication systems across the organization work together well. Some groups may have highly structured systems, while other systems may not be structured enough. Some systems may have grown organically and are not sufficient now that the organization is larger. Understanding existing systems will help you identify which changes will make a difference.

► Measure your communication efforts. Set goals and expectations, and specify how communication will be evaluated. Make people accountable for results.

► Learn whether people view communication systems as just more paperwork or another idea imposed from above. Involve groups in creating or adjusting the systems. This will give them a stake in the outcome and a sense of ownership over the process.

► Avoid building your communication structures around one person's personality or skill. For example, you may have a charismatic CEO who gives rousing speeches to inspire employees. He or she may decide that all managers should give rousing speeches to their groups. The odds are low that this will be effective over the long term.

► Consider whether communication systems work as well during stressful, adverse times as they do during good times. Stress points out the fracture lines and makes it clear where the breakdowns occur. Ask a communication specialist or one of your direct reports to study this issue and develop recommendations.

Encourage open exchange of information and viewpoints

▼

An open exchange of ideas, opinions, and views is necessary for a successful organization. Think about the problems and tragedies that have occurred because people did not think it was all right to deliver bad news, counter those in charge, or offer suggestions that were different from the norm. Fast-moving change requires organizations to constantly adjust, regroup, and move on. Openly exchanging ideas is critical to making this work. Consider the following suggestions:

▶ Encourage people to contribute ideas. When they do, listen carefully and thank them. Use their ideas or information whenever possible.

▶ When people give you recommendations, ask about the other options they considered. Ask whom they consulted for their ideas and points of view. This will help set the norm that you want people to exchange ideas.

▶ Ask for feedback about whether you tend to "shoot the messenger"—to punish the bearer of bad news.

▶ Whenever someone cuts off another person's ideas or is inappropriately critical, call the person on that behavior and remind him or her to be more open to the ideas of others.

▶ Learn to value diverse and unusual views. When you hear an idea that does not seem to make sense, don't dismiss it immediately. Take time to consider it, even if it seems implausible. Although this approach may seem uncomfortable, over time you will benefit from a wider range of information and ideas.

Discuss how people from other countries or cultures express their opinions.

▶ Analyze your typical reaction to outspoken people in your area. Do you look forward to hearing their views? Or do you dread their presence at a meeting because you think they will slow things down or create conflict? Your reactions will determine how people interact with you and the quality of information you receive.

- Guard against viewing dissension, differences of opinion, and disagreement as obstacles. Showing even subtle frustration with people who express their views will inhibit them from speaking out in the future.

- Give people options for expressing their views. Don't force everyone to talk to you face-to-face. Ask people to convey their ideas and opinions in a way that is comfortable for them, with the understanding that you may wish to contact them later with clarifying questions.

- Monitor how well you exchange information with people from different levels, functions, and cultures. You will be less effective if you interact only with select groups and individuals.

Provide others with open access to information

▼

People who get the information they need can do their jobs more efficiently and effectively. Consider the following suggestions:

- Ensure that you provide the information people need to do their work. For example, when you delegate work, ask what the person wants and needs to know to complete the assignment.

- As you leave a meeting, think about what you learned that others should know. Decide how and when you're going to share the information.

Encourage people to take advantage of informal opportunities to share information.

- Be a role model for providing open access to information. Actively discourage people from hoarding information as a source of power or influence.

- Ask for feedback about how well you share information. Act on the feedback, so people see that you are trying to communicate more openly.

- Meet with your team and discuss the organization's current communication practices. Strive to get below the surface, and get past statements like "We need to communicate more." Address questions such as:

  ▷ What do we need to communicate about that we currently are overlooking?

    ▷ What information are you missing or not receiving that you need in order to do your work?

    ▷ What communication do you need from me that you do not get now?

    ▷ What are our barriers to communication?

    ▷ What information do people want access to?

▶ Make sure people across your organization know how to get in touch with each other. For example, do people in the office know how to reach telecommuters and contract employees? Keep contact lists up to date and accessible.

▶ Determine whether people can easily find out what time it is in the countries in which you have facilities or offices. This will give them a better sense of when people are in the office. Post the information on your intranet.

▶ Analyze how people in your area currently get information. What works well and what should be improved? Identify two or three areas you would like to improve. Then talk to people in your area about how to make changes.

▶ Sponsor a knowledge management improvement team to dramatically increase your area's or organization's ability to manage the knowledge you have.

▶ Talk to your peers about information sharing between groups. Pull together key people from each group to explore issues, come up with a plan, and lead implementation.

▶ Learn about open access to information across the organization. Depending on your organization's culture, you may find that it ranges from information hoarding to lack of information to timely, relevant information.

Use communication methods appropriate to the situation

How you communicate is as important as *what* you communicate. Before you send a message, choose a method that will work best for your purpose and your audience. Consider the following suggestions:

▶ Consider what method will be most effective to convey your message. Choose the method based on the type of message, the person to whom it is going, and practical considerations like whether it is during regular work hours or off hours.

▶ Deliver certain messages in person: important changes, complicated or controversial issues and decisions, bad news. This will allow you to check the person's understanding of the message and get immediate feedback through verbal and nonverbal responses.

Talk about communication methods and how to use each one effectively.

▶ Use more than one method to deliver an important message. For example, announce an initiative in a meeting and then in an e-mail; follow up by talking to each individual on your team. Even if people don't go to the meeting or read their e-mail, they will hear about it in person.

▶ When a dialogue is needed and a face-to-face meeting is not possible, use the telephone, online chat, or videoconference.

▶ Use videoconferences when you need to see participants who cannot be in the same location.

▶ Choose voice mail or e-mail when the message doesn't need to be delivered in person, when it is after hours, or when the person is out of the office. Organize your thoughts so that your message will be clear and concise. Make yourself available for the person to reach you, especially when it is a message that should have been delivered in person.

▶ Use e-mail as part of the communication process when you want to document your message or send attachments. Recognize that the effectiveness of e-mail depends on your writing skills and the reader's willingness to read thoroughly.

▶ Work with your organization's communication experts for ideas on how you can most effectively use videoconferencing, Live Meetings, and online chats to achieve your objectives.

▶ Monitor long e-mail chains for signs that issues are not getting resolved and are getting worse: more and more people are becoming involved, emotions running high, negative assumptions or interpretations being made. Stop the e-mail conversation and arrange for a conference call or a meeting of the people involved. Let everyone know that you're scheduling a meeting and ask that the e-mail conversation stop.

▸ Consider communicating messages in both written and oral forms to people who are working in a second language to help ensure that your message is clear. Remember to use simple words to express your thoughts, especially if you are uncertain what the other person's language skill level may be. Avoid jargon. Ask questions to make sure that the person understood. For example, "How do you think my recommendations would work for you?"

▸ List the communication methods that are used in your organization. Identify which ones are used most frequently and which ones people pay the most attention to. You may find that they are not the same.

Keep people up to date with information

▼

Look at communication plans that outline how, when, and with whom information will be shared.

Timely sharing of information is critical to many, if not most, work situations. Work processes rely on the smooth flow of information among people inside and outside of the organization. Consider the following suggestions:

▸ Include a communication plan as part of the planning and execution of any major project.

▸ Identify the type of updates and amount of information that need to occur daily, weekly, or monthly. What kinds of decisions do people make? Do they have the information they need to make those decisions? Clarify how you can help and what information you can contribute.

▸ Identify typical obstacles to sharing up-to-date information: projects may move fast, you may be traveling, you might not have time to follow through on all details. Determine what you will do to counteract each obstacle—for example, delegate specific responsibilities while you're traveling.

▸ On a three-month calendar, mark dates of major projects and initiatives. Plot out a communication schedule for updating people on milestones, such as the completion of a crucial phase of a project.

- Ask your manager to identify the kinds of information he or she is most interested in receiving from you and how he or she wants to get that information. Check regularly to see if you are providing the desired amount of information in each area.

- When you get an e-mail directed specifically to you, consider whether the information would be useful to other people in your area or across the organization. If so, forward the e-mail as is, or modify it to fit the circumstances. People need to know what is going on in other functions so they can understand how their work affects the broader organization.

Make sure people have no "surprises"

▼

People don't like surprises, especially when the surprises are negative. Therefore, it is critical that you share information so people won't be caught off guard, or ill prepared. Even when you know the other person will be angry or displeased, it is better to say something before the person hears the bad news from another source. Consider the following suggestions to help you avoid unnecessary surprises:

- When you get information that affects individuals on your team, tell them about it as soon as possible. People expect that their managers will share information with them. Your example will also encourage them to share news—especially bad news—with you.

- Give your manager any information that may have negative implications for your area. Make sure your manager hears the news from you.

- Meet regularly (at least monthly) with your peers in other areas of the organization to share information and prevent surprises.

Talk about the best timing and setting for a particular message.

- Get ahead of the rumor mill by anticipating and debunking rumors. Candidly explain an issue and how it will affect your team. Over time, you will build credibility with the team members, and they will come to trust your information.

- When there is a crisis, tell people as much as you can, even if you don't have all the details. Explain that you will share details as they become available. If you wait until you know more, you could find yourself in damage control mode and give the impression that you're out of the loop.

- Present surprising or bad news calmly, especially if it is politically charged or potentially job-altering information.

- Realize that people may have strong emotional reactions to certain information, both positive and negative. Recognize and empathize with their emotions, and give people time to process how the information will affect them.

- Make yourself available while a situation unfolds. Encourage people to come to you with questions and concerns.

- Allow yourself time and space to absorb and process your own emotional reaction to negative information. Allow people to see that you are human and that the news affects you as well.

Facilitate discussions to ensure that everyone's viewpoint is heard

When you lead a discussion, it is your responsibility to ensure that all participants have a chance to express their views and that those views are received respectfully. Consider the following suggestions:

- Provide opportunities for people to participate. After you invite people to share their ideas, sit back and listen. Monitor any tendency you have to dominate the conversation or to shift it to your point of view.

- Assess your willingness to hear people's views and your level of patience when they speak. Guard against immediately evaluating and critiquing what others say. Nothing curbs participation faster than interruptions, criticism, sarcasm, visible impatience, and "yes, but" answers.

Coach people on how to present their honest point of view in a constructive manner.

- Ask open-ended questions, which are excellent tools for monitoring and facilitating discussions. Asking the right questions can be more important than knowing the answers.

- Draw out quiet or reticent team members. They may never speak up unless you request their ideas. Without their input, you might miss valuable information and perspectives. Consider letting these people know ahead of time that you will be asking for their input. This will give them time to prepare.

▸ Offer alternative ways for team members to give their input, especially if they are uncomfortable speaking in a large group. For example, break the group into pairs for discussion and ask each pair to report back, or invite people to send you written comments and ideas.

▸ Read about the effects of gender and culture on group interaction. Monitor your facilitation skills to ensure that you respect differences during meetings.

Structure creative ways to obtain input from others

▼

Effective leaders work best in a culture in which people openly contribute their ideas and thoughts. This does not happen automatically; leaders and team members need to take deliberate steps to create such an environment. Consider the following suggestions:

Discuss which words and phrases work best to draw out ideas and solicit feedback.

▸ Assess how you currently obtain input from people within and outside of your group. You may find that you always use the same method, which is not necessarily effective with all groups and individuals. For example, do you count on people to be proactive, or do you ask for specific pieces of information? Do you talk with people directly or do you use e-mail only?

▸ Review your options for soliciting and receiving input, and think of one way you could use each method. For example, you could invite people to e-mail you, leave voice-mail messages about a certain topic for a week, create an online forum where people can post their input, invite people across the organization to lead brown-bag discussions, or conduct surveys.

▸ If some of the people in your group work at other sites, identify your options for collecting their input. Ask them how they would like to participate and then work together to specify action steps, deadlines, and accountability.

▸ Be patient when you solicit input. People may need time to develop their ideas, or they may prefer to establish a relationship before they discuss business. Don't expect (or demand) that everyone will communicate the way you do.

- Use structured information sharing: debriefing sessions during and after projects, posting competitive information, documenting best practices, teaching newly acquired skills.

- Identify people who find creative ways to collect and distribute ideas and knowledge. Talk about how they set up their processes, learn the pros and cons of trying new methods, and solicit tips and recommendations for your group.

Communicate the message that every idea is worthy of consideration

▼

Discuss the fact that people who habitually disregard ideas have a hard time convincing others that they are serious about wanting to hear candid views.

Valuing the ideas of others is an important element of fostering open communication. Set the tone for your part of the organization by consistently sending the message that you appreciate ideas and contributions. Consider the following suggestions to help you communicate this message:

- Advocate the view that contributing ideas and knowledge is a part of everyone's job, regardless of function or level of responsibility. Challenge the belief that leaders come up with the ideas and everyone else follows, or that leaders are interested only in their own ideas.

- Actively seek ideas from every level, from the head of the organization to hourly workers. Valuable ideas can and do come from people in all roles. People are more likely to share their ideas if you ask them directly.

- Specify the types of ideas you're looking for. If you are brainstorming, stress that all ideas are welcome. If you are refining ideas or planning implementation, specify that you are looking for ideas in those areas. It can be frustrating for everyone if you're looking for specific planning ideas and someone wants to brainstorm.

- Be receptive to the ideas you hear. Part of open communication is being willing to listen to a wide range of ideas. Even if you think an idea has no merit, show your willingness to hear it so you don't shut off the flow of ideas.

Encourage others to express their views, even contrary ones

▼

Speaking candidly is hazardous duty in some organizations. People personalize messages, act defensive, become angry, and get even. In such an environment, individuals believe that what they *don't say* won't hurt them. The irony, of course, is that it does. Problems remain problems, great ideas wither on the vine, and people get frustrated. To support candid exchanges in your area, consider the following suggestions:

▸ Share your expectation that you want people in your area to speak candidly, without being brusque or rude. Provide examples of how to phrase a viewpoint honestly yet tactfully.

Suggest ways to react appropriately to contrary views.

▸ Recognize that you are a model for the people who report to you. They notice whether or not you are open to hearing candid views. If you waffle, get defensive, or go on the attack, it will contradict your stated intention.

▸ With your direct reports, discuss real or hypothetical situations in which it would be tempting to shade the truth or hide information. Work through the details and reinforce the conviction that expressing straightforward viewpoints is helpful.

▸ If you suspect that people are holding back or being less than frank, talk to them individually. They may be reluctant to speak in front of other people or fear retaliation. They may also feel that their thoughts are not fully formed and don't want to commit to a position before they've had time to think it through.

▸ Ask selected colleagues to give you feedback on your willingness to hear candid viewpoints. Analyze the feedback to look for patterns. If necessary, create a plan to be more receptive.

Express reactions and opinions without intimidating others

▼

Leaders are typically confident and self-assured individuals. While these characteristics contribute to their success, they can also intimidate others. To develop your ability to express your opinions without intimidating other people, consider the following suggestions:

- Recognize that simply due to your role, others may perceive you as intimidating, even if you don't intend to be.

- Before you offer your opinion, ask other people for their views. Listen intently and try to find some areas of agreement that you can refer to as you express your reaction or opinion.

- Assess how you typically state your views. Do you make definitive—and intimidating—statements like "That will never work," "We can't possibly do that," or "You haven't thought that through"?

- Use "I statements" and "whole messages" when you express your opinions. "I am not sure we have fully explored the alternatives on this issue" sounds less intimidating than "You have not investigated this issue fully." Whole messages, which include observations, thoughts, feelings, and goals, provide the context for an "I" message.

- Determine whether you are offering an opinion or trying to convince people that you're right. If you are trying to convince people, your passion for the subject may make you seem intimidating.

- Ask colleagues at various levels in the organization whether you come across as intimidating when you express your opinions. Listen carefully to feedback. Instead of arguing or becoming defensive, think of ways you could come across as less intimidating: change the words you use, your tone of voice, your body posture.

Point out behaviors that make people seem intimidating.

- If you see the ability to intimidate as a positive attribute, analyze its effectiveness. When do you use intimidation? What does it accomplish in the short term and the long term? Look at examples of intimidating leaders. How effective are they over the long term? See if you can find more effective ways to accomplish your goals.

- When you react strongly, point out that it is a reaction, not a decision. Sometimes it can be helpful to explain your behavior.

20
Speak Effectively

Few things cause more anxiety than having to speak in front of a group. Yet, because you are a leader, people will expect your communication skills to be smooth, polished, and organized. Learning to speak effectively to groups—regardless of their size—takes understanding of what makes public speaking successful, thorough preparation, and practice.

Regardless of your current comfort level with public speaking, you can improve your skills and presentation manner to become a more engaging speaker who communicates well and feels comfortable making presentations. Remember, people want you to do well—audiences are looking for information, and the more comfortable you allow yourself to be, the more connected your audience will feel to you and to your message.

In this chapter, we will cover the following areas:

▼

- ▶ Assess your current skills
- ▶ Manage anxiety effectively
- ▶ Prepare and deliver clear, well-organized presentations
- ▶ Adapt content and level of detail to your audience
- ▶ Speak effectively in front of a group
- ▶ Demonstrate poise in front of a group
- ▶ Use a smooth, polished delivery style
- ▶ Speak with enthusiasm and expressiveness
- ▶ Speak clearly and concisely
- ▶ Get your point across when you're speaking
- ▶ Actively engage the audience's interest
- ▶ Gauge audience reaction and make appropriate adjustments
- ▶ Use nonverbal behavior to emphasize key points
- ▶ Use audiovisual aids smoothly and effectively
- ▶ Use humor effectively in group discussions and presentations
- ▶ Answer questions clearly and concisely

Assess your current skills

▼

Videotape people giving presentations. Review the tape with them, discussing skills that are strong and those that can be improved.

Before you can become a more polished speaker, you need to assess your skills candidly. It could be a painful experience—or you could be pleasantly surprised that your skills are not as hopeless as you thought. Consider the following suggestions:

▶ Write down situations in which you believe you do a poor, adequate, or excellent job of speaking. Note situations when you are comfortable, when you are uncomfortable, when people respond well, when they are disengaged or bored, when you feel articulate, and when you feel tongue-tied.

▶ Ask your coworkers, manager, friends, and family how well you express yourself. Compare their perceptions to your assessment. Are there similarities? What are your strengths? What would you like to improve?

▶ If you really want the unvarnished truth, videotape yourself giving a presentation. As you watch and listen to yourself, are you:
  ▷ Impressed with what you say and how you say it?
  ▷ Interested in what you say?
  ▷ Understanding the main points of the presentation?
  ▷ Seeing a confident, capable speaker?
  ▷ Comfortable with your style, pace, and intonation?

▶ As you review the tape, consider the following questions. Do you:
  ▷ Speak at the right pace and with varied intonation?
  ▷ Show appropriate enthusiasm for the topic?
  ▷ Use lively, engaging language?
  ▷ Drop your volume at the end of sentences or phrases?
  ▷ Speak too quickly and run words together?
  ▷ Give so much detail that the audience becomes numb?
  ▷ Ramble through an unorganized presentation?

▶ Make two columns on a sheet of paper. In the first column, list obstacles that keep you from expressing yourself effectively. For example, you might be unprepared or caught off guard, you might not set aside enough time to prepare, you might think you can "wing it," or you might be intimidated by people in the audience. In the second column, write down what you could do to overcome the obstacle. Ask an experienced colleague or your mentor to help you put your ideas into practice.

Manage anxiety effectively

▼

Even the most polished, competent presenters experience nervousness in some situations. While you may never entirely eliminate presentation anxiety, you can take steps to manage it and make it work for you. Consider the following suggestions:

▸ Prepare as much as you need to, not as much as your colleagues need to. Some people only need to glance at their notes before speaking in front of 500 people. You, on the other hand, may need to go through your presentation seven or eight times before you feel comfortable talking to coworkers you see every day. Do what you need to do to feel prepared.

▸ Come to grips with your fear of making a mistake. The belief that a good presenter never makes a mistake is both untrue and unhealthy. The key is to regain control after an error occurs. If you pick up and go on, so will the audience.

Outline the techniques you use to manage anxiety.

▸ Identify the message you give yourself through your "inner critic." For example, you might believe that you are an introvert who will never be comfortable talking to groups or that you can't talk about technical subjects. Become aware of your inner dialogue and substitute a positive message each time you criticize yourself. When you hear yourself saying "This is going to be awful," replace the thought with a positive one: "I'm prepared for this" or "This will go better than I expect because it always does."

▸ Visualize giving an effective presentation. Imagine the room, the audience, and your position in the room. Mentally go through each step—your walk to the podium, your opening line, each key point, your conclusion, and your walk back to your seat amid thunderous applause. You can also visualize having an effective discussion with another person. Imagine the conversation: the words you use to put the person at ease, how you start the conversation, how the person responds, what you say next, and so on.

▶ Remember this adage: If you are not a little nervous when you speak in front of a group, you don't care enough.

▶ Realize that anxiety decreases with experience, but it doesn't disappear. Many people who look calm and collected are not. Anxiety is not nearly as noticeable to your listeners as it is to you.

▶ Concentrate on your message and your audience, not on yourself and your performance.

▶ If you stutter or stumble, stop, take one or two deep breaths, and then continue. If that does not work, say something about the mistake, such as "Obviously, this point is important to me." This will help you refocus and engage the audience in helping you, which they will.

▶ Remember that most people are looking for information, not perfection. They want to be reasonably engaged in your speech and will forgive some mistakes as long as you are obviously prepared and making an effort.

▶ Sometimes the thought of talking with certain individuals can make you anxious. If so, prepare what you want to say and how you will say it. Practice several ways to discuss or present the message so that you know you can handle a number of different responses.

Prepare and deliver clear, well-organized presentations

▼

Audiences appreciate a well-designed presentation. Because they have to process a great deal of information as they listen to you, it helps to use a clear structure and comprehensible language. Consider the following suggestions:

▶ Carefully decide the purpose of the presentation (to inform, to convince, to entertain). Consider what you want to accomplish, your audience's goals, and the impression you want to convey. You might want others to see you as smart, as someone who accomplishes things in spite of difficult odds, as someone they want to work with. Keep these goals in mind as you plan the presentation.

▶ People form their first impressions of you during the introduction portion of your presentation. This is your chance to establish the right tone and give people the sense that they have something to look forward to.

▶ Do three things in your introduction: capture the audience's attention, provide appropriate background information, and introduce your key messages. Use the opportunity to set the stage.

▶ To grab the audience's attention, try one of these ideas:

　▷ Use a dramatic statement.

　▷ Ask a question that requires a response from the audience.

　▷ Refer to a recent or well-known event.

　▷ Tell a story from your own experience.

　▷ Cite a quotation from an authoritative source.

Don't flood people with feedback. Focus on things that will make the most difference. Think targeted, not comprehensive.

▶ Determine your key messages. Choose no more than five.

　▷ State your key messages in simple, declarative sentences.

　▷ Express them as precisely and vividly as possible.

　▷ Include only one idea in each key message.

　▷ State all main ideas positively, if possible.

▶ When you form your key messages, make sure each one directly supports your purpose. There may be several points you could make about the topic, but you need to limit yourself. Choose only material that will help you achieve your purpose.

▶ Recognize that you can't cover all the details or multiple subthemes within a presentation. Presentations are illustrative, not comprehensive. Focus only on your key messages. If you have additional material that would be helpful, put it in a handout.

▶ Consider using a rhetorical device, like a metaphor, story, theme, word, comparison, or quote that you refer to throughout the presentation. The repetition will unify your presentation. For example, "In the past, our results were like a roller-coaster—up and down and all over the place."

▶ Choose supporting material that adds interest, clarity, persuasion, and impact. Vary the types of supporting data for each main idea. Select from examples, anecdotes, statistics, comparisons, explanations, and quotations.

▶ Organize your material. Some structures you could try include:

▷ Problem-solution: Present a problem, suggest a solution, and indicate likely benefits if your solution is used.

▷ Classification: Group your key messages into categories or a process. For example, research and development, engineering, manufacturing, sales.

▷ Chronology: Arrange events in sequential order.

▷ Climax: Arrange your key messages in order of increasing importance, ending with the most compelling and convincing.

▷ Simple to complex: Arrange the main points from simplest to most complex. Use this for difficult or complicated topics.

▷ Proposition-support: State your key messages and support them with evidence.

▶ In your conclusion, summarize your key messages and tell the audience what you want them to do and why. In other words, answer the questions "So what?" and "What's in it for me?"

▶ Use the template on the following page to help you organize and coordinate your content, nonverbal actions, and presentation aids:

▶ After you create the first draft of your presentation, check for continuity. For example:

▷ Check the flow of the presentation. Look for missing steps and logical leaps.

▷ Assess whether you are going on tangents.

▷ Use the same terminology to refer to the same thing throughout the presentation.

Presentation Template			
Purpose			
Introduction	*Attention getter* *Background* *Overview of key messages*	**Presentation aid(s)**	**Nonverbal actions**
Core Content	**Key message #1** *Supporting material* *Transition statement*	**Presentation aid(s)**	
	Key message #2 *Supporting material* *Transition statement*	**Presentation aid(s)**	
	Key message #3 *Supporting material* *Transition statement*	**Presentation aid(s)**	
	Key message #4 *Supporting material* *Transition statement*	**Presentation aid(s)**	
	Key message #5 *Supporting material* *Transition statement*	**Presentation aid(s)**	
Conclusion	*Summarize key messages* *Implication statement*	**Presentation aid(s)**	

▸ Retain an overall tone to the presentation, even if you have a few shifts to break the tension. (Don't veer off in a wildly different direction. If you do, people will focus on your change of tone instead of your content.)

Adapt content and level of detail to your audience

▼

People generally respond best to messages that are clear and unambiguous. They want to know what the topic is, some relevant and pertinent facts, and why it matters to them. Thoughtful preparation can make this possible every time you give a presentation. Preparation for informal settings can be helpful too, especially when it is essential that you communicate effectively. Consider the following suggestions:

▸ Analyze your audience as thoroughly as possible. Talk to people who will be in the audience or discuss your presentation with other people who have presented to the same audience.

▹ Who will be there?

▹ What do people know about the topic?

▹ How diverse is the audience? Can you discuss the topic or issue in a way that includes and relates to everyone?

▸ Learn why people want or need the information. Do they need to make a decision? Do they need background? Do they need more information to implement decisions? Use this information to guide what you say and how you say it.

Talk about ways to learn about an audience prior to giving a presentation.

▸ Recall other conversations or meetings with this individual or group. What worked well? What did the person or group respond to? Use strategies that were successful in the past.

▸ Appeal to the different perspectives represented in the audience by emphasizing several elements of your topic. Choose ideas and supporting material that will be relevant and convincing to them.

▸ Direct your content toward the level of knowledge of the decision makers in the audience, but also be prepared to provide background information for those who are less informed.

Speak effectively in front of a group

▼

Most people have a good idea of what they need to do to speak effectively in front of a group: prepare, relax, and be articulate. The piece they usually ignore is practice. To speak effectively in front of people, you actually have to speak in front of people. Consider the following suggestions:

▶ Before you start preparing, learn more about the situation and whether there is a format you should follow. This will help you determine how formal you should be, whether you can use humor, and whether you will have opportunities to interact with the audience.

▶ Whenever possible, actively involve your audience during a presentation. They will feel like you're talking with them, rather than at them.

▶ Manage the experience when you include interaction in your presentation. Decide when and how to involve the audience, keep people on topic, draw disparate thoughts together, play off the ideas and energy of the listeners, and keep the focus on your message.

Schedule practice sessions, especially before people speak at high-impact occasions.

▶ When you ask questions, make them targeted enough that people know what you're asking but not so specific that people will hold back because they fear giving a wrong answer. Questions about experiences, preferences, and opinions on a public matter are safe.

▶ Take your topic seriously, but don't take yourself too seriously. If you're too serious, people will sense that if they challenge your message, they will be challenging you personally. It will make you seem unapproachable and defensive.

▶ Talk about how people will benefit from your message. Show how it connects to other initiatives, both present and future. If you can, tie your idea or solution to an already acknowledged problem.

▶ When you are presenting to an online or video audience, remember that time delays may occur. Pace your presentation and summarize your key points so that if people missed something, they have a chance to hear it again. Remember to look directly at your Web camera during your presentation.

Demonstrate poise in front of a group

▼

In a practice session, raise your hand every time people say "uh," "umm," or other filler words. This will help them decrease their use of these words.

As a leader, you probably give presentations to many groups, including employees, direct reports, peers, upper-level leaders, and customers. Demonstrating poise will give people confidence in your message and your leadership. Consider the following suggestions:

▶ Know your topic. Be ready to talk about it broadly and in detail, and to answer a wide range of questions.

▶ Use nonverbal actions that show your conviction. Project your voice, smile, and use broad gestures.

▶ Be genuine. You will be convincing because you believe in what you are saying.

▶ Enjoy yourself and the speaking process. Your listeners will detect your confidence and also enjoy themselves more.

▶ Avoid distracting mannerisms, such as speaking in a monotone, mumbling, repeating, saying you're sorry, appearing unprepared, being vague, jingling change in your pocket, and saying "ah," "um," "like," and "you know."

▶ If you tend to appear timid or uncertain, choose words that will emphasize your message. Use words that are more dramatic and powerful than you would generally use in order to express your certainty.

▶ If you don't feel confident or enthusiastic about your idea, determine why and resolve the issue. Otherwise people will pick up on the contradiction between your words and your attitude.

Use a smooth, polished delivery style

▼

People expect leaders to be experienced communicators, at ease with groups and in command of their message. The extent to which you present with polish and poise will add to your message. Consider the following suggestions:

▶ Many leaders are experienced communicators who have weathered both positive and negative situations. Reflect on your experiences:

> ▷ Which communication experiences have been most successful for you?

> ▷ How can you use those experiences and successes in your current position?

> ▷ Which negative communication experiences taught you lessons?

Arrange for people to work with a coach in order to polish their skills.

▸ Although each opportunity is not a formal presentation, try approaching all of your messages as if they were. It will teach you how to lend high impact to your communication delivery.

▸ Be sure to do your homework. Effective preparation and accurate information are the keys to credibility.

▸ Match your delivery to the message. For example, if you are trying to energize people, show enthusiasm. Also determine when you should be a role model for how people can respond to your message. For example, if you are delivering an alarming message, do so in a calm manner.

▸ In general, dress at the level of your audience or one step above. However, if an audience expects you to dress "in uniform" despite their casual attire, meet that expectation.

▸ Keep it simple and be concise. Simplify your message to clarify complex issues, but do not be simplistic. Get to the point and focus on what is important to the audience.

▸ Package your message attractively. Use compelling stories and interesting visuals.

Speak with enthusiasm and expressiveness

People tend not to listen to speakers who are not interesting. Presentations are even more challenging. No one likes to listen to a person who drones. If you want to engage, motivate, inspire, captivate, energize, or wake people up, you need to be enthusiastic and expressive. Your ideas deserve the best delivery you can give them. To inject energy into your presentation or discussion, consider these suggestions:

▸ Note how dynamic leaders communicate their enthusiasm and adapt some of their techniques.

Together, identify two individuals who express themselves effectively and determine what makes them effective.

▶ Use your voice to show your interest and passion during a dialogue. Vary your tone of voice and inflection.

▶ Watch people react to enthusiastic speakers. List behaviors that indicate a positive or negative response. The next time you are presenting or leading a discussion, check to see what types of reactions you're receiving.

▶ Don't force enthusiasm. You don't have to be overly animated to show you're excited about an idea. Relax and let your natural enthusiasm and commitment to your message show.

▶ Develop your expressive skills outside of work.

  ▷ Read children's books, novels, or plays aloud. Act out all the parts. Use a different voice for each character. Make sound effects.

  ▷ Take an acting class. Learn about movement, conveying a message, projecting your voice, matching body language to words, and dealing with stage fright.

Speak clearly and concisely

▼

Have people practice illustrating their points to be sure they don't give exhaustive detail.

Think of how you react to someone who mumbles. How about someone who is wordy? How many minutes pass before you start thinking of something else? It's easy to become impatient with people who can't deliver a message clearly. To be sure this doesn't happen to you, consider the following suggestions:

▶ Use clear, concise language, even in casual conversations. This will help you be aware of the need to speak clearly and will give you more chances to practice.

▶ Use short, simple sentences. Complex sentences may work well in documents, but they can be confusing and difficult to understand when they're spoken.

▶ Don't lard your message with too much detail. It is easy to lose the momentum and energy in your presentation. Focus on relevant, well-chosen details and share additional information during a question-and-answer session.

▸ Pay attention to how people react to you during discussions and meetings. If they lose eye contact with you or get restless, you may be straying from the topic or giving excessive or irrelevant detail.

▸ Watch your use of "business speak." People are more interested in your ideas than in whether you know the latest jargon. If you use too much jargon, they won't hear your message.

▸ If you sense that you are on a tangent, pause and segue back to your message. Acknowledge that you were off track and reiterate your main point.

Get your point across when you're speaking

▼

People are bombarded with information. They are more likely to remember a message that is told directly. Consider the following suggestions:

▸ Know what point you're trying to make. This sounds simple, but many people don't spend enough time on this step. Be able to state your point in a single, precise sentence.

▸ Be equally precise about your key messages. Write each message in a sentence of five to eight words. Then elaborate on it with two or three sentences (no more). This will ensure that you know exactly which messages you want and need to communicate.

▸ Assume that people will remember only one or two things you said. Emphasize the points you want them to remember.

▸ Make your message memorable. Use examples and anecdotes to illustrate your points. Stories give people something to relate to and remember.

Get people to move beyond generalities. A few well-chosen details will make the presentation more compelling.

▸ When you explain a complicated point, begin with an example (concrete) and then move to an explanation (more abstract).

▸ Avoid clouding your message with extraneous detail. Give people a chance to ask questions if they want more details.

▸ Once you have made your point, ask listeners for their reactions. Are they talking about your main point? Was it clear? This will give you an opportunity to restate your point more clearly if necessary.

Actively engage the audience's interest

▼

Presenters aren't guaranteed the attention of their audiences; they have to earn it. To engage your audience, consider the following suggestions:

► If you are presenting to an audience that does not know you, walk around and talk to people before you speak. Ask about their interest in your topic and give them some background information about you. Incorporate what you learned into your presentation. For example, share an anecdote or quote (with the person's permission).

Remind people that they have approximately 30 seconds to engage the audience.

► Pause for a moment before you begin to speak. Let the audience's expectation build.

► Indicate clearly what impact your ideas are meant to have on the audience. They will be more interested in your presentation if they know how it affects their daily lives.

► If you want an interactive session, ask questions of the audience within the first five or ten minutes of your presentation. As you speak, if you are not getting questions and comments, continue to ask questions about their point of view.

► If your audience contains people with varying degrees of expertise in the topic, provide background information to those with less knowledge. For example, say, "Some of you are already familiar with _____ . For those who aren't, I'm going to take a couple of minutes to provide some background."

► To keep people from getting restless, try some of these ideas:
  ▷ Vary your vocal projection, pitch, and pace.
  ▷ Make eye contact with individuals.
  ▷ Ask a question.
  ▷ Use a visual aid.
  ▷ Tell an anecdote or a firsthand story.
  ▷ Use appropriate humor.

Gauge audience reaction and make appropriate adjustments

▼

Encourage people to practice improvising when things go wrong.

Successful presenters know the importance of watching their audience's reactions to ensure that their presentations are on target. They monitor whether the audience's attention is wavering and immediately take steps to get people back on track. Consider the following suggestions:

▶ Pay attention to the audience. Note their body language to see if they're engaged. Are they looking at you and nodding their heads? Or are they looking around and talking to each other?

▶ Invite questions from your audience. Their questions will help you identify any points that are unclear. If you need to clarify a point, use a concrete example.

▶ If you sense that your audience is lost, pause after you finish your point. Briefly recap what you have said so far, using simpler language or less detail.

▶ Watch more experienced colleagues in situations when the audience loses interest. How do they acknowledge it? How do they get people back on track? Identify at least three techniques that you can try.

▶ Role-play situations with your colleagues in which audience members get lost, restless, or otherwise disengaged. Give each other specific feedback on what works well and what is ineffective.

▶ Ask some colleagues to attend one of your presentations and provide feedback about audience reactions. They will be able to pick up on more subtle reactions than you are able to pay attention to. Use their feedback to fine-tune your ability to detect and interpret audience reactions.

Use nonverbal behavior to emphasize key points

▼

Nonverbal behavior tells the story behind the story; it can verify your words or undermine them. Be aware of and choose your nonverbal actions to enhance your words. Check the following areas:

▶ *Facial animation.* Your face displays your attitudes and emotions, so make sure your expressions match your content and your intent.

Find opportunities to smile. Smiles indicate humor, warmth, irony, or empathy. A smile will convey your personable side.

▸ *Eye contact.* Eye contact conveys your confidence and your interest in the audience. Make eye contact with many members of the audience; avoid gazing exclusively at one person or at a spot above people's heads.

▸ *Vocal variety.* Develop an effective speaking voice that varies in pace, pitch, volume, and tone. While many people are not naturally endowed with melodious voices, most have the potential for a wider range of pitch and tone.

Determine whether people's nonverbal actions enhance their message or distract from it, and why.

▸ *Gestures.* Use gestures to emphasize and reinforce your statements. Allow gestures to flow naturally from your message. For example, if you are excited and enthusiastic about your message, use more frequent and expansive gestures.

▸ *Stance.* Adopt a relaxed stance, and move in ways that complement and support your message. A rigid posture usually conveys nervousness, and random walking or other movements tend to be distracting.

▸ *Dress and appearance.* Dress appropriately for the audience and the situation. First impressions often begin with how someone is dressed. If people are preoccupied with your clothes, they won't listen as intently to your message.

Use audiovisual aids smoothly and effectively

▼

Many people believe that if they use audiovisual aids, they won't have to look at the audience, won't lose their place, and won't have to prepare formally. They usually end up overusing the aids, to their detriment. Consider the following suggestions:

▸ Use an audiovisual aid only when it is necessary: when you need to portray something that is difficult to explain—in other words, when a picture is worth a thousand words.

▸ Consider using a wider variety of audiovisual aids than PowerPoint slides. For example:

  ▷ Show a photograph or a map when you describe a place.

  ▷ Hold up a sample when you're introducing a new product.

▷ Show a map when you're describing a journey.

▷ Play music to evoke another era.

▷ Play a video clip.

▶ Avoid creating complex or highly detailed visual aids. When you need to explain a subject in detail, use a series of simple visuals rather than a single complex visual.

▶ Put key words instead of entire sentences on the slide.

▶ Practice the 1x5x5 rule: one slide, no more than five lines, five words (or fewer) per line.

▶ Use a consistent style on all visuals, including type fonts, color, and position of words and images.

▶ Proofread your visual aids. Spell-check won't catch words that are used incorrectly. Catch typographical errors by starting at the last word and working your way backward, one word at a time.

▶ Look at your visual aids from the back of the room where you will be presenting. Make sure you can see them clearly and read the words. Adjust them as necessary before your presentation.

Challenge people to give a presentation without using PowerPoint. They will stand out from the crowd.

▶ In general, provide handouts in advance only if people need to see them during the presentation. If they do not, distribute them after your presentation. Otherwise the audience will read your handouts instead of listen to you.

▶ Practice giving your presentation with your audiovisual aids. Introduce the aid, display it, describe it, show why it's relevant, and make the transition to your next point.

▶ Avoid standing between the visual aid and the audience. Also, resist the tendency to lower your voice while you use an audiovisual aid.

▶ If you have an equipment problem, tell the audience. If you can solve the problem quickly, ask the audience to wait for a few minutes or take a short break. If you can't solve the problem quickly, continue your presentation without the visual aid.

Use humor effectively in group discussions and presentations

▼

Used well, humor is a wonderful aid to communication, helping you defuse emotion, build relationships, and improve morale. Used poorly, humor can hurt people, create distance, and create an uncomfortable workplace. To use humor effectively, consider the following suggestions:

▸ Recognize that humor is a high risk/high reward stylistic element. Organizational leaders often use humor to help listeners maintain their perspective in a challenging situation, or to wryly illustrate a serious point. If you use humor well, people are likely to have a more favorable impression of you than if you don't. If you use humor poorly, however, it may be worse than if you used no humor.

Talk about the type of humor that's appropriate in the organization.

▸ Seek feedback from a trusted colleague or team member on how you currently use humor. You may think you are always using appropriate humor and may be surprised to find out that people view it differently. Or you may find that you are using humor well and people would like you to use it more frequently.

▸ Humor is highly personal. When you use humor, consider what effect your words will have on all the people you are talking to. Be especially sensitive to gender, diversity, religion, and other potentially charged issues.

▸ Humor is cultural. What is funny in one culture may not be in another.

▸ Do not use sarcasm during presentations. Even though people might laugh, at some level they will wonder when you will make them the target.

▸ If you feel uneasy about a joke or an image, don't use it. The risk of alienating your audience is not worth it.

▸ Choose humor that will be understood by a general audience. If you have to explain why something is funny, don't include it.

▸ Watch how others use humor in business settings. Choose two or three effective methods and incorporate them into your repertoire.

▸ Spend time with friends and colleagues who display a good sense of humor. Note what they say and how they use humor.

▶ Collect a few humorous books and DVDs, and bookmark online sources. Stay up to date on the type of humor that is popular with your team and your colleagues.

Answer questions clearly and concisely

▼

Answering questions is a familiar interaction; most people field questions every day from their coworkers, family, friends, suppliers, customers, and other groups. Questions help you determine how well your message is understood, what you need to clarify, and what you need to emphasize. Consider the following suggestions:

▶ Before a presentation or team discussion, think of as many potential questions as possible, especially difficult or hostile ones. Prepare strong answers that relate to your key messages. You still might be surprised by a question, but preparation will take away much of the "what if" anxiety.

▶ Determine the intent of the question. Otherwise, you may give an answer that is literally correct but ignores the larger issue that concerns the questioner.

▶ Speak to everyone in the group when you answer questions. This will focus people's attention on you instead of on the questioner. If you are in a large group, repeat the question before you answer it.

▶ Answer concisely. Research shows that answers that last 10 to 40 seconds are the best. Shorter answers can seem too abrupt, and longer answers can seem too elaborate.

During a practice question-and-answer session, try to pull people off message through your questions.

▶ When you answer lengthy or multifaceted questions, first restate the question more concisely. Then give a brief synopsis of your answer before going into details.

▶ Be honest. If you don't know the answer to a question, say so. An honest answer will give you and your message more credibility.

▶ Focus on getting information to the questioner, not on preserving your pride. If someone else can better answer a question, invite that person to respond. This will still show your expertise, because you know who has the answer.

▸ Acknowledge and empathize with the emotion behind an aggressive or hostile question, then paraphrase it in neutral terms. Answer by addressing the substantive issue, then adding neutral or positive details.

▸ If you have requested that questions be held until the end and someone interrupts with a question, offer to answer it at the conclusion of your remarks. If you keep taking questions, you could get sidetracked into areas that are not relevant to your key messages.

▸ Provide a "capper" (recap) after the last question. The question and answer session might end on a question that is unrelated or peripheral to your topic. A capper will help you finish with the key message that you most want the audience to remember.

21
Listen to Others

Listening is a hallmark of a good leader. How you demonstrate your understanding of what people say determines whether they feel heard. By taking the time to polish your listening skills, you build others' trust and confidence in you. You also will help people say what they mean.

Studies show that up to 80 percent of communication is nonverbal. So, knowing how to read others and how to ask follow-up questions are important skills to develop. When you become known as someone who is a good listener, people will feel comfortable sharing their honest opinions with you and will perceive you as someone who is engaged, present, and concerned about the issue at hand.

In this chapter, we will cover the following areas:

▼

- ▶ Evaluate your current listening skills
- ▶ Listen willingly to concerns expressed by others
- ▶ Listen attentively and with empathy to concerns expressed by others
- ▶ Exhibit appropriate nonverbal behavior to show receptivity to others' spoken messages
- ▶ Listen carefully to input
- ▶ Ask questions to clarify others' points of view
- ▶ Listen actively, reflect, and summarize others' comments to ensure understanding
- ▶ Interpret nonverbal messages
- ▶ Listen patiently to others without interrupting
- ▶ Listen well in a group

Evaluate your current listening skills

▼

As you coach, be a role model for effective listening.

Before you can effectively improve your listening skills, you need to evaluate them. Consider the following suggestions:

▸ Solicit feedback on your listening skills from coworkers, other leaders, friends, and your family. Choose people who will give you the unvarnished truth. Find out how effectively you listen to individuals both one-on-one and in group settings.

▸ Assess your typical behavior when you listen to people. Do you frequently:
  ▹ Interrupt?
  ▹ Show impatience?
  ▹ Suggest solutions before the problem is fully explained?
  ▹ Misinterpret what the person said, causing him or her to correct you?
  ▹ Spend more time talking than listening?
  ▹ Let your mind wander and miss what was said?
  ▹ Think about your response instead of listening to the speaker?

▸ Review the feedback you received. What patterns do you see? List some of the reasons you don't listen to people. For example, perhaps you:
  ▹ Don't have enough time for the conversation.
  ▹ Don't feel like making the effort.
  ▹ Think you know what the person will say.
  ▹ Don't respect the person.
  ▹ Don't like the person.
  ▹ Believe the person's opinions are irrelevant.
  ▹ Think the person is boring.

▸ Identify the top thing you could do to improve your listening skills. Treat it like any other project: pick your goal, make a plan, take action, measure your progress.

▸ Ask two or three people to help you measure your progress. As you work on your listening skills, try not to become frustrated. Typically, it takes people much longer to recognize a change in your behavior than you would like. Remember that they can't measure your intention to listen better; they can only see your behavior.

Listen willingly to concerns expressed by others

▼

Do you often learn about work concerns through a third party? Are you frequently surprised? Do people let you know what is happening on their projects, what they think, what their concerns are? If people don't communicate directly with you, perhaps it is because they think you are not interested, are unwilling to listen, or will become upset when you hear something you do not like. Consider the following suggestions:

▸ People need to know that you care about what's happening with them, their work, and their ideas and opinions. Ask people, and then listen when they talk with you. Listening is a key element that will help you create and sustain relationships.

▸ Listening is essential to engage employees. If you want your people to feel ownership for results and commitment to you and the organization, listening will help you foster this environment.

▸ Assess your attitude toward your employees and your willingness to make an effort to understand each of them. Regardless of how you feel about particular team members, recognize that each person has a part to play in your group or organization. Building a positive relationship will help you work together more effectively.

Help people understand that listening to a problem doesn't mean they are obligated to solve the problem.

▸ If you are unwilling to listen to people, identify the reasons. For example, you may expect the worst, be uncertain of your ability to solve a problem, or be afraid that people will get emotional. Once you know why you don't want to listen, you can face the issue and listen despite your fears or concerns.

▸ Offer to serve as a sounding board. Sometimes people simply need to express their concerns or frustrations.

Listen attentively and with empathy to concerns expressed by others

Empathy isn't about whether you feel the same way as the other person feels; it's about whether you care about how the person feels and respond appropriately. As you listen to concerns expressed by others, consider the following suggestions:

▸ Focus on the moment. You may have several things you would prefer to do other than listen, but your priority is to be present and pay attention to the person speaking.

▸ Listen carefully so you will understand what the person is saying, why it is important to him or her, and what he or she wants.

Explain that empathy involves understanding another person's point of view, not a deep emotional connection.

▸ Play an active role in the conversation. Ask pertinent questions that show you are listening attentively. This will encourage the person to continue and help you stay engaged in the conversation.

▸ Identify the person's main message. Also develop an understanding of how important the topic is to the person, and why.

▸ Notice the speaker's vocal pitch, intensity, and pace, and whether it differs from the person's usual way of speaking. The words may be neutral, but how they are spoken will give you clues about how important the topic is to the individual.

▸ To identify the speaker's feelings or how important the message is, listen for words like *happy, sad, worried, upset, annoyed.* Also watch for nonverbal clues to the speaker's mood. Use a reflective statement to show that you recognize the speaker's feelings.

▸ Refrain from problem solving, unless the person asks for ideas or suggestions. Often people need someone to listen more than they need an immediate solution.

▸ As you listen to people, try to put aside your own point of view and feelings. Otherwise you may find it difficult to truly listen and may start advocating your point of view.

▸ Identify people who are considered skilled listeners and watch them in action. Take note of how they convey interest and empathy. What are their nonverbal actions? What questions do they ask? How do people respond to them?

Exhibit appropriate nonverbal behavior to show receptivity to others' spoken messages

▼

Your nonverbal actions help establish the atmosphere for a conversation. They show whether you are interested, engaged, patient, bored, annoyed, dismissive. To exhibit appropriate nonverbal behavior, consider the following suggestions:

▶ Shift your attention to another person as the first step to being receptive. As you make a genuine effort to listen, your nonverbal actions will start to fall in line.

Have people practice using appropriate nonverbal behaviors during a coaching session.

▶ Use a tone of voice that shows receptivity. A monotone makes you sound bored or disinterested. Use a range of pitches and emphasize words to show that you are engaged in what the person is saying.

▶ Stop doing other things when a person is talking, even if you are talking with him or her on the phone. Research shows that people can tell when someone is occupied during phone conversations. You cannot attend to the person and do something else at the same time.

▶ Use concrete nonverbal actions to indicate that you are receptive: put aside other work, smile, make eye contact, look interested, lean toward the person as you're speaking.

▶ Learn about nonverbal behaviors in other cultures by talking to experts or reading books. When you work with people from different cultures, use behaviors and gestures that show receptivity within their culture.

Listen carefully to input

▼

Anytime you work with people, you need to know how to listen to input. On the surface, it might seem easy—people talk, you listen. Unfortunately, it's not that simple. As a leader, you need to hear two things: what people are saying and what they're not saying. Consider the following suggestions:

▶ As a person talks, identify what he or she is saying. What is the main idea? What does the person think? Why? How important is it to the person? What are the facts? What is opinion?

▶ Ask questions and listen until the message is clear, you know what the person thinks, and why it is important to the person.

▶ If the viewpoint or message does not make sense, ask more questions and learn the context for the speaker's message. Figure out what background information you need in order to understand his or her viewpoint.

▶ Ask clarifying questions to confirm the main thoughts or ideas. This is especially useful when you are listening to people who include a lot of detail or who tend to ramble.

▶ Accept silence as part of a conversation. Even though it may make you uncomfortable, don't try to fill every moment with words. People need sufficient time to shape their thoughts. Waiting for people to speak will communicate your willingness to listen and give them a chance to express themselves more fully.

▶ Recognize that some people are reluctant to share their thoughts with leaders. If you want to hear from individuals, you're going to have to seek them out. You're also going to have to be especially vigilant about listening, and not pontificating about your own ideas.

Talk about whether people's questions elicit the type of information they need.

▶ Watch your talking-to-listening ratio. Make sure you are listening more than 50 percent of the time, especially if you want to know what someone thinks.

▶ Be aware of any tendencies you have to tune out while a person is talking to you. This is a classic example of actions speak louder than words. Your actions will drown out what the person is saying and she or he will be convinced that you don't care.

▶ Recognize that some people may equate listening with agreement. They may not feel heard if you don't do what they say. State up front what you intend to do as a result of the conversation, for example, "I'm asking several people about this issue. Next week I'm going to make my decision, based in part on the input I receive."

Ask questions to clarify others' points of view

▼

Asking effective questions is a skill. You need to learn what to ask, how to phrase your questions, and when to ask them so that people will be receptive, not defensive. Consider the following suggestions:

▶ Ask questions to understand, not challenge, the person. Be aware of your body language and your tone of voice—both reveal your attitudes toward the speaker and the topic. The person might get the impression that you're challenging him or her personally rather than ensuring understanding.

Point out when questions sound challenging instead of curious.

▶ Listen carefully to the answers you receive. You may find that the conversation goes in a direction you didn't expect, but the information you receive is richer.

▶ Learn how to use open-ended questions to clarify what people are saying: "Tell me about…," "Describe…," "What happened next?" Open-ended questions give the speaker a chance to give more information. Contrast this type of question with closed questions, which can be answered with a yes or no.

▶ Guard against asking too many questions at one time. If you pepper a person with questions, he or she may get frustrated, become defensive, feel like you're more interested in getting through your list of questions than in hearing the answers.

▶ Realize that all your questions may not be answered at one time. People may get overwhelmed or may not have all the answers. Know when to pull back and continue the conversation later.

▶ When you end a conversation, ask if you can follow up later with additional questions. Sometimes questions won't occur to you until you've had time to think.

Listen actively, reflect, and summarize others' comments to ensure understanding

▼

Paraphrasing, reflecting, and summarizing are three active-listening skills that can significantly improve your communication. These skills let the speaker know that you are listening and help you understand what is being said. Active listening is much more effective than passive listening. Consider the following suggestions:

Paraphrasing: A paraphrase is a brief restatement of what another person said. It focuses on content: information, ideas, facts, opinions. Here is an example:

> ▷ *Person #1:* I can't figure out what to do with Sarah. She wants to be more involved with planning, but she doesn't understand the business context. Her ideas are interesting but they require changes that we don't have the time or money to explore.

> ▷ *Person #2:* You think her ideas are intriguing but they would be difficult to implement.

To develop your skill in paraphrasing:

▸ Make your paraphrase shorter than the original statement.

▸ Practice paraphrasing with a colleague who can give you informed feedback.

Reflecting: Reflective statements are short declarative statements that repeat the speaker's emotions or feelings. They help you create rapport, give the speaker a chance to vent his or her emotions, and allow the speaker to feel understood. Here is an example:

> ▷ *Person #1:* Since I've become a unit manager, I'm not sure how I'm doing. I don't know if I'm really in control. Sometimes I think I made the wrong decision in accepting this promotion.

> ▷ *Person #2:* You're worried that you may have made a mistake in taking the new position.

Talk about how to put people at ease during a conversation. Individuals who are too intense or overly eager to listen may make others uncomfortable.

To create reflective statements:

▸ Listen for words that indicate feelings: excited, glad, concerned, depressed, irritated.

▸ Watch for nonverbal clues to the speaker's mood.

Summarizing: A summary statement briefly restates both content and feelings. It helps you identify the key elements of a situation, shows that you are making an effort to understand a person's point of view, and promotes further discussion.

For example: "As I understand it, you think the problem with the first-line supervisors is their perception that they do not have enough responsibility and authority."

To practice creating summary statements:

▸ During meetings, create summary statements on your copy of the agenda. (This will also help you remember what was said during the meeting.)

▸ Write summary statements as you listen to interviews, podcasts, or radio and television.

Interpret nonverbal messages

▼

Talk about reasons why words and nonverbal actions might be inconsistent.

If you listen only to someone's words, you're not going to get the whole message. Communication studies show that 70 to 80 percent of the meaning in a message is communicated nonverbally. Nonverbal actions fill in the details, provide clues about attitudes, and help you understand how someone really feels about a topic or issue. Consider the following suggestions:

▸ Pay attention to nonverbal behavior. For example, if someone looks tense but is speaking calmly, coolly, and objectively, it might help to say, "It looks like you're concerned about this situation." This will encourage the person to tell you what he or she is concerned about.

▸ Compare the person's words with his or her nonverbal actions. If the actions and words appear to contradict each other, this is a clue that something is going on under the surface.

▸ Pay attention to the person's vocal intonation. Listen for shifts in tone or emphasis. Also notice whether the person's level of enthusiasm matches his or her words.

▸ When appropriate, inquire about contradictory behavior. "You said it was okay that Jeff did not deliver his part of the project on time, but you sound very angry and frustrated." Speak quietly, without judgment, and in a tone of voice that indicates you are checking your understanding. This approach will allow the person to tell you whether you interpreted the behavior correctly.

- Be aware that nonverbal behaviors vary among cultures. Learn about the differences before you try to interpret the actions of a person from a different country or culture.

Listen patiently to others without interrupting

Interruptions shift the focus to the interrupter and stifle the flow of ideas. They also can be used to intimidate people, especially when they come from someone with more expertise or from a different level of the organization. As a leader, you need to understand how frequently you interrupt others and recognize the effect it has on your group. Consider the following suggestions:

- Become aware of how often you interrupt people. Over the next month, ask people to point out when you interrupt them. Keep track of each incident and analyze it by asking the following questions:
  - ▷ Whom did you interrupt?
  - ▷ What was the situation?
  - ▷ What was the topic?
  - ▷ Why did you interrupt?
  - ▷ How did the person react to the interruption?

- Look for patterns. Do you tend to interrupt only in certain situations, such as when you talk to a specific individual or about a certain issue? Raising your awareness level will help you catch yourself.

Identify situations in which people interrupt because of disinterest, time constraints, or other reasons.

- Ask others if they consider your interruptions disruptive. Some interruptions may be helpful. They may add to the conversation by stimulating the other person to expand on his or her ideas. If it seems to contribute to the conversation, it may not be important that you stop.

- If your interruptions are disruptive, set realistic goals for changing your behavior. Avoid sweeping declarations like "I will never interrupt again." Instead, focus on one event at a time: "I will not interrupt during this meeting."

Listen well in a group

▼

It's not always easy to listen when you're in a group. Sometimes the topic does not involve you directly, or you believe people are going on and on about an issue that could be resolved easily. However, because much work is done in groups, you need to learn how to listen well and demonstrate that you are involved and are a team player. Consider the following suggestions:

▸ Resist doing other things during group discussions. Wait until the meeting is over before you do paperwork, have a side conversation, or check your messages.

Give people timely feedback on how well they listen.

▸ During the discussion, ask relevant questions. This will help you be a participant, not just an observer.

▸ Sit with the group. Don't automatically head for the back or the side of the room, where you can ignore the main activity.

▸ Challenge yourself to learn something from the speaker, even if the discussion does not pertain to you or your area of responsibility. For example, watch how the speaker tries to influence others, builds support for his or her position, or the way in which he or she uses visual aids.

22
Write Effectively

Effective business writing is clear and concise. Whether or not you are required to do a lot of writing in your job doesn't matter—managers often communicate through e-mail and online presentations. By sharpening your writing skills, you'll be able to communicate with more impact.

Many people hate writing—and while it may not be your favorite task, you can improve your writing with a little study and practice.

In this chapter, we will cover the following areas:

▼

- ▶ Define the purpose of your document
- ▶ Prepare persuasive written materials that provide a solid rationale for your position
- ▶ Adapt written communications to the audience
- ▶ Use the appropriate format for your message
- ▶ Clearly express ideas and concepts in writing
- ▶ Write in a constructive and professional manner
- ▶ Prepare written materials in a timely and efficient way
- ▶ Use style effectively
- ▶ Follow the basic rules of grammar
- ▶ Be familiar with the parts of speech
- ▶ Avoid common mistakes in writing
- ▶ Edit your documents
- ▶ Review and constructively edit the written work of others
- ▶ Write compelling e-mails that people want to read

Define the purpose of your document

▼

Discuss criteria that will make the document successful.

Many writers have a topic, but they don't have a purpose for their documents. If you don't have a purpose, you run the risk of muddying issues, confusing readers, and wasting their time. Consider the following suggestions:

► Pinpoint precisely what you're trying to persuade people to think or do. Often writers have a vague sense of what they want to accomplish but their ideas lack specificity. If it is not absolutely clear to you, it will not be clear to your readers.

▷ State your topic in a single word or a phrase. For example, a topic might be "sales prospect tracking."

▷ Find your purpose by asking "What about [your topic]?"

▷ Write your purpose in a complete sentence. To continue the example, your purpose could be "Persuade the account managers to consistently use the online version of the prospect status sheet."

► If you are unsure of your purpose, review this list for ideas.

▷ Advocate an idea.

▷ Gain approval for funding.

▷ Inspire or initiate action.

▷ Persuade people to try a new process.

▷ Sell a product or service.

▷ Update team members on progress.

Prepare persuasive written materials that provide a solid rationale for your position

▼

Persuading people through writing is different from persuading them face-to-face. You don't have the advantage of seeing the person's response so you can fine-tune your message on the spot. However, writing gives you the opportunity to polish your message and be precise. Consider the following suggestions:

► Realize that you may not know how to state your position until you wrestle with the material for a while. Expect to write several versions of important communications. Sharpen your message as you work on successive drafts.

Commiserate over the struggles and successes of writing.

▶ Prepare an outline, especially when you're writing a report or a long document. As you're preparing your outline, list the pros and cons of your position. Make arguments for and against your viewpoint. You need to be aware of multiple perspectives, even if you don't address all of them in your document.

▶ Include only relevant facts and supporting material. Irrelevant material will weaken your argument. However, don't necessarily exclude conflicting or contradictory facts. Address them, and show why they do or do not play a role in your conclusion.

▶ Link your proposal to acknowledged problems and opportunities. Then focus on selling the solution. Show how your position will bring value or benefit to the reader—will save money, increase productivity, solve a problem, avert trouble, or improve job satisfaction.

▶ Identify the type of support material that your readers will find most compelling. Talk with the people who will play a central role in getting your ideas accepted. Get their input on how to position your message.

Adapt written communications to the audience

▼

In this era of information overload, you're competing for your audience's attention. Adapting to their tastes and expectations is an effective strategy for reaching them. Consider the following suggestions:

▶ Learn about the point of view of the audience. Answer the following questions:

▷ How is the issue or topic important, relevant, timely, or significant to the readers?

▷ What do people already know about the subject or issue?

▷ What do they expect to learn from reading this document?

▶ Find out what style the audience is used to and what appeals to them. For example, assess how formal or informal they are, and whether humor appeals to them.

- Determine when people will need the information and how detailed it needs to be. For example, you might be able to send e-mail with key messages and include a more detailed attachment.

- Choose a format that will appeal to the audience. One audience might prefer a short document with brief paragraphs and bulleted lists, while another audience might feel cheated if they don't get three single-spaced pages brimming with detail.

Discuss how best to shape and deliver a potentially controversial message.

- Position your message to appeal to the audience. Imagine that you have to announce a policy change. Your readers might like some background on how you made the decision, a description of the options you considered, the part they will play in implementing the change, and the benefits you expect from making the change.

- Use terminology and jargon that your readers understand. Many writers use language that makes sense to them and don't think about whether the readers will understand it. Scan your document for insider words and acronyms, and rephrase them.

- Periodically ask a cross section of your audience for feedback on your documents. This will give you a better idea of what people ignore and what they actually read.

Use the appropriate format for your message

Packaging and format make a difference in whether or not people will read your documents. Consider the following suggestions:

- Before deciding on a format for your message, think about what you're trying to accomplish. Also consider what your readers are expecting.

- Use a standard template or format when one is available. A familiar format makes it easier for readers to quickly find the information they need.

- If you are unsure which format will be most effective, test two or three to see which one is most appropriate for your ideas. Ask colleagues to read your documents and give their opinions of which format is most successful.

▶ Include a table of contents for documents that exceed 10 pages. This will help people find the material they need. It will also help you verify that you included all the necessary sections.

Help people create templates for types of documents that they often need to write.

▶ Consider including an executive summary. This will alert people to your main points. It will also give them a quick overview of your topic in case they don't have time to read the entire document.

▶ Organize your information in a logical sequence. For example, arrange it from general to specific, from most important to least important, or in chronological order. Also try comparing and contrasting facts, categorizing them, or showing cause and effect.

▶ If you are sharing technical information with a nontechnical audience, include examples of how the concept or information can be applied. Show how the concept plays out in real life. Give illustrations and examples to which your audience can relate. Be sure to ask others to tell you when you have lapsed into using technical terminology without clarifying the terms.

▶ If you are writing for a technical audience, present an in-depth treatment of the issue. Use terminology that demonstrates your sound understanding of the topic; technical terms and concepts are appropriate, even desirable.

Clearly express ideas and concepts in writing

People like to read clearly written documents. They typically don't have time or patience to wade through unnecessary details; they just want the pertinent facts. Consider the following suggestions:

▶ Remember that your job is to convey a message, not display your vocabulary. Sometimes people become overly formal and stilted when they write. Focus on making your points, not on impressing people.

Share your process for getting started on a writing project, especially if you tend to procrastinate.

▶ Be concise and focus on the issue. If you have a hard time deciding what to include, make two columns on a page. On one side, list the necessary information; on the other side, list the "nice to have" information. This will help you identify the critical points.

- Start with a simple outline. Write your topic, your purpose, and your key messages. Don't use any adjectives, adverbs, or additional clauses. You can add details in your first draft.

- Reduce the number of words you use. For example, "We need to sit in the same room and talk about the issues that we face in trying to expedite the process necessary to get the work done" could simply be "We need to meet and discuss the process we use."

- Check for elements that will make your document difficult to understand. For example, look for contradictions, vagueness, and unnecessary details or tangents. These will interfere with your main points and discourage your readers.

- Ask several experienced writers and editors for feedback on how clearly you write. Are you wordy? Do you include unnecessary information? Does your writing lack structure? Determine the top two things you could do to improve your writing, and start practicing them this week.

Write in a constructive and professional manner

Analyze examples of excellent business writing. Look for and share samples from Business Week *or* The Wall Street Journal.

How would you feel if people formed their first impression of you based on your writing? Perhaps you would be thrilled, because you're more eloquent on paper than in person. Or perhaps you would feel cheated, because writing has never been your strong suit. In reality, people do judge you by your writing. To write in a professional manner, consider the following suggestions:

- Look at every communication as a reflection of you and your organization. Always assume that your message could be forwarded to a recipient outside of the company, or saved in a database. Don't write anything you'll regret later.

- Writing in a professional manner takes more than good intentions. Monitor your documents for the next month. Check for typographical errors, the appropriateness of your tone and style, level of detail, and clarity.

▶ Check your level of formality. If you are overly formal, it may look like you are trying to distance yourself from the material and your readers. If you are too familiar, readers may think you are not serious enough.

▶ If you are writing for an international audience, watch your use of jargon, slang, and idioms. They will not be commonly understood around the globe.

▶ Gauge the appropriateness of using humor. Humor can be misconstrued more easily in writing than in speaking, because you don't have the advantage of using intonation, gestures, and other nonverbal cues to clarify your intentions.

Prepare written materials in a timely and efficient way

▼

Many people dread writing, especially when they have a deadline. They proceed in fits and starts, and put off writing until the last possible moment. To start promptly and write efficiently, try these suggestions:

▶ Don't wait for inspiration to strike—you could wait years for this to happen. Instead, schedule time to write, and write during that time. Be disciplined.

▶ Set aside 30-minute blocks for writing. This is a manageable amount of time to endure if you dread the process, and it's usually a small enough chunk to carve out of a busy schedule.

▶ Set small goals that you can achieve in 30 minutes. For example, write an outline or one paragraph.

Suggest that people set up a schedule for writing and editing. Writing takes a lot of effort that people often are not prepared to exert.

▶ Go to a place where you can shut the door and not be interrupted. Writing takes concentration; give yourself the space and time to do it well.

▶ Begin writing the section you are most familiar with or the one you like the most. Don't feel that you have to start at the beginning and plow through until you reach the end.

▶ If you have trouble getting started, write for five minutes without stopping. If you can't think of enough to write about the topic, write about something else. Just keep writing.

▶ Don't get stuck trying to think of the perfect word; you can find a better word later. To make sure that you go back to that part of your document, highlight the word or use capital letters. If you are using Microsoft Word, use the tracking feature and insert comments to remind yourself to revisit that section.

Use style effectively

▼

Think of authors you admire, whose books and articles you always read. What makes the writing compelling? One reason is style. Style turns reading into an experience. Whether or not you recognize it, you already have a style. People have expectations of your writing—they already know whether they will enjoy it or endure it. To enhance your style and make your writing more inviting to others, consider these suggestions:

▶ Ask for feedback about your writing style. Get details about the words you use, the rhythm and pace, whether your writing seems formal or informal, and so on.

Help people decide when to use a casual style or a formal style.

▶ Be aware of style when you read magazines, books, academic journals, e-mails, and online information. Describe your general impression of each: Is it formal, informal, academic, brisk, plodding, lively? What makes it that way? Look at elements like word choice, sentence length, the amount of detail and explanations, and point of view. Is the author writing in the first (I, we), second (you), or third (she, he, they) person?

▶ Raise your standards by reading excellent writing. Look for well-written articles, essays, biographies, reports, and novels.

▶ Remember that writing is not speaking. Writing gives you time and space to choose the right word, use the right tone, and strike the right note. Viewed this way, writing is a luxury, not a chore. You can literally think before you write.

▶ Consider taking a writing class or working with a writing coach to develop your style. Individualized feedback and group discussions will develop your knowledge and appreciation of style.

▶ Ensure that your writing style is consistent with your organization's culture, others' expectations, and the content of your message.

Follow the basic rules of grammar

▼

Hand out grammar "cheat sheets" and suggest that people play a game of grammar trivia with their team. Make it fun.

Grammar. If you rolled your eyes when you read this word, you're not alone—many people find grammar a bewildering and boring subject. However, learning grammar is not impossible. If you can learn the rules of tennis or chess, you can learn the rules of grammar. Consider the following suggestions:

▶ Reacquaint yourself with the basic elements listed here, then forge ahead and learn more about how they interact.

▶ Invest in a high-quality, up-to-date dictionary (the current edition of *Merriam-Webster's Collegiate Dictionary* is a good choice) and a grammar guide such as *Grammar Girl's Quick and Dirty Tips for Better Writing* (Holt Paperbacks, 2008).

▶ Take one evening to read Strunk and White's *The Elements of Style*. It's a classic book, a quick read, and a great way to become familiar with basic grammar and style issues.

▶ Bookmark Web sites that focus on language and usage.

Become familiar with the parts of speech

▼

Refer people to "Grammar Girl" for podcasts and quick articles on easy ways to remember grammar and improve writing.

Words fall into eight categories according to how they are used in sentences. These categories, or parts of speech, are nouns, pronouns, verbs, adjectives, adverbs, prepositions, conjunctions, and interjections.

In its most basic form, a sentence consists of a subject (a noun or pronoun) and a predicate (a verb): *Tom works.* Various kinds of modifiers may be attached to both subject and predicate: *Tom, the division manager, works until seven almost every evening.* A verb must agree in number with its subject, and a pronoun must agree in number with its antecedent— that is, both elements must be either singular or plural.

A noun *(manager, office, desk)* refers to a person, place, or thing. A pronoun *(she, it)* refers back to a noun (the pronoun's antecedent). Make sure that it is clear to whom or to what a pronoun refers.

A verb *(do, be, go)* indicates an action or a state of being. The infinitive form of a verb incorporates the word to: *to do, to be, to go.* Avoid splitting an infinitive *(to boldly go)* unless you have a good reason to do so, but don't write a tortured sentence merely to avoid a split infinitive.

Adjectives and adverbs are modifiers that describe nouns and verbs. Place them as close as possible to the words they modify in order to avoid confusion or an unintended meaning.

A preposition *(of, to, in)* links a noun to another word. A conjunction *(and, but)* is a connector. An interjection *(wow)* is an exclamation.

Avoid common mistakes in writing

It's relatively easy to learn to recognize—and thereby avoid—some common mistakes. Don't try to memorize them all. Instead, get to the point where you are prompted to look up a word or grammar point because you know there's "something about this word."

▸ Ask an editor to check your work for common mistakes. Make a list of the kinds of problems this person points out to you and keep it near your computer to use as a guide for proofreading your work.

▸ Avoid making up words. Businesspeople are notorious for making up new words by adding suffixes *(-ful, -ity, -ization)* and turning nouns into verbs *(author, impact)*. While part of the charm of English is its flexibility, stretching it too far will reflect poorly on you.

▸ Among the errors most often made by good writers are dangling and misplaced modifiers. A dangler modifies a word that is implied but doesn't appear in the sentence; the solution is to make that word explicit:

Incorrect: *Having reviewed the report, your conclusions appear to be correct.*

Correct: *Having reviewed the report, I find that your conclusions appear to be correct.*

Carelessly placed modifier: *The group only meets in the mornings.*

Well-placed modifier: *The group meets only in the mornings.*

▸ Use *myself* correctly. It is a reflexive pronoun—the doer of the action is the same as the receiver: *I burned myself on the stove.*

Incorrect: *Miranda or myself will check on the refund.* (Myself will check.)

Correct: *Miranda or I will check on the refund.* (I will check.)

Incorrect: *Send the forms to Alma or myself.* (Send the forms to myself.)

Correct: *Send the forms to Alma or me.* (Send the forms to me.)

Ask people to pick one writing skill they want to improve in the next three months. Check in with them periodically to keep them accountable.

▸ Use singular pronouns and the singular form of verbs with *someone, anyone,* and *anybody*:

Incorrect: *If anyone wishes to go, they should call . . .*

Correct: *If anyone wishes to go, he or she should call . . .*

▸ Use inclusive language that excludes neither women nor men. If you find "he or she," cumbersome, use the plural or look for another way to structure your sentence.

Exclusive: *An applicant must write a letter and include his résumé.*

Inclusive: *Applicants must write a letter and include their résumés.*

Inclusive: *You must write a letter and include your résumé.*

Inclusive: *To apply, write a letter and include a résumé.*

▸ Use apostrophes correctly. An apostrophe generally indicates either a contraction (*it's* for *it is*) or a possessive (*the manager's office*). Beware of adding an apostrophe to a plural:

Incorrect: *The Smith's founded the company.*

Correct: *The Smiths founded the company.* (plural)

Correct: *The Smiths' company is doing well.* (plural possessive)

▸ Write each item in a bulleted list to fit a parallel structure: begin each item with a verb, for example, or make each one a question.

▸ Use *i.e.* ("in other words" or "that is to say") and *e.g.* ("for example") correctly, and use them sparingly. In either formal or colloquial text, you are probably better off using the words than the abbreviations.

▸ Distinguish between *comprise* (to include) and *compose* (to form by putting together). The whole comprises the parts; the parts compose the whole.

- Become familiar with other potentially confusing pairs of words:
  - ▷ *accept* (take, believe) and *except* (but)
  - ▷ *allude* (make reference to) and *elude* (escape, evade)
  - ▷ *imply* (suggest in a subtle manner) and *infer* (understand to mean)
  - ▷ *ambivalent* (of two minds) and *ambiguous* (lacking clarity)
  - ▷ *fewer* (for numbers: fewer pens) and *less* (for quantities: less time)
  - ▷ *continual* (has breaks in the action) and *continuous* (uninterrupted)

- Avoid confusing words that sound the same: *it's* ("it is") and *its* (possessive); *you're* ("you are") and *your* (possessive); *who's* ("who is" or "who has") and *whose* (possessive); *they're* ("they are"), *their* (possessive), and *there* ("at that place").

- Avoid run-on sentences.

  Incorrect (run-on): *My findings show that a merger is the only solution, we need to take action on the plan now.*

  Correct: *My findings show that a merger is the only solution. We need to take action on the plan now.*

- Use sentence fragments (which lack either a subject or a verb) sparingly. Here are two examples:
  - ▷ *Packed full of tips and how-to's.*
  - ▷ *To prove that the project worked.*

- Avoid ending a sentence with a preposition if you can do so gracefully.

Edit your documents

All writing needs an editor. Depending on the situation and the document, you may be able to edit your own work, or you may need to enlist an editor. In either case, editing will make your work clearer and help you communicate your thoughts more effectively.

- Analyze the tone of your writing. What tone do you want to convey? Are you using the proper words to do so?

> ▸ Look for sentences that seem out of place. For example, does any of the language sound inappropriate or unnecessarily forceful compared with the rest of the document?

Invite an experienced editor to a coaching session so people can ask questions and get a better sense of the editing process.

> ▸ Determine whether your content passes the following test: Everything needs to be there for a reason, and that reason must be clear to the reader.

> ▸ Focus on the action in each sentence and state it succinctly. For example, use "investigate" instead of "conduct an investigation," and "decide" instead of "make a decision."

> ▸ Circle the passive verbs that can create flat, tepid writing, in your document and turn some of them into active verbs. For example:
>   ▷ *Managers are motivated by the idea of quality.* (passive)
>   ▷ *The idea of quality motivates managers.* (active)

> ▸ If you have difficulty cutting text, try the following:
>   ▷ Cross out all unnecessary adjectives, adverbs, and descriptive clauses.
>   ▷ Change passive verbs to active verbs.
>   ▷ Address only one idea per sentence.

> ▸ Check your work for redundancies such as *2 p.m. this afternoon, duration of time, red in color, advance planning, small in size, past history.*

> ▸ Delete wordy clichés: *at this point in time, per your request, above and beyond.*

> ▸ Limit your use of adverbs like *absolutely, totally, really, incredibly, extremely.* They can make your work sound like a marketing brochure.

> ▸ Refer to men and women in the same way. For example, don't refer to women by their first names if you are referring to men by their full names. Don't describe how women look unless you are also going to mention the men's appearance.

> ▸ Use your word processor's spell-check utility, but be aware of its shortcomings. It checks only for correct spelling, not whether you have used the correct word: If you type manger instead of manager, the spell-checker will not detect the error.

▶ To catch words the spell-check program may have missed, begin proofreading your documents at the end and working back toward the beginning. This will help you pay attention to the words, not the meaning.

▶ Ask an editor to review your document. It is always helpful to have another person look at your work to verify that you caught all the typographical errors and that your message is clear.

Review and constructively edit the written work of others

▼

Managers frequently need to review the work of others, such as editing the work of a direct report or commenting on a colleague's position paper. Reviews can focus on content, grammar, style, or other elements. Consider the following suggestions:

▶ Understand your role as an editor. In most cases, your task is to help the writer make the document as clear as possible, not to rewrite it in your own words.

▶ Find out how thoroughly the person wants you to edit. Is he or she looking for feedback on the tone and content, on inconsistencies and typographical errors, or both? Agree on the kind of review you will do before you begin.

If people are upset by edits, remind them that editing is meant to help writers convey what they actually mean to say.

▶ Before you start to edit, read the entire document to get an overall sense of what the writer is trying to accomplish. If you have questions as you read, write them on a separate piece of paper. You may find that the author answers your questions later in the document.

▶ Check your content questions with the writer before you modify the document in order to avoid unnecessary and incorrect changes.

▶ Analyze whether the tone or style conflicts with the message. If it does, help the writer identify a tone that would be more appropriate for the document.

▶ If you suggest significant changes, explain how they will make the document stronger.

▸ Communicate your edits in a positive way. Remember that writing is difficult for many people and the editing process can be painful. Consider how you would feel if you heard this feedback.

▸ Identify three or four people whose work you have edited. Ask them whether your edits were helpful and if they have any suggestions for improving the process in the future.

Write compelling e-mails that people want to read

▼

E-mail can be a source of frustration and overload when it's used poorly. To make the most effective use of e-mail, consider the following suggestions:

▸ Think about what you put into e-mail, especially when it involves sensitive company information. E-mails can be stored permanently. You may think you're deleting them, but a skilled person can retrieve e-mail weeks, months, and even years later. As you write, consider how your message would sound being read aloud in court.

▸ Write for a wide audience, even when you think your e-mail will go only to your intended recipient. E-mails can be forwarded to other people without your knowledge.

▸ Make your subject line count. Some people won't open an e-mail unless the subject line clearly indicates that it is important for them to read it. Place a person's or company's name in the subject line to help avoid spam filters.

▸ Put the most vital information at the beginning. You can't be sure that someone will read the entire message.

▸ If you address e-mail to a wide audience, begin with a line stating what the e-mail is about so that people can delete it if it is not relevant for them.

▸ Check the spelling and grammar in your e-mails. E-mail can be casual, but not sloppy.

- When you send e-mails to colleagues in other countries, avoid jargon. Your terminology may be unfamiliar, and colloquialisms literally may not translate. Also gauge the level of familiarity you adopt; some cultures require a more formal tone than others.

Ensure that people put vital information in the first paragraph of an e-mail.

- Establish e-mail guidelines with your group. Consider factors such as:
  - ▷ How often e-mail should be checked.
  - ▷ What kinds of communication e-mail should *not* be used for.
  - ▷ Whether you want to allow jokes or non-work items to be sent to company lists, and if so, with what guidelines.
  - ▷ How quickly you expect your colleagues to respond to e-mail messages.

- Find out how the people in your IT department want to handle attachments. For example, they may discourage sending attachments to large groups of people. Or they may prefer that you attach shortcuts or links instead of the entire document.

23

Establish Relationships

Establishing positive relationships with people in your organization fosters a friendly, open work environment where employees feel that they can contribute ideas, creativity, and feedback. You can take steps to improve your people skills and be a model to others. Understanding how relationships work in your organization is a good place to start.

As you focus on relationships, take the time to consider how people perceive you and how you can improve the way you relate to people. Sometimes small changes can make a big difference. If you need help, consider finding a coach who can provide feedback and suggestions.

In this chapter, we will cover the following areas:

▼

- ► Be open and friendly to put people at ease
- ► Show genuine interest in the needs and concerns of others
- ► Relate to others in an accepting and respectful manner regardless of their organizational level, personality, or background
- ► Leave others feeling better after you have interacted with them
- ► Adjust interpersonal style and communication to a variety of people and situations
- ► Respond appropriately to subtle or nonverbal cues from others
- ► Treat people with respect
- ► Treat people fairly
- ► Develop effective working relationships with your direct reports
- ► Develop effective working relationships with your peers
- ► Develop an effective working relationship with your manager
- ► Develop effective working relationships with higher management
- ► Compromise to build give-and-take relationships with others
- ► Build relationships with direct reports in other locations
- ► Cultivate networks of people across a variety of functions and locations within the organization
- ► Leverage networks to get things done

Be open and friendly to put people at ease

▼

List behaviors that make people seem approachable.

An open and friendly manner can help you build relationships by making you more approachable. It can also put people at ease, dissipate a negative atmosphere, and help people work cooperatively. Consider the following suggestions:

► Ask trusted coworkers or friends about their first impressions of you. Do you seem friendly and easily approachable, or do you seem intimidating and gruff? Do your gestures and speech patterns make people comfortable or uncomfortable? List specific behaviors that people use to describe you.

► When you meet someone, use a culturally appropriate manner to communicate welcome, respect, and interest. For example, in a Western culture, help the person feel at ease by initiating a conversation.

► Show interest in people as individuals. For example, pay attention to what they say about their interests, likes, and dislikes. A colleague might mention her garden; take the cue to talk about gardening.

► Use humor to ease awkward silences or tension, and to break the ice when you're meeting new people. Appropriate humor helps people see your personable side.

► Consider your body language. If your presence seems to make others uncomfortable, ask a coach for feedback about your body language and find out how you could be more approachable. For example, hold yourself in a relaxed manner, smile, and nod to encourage others as they talk.

► Be visible to your team. Frequently walk around your area, check in with people, and talk to them about their work. Make sure to stay in touch with team members in other locations—a quick e-mail can help them feel included and appreciated. This will make people feel more at ease with you, and they will feel more confident that you understand their issues.

► If you choose to adjust your personal style, do so gradually and consistently. People may be suspicious about an abrupt change from a distant or heavy-handed style to a friendly and approachable style. Changing too quickly can make your relationships uncomfortable.

▶ Tell people about your communication style ahead of time so they will not be taken by surprise or offended. People appreciate managers who communicate openly and directly while still respecting their feelings and differences.

Show genuine interest in the needs and concerns of others

▼

Taking an interest in other people and their needs is a necessary step in building positive relationships. This does not mean that you have to engage in long conversations about their personal lives. Instead, show that you care about what they think and what they are doing. Consider the following suggestions:

▶ Recognize that it is important for leaders to show interest in people and their needs. You accomplish your work through other people. If you don't know what they're interested in or what they need, you won't understand what motivates them or be able to garner their support.

▶ Commit to understanding others, even if you don't agree with them. Adopting this mind-set may make it easier for you to listen and show interest in people's views.

▶ Ask open-ended questions about people's work—what they enjoy the most, what gives them the most satisfaction, what their biggest challenges are. Ask what they want from you and how you can help them be more successful.

▶ Use active listening skills such as asking open-ended questions, paraphrasing, reflecting, and summarizing. Active listening helps you focus on the person who is talking.

▶ Recognize that spending time on relationships is an investment. The amount of time you devote to others will pay large dividends in terms of your ability to accomplish your goals.

Be a role model; show genuine interest in the people you coach.

▶ If you have difficulty generating interest in certain people and situations, examine the reasons for it. You may have a personality conflict; you may be bewildered because people seem to be bothered by things that don't affect you. Once you address the root cause, you can begin to show more genuine interest.

▶ Identify leaders who show genuine interest in others and watch them in action. How do they convey interest and empathy? What are their nonverbal actions? What questions do they ask? How do people respond to them? Note how their behavior affects their reputation and skill as leaders.

Relate to others in an accepting and respectful manner regardless of their organizational level, personality, or background

▼

Successful leaders know how to get along with people across the organization, regardless of their personalities or backgrounds. They understand that cordial, effective relationships help people work together productively. Consider the following suggestions:

Have people practice expressing opinions and disagreements in ways that are constructive and respectful.

▶ When you meet a new colleague, concentrate on developing a rapport that will allow you to communicate effectively. Focus on what you need to do to make the relationship work, not on whether you like the person or whether he or she is different from you.

▶ Learn more about people in your organization. Find out how their interests, experiences, and perspectives are similar to and different from your own. Understand each person as an individual, not as the representative of a group.

▶ Develop an appreciation for people's differences. Learn about their careers, what brought them to the company, what they're trying to accomplish. This will help you understand their viewpoints and give you a broader perspective on their reactions to events and issues.

▶ Adopt the attitude that you can learn something from each individual, even those who are difficult to work with. Look for a skill, approach, or outlook that each person can teach you.

▶ Observe the way people in other groups interact. Take note of behaviors you could use to be more effective when you work with them. For example, people from other cultures or backgrounds may have different expectations about nonverbal behavior, sharing personal information at work, or interacting with coworkers.

▸ Be wary of basing your opinion solely on another person's experience with an individual. Develop your own relationship with the person, and go into it with an open mind and a positive attitude.

Leave others feeling better after you have interacted with them

▼

Work can be stressful. Part of your job as a leader is to maintain a positive atmosphere in which people can accomplish their goals. Even in tense or unpleasant situations, you can show a concern for others that will help them feel better after you talk. Consider the following suggestions:

▸ Think of concrete ways you can make people feel better. For example, talk about people in a way that makes them feel valued. Discuss situations in a graceful way instead of complaining, getting bitter, or being cynical.

▸ Make yourself accessible, and encourage others to come to you with problems or concerns. Knowing that you are available and willing to help will make people more likely to seek you out.

▸ Improve your listening skills. Check your understanding of others' feelings and concerns by asking open-ended questions and paraphrasing their comments. Nod and make eye contact as you listen.

▸ Use humor to relieve stress. Humor can take away the initial "bite" and help people get perspective on a situation.

▸ Realize that humor needs to be used at the right time and in the right way. For example, use humor to help people cope more effectively with a serious situation, not to distract them. People may feel more stressed if they think you're trying to minimize the seriousness of a situation or to paper over it with a positive attitude.

Observe people to see if they encourage individuals who have been having a difficult time.

▸ Consider how your personal style affects people. For example, if you have a strict or demanding leadership style, people may feel intimidated, overwhelmed, or nervous when they're interacting with you. Learn how you can adjust your style so that you leave people feeling better, not worse.

▸ When you must communicate negative information, offer your help, support, and sympathy. This will let people know that you recognize the gravity of the situation and that you want to help them.

Adjust interpersonal style and communication to a variety of people and situations

Effective leaders are versatile and adaptable. They understand that one style of interaction does not fit every person or situation. Consider the following suggestions:

Encourage people to discuss communication styles with their teams so they can recognize when someone's style is different from their own.

▸ Base your approach on the needs of the person, task, and situation. For example, an experienced employee facing a daunting task may need to know that you have confidence in his or her abilities. A new employee may need encouragement plus training.

▸ Use a personality test such as the Myers-Briggs Type Indicator® to gain insight into your personal style and those of others. This will help you understand why the detail people get so frustrated when big-picture thinkers start brainstorming during a project planning meeting.

▸ Pay attention to the interpersonal styles of your team and other colleagues. Then consider how your style typically interacts with theirs. For instance, if you tend to be gregarious and assertive, your style may put off people who prefer quiet, calm interactions.

▸ Recognize the value of adapting your interpersonal style. People respond more favorably to leaders they feel comfortable with, and adjusting your style is one way to make them comfortable. Expect that you will need to adapt to others, not that they will adapt to you.

▸ Think about how you adapt your style in your personal life. You probably interact differently with family members and friends depending on their personalities, your history, the situation, and your relationship. Do the same at work.

▸ Be careful about how and when you adjust your interpersonal style. You may be viewed as manipulative if you change styles suddenly. Also, people might believe you are showing favoritism if you use drastically different styles with different people.

Respond appropriately to subtle or nonverbal cues from others

Have you ever experienced a situation in which everyone appears calm, but the atmosphere is charged? In those cases, your best strategy is to look for nonverbal cues to guide your actions. Consider the following suggestions:

▸ Make a list of the cues you should look for: vocal tone, intensity, and inflection; eye contact; body language; word choices; where people are sitting or standing in the room.

Discuss how nonverbal cues differ between genders and cultures.

▸ Become a student of how people show their reactions nonverbally. For example, watch how people behave when they are receiving praise or being treated respectfully. In meetings, watch how people respond nonverbally when they are interrupted or when their ideas are not taken seriously.

▸ If you have received feedback that you aren't responding to nonverbal cues, get more information. Have a candid discussion with a trusted colleague or friend, and press him or her for details. For example, you may be so focused on communicating your point that you don't pay attention to how people are responding to you. Or you may not understand the messages people are sending through their actions.

▸ Realize that nonverbal behaviors vary by culture and region. For example, in some cultures direct eye contact is expected, and in others it is considered rude or confrontational.

▸ When you recognize negative nonverbal responses, allow others to talk while you assess the mood and the situation. Adopt a listening and learning role for a while.

Treat people with respect

▼

Consistently showing respect for others is essential for creating and sustaining a productive environment. Consider the following suggestions:

▸ Check out your assumptions about how people prefer to be treated. Many individuals assume that all people define respect in the same way and are surprised to find that their impressions are incorrect. When in doubt, ask questions.

▸ Assess whether your intentions match your behavior. You may not intend to be rude or disrespectful, but nonverbal behaviors can give the impression that you aren't interested in listening, you don't think others' views are important, or you don't care about their feelings. Ask for feedback about the impressions you give others.

> ▸ Identify the circumstances in which you do not treat others with respect (when you are stressed or behind schedule, for example), and make a conscious effort to change your behavior. Being aware of your tendencies will help you change them. As you approach a deadline, for example, remind yourself of the need to be respectful toward your colleagues.

> ▸ Confront issues, not people. Placing blame on others or making personal attacks fosters an atmosphere of disrespect. Focus on issues and respect other people and their ideas, even if you don't agree with them.

When people are stressed, talk about how to monitor moods, actions, and words to ensure that they remain respectful toward others.

> ▸ Respect others' privacy. When you must confront someone or handle a delicate situation, do it in private. This will show respect for the other person's feelings and reduce the chance of potentially damaging gossip.

> ▸ Don't use inappropriate or hurtful sarcasm. Identify occasions in which you use sarcasm in ways that offend others, or where you use sarcasm to avoid talking honestly about a difficult situation. Replace sarcasm with appropriate humor.

> ▸ Study other cultures to understand different perceptions of respect. People with backgrounds different from yours may have different ideas about how to convey respect. Understand expectations for respectful behavior and act accordingly.

Treat people fairly

▼

Perceptions of unfair treatment can arise in many situations. For example, people might perceive unfairness in amount of work, types of opportunities and assistance they receive, or opportunities to influence a decision that affects their work. To ensure that you treat people fairly, consider the following suggestions:

> ▸ Pay attention to any feedback you receive that you show favoritism or treat some individuals differently than you treat others. When you receive feedback, keep the following in mind:
>> ▷ Listen carefully so that you understand the situation. Take care to not argue or defend yourself.
>> ▷ Summarize the person's concerns and feelings.

> ▷ Consider asking the person what he or she thinks would be fair in the situation.

> ▷ After you understand the point of view, discuss what you could do differently.

> ▷ If you do not understand or know what to do, or if you feel angry or hurt, let the person know you heard what he or she said. Say that you want to think about the situation, and then consult with someone, such as your manager, coach, or HR representative.

▶ Recognize everyone involved in a project—not just the stars. People want to know that you notice and appreciate their efforts.

Ask for a description of fair treatment in a number of work scenarios.

▶ Examine how you assign work:

> ▷ Look at the assignments you give to each team member. Analyze each person's abilities, the visibility and complexity of the assignments, and the person's interest in the assignments.

> ▷ Determine whether the assignments are equitable, given the skills of each individual.

> ▷ Ask your team members for their opinions on the current distribution of responsibilities. Address any concerns they have.

> ▷ If people believe they should have more challenging assignments, tell them what skills, competencies, and experiences are required.

▶ Avoid taking sides in disagreements between or among employees. Instead, facilitate a discussion.

▶ Explain your decisions, especially when they affect people's roles and their work. When people understand the rationale behind a decision and feel as if they have been a part of the process, they are more likely to perceive you as being fair.

Develop effective working relationships with your direct reports

▼

Managers are often the most significant factor in whether direct reports enjoy their jobs. Every other aspect of the job may be perfect, but if the relationship with the manager is poor, direct reports will become unhappy. To develop effective relationships with your direct reports, consider the following suggestions:

▸ Be accessible. Spend time each day in your employees' work area and talk about their work. Remind people in other locations to feel free to call or e-mail you. This will show your interest and give you opportunities to hear firsthand about daily issues and frustrations.

▸ If you typically don't spend a lot of time with your employees, gradually increase the frequency of your visits or other communications. A drastic change may cause them to think that you are unhappy with their work and you're checking up on them.

▸ Establish an open-door policy. If this is not a good option (if you travel frequently, for example, or have employees in other locations), set aside regular blocks of time to discuss concerns. Announce your schedule, put it on your electronic calendar, and tell each direct report personally.

▸ Stick with your policy once you start it. Insincere attempts to appear approachable may worsen communication instead of improve it. For example, if you establish times when you will be available and then consistently schedule other events at these times, people may conclude that you are all talk and no action.

Ask people whether they focus on their direct reports' feelings and concerns, not on their own.

▸ Share some of your personal interests. People will feel more comfortable sharing their interests with you if they see that you are willing to reveal information about yourself.

▸ If you invite people to discuss problems, be prepared to respond appropriately. Be a problem solver rather than a problem reactor.

▸ If individuals wish to discuss personal problems, be willing to listen. Take care, however, not to take on roles for which you are not professionally trained, such as that of financial or family counselor.

Develop effective working relationships with your peers

In your career, you probably have had both positive and negative experiences with peers. You know how their support can help you achieve your goals and how their opposition can stymie progress. The question is not whether to build relationships with your peers, but how. Consider the following suggestions:

▶ Prepare a list of the peers with whom you work regularly. Rate the quality of your working relationship with each person on your list:

1 = Work poorly together
2 = Have an adequate working relationship
3 = Work reasonably well together (room for improvement)
4 = Work very well together

Peers	Quality of Working Relationship
	1 2 3 4
	1 2 3 4
	1 2 3 4
	1 2 3 4

▶ Identify obstacles and problems in the relationships. Determine what you can do to resolve these issues. In many cases, the solution may be obvious once you describe the problem.

▶ If you want to improve a relationship, set measurable goals and establish milestones for taking action. Be precise about what you're going to do and why you're going to do it.

Have people compare a positive peer relationship with one that is thorny. What makes the difference?

▶ As you work with your peers, try to recognize when you're on the verge of damaging a relationship over a small issue. Take a step back and think about the larger context. Is it worth alienating a peer just to make a point?

▶ As you improve your relationships with your peers, monitor whether they are more willing to volunteer information, provide feedback on your ideas, and discuss issues with you. You'll know you're making progress when you start getting input from peers who have never offered it in the past.

Develop an effective working relationship with your manager

▼

Your relationship with your manager greatly affects your job satisfaction. It is in your best interest to make the relationship as positive as possible. Consider the following suggestions:

- ▶ Help negotiate your manager's expectations of you. Set up a meeting to discuss your role, compare perspectives, and develop a shared understanding of goals and expectations.

Ask people to write a description of the type of relationship they would like to have with their manager.

- ▶ Learn about your manager's professional and personal goals, and determine how you can help him or her achieve them.

- ▶ Identify your manager's strengths and weaknesses, and use your skills to complement or compensate for them.

- ▶ Let your manager know what you are learning from him or her, and what he or she has done that you like or respect. Managers appreciate positive feedback too.

- ▶ If you have an unpleasant or even hostile relationship with your manager, recognize that you're probably going to have to be the one to improve it. Set your expectations accordingly. You don't have to become friends, but you need to find a way to work with each other. Start by taking the high road: treat your boss with courtesy, don't talk behind his or her back, follow through on your commitments.

Develop effective working relationships with higher management

▼

Look for projects in which people will work with higher management on broad organizational problems.

Senior-level managers can help you obtain the support you need for your area, give you insights into the strategy of the organization, and provide opportunities to advance your career. Consider the following suggestions:

- ▶ Take advantage of opportunities to associate with higher-level managers. Establish rapport by discussing something you know they are interested in or providing information about an initiative they're sponsoring.

- ▶ Focus on providing information that will be of interest to higher-level managers. If you just try to publicize your accomplishments or opinions, you will be memorable, but for the wrong reasons.

- ▶ Identify two or three senior managers whose areas intersect with yours. Discuss common goals and ways you can work together to achieve them. If it seems appropriate, volunteer to act as a resource to their teams.

▶ Serve on a committee or work on a special project with higher-level managers. This will give you a chance to interact in both structured and unstructured situations in which they will have opportunities to witness your skills, ideas, and enthusiasm firsthand. Find opportunities to maintain the relationships after the committee or project work is done.

Compromise to build give-and-take relationships with others

▼

Building reciprocal relationships requires both compromise and responsiveness on your part. By conceding relatively unimportant points and offering to share resources, you can create and maintain relationships that will serve you well. Consider the following suggestions:

Check that people support others whenever possible. Their influence will increase when they build give-and-take relationships.

▶ Keep in touch with people, so you can volunteer help when it is needed. Showing awareness and concern for others builds solid relationships.

▶ When you think compromise may be required, classify your issues into three categories:

▷ Issues that can be dropped or put aside without penalty to you. Use these issues first as conciliatory gestures in negotiations.

▷ Issues that are nice to have, but not essential. These are the next offerings you can make.

▷ Must-have issues. Hold out the longest for these.

▶ Resist the urge to forward your request to a higher level in the organization when someone cannot help you. This tactic will alienate the person whose support you will need in the future. Instead:

▷ Believe he or she does want to help, but really does not have the time or resources.

▷ Make your request again, emphasizing your common goals or the importance of the need.

▷ Give the person direct feedback about the impact of his or her refusal.

▶ Don't be too busy to listen to another person's requests; this can brand you as a manager who uses others, a reputation that can hurt you. Other managers may not want to work with or promote individuals who do not know how to give as well as take.

- Before agreeing to help, make sure you understand exactly what the other person is requesting by asking questions and investigating the issues. If possible, write down and agree upon the resources you will contribute.

- If you truly are too busy to help, the following tips can help you say no without jeopardizing the relationship or future support:
  - ▷ If the task is not integral to you, suggest someone else who could help.
  - ▷ If it is integral, make sure there is no possible way you can take it on. Look for ways to rearrange your current priorities to allow you to accommodate the request. Or try to identify a peer or a team member who could temporarily or permanently assume one of your other responsibilities.

Build relationships with direct reports in other locations

Depending on your organizational structure, your direct or indirect reports may be located in other cities, states, or countries. Some of the biggest hurdles to building relationships with them are logistical: different time zones, different languages, lack of opportunity to meet face-to-face, reliance on e-mail and voice mail as the main communication vehicles. To overcome these obstacles, consider the following suggestions:

- Set the expectation that you will speak regularly with each individual and that the team will have opportunities to interact. For example, you might have a weekly phone call with each person and a weekly videoconference call with the team.

- Arrange to meet your direct reports throughout the year. At a minimum, you should meet each person at least once. If it's feasible, try to get together every month or once a quarter. Also take advantage of events, such as professional conferences, to gather your team.

Recommend weekly phone calls with direct reports in other locations.

- Think of e-mail as a way of having a friendly chat like one that you might have with someone walking down the hall: How are you? Did you have a good weekend? Do you have any questions or concerns?

- Include all team members in communications and decisions, and schedule team meetings so that remote workers can join in by telephone or videoconference. E-mail documents to each person before a meeting.

▶ If you don't see each other often, it's important to be very clear about expectations and assignments, and to follow up regularly. This will help you catch issues quickly and give you additional opportunities to build your relationships by working through problems together.

Cultivate networks of people across a variety of functions and locations within the organization

▼

Effective leaders have networks that extend beyond their immediate area to include key people in other functions, locations, and organizations. These relationships provide leaders with the flexibility, resources, and strategic advantages they need to succeed in a fast-paced business world. Consider the following suggestions:

▶ Determine whether the structure at your organization is formal or informal. This will help you determine your strategy for creating connections with other groups.

▷ If the structure is formal, make sure you understand the protocol. Work through the structure to create relationships with people in other levels, functions, and locations.

▷ If the structure is informal, find a mentor to help you navigate the organization and figure out whom you need in your network. An experienced colleague can guide you in building relationships with people from all areas of the organization.

▶ List the groups you work with inside and outside of your organization, and list your contacts in each. Include their names, their functional responsibilities, the ways in which they can support you, and the support you can offer them. If you do not have a contact for each group, identify people you would like to meet.

Suggest that people co-chair an event, such as a summer picnic or a holiday party.

▶ Serve on cross-functional committees to work with leaders in other areas. Make an effort to stay in contact with these people once your involvement with the committee has ended.

▶ Attend company social events to meet people from other functional areas and organizations. Company picnics, award banquets, open houses, charity events, and customer events are excellent ways to meet people informally.

▸ Get to know your vendors, suppliers, and customers better. This will help you work with them more effectively and creatively. Also, because you will understand each other better, it will help you to both provide and receive better service.

▸ Build relationships with others in your profession by joining a professional association or attending trade shows. Networks can provide professional development, business opportunities, and resources to do your job better. In addition, building your reputation externally can often help you increase your status within your organization.

▸ Broaden your circle of acquaintances. Introduce yourself to people you have wanted to meet. Consider setting a goal to become acquainted with a certain number of people each week.

▸ Find a well-connected person who would be willing to act as your mentor. This person can provide valuable information about key people in other functional areas, such as who has the authority or influence to get things done, who can provide advice or political support, or who has experience or skills in an area relevant to yours.

▸ Develop relationships with key people in other functions and at other levels in your organization. Find ways to stay in touch with them— common interests, projects, committees—and communicate regularly.

Leverage networks to get things done

▼

Effective leaders leverage their relationships with people inside and outside the organization to get things done. They know how and when to involve others, gain support, and mobilize them for action. Consider the following suggestions:

▸ If you need practical assistance—advice on a proposal, another person's time, priority for your project—state your needs in person; if that's not an option, use the phone or e-mail. Be prepared to negotiate and adjust your plan in order to receive the assistance that you need.

▸ If you need support from several people, think about the best way to present your position so others will see mutual benefit in supporting you.

▶ Treat other network members with respect. Always ask for people's help; never demand it or try to manipulate people. Keep in mind that strong networks are built on mutual respect.

Study the organizational chart and discuss who should be in a person's peer network.

▶ Realize that asking for help after having no contact for a long time may feel manipulative to some people. A colleague who hasn't heard from you in several months may not be responsive to your request for support. Although it takes time and effort to maintain regular contact, the benefits of doing so are well worth the investment.

▶ Identify the people in your organization who successfully leverage their networks to achieve results and influence others. Take them to lunch and find out how they do it.

24
Manage Disagreements

Managing conflict and disagreements is one of the stressful aspects of being a manager. People get stuck in disagreements when they cannot see past their own opinion or position. Try to see conflict as an opportunity for growth, creativity, and new solutions. Conflict and disagreements can be good—when they're managed well.

As you improve your skills at dealing with conflict, negotiating, and helping others express themselves with respect to all involved, you can create a spirit of cooperation that fosters openness, directness, and the advancement of ideas.

In this chapter, we will cover the following areas:

▼

- ▸ Analyze your conflict-management style
- ▸ Address your reluctance to manage conflict
- ▸ Understand how others react to conflict
- ▸ Encourage people with opposing viewpoints to express their concerns and interests
- ▸ Address and resolve conflict directly and constructively, focusing on issues rather than people
- ▸ Facilitate the discussion and resolution of conflicts or disagreements
- ▸ Express disagreements tactfully and sensitively
- ▸ Use active listening to reduce conflict
- ▸ Preserve relationships in heated or difficult situations
- ▸ Negotiate effectively to achieve win-win outcomes that meet the interests of all parties
- ▸ Minimize recurrent conflict
- ▸ Resolve conflict among your employees

Analyze your conflict-management style

▼

Discuss whether the need to be liked prevents people from addressing conflicts.

People often have typical responses to conflict—they might avoid it, try to "keep everyone happy," or charge into the middle of it, set on winning. Others approach each situation differently, depending on the conflict, the people involved, the issues, and so on. To analyze your style of conflict management, consider these suggestions:

▶ Reflect on your conflict-management style and recall feedback from others. Do you try to ignore conflict and hope that it will go away? Or do you get locked in battles with others, thinking that they are wrong and you just cannot let them win?

▶ Talk with trusted others about what they see as the impact of your approach to conflict. When you do this, focus on listening to the feedback rather than on defending yourself and explaining your actions.

▶ Keep a journal or log charting your disagreements and conflicts with others, using the chart below.

Conflict Log

Issue	My Perception of Others' Concerns	My Response (describe)	(circle one)	
			Aggressive	Collaborative
			Withdrawal	Agreeable
			Aggressive	Collaborative
			Withdrawal	Agreeable
			Aggressive	Collaborative
			Withdrawal	Agreeable
			Aggressive	Collaborative
			Withdrawal	Agreeable
			Aggressive	Collaborative
			Withdrawal	Agreeable

Aggressive: trying to convince the other person you are right, insisting on winning the point.

Collaborative: working through issues to arrive at a mutually satisfactory agreement.

Withdrawal: avoiding or withdrawing from conflict situations.

Agreeable: deferring to the other person's point of view.

> ▶ Identify the people and situations that are a challenge for you to approach collaboratively. Analyze what it is about the situation or the person that causes you to get caught in less-than-cooperative behavior.

Address your reluctance to manage conflict

▼

Effectively working through conflict results in stronger working relationships and encourages creative solutions. On the other hand, avoiding or ignoring conflict can damage relationships and inhibit the expression of valuable opinions. To address your reluctance to manage conflict, consider the following suggestions:

> ▶ Make a decision to view conflicts as problems to be solved. If you resolve disagreements early, you can often avoid conflict.

> ▶ Ask yourself: What am I concerned about? What prevents me from approaching this head-on? What am I afraid of? As Franklin D. Roosevelt said, "The only thing we have to fear is fear itself." Once you know the barriers, you can evaluate probabilities and risks more accurately.

> ▶ After you identify your fears, use your problem-solving skills to determine what you need to do to reduce the probability of the fears being realized.

Pay attention to situations in which people are reluctant to address conflict. Discuss the reasons and tactics for taking action.

> ▶ When you are reluctant to approach a conflict, determine what the consequence will be if it continues. This technique will help you identify serious situations that will worsen if you ignore them. Use this approach to motivate yourself to take action.

> ▶ Talk with people who address conflict well. Ask how they assess a situation, what they do to make themselves address the issues, and how they keep discussion focused on a win-win solution.

> ▶ Ask others to give you feedback on your current approach to conflict. Also ask for ideas on what you could do differently. It is easy to get locked into behavior or approaches that are not working.

Understand how others react to conflict

▼

People on your team, others in the organization, and your customers each have their own ways of reacting to conflict. If you pay attention to these differences, you can work more effectively to ensure that issues get raised, people share feedback, and ideas and differences of opinion are aired. Consider the following suggestions:

▸ Assess your team members to understand who is reluctant to raise issues and provide feedback, who has difficulty resolving conflict, who stirs up situations, and who gets caught in win/lose battles.

Help people learn how individuals typically respond to difficult situations.

▸ Recognize that culture may have an impact on people's willingness to address conflict and govern the way in which they do. In some cultures, people do not disagree with those in charge. In others, disagreement is raised subtly.

▸ Notice the impact that your style of dealing with conflict and differences has on people. Some may not understand or agree if you seem unwilling to address performance issues. Others may react if you show strong emotions when you are angry. You can expect that if your reaction to conflict is different from those around you, it may have an impact. You may get less feedback than you want, and people may become frustrated.

▸ Customers also have their own ways of reacting to conflict. Analyze the type of feedback you get from your customers. If you do not hear both the good and the bad, find ways that the customer will view as safe or helpful means of giving feedback. It is dangerous to have customers who do not provide feedback—you can lose them and not know what went wrong.

Encourage people with opposing viewpoints to express their concerns and interests

▼

Although diverse points of view can create conflict, they are essential to a thriving organization. Without differences of opinion, organizations fail to develop and fail to adapt to changing circumstances. Successful leaders are adept at encouraging expression of a variety of viewpoints, creating an atmosphere of respect in which people engage in a healthy interplay of ideas. Consider the following suggestions:

- ▸ Ask for differing points of view. When an issue comes up, ask for others' opinions. Carefully monitor your reactions; do not disagree energetically. Instead, ask people to say more and pursue their points of view until you understand them.

Watch how people react to conflicting viewpoints. Discuss whether they think their reactions help or hurt resolution of issues.

- ▸ Create team norms for discussions to ensure that all participants contribute equally. Include listening actively, not criticizing, asking questions, and contributing ideas.

- ▸ Make a point of talking with people whose perspectives differ from your own. Look at it as an opportunity to learn more and to explore new ways of thinking.

- ▸ Monitor how you and others respond to people who have different viewpoints. Note when you feel resistance to others' ideas and assess why you are having this reaction.

- ▸ If team members seem uncomfortable about encouraging the expression of different viewpoints, structure discussions to solicit opposing viewpoints. Ask: How else could this issue be seen? What would be another way to look at this? How else might we approach this?

- ▸ Organize meetings so that all people can share their views. For instance:
  - ▷ Arrange seating so that all participants can see and hear one another.
  - ▷ At the start of a meeting, ensure that everybody has an opportunity to add items to the agenda.
  - ▷ Ask quiet group members for their opinions.
  - ▷ Control dominating speakers by bringing their points to a close and moving the discussion forward.
  - ▷ If you are using teleconferencing or videoconferencing, be sure to include all participants in the discussion.

- ▸ After a meeting, note whether different opinions emerged. Consider whether you reacted openly to all of them, not just to the most popular or most confidently expressed ones.

▸ Identify the people on your team whose opinions typically garner the greatest or least support, and try to determine why. Do the people whose ideas are accepted express themselves well verbally? Do they tend to voice only popular opinions? Are the people whose ideas tend to be less popular more reserved or less articulate?

Address and resolve conflict directly and constructively, focusing on issues rather than people

▼

Disagreements and conflicts are inevitable, so finding direct and constructive ways to handle them is important. Consider these suggestions to address conflict more constructively:

▸ Decide that you want to resolve conflicts by finding the best solutions and maintaining the best relationships possible.

▸ Approach conflicts from a win-win perspective. Realize that it is important to address others' needs, including their need to "save face."

▸ Depersonalize conflicts. View them as differences in ideas, priorities, or approaches rather than as clashes of personalities or egos.

▸ Whenever possible, create a plan for dealing with a conflict rather than trying to confront it without preparation.

When people face difficult conflicts, help them identify two or three win-win solutions.

▸ At the beginning of a discussion, express your interest in a resolution acceptable to all parties. During the discussion, use the following guidelines:

▷ Focus on understanding others. You can't resolve an issue if your focus is on getting others to see why you're right.

▷ Avoid saying "You're wrong about . . ." or "What you're saying doesn't make sense."

▷ Restate each person's position to see if you understand it.

▷ If the tone begins to get personal, reiterate the issues and ask people to focus on them exclusively.

▸ Write a detailed agenda for meetings in which a conflict needs to be addressed. This will give everybody the same expectation for what needs to be accomplished and will help the group stay on track.

- Consider whether it is necessary to talk with the parties involved before a group session in order to help them get focused on a win-win solution.

- If conflict erupts during a meeting, ask the group to list the relevant issues. If you're meeting in person, capture the ideas on a flip chart; if you're on a conference call, e-mail the issues to everyone on the call. Have people refer to the list during the rest of the meeting.

- When you witness a conflict, evaluate the parties' skills at focusing on issues rather than people. Try to discern whether behaviors or words seem to create greater personal offense. Also note what people do to keep the conflict impersonal.

Facilitate the discussion and resolution of conflicts or disagreements

▼

Handling disagreements at work can be tough. You may have to deal with forceful egos, with people's strong belief that they are right, or with childish behaviors. Consider the following suggestions:

- Fundamentally, all conflict is about who gets to decide an issue or who is right. Recognize that you and others get into conflicts because the issue is important, because one or both of you believe your respective views are right, or because you disagree about who should be the decision maker.

- When you facilitate a conflict, acknowledge that there are different views. Explain that you want to talk about them in a productive manner in order to reach a good solution.

- Encourage people to clarify their positions. Ask open-ended questions starting with *tell me about, explain,* or *how do you feel about.* Avoid asking questions that can be answered yes or no.

Lead people through a discussion that challenges them to see the validity of other views.

- Paraphrase each person's views to confirm that you understand them. This will assure that you are listening intently.

- Invite the people involved to define the problem or issue at hand and to express their position in specific terms. This will help you identify any false assumptions you have about their views. It will also show that you're interested in hearing their views.

- Review areas of agreement. Also take this opportunity to reemphasize the overriding priority or objective toward which you all are working.

- Look for a common goal about which all of you can agree. Conflicts often get resolved because the participants agree that resolution is more important than continuing to disagree.

- Identify options and solutions that will allow all parties to get what they need. Also acknowledge that all parties may need to compromise on some issues.

- Sometimes people disagree on so many issues that resolution seems impossible. Break larger conflicts into smaller ones and continue this process until you have identified basic disagreements. However, don't get lost in minutiae and avoid disputes over petty details.

- Go for a time-limited solution when you are stuck. You may be able to get a resolution in which everyone agrees to try something for a limited period of time.

- Once you have reached an agreement, set a date to review how the solution is working.

Express disagreements tactfully and sensitively

Coach people to listen and understand others before stating their own point of view.

When you have strong feelings about an issue, expressing disagreement can be a challenge. Your tone of voice and choice of words may not be particularly tactful or sensitive. Consider the following suggestions to help you express yourself appropriately:

- Assess the dynamics of the situation before you speak. Determine whether the other person is in a receptive frame of mind and whether you are calm enough to address the issue constructively.

- Use active-listening skills to draw out information and help pinpoint the real source of the disagreement. For example, paraphrase statements to show your understanding, use reflecting statements to acknowledge emotions, and use summary statements to recap your conversation.

▸ Monitor your body language. Do you look receptive? Are your arms crossed or relaxed? What expression is on your face? Use appropriate nonverbal behaviors when you express disagreement.

▸ Wait until the other person is finished before you begin to speak, even if you believe you understand the argument. Interruptions often appear to be insensitive.

▸ Acknowledge the value of the other person's opinion before you express disagreement. Then simply state your point of view rather than lecturing the person about why you're right.

▸ Be direct, concise, and forthright as you state your position. Outline your rationale and provide examples to clarify it.

▸ Refrain from using loaded words that insult or attack the other person. Also, resist using sarcasm.

▸ Try not to make assumptions about what the other person's response will be. If, for example, you predict that the other person will react negatively to what you say, your tone might be aggressive or defensive.

Use active listening to reduce conflict

Too often, parties involved in an argument spend most of their time talking instead of listening. While one person is speaking, the other is busy preparing a rebuttal or thinking of ways to support his or her viewpoint, rather than listening to what is being said. In addition, most people immediately judge the statements of others. How can you hold a more productive discussion? Consider the following suggestions:

Point out how listening skills contribute to or hinder the ability to handle conflict.

▸ Over the next month, each time you sense that an argument is about to begin, switch from a defensive position to listening mode. To accomplish this, use the following technique:

  ▷ Listen carefully to what the speaker is saying.

  ▷ Give the speaker your full attention, without thinking about how you are going to respond, and without judging the speaker's statements.

  ▷ Show that you are really listening by using nonverbal behavior: lean forward, raise your eyebrows, nod your head.

> ▸ Avoid questions that can be answered yes or no. These questions often start with *is, are, could, would, do, did,* or *should.*

> ▸ Periodically paraphrase what the speaker said to ensure that you understand what was meant, and to let the speaker know that you are truly listening. Reflect the feeling as well as the content of the message.

> ▸ As the discussion progresses, determine whether your interpretations are accurate. If you are listening well, you will probably hear comments like "That's exactly what I meant" and "That's right! I think you understand my problem."

Preserve relationships in heated or difficult situations

▼

Conflict can erode relationships—one of your greatest assets—unless you take care to preserve them. To ensure that you don't burn your bridges, consider the following suggestions:

Discuss the implications of allowing disagreements to harm work relationships.

> ▸ In heated moments, keep the larger picture in mind. While it is important to resolve the issue, the quality of the decision is not the only priority. You and the other person are most likely going to be working together for a long time, and you need to maintain your relationship.

> ▸ Assume that the other person has good intentions and a reasonable point of view. If you don't, this will be communicated to the other person through what you say and how you say it, and your ability to resolve the issues will be damaged.

> ▸ Frame difficult situations positively by asking "What do you think is the best course of action now?" rather than "How could this have happened?"

> ▸ Avoid assuming that others do not like you or are unkind merely because they hold opinions that differ from yours.

> ▸ Try to maintain a balance of power between you and the other person by ensuring that you both have equal amounts of time to speak.

> ▸ When people get angry or defensive, remain calm and show interest in their needs as well as your own.

- ▶ If you sense that you've insulted somebody during a heated discussion, apologize and rephrase your comment in terms of the problem, not the person.

- ▶ If you feel that you avoid conflict at all costs to preserve relationships, deal with issues before they become conflicts. It is much easier to talk about an issue before emotions run high.

Negotiate effectively to achieve win-win outcomes that meet the interests of all parties

Ask people to describe both successful and unsuccessful negotiations and to extract lessons from their experiences.

To negotiate effectively, you need to know other people's position and needs, come up with creative alternative solutions, and specify clearly how your objectives will benefit the other person or persons involved. Consider the following suggestions:

- ▶ Go in with the perspective that other people mean well, are trying their best, and want the best solution. This mind-set will help you look for win-win solutions.

- ▶ Before presenting your point of view, investigate others' positions and needs. What is important to them? What are their goals? What can you do for them? The answers to these questions will help you frame your points during the discussion.

- ▶ Listen carefully to what people are saying. Try to identify the needs behind their requests. If you understand their needs, you will be more likely to generate alternatives from which everyone can benefit.

- ▶ Refrain from getting into a win/lose battle in which each alternative calls for one party to benefit and the other party to be defeated. If the discussion reaches that point, note this fact to the others and communicate your desire for everyone to get something out of the agreement you reach.

- ▶ Be careful not to burn bridges. If you succeed at the expense of others, future attempts to influence the same people may fail. They may also take advantage of a future opportunity to benefit at your expense.

- Be prepared to bargain. Think about the resources you have to offer that would be of value to each person or group you want to persuade.

- Don't be too committed to reaching an agreement quickly. Alternatives may not be readily apparent.

- If you are presented with new facts, make sure you understand them before you proceed. As an alternative, postpone the discussion and take time to get up to speed on the new information before you meet again.

Minimize recurrent conflict

▼

Recurring conflict decreases productivity and harms working relationships. It usually occurs because a root-cause issue has not been addressed, or because individuals or groups of people continue to have difficulty getting along. To minimize recurring conflict, consider the following suggestions:

- Avoid labeling a recurring conflict as a personality conflict, even if it appears to be one. It is much harder to resolve a personality conflict than other kinds of conflicts. Instead, focus on each person's goals and issues. View the issue as you would another problem. What is each person trying to accomplish? What is the underlying issue?

- If past problem-solving efforts have not worked, change your approach. The most common reason for failure is that the root cause has not been addressed or motivation is not strong enough to stop the behavior or to resolve the conflict.

Use the "five whys" technique to help people pinpoint the root cause of a recurring conflict.

- If people lack motivation to resolve the conflict:
  ▷ Increase motivation by finding out why it is in the interest of each party to address the conflict. You can literally ask "Why is it important to you that these conflicts be resolved?" or "What would cause you to be more interested in resolving these conflicts?"
  ▷ Occasionally, you may need to set some limits, such as making it clear that the conflict cannot continue. Point out that the conflict is creating a negative impact and that you view the lack of resolution as a performance issue for the parties involved.

Resolve conflict among your employees

▼

Handling conflict between employees is a sensitive issue. While it's important not to interfere too much, your intervention may be necessary at times. Consider the following suggestions to help you choose an appropriate and productive level of involvement:

► Encourage your employees to resolve their conflicts themselves and not come to you for resolution.

► Coach a reluctant person on how to resolve conflict. If necessary, role-play a conflict-resolution situation to give the person an opportunity to practice.

Role-play situations in which people listen to views they find objectionable. Together, settle on appropriate ways to respond.

► Get feedback from your employees on your current level of involvement in their conflicts. Are you involved too much, not enough, or an appropriate amount?

► When conflict that does require your intervention (such that the employees cannot resolve it themselves) arises, follow this procedure:

▷ Help the individuals involved define the problem in specific, observable terms. Ensure that each person listens to the others.

▷ Help them identify areas of agreement.

▷ Have them brainstorm alternative approaches and determine viable solutions.

▷ Ask them to create a problem-resolution plan. If they are unable to do this cooperatively, it may be necessary for you to step in and determine the best course of action.

▷ Set up future meetings during which they can discuss how things are going and whether the chosen approach is working.

25

Increase Cultural Competence

As a manager, you work with people from various cultures, backgrounds, home countries, lifestyles, generations, and beliefs. If you are sensitive, respectful, and open to learning, it will help others see beyond their own beliefs and perceptions to welcome new ideas.

Differences often create conflict. That's why you need to be able to discern what the differences are and then, more importantly, to find commonalities. People need to be reminded that we are all individuals, with similar goals, objectives, and priorities that are expressed in different ways. Bridging cultural gaps and increasing a sense of common vision, purpose, and respect helps your organization do business in a way that works globally and locally.

In this chapter, we will cover the following areas:

▼

- ▶ Assess your beliefs about valuing diversity

- ▶ Increase your sensitivity to issues of culture and diversity

- ▶ Address prejudice or cultural bias in yourself

- ▶ Seek out culturally diverse ideas and points of view to achieve business success

- ▶ Help people from diverse cultures/backgrounds/lifestyles succeed in the organization

- ▶ Seek out opportunities to involve or integrate those from different cultural backgrounds

- ▶ Recruit for and promote workforce diversity

- ▶ Adapt to cultural norms and expectations

- ▶ Relate well to a variety of people regardless of their cultural background

- ▶ Create an environment in which people from diverse backgrounds feel comfortable

- ▶ Accommodate the needs of a diverse workforce

- ▶ Focus on the goal of valuing the individual

- ▶ Address prejudice and intolerant behavior in others

Assess your beliefs about valuing diversity

▼

Explore how people's views have been shaped by culture. Talk about how they can recognize the cultural assumptions they make.

A helpful step in learning to value human diversity is to understand your own values and beliefs. It is important to see how beliefs contribute to making you who you are and to recognize that other people may not agree with your beliefs or understand them. Consider the following suggestions to help you assess your own attitudes, assumptions, and feelings about people who are different from you:

- Identify the influences in your life that have affected who you are and what you believe: your nationality, ethnic origin, gender and religion; places you have lived; your education; your experience with people from other cultures. How do these factors influence you?

- Keep track of comments and feedback suggesting that people perceive you of having a specific cultural view. For example, you may have received feedback that you misread people from a particular culture. This is a helpful way to learn about your own belief systems.

- Ask others to describe how they see your culture affecting you and the decisions you make. Also ask them how their own background influences them; this could help you recognize influences in your own life.

- Learn about and value your own culture, background, and heritage. Expand your definition of culture to include educational background and values, economic status, religious beliefs and affiliation, rural/suburban/urban focus, and so on. Culture shapes factors such as:
  - ▷ *Belief systems:* anything you think of as an original truth, assumptions you make about the world.
  - ▷ *Norms:* appropriate and inappropriate behaviors.
  - ▷ *Values:* what is important to have, to know, and to be.

Increase your sensitivity to issues of culture and diversity

▼

As a leader, you need to push yourself beyond your comfort level to develop your knowledge of and sensitivity to diversity issues. Doing so can help you more fully understand, appreciate, and maximize the talents of others. It can also help you find ways to grow your business and handle business situations. Consider the following suggestions:

▸ Establish relationships with people who are different from you. Although it is a natural tendency for people to surround themselves with people who are similar to them, connecting with people of different backgrounds will help you learn about the unique perspectives others have to offer.

Be sensitive to whether the people you're coaching want to discuss their differences openly.

▸ Ask people from a variety of backgrounds for help in understanding their experiences, perspectives, and culture.

▸ Some people won't want you to recognize their differences. Others may see your overtures to support underrepresented groups as threatening. Make sure your message always returns to the central issue—how to recognize and enable each person's unique talents.

▸ Consider your actions from the point of view of a person with a different background. In some cultures, for instance, it is not common to ask for help; it may be an indication of deficiency or a form of losing face. Pay attention to the person's background and how it differs from and is similar to your own culture.

▸ Get into the habit of looking at how decisions affect people and how individuals view the same situation differently.

▸ Over the next few weeks, monitor the assumptions you make about people. Some people find it difficult to acknowledge that their assumptions and cultural beliefs significantly affect how they see others. Consider the following example: In a U.S. company, a white male manager walks past the office reception area and sees two black men laughing. He concludes that they do not take their jobs as managers seriously. Next he passes two women talking to each other at the mail station and assumes they are gossiping. Just before he reaches his office, he passes two white men talking and chuckling, and he thinks nothing of it. This manager has made assumptions without listening to the actual conversations. Instead, he has used external differences to draw conclusions. Making assumptions is often an unconscious process, not a deliberate one—which is why assumptions can be so difficult to catch. Catch yourself making inaccurate assumptions about people and situations. For example, you might think that a woman from France will not be successful as a sales representative in Japan. On what basis did you make that judgment? How do you know it is accurate?

Address prejudice or cultural bias in yourself

All of us have cultural points of view and biases. It is important to understand how culture affects you so you can work to eliminate prejudgments based on outdated or inaccurate cultural viewpoints. To take the lead in examining your prejudgments:

▸ Identify your own prejudgments. You may believe you have none, but that is unlikely. Prejudgments are a shorthand way of thinking and can be based on cultural values, experiences, or stereotypes. They may include beliefs such as:

  ▷ Older workers not only have a hard time learning new technologies, they don't want to.

  ▷ Americans are arrogant.

  ▷ Men are less sensitive and less considerate than women.

  ▷ Accountants are bean counters who can't see beyond numbers.

  ▷ French people are arrogant.

  ▷ The British are hopelessly bureaucratic.

  ▷ Gay people are not tough.

  ▷ Women are less committed to their careers than men are.

  ▷ Japanese people aren't creative.

  ▷ Younger workers are interested only in themselves.

Talk with people about the ways we show bias, such as telling "harmless" jokes.

▸ Become aware of your prejudgments by listening to feedback from others, taking diversity training, or simply questioning your own assumptions. Notice the impact your behavior has on others. Do you:

  ▷ Have higher career aspirations for your male employees than for your female employees?

  ▷ Give less feedback to people of a different race for fear of being accused of racism or discrimination?

  ▷ Shy away from talking with employees who do not speak your language well?

▸ Challenge your prejudgments. Take the time to get to know people. Work to eliminate prejudgments that are hurtful and unfair to others.

- ▶ Model inclusive, respectful behavior that doesn't prejudge people. By including a wide variety of people in your world, you can serve as a model to others.

- ▶ Listen to feedback from others. If it does not make sense to you, find a trusted adviser, preferably from the same culture as the person giving you feedback, to help you sort it out and learn what it means.

Seek out culturally diverse ideas and points of view to achieve business success

The diversity in your organization is a huge resource, often untapped. Research has shown that diverse groups often generate more creative, useful ideas than homogenous groups. Tapping the power of diversity can help your team and your organization reach their greatest potential. To seek out new ideas and perspectives, consider the following suggestions:

- ▶ View diverse ideas and points of views as tools to help you achieve your goal. For example, if you want to expand into the Latin American market, consult with Latin Americans to help you develop a successful strategy.

- ▶ Consult with and involve people from the organization who are knowledgeable about different cultures.

- ▶ Expand your definition of diversity beyond skin color and national origin. Consider such factors as job function, educational and professional background, linguistic background, gender, and personality style.

Challenge people to go beyond visible signs of diversity and become more aware of other types that exist in the organization.

- ▶ Learn more about your direct reports. You may find that people have views and skills that you didn't know about. Talk to people about their interests and viewpoints. Ask them to describe how they could use their unique talents and perspectives to contribute to the team's performance.

- ▶ Develop a group of informal advisers that you can consult on diversity issues. Recruit people from a wide range of organizations, industries, and cultural backgrounds. Make sure you include people in creative fields—they make a habit of thinking about issues in new ways.

- People may be hesitant to share views that go against traditional thinking. Offer several options for communicating with you, such as e-mail, face-to-face or phone conversations and group meetings.

- If your team is fairly homogenous, ask for input from other teams in the organization. It's likely that they will have a different perspective.

- Once you have consulted with others, allow their information to influence your plans and actions. It is frustrating to be asked for input and never know what happened to it.

Help people from diverse cultures/backgrounds/lifestyles succeed in the organization

It is often challenging for employees who are different from the majority to succeed in an organization. Leaders can help people succeed by appreciating their contributions and being sensitive to the different sorts of support they require. Consider the following suggestions:

Discuss whether the skills considered necessary for high-potential employees reflect bias and limit the possibility of success for some people.

- Provide specific and constructive feedback to all employees. Sometimes leaders are uncomfortable sharing feedback because they are uncertain about how it will be received. Remember that it is your job to help all employees do their jobs more effectively, not just those who look or act like you.

- Invite people to talk with you if they feel their opportunities in the organization are being limited. Realize that some people may not feel comfortable talking to you directly. Provide access to others, such as a human resources representative, whom people can contact to discuss this issue.

- Create an environment in which it is safe for everyone to ask for support or information. People may hesitate to ask for help or support because they fear they will be seen as weak. You may need to emphasize that requesting assistance is an appropriate and valued practice in your organization's work culture.

- Give all employees frequent opportunities to stretch—to take on assignments just beyond their current comfort levels.

- Provide mentors and support people for those who are new to the organization. Pay particular attention to people who are different from the majority culture. They will probably find it more difficult to fit in and may question whether they truly will have good opportunities.

- Recognize that many of the skills considered necessary in business—assertiveness and straightforwardness, for example,—are cultural preferences.

- If some of your employees have limited skills are limited in the language you use to conduct business, work with HR to institute a voluntary in-house language-training program.

- Explore opportunities for grants, scholarships, and other funding to help people further their education. Allow them to arrange their work schedules to accommodate classes.

- Suggest that your organization create resource groups for people with common backgrounds.

Seek out opportunities to involve or integrate those from different cultural backgrounds

▼

Discuss the business reasons for focusing on diversity.

As in society at large, people in organizations tend to group themselves according to gender, ethnic background, and job function or level. Even though this is a natural tendency, effective leaders recognize that it is not always beneficial to the success of individuals or the organization. To help your team profit from diversity and to enable each person to feel more included in the organization, consider the following suggestions:

- Meet individually with each person on your team. Talk about the organization and find out what the person would like to learn about in more depth. Arrange for individuals to meet with people from other areas to broaden their understanding of the organization.

- Set up a mentoring program in your department, pairing new or less-experienced people from diverse backgrounds with veteran employees who can provide encouragement and guidance.

- Have people work in teams on various projects, and be sure each team is diverse in as many ways as possible: cultural background, age, gender, job function and level.

- Make sure your team includes people from the same demographic groups as your customers. This will give you some insight into how your customers think, what they find important, and how you can serve them most effectively.

- If individuals seem reluctant to become involved, respectfully ask if there is anything you can do to help them participate more actively. Recognize that there are several ways to be involved; don't insist that everyone approach things in the same way.

- Build a support network with colleagues who are interested in more effectively leveraging diversity. Explore ideas, share best practices, and hold each other accountable for changing ineffective practices.

- Learn from successful practices at other organizations. Do some research on your own, or ask an HR representative to track down information for you. Then discuss best practices with people at your organization and determine how you can adapt them for your situation.

Recruit for and promote workforce diversity

Successfully recruiting people from diverse backgrounds sometimes involves long-term, concerted efforts with others throughout your organization. To help you with this process, consider the following suggestions:

- Develop specific strategies to increase your flow of applicants from a range of backgrounds. Draw on target populations by advertising in a variety of media including magazines, Web sites, social media groups, and international job fairs. Recruit from colleges and universities with a diverse student population.

- Use internships to bring more diverse people into your organization and help them gain on-the-job experience and skills.

- Be willing to hire people with nontraditional backgrounds and skills, and implement support systems to get them up to speed quickly so they feel like part of the group.

- Seek referrals from employees to find promising candidates from a variety of backgrounds.

▸ Study other companies or even other units within your company. Can you use any of their initiatives?

Hiring is the first step. Retaining, developing, and promoting people is the next critical step. Consider the following suggestions:

Ask people how they currently recruit employees from diverse backgrounds. Brainstorm additional ways they can find talent.

▸ Look for opportunities to develop people from diverse backgrounds and to prepare them for positions of responsibility. Tell them about the options in their present careers, as well as other career opportunities within the organization.

▸ Look at career paths and opportunities in your area with a fresh perspective. Aggressively attempt to eliminate intentional or unintentional discrimination or favoritism based on language skill, academic achievement, or indirect measures of past performance.

▸ Publicize available career paths and the skills they require.

▸ Form an officially recognized and supported steering committee to address issues of diversity. Invite team members who represent a diversity of backgrounds to join the committee.

Adapt to cultural norms and expectations

▾

Entering an environment where the norms and expectations differ from yours can be like entering a new world. You may feel a new urgency to observe and listen in order to absorb as much as possible about new rules and expectations. Consider the following suggestions:

▸ When you're in a new culture, note your assumptions about it. During the next few weeks, determine whether you were correct.

▸ Make a list of the aspects of the culture that are most difficult for you to adapt to, and think about why they are particularly challenging.

▸ Be patient with yourself. Adjusting to a new culture is a long process.

▸ If you're having a strong response to a situation, compare your response to those of the people around you. This could be an area in which you need some extra help to adapt.

▸ Talk with your boss, a mentor, or a colleague about the organization's policy on adapting to cultural norms. There may be some norms that your organization chooses not to adapt to. Be aware of how these delicate situations are handled.

▶ Ask specifically what is not okay or not accepted in the culture. It is okay for you to inquire; it is much better to ask than to assume you know.

▶ Observe others. For example, notice the pace of how people speak, move, and work. Observe whether bosses are treated deferentially. Learn how people treat time. Determine what you need to adjust in your own behavior in order to adapt to local expectations.

Point out when people are holding back because they fear offending someone from another culture. Explore their reluctance.

▶ Recognize that culture shock is entirely normal and can cause frustration, sadness, anger, and disorientation. If you feel you are having an especially difficult time adapting to a new culture, seek professional counseling or coaching from a seasoned cross-cultural traveler.

▶ If you find yourself lecturing to others about how you do things at home or in your previous organization, try to focus more on learning about your host culture or new organization.

▶ Continue to pursue your hobbies and interests in the new culture, adapting them to locally available products and venues. If you enjoy cooking, try new recipes with local ingredients. Become a fan of a local sports team. Attend concerts or go on day trips outside of your city.

Relate well to a variety of people regardless of their cultural background

▼

Successful leaders know how to get along with people from all cultural backgrounds. The skill of adapting to a variety of personality types, working styles, and cultural experiences is indispensable when you're managing people. To hone your skill at relating well to many people, consider the following suggestions:

▶ When you meet people, concentrate on developing effective working relationships. Focus on what you need to do to make the relationship work. Take the first steps. Do not assume the other person will.

▶ Suspend judgment based on people's background or experience.

▶ Get to know all of your direct reports so you can relate to them as people, not just as employees. Learn about their backgrounds, what's important to them, their goals, and so on.

▶ When you are having difficulty with someone, ask for advice from others, particularly people who get along well with the person.

▶ Learn about the cultures—including communication style preferences— of your direct reports, and consider how cultural differences might play a role in your interactions with them.

▶ Focus on and appreciate people's strengths. This will help you be more tolerant. Sustained effort and concentration will help you improve your working relationship with each person.

▶ Offer an opportunity for your group to voluntarily take personality or working-style inventories, such as the Myers-Briggs Type Indicator®. Ask an HR representative or an outside consultant who is certified to discuss results with each person.

Discuss what people have learned from colleagues with backgrounds different from their own.

▶ Work with a coach to strengthen your ability to work with a variety of people. Find out what areas you should focus on first. As part of the process, you may want to seek formal or informal 360-degree feedback to find out how different groups perceive your abilities in this area.

▶ When you feel that an encounter with a person who is different from you has gone poorly, check in with a friend or colleague who has strong skills in this area to learn what you might have done differently.

▶ For one month, keep track of the success of your interactions with all team members. Make notes on those that went especially well or poorly and look for any patterns related to cultural background.

Create an environment in which people from diverse backgrounds feel comfortable

▼

Creating an environment of respect, appreciation, and acceptance for everyone goes beyond simply tolerating people who are different. You must welcome and involve them so that they feel comfortable and understand that they play a significant role in your group. Consider the following suggestions to help you create a more accepting and respectful environment:

▶ Decide to accept and appreciate others. This is simple to say but sometimes difficult to do. Choose to focus on the positives of each person.

► Send people a clear message that they are a valued part of the group. For example, recruit people for projects rather than waiting for them to ask to be involved. Include them in all aspects of a project, including decision-making and problem solving sessions.

Talk about increasing overall diversity in a group, rather than simply hiring one or two employees who look different from the rest.

► Seek to understand a person as an *individual* as well as a *member* of a group. Viewing a person only as an individual (ignoring his or her cultural background) or only as a representative member of a group (ignoring the person) almost always leads to incorrect assumptions.

► Deal with discomfort within the group that stems from differences; don't let it simmer. When a conflict emerges between people from different cultural groups, separate the issues from the people involved in them. Try not to let disagreements become personal.

► Don't let people get away with disrespectful behavior toward coworkers. Pay attention to the words and tone they use and the attitudes they indicate.

Accommodate the needs of a diverse workforce

▼

To seriously address the needs of a diverse workforce, an organization must have systems and policies that are sensitive to and accommodate those needs. Consider the following suggestions:

► Identify the areas in which the organization can and should have common business processes and polices, and areas in which they need to be different for legal, cultural, or business reasons.

► Choose a common language for business meetings and provide opportunities for people to learn that language.

► Realize that there will be times when key communications should be translated into multiple languages, even though business is conducted in a common language.

Discuss how to leverage diversity without becoming fixated on it.

► Offer flexible benefits packages that readily allow for individual preferences—elder care, vacation time, health care providers—in benefits.

► Promote programs designed to recruit and retain specifically targeted groups of employees. Baby boomers, for example, might be drawn to flexible schedules or job sharing to enable them to care for elderly parents.

▸ Show sensitivity in your physical work environment. For example, display artwork representing a variety of cultures. Recognize, though, that this alone—in the absence of more substantial acknowledgment of diversity—can be seen as a superficial attempt to achieve political correctness.

Focus on the goal of valuing the individual

▼

Your efforts to manage diversity can easily stir powerful frustrations and other emotions within your organization. Those who have stifled feelings of frustration for years may suddenly voice their anger. Some may see a diversity program as a "quota" plan that will advance others' careers at the expense of their own.

To be effective, you need to keep sight of the overall goal—to value the individual—and communicate the purpose clearly and repeatedly. Valuing diversity is a means of valuing everyone. Consider the following suggestions:

▸ Clearly communicate that diversity refers to everyone. In your discussions, use a broad definition of diversity: personality, age, profession, family status, country of origin, culture, urban/suburban/rural, and so forth. People who might otherwise consider themselves irrelevant to the discussion can feel they are full participants, while those who consider themselves overlooked will be heard.

Pick up on signs that people do not value the diverse views of the individuals they work with. Delve into this issue to learn more.

▸ Emphasize the importance of understanding and respecting each other's view of the world. Encourage people to share their worldview. Draw on people's travel experiences as a way of illustrating differing worldviews.

▸ Be clear about your intent. Some people don't want their differences to be recognized or emphasized. Others may see your overtures to underrepresented groups as threatening. Make sure your message always returns to the central issue—how to recognize each person's talents and enable the organization to use them effectively.

- Realize that some people have suffered through poorly designed or conducted diversity programs or sensitivity sessions, and may already be defensive and skeptical. Accentuate the positive. And accentuate the benefits to the business.

- Provide feedback on valuing diversity and cultural differences as part of the performance management process.

- Hold managers accountable for respecting and using the diversity of their workforce.

Address prejudice and intolerant behavior in others

Provide feedback to people who intentionally or unintentionally insult, ignore, or treat poorly people who are different from them.

As a manager, you have the opportunity and the responsibility to take the lead in defining acceptable workplace behavior. Your actions strongly influence the conduct of your group. If you refuse to accept prejudice and intolerant behavior, others will as well. Consider the following suggestions:

- Confront aspects of your organizational culture that keep capable employees from being fully included and successful within your organization. For example, some organizations may be reluctant to promote an individual whose primary language is not the same as the standard language of the organization, or reluctant to select a person with an educational background that is out of the ordinary.

- Challenge prejudiced or intolerant remarks immediately. Say "That comment is not appropriate" or "Comments like that are not welcome here." If the person defends his or her behavior, simply reassert its inappropriateness. Your goal is not to humiliate the person, but to stop the comments.

- Treat a consistent pattern of intolerant behavior as a performance issue. Follow your organization's disciplinary procedures.

26

Establish Trust

Without trust, there is no relationship—and business is built on relationships. Building trust with employees, shareholders, and customers is the foundation to sustaining success. As a manager, you are responsible for inspiring trust as well as establishing your own ethical behavior and modeling it to your group and your organization.

Be a manager who keeps your word. Set high standards for ethical behavior. As others see your commitment to ethics, they'll be inspired to better behavior and practices. In ethics, one person's actions really do matter.

In this chapter, we will cover the following areas:

▼

- ▸ Model and inspire high levels of integrity
- ▸ Evaluate others' perceptions of your integrity
- ▸ Show consistency between words and actions
- ▸ Lead with values such that others will respect and follow you
- ▸ Live up to commitments
- ▸ Do not undermine others for your own gain
- ▸ Accept responsibility for your mistakes
- ▸ Recover from violating trust
- ▸ Do not distort facts with your own biases and agendas
- ▸ Protect confidential information
- ▸ Communicate across constituencies without compromising the integrity of the message
- ▸ Address questionable business practices
- ▸ Confront actions that are or border on the unethical
- ▸ Encourage discussion of ethical considerations before decisions are made
- ▸ Align the organization's systems and processes with its ethical standards
- ▸ Understand community issues relevant to the business
- ▸ Develop collaboration between business and community
- ▸ Contribute to community organizations
- ▸ Encourage responsible use of resources
- ▸ Support efforts to improve stewardship
- ▸ Seek alternatives to business practices that are harmful to the environment

Model and inspire high levels of integrity

▼

Demonstrate a high level of integrity. Talk with people about your belief in the importance of integrity.

Modeling is the best way to reinforce your organization's ethical principles and foster an environment in which people practice sound business ethics. Consider the following suggestions to help you model ethical behavior:

▶ Actions speak louder than words. Be aware that people pay attention to what you do, your attitude about things, how often you help people, as well as what you say. Even if you act with impeccable integrity 95 percent of the time, they'll remember the 5 percent when you didn't.

▶ Observe leaders within your organization who model and inspire a high level of integrity. Analyze why they are considered ethical. What specific behaviors, actions, or words indicate this?

▶ Initiate discussions of ethical considerations before decisions are made, even if people don't want to take the time. Being on the wrong side of an ethical issue can bring down an entire company.

▶ Stand up for what you believe is right, whether you are working with senior leaders, colleagues, people outside your organization or function, or your own team.

▶ Scan newspapers, business journals, and web sites for case studies in ethical and unethical behavior and talk about them with your team. Discuss what your team would do in similar circumstances to give people an opportunity to explore the issues, learn how their colleagues think, and build their capacity to talk about ethical concerns.

Evaluate others' perceptions of your integrity

▼

Discuss how perceptions of integrity are formed and how they affect an individual's reputation.

Your effectiveness as a manager and a leader is severely compromised if people have doubts about your integrity. What is characteristic of you?

Evaluate yourself on a scale of 1 to 3:
1 = very unlike me   2 = like me   3 = very like me

	What I believe	What I think others think
I consistently . . . : ▸ Keep promises and agreements. ▸ Give honest and complete answers to questions and challenges. ▸ Protect confidential or sensitive information. ▸ Admit when I've made a mistake. ▸ Consider the trust and confidence of my coworkers to be important. ▸ Make an effort to foster open, honest, and sincere communication. ▸ Encourage others to question practices they cannot support. ▸ Make use of the company's written code of ethics to guide me in making ethical decisions. ▸ Demonstrate consistency between my words and actions. ▸ Allow time for others to ask questions.		

Show consistency between words and actions

▼

People judge your actions, not your intentions. If your words and your actions are consistent with your principles and values, it will build trust. People will believe they can count on you. Consider the following suggestions:

► Stand up for what you believe is right. Don't allow yourself to be swayed by what others would like you to say.

► Give full and honest answers to tough questions. If you prevaricate, hedge, or give long-winded, circuitous answers, people will believe you're lying, trying to save yourself or someone else, or simply lacking integrity. If you can't share details, explain why. People will appreciate your candor.

► Be aware of your values. People may be inconsistent when they are not being honest with themselves about what they really want or need.

► Avoid making statements that others may misinterpret as promises. You might not realize that people think you promised to do something. Choose your words carefully and be very clear about next steps and precisely what you're going to do.

► Ensure that your nonverbal actions align with your words. For example, if you claim that you are interested in hearing employees' concerns and then avoid eye contact when they talk to you, your verbal and nonverbal messages are inconsistent.

Ensure that people have defined their personal code of ethics. Use phrases such as "I believe . . ."

► Be aware of situations in which you are acting against your stated words. People will be confused by your mixed messages. If this happens frequently, you'll lose credibility.

► Deliver a consistent message to different audiences. While you need to consider your audience in formulating the tone and wording of your messages, be sure that the underlying idea or opinion remains the same. Stating a strong opinion to your peers and then watering it down for your manager will only raise questions about your integrity.

Lead with values such that others will respect and follow you

▼

Leaders cannot lead unless others are willing to follow. In most organizations, people will not follow someone just because he or she has the title of leader or manager. People will follow when they share the vision, the direction makes sense, and they trust the leader.

There are countless examples of leaders who are out for themselves at the expense of other people, the environment, the success of the organization, individual stakeholders, and even the economies of nations. People look for leaders who care about the long-term success of all stakeholders. Consider the following suggestions:

▶ Think of the leaders you respect and why you respect them.

Have people identify whom they respect and what values those individuals demonstrate.

▶ For what do you want to be respected? Given what you do and how you do it, what values are you communicating that are important to you?

▶ What about your vision gets others excited and engaged?

▶ Does your vision inspire confidence and the respect of others?

▶ If you do not have a vision that matters to you, spend the time to find one. Use meditation to focus on what is important to you. Talk with others about what you value and what you want to be able to do. Work with your team to create a vision that excites and motivates you and others.

Live up to commitments

▼

Follow-through on commitments is an essential component of building trust and integrity. As you find yourself committing to deliverables, think about the following:

Situation	Implication
Do you commit by saying "I'll try to get that done"?	The word "try" is weak and can be perceived as giving yourself an excuse in advance. If you can't be confident about the outcome, state what you will do, while being realistic about potential barriers.
Do people frequently follow up with you on things you have agreed to do?	This could be a signal they do not trust you to fulfill your commitments.
Do you find yourself saying yes to others when you know you should be saying no?	You are likely over-committing. When you cannot deliver, others will lose their trust in you.
If you run into an obstacle that will prevent you from meeting a commitment, do you let others know in advance?	It is always more effective to be straightforward about problems than to wait for the due date to offer an explanation.
Do you communicate the outcome of activities you've completed?	Even though it might be obvious to you that you've completed something, it might not be as apparent to others. A status update will ensure that others are not left wondering whether you followed through.

To ensure that you live up to your commitments, consider the following suggestions:

▶ Do not make commitments you cannot keep. Make realistic time and resource estimates. If you have not had experience in an area, ask a more experienced colleague to give you estimates, and then add time to accommodate your learning curve.

▶ Attend meetings and appointments you've agreed to. If you can't attend or will be late, contact the meeting organizer.

▶ If you are not going to make a deadline, let those who will be affected know ahead of time and tell them when you will be done. Make certain this happens as infrequently as possible. If it happens often, you're probably setting unrealistic deadlines.

Tell people who overcommit that this behavior can become a serious integrity issue, resulting in lost trust.

▸ Identify what prevents you from keeping your commitments. For example, you might procrastinate, or perhaps you're a perfectionist. Plan a series of small steps that will help you be more consistent.

▸ Use a good electronic or paper time-organization system. The key word here is *use*. It won't do you any good if you never look at it.

▸ Tell your coworkers you are trying to be more reliable and ask for their help. Realize that once you talk about it, they will expect to see results, or at least a strong effort.

Do not undermine others for your own gain

▾

People who deliberately make themselves look better at the expense of others often operate in highly competitive, win-loss environments. Other people want so much to be seen well that their behavior is consistently self-aggrandizing, sometimes dismissive of others, and frequently destructive to teamwork.

Consider the following suggestions:

▸ Listen to feedback. Do people:
  ▹ "Kid" you by sarcastically saying "And what did you do?"
  ▹ Tell you that you put others down?
  ▹ Say that you only look out for yourself?

Have a serious discussion with people who are so interested in their own success that they undermine others. This behavior will not go away on its own.

▸ Be honest with yourself about whether you believe that the most important thing is to win or to be seen as better than others, regardless of the consequences. If you believe this:
  ▹ Recognize that you need a new mental model of how to act at work. You're going to need a new set of behaviors, and it's going to take time and effort to learn them. The payoff will be worth it.
  ▹ Ask someone you trust for feedback on the impact of your behavior.
  ▹ Realize that your behavior invites other people to act the same way toward you. In other words, it can be a vicious circle.

- Learn to recognize when you are undermining others. For example, you:
  - ▷ Talk behind others' backs.
  - ▷ Start rumors.
  - ▷ Make insinuations.
  - ▷ Question people's background, intelligence, or competence.
  - ▷ Describe people or their actions in a misleading way.
  - ▷ Attack people personally, not merely disagree with their ideas.
  - ▷ Make bitter, sarcastic remarks that cast doubt on people or their work.

- Realize that people are going to have a hard time believing that you've turned over a new leaf. They'll probably mistrust you for some time; it will take absolutely consistent performance on your part to change people's perceptions of you.

Accept responsibility for your mistakes

Mistakes can prompt you to look inward and evaluate your limitations and shortcomings, learn more about yourself, and behave differently. Consider the following suggestions:

- When you make a mistake, say so. Apologize, fix it, and make amends. Do not explain your behavior unless you're asked.

- When you are confronted by others about a mistake you made, listen to their concerns and feelings. You'll probably want to defend yourself but hold back. Make sure you understand what they're telling you. Later, reflect on their feedback and determine what is useful and what you want to act on.

- Identify what you do when you are not taking responsibility for your mistakes. For example, your tone of voice might be defensive, and you might interrupt people and start explaining why you acted as you did.

- If you are frequently defensive, examine the reasons behind your difficulty in taking ownership for your mistakes:
  - ▷ Do you expect yourself to be perfect?
  - ▷ Do you need to always be right?

> ▷ Do you tend to maximize negative feedback and minimize the positive aspects of a situation?

> ▷ Do you get emotional when you make a mistake?

> ▷ Do you want to "look good"?

> ▷ Do you want others to know that you thought what you were doing was good or right?

Be a role model for taking responsibility for your mistakes. Discuss what you learned from the situation and the process you used.

▸ When you make a mistake, figure out what you can learn from the situation. Talk about it with a friend or write it down—whatever works best for you. Try to get past merely saying "I'll never do it again."

▸ Increase your understanding of the situation. For example, why did it happen, what factors led to it, and what could you do differently in a similar situation?

▸ When you make a mistake, consider whether you made similar mistakes in the past. Try to figure out if you're falling into patterns of behavior that make you miscalculate, misread situations, or make wrong decisions.

▸ Focus on your own role in the mistake. Of course you need to understand the part others played, but don't dwell on what others did or didn't do.

Recover from violating trust

▼

Nothing is as damaging to a person as a breach of his or her integrity. Therefore, it is critical that you take remedial action quickly rather than get mired in frustration, guilt, or defensiveness. Consider the following suggestions to help you regain lost trust:

▸ If you are doing something unethical, stop doing it and make amends.

▸ If you know what you are doing to damage trust, stop doing it. That may sound obvious, but some people think they can continue without others knowing.

▸ If you do not know what you did to damage trust, find out. Ask others. Listen. Don't defend. Don't explain yourself.

- Expect that you might disagree that what you said or did showed a lack of integrity or violated trust. People usually behave in ways they can justify or that they decide is all right. It is critically important, however, that you truly understand how the other person was affected. To rebuild trust, you need to understand what you did from the other person's point of view.

- If you sense that you have violated somebody's trust, talk with that person directly as soon as possible.
  - ▷ Explain that you believe you may have violated a trust, and ask for confirmation.
  - ▷ Paraphrase what the other person says to confirm that you understand.
  - ▷ Apologize in a respectful manner.
  - ▷ Ask what you can do to repair any damage that has been done.
  - ▷ Follow through.

When people have violated the trust of others, talk about the issue. Find out whether they are interested in working to regain others' trust.

- Be aware that you may need to do penance for the offense. For example, you may need to listen repeatedly to the person expressing his or her anger or disappointment. If you are important to the person and you have seriously violated his or her trust, the person will not get over it quickly; it will take time.

- Ask what the person will need from you to begin to trust you again.

- Continue to behave in a trustworthy way even when the situation does not seem to improve. It won't get any better if you return to the old behavior.

- If you have received feedback that you are not trusted, learn more. Ask people you trust to tell you what you do or neglect to do that makes people not trust you. Recognize that it might be difficult for people to be honest with you about this issue. As they speak, just listen. Don't say anything. This is the time to listen, not defend yourself.

Do not distort facts with your own biases and agendas

▼

People are wary of those who twist or distort facts in order to win arguments or get their way. Behaviors that cause this impression include focusing on only one side of an issue, using facts selectively, and refusing to acknowledge ideas that don't fit a theory. To avoid distorting the facts, consider the following suggestions:

▶ When you study an issue, take into account all the facts, not just the ones that support your view. After you draw conclusions, ask a savvy colleague to review them and see if they seem biased.

▶ As you examine a situation to find facts, interview people who are directly involved and people who have differing perspectives. Make sure you talk to people who often have a viewpoint different from yours.

▶ If you feel strongly about a situation, take a few minutes to write down your thoughts, opinions, and feelings about it. (Be as honest as you can be; you can always tear it up later.) Identify bias by looking for words and phrases that express emotion. Use this exercise to sift through your reactions and biases and uncover facts.

▶ Assess whether your list of facts includes those that don't necessarily support your point of view.

▶ Check your perception of the facts by discussing them with a colleague. He or she might have additional information or be able to point out details that you missed.

If you notice people talking disparagingly about others, challenge them to go to the individuals and be straightforward about their concerns.

▶ To get opinions out in the open, state your bias candidly during a group discussion, and invite others to do the same. Then people will not have to wonder about hidden agendas.

▶ Recognize that having a biased view is not necessarily negative, though you do need to be aware of your biases and how they might cloud or color your judgment.

▶ You might not realize you're biased until you hear yourself talking about an issue. Your nonverbal actions and vocal inflections can reveal your true feelings. Record yourself talking about a situation and check for biases.

Protect confidential information

▼

Leaders have access to sensitive information: personnel records, compensation figures, proprietary technical information, corporate secrets. How you handle this information and to whom you choose to impart it reflects on your integrity. Consider the following suggestions:

▶ Don't promise confidentiality when you can't deliver it.

Ensure that people have read the organization's ethical guidelines.

▶ Resist talking about things you shouldn't talk about, even when you're tempted.

▶ Read your corporate code of ethics for guidelines on handling sensitive or confidential information. Also find out if there is a handbook that details common ethical concerns for your field. These documents can be a good source of guidance.

▶ Know what kinds of information you could be compelled to share, whether by law or company policy. When one of your direct reports wants to talk to you privately about an issue, make sure he or she understands that there are types of information that you can't keep confidential.

▶ Understand that your organization's culture determines how confidentiality is addressed and maintained. Inevitably, you'll face potential exceptions to these rules. When this happens, will you be able to say that you are comfortable with your knowledge and the actions you took?

▶ Be aware of policies and laws about health care information, providing references, and intellectual property.

▶ If you work with intellectual property, ask the organization's attorney to talk with your team about concerns and procedures.

▶ Ask yourself the following questions to determine how well you protect confidential information:

  ▷ Do you protect employees who are willing to take the risk to reveal their concerns?

  ▷ Do you foster an environment in which employees can talk with supervisors about issues without their names being revealed?

▷ Do you keep your door shut or go to a private office when you are discussing confidential information?

▷ Do you keep sensitive files, documents, and correspondence secure?

Communicate across constituencies without compromising the integrity of the message

▼

Provide feedback to people who give others conflicting versions of the same message.

Leaders often need to share messages with several constituencies across the organization. While they might tailor delivery to the audience, the core message needs to be the same. If people hear conflicting versions, they won't find the information credible, and they'll wonder what you're hiding. Consider the following suggestions:

▸ To prepare your message, state your purpose in one declarative sentence. Then write down three to five key messages that you will use in every communication about the topic.

▸ Tailor the level of detail to your audience, but always cover your key messages. Use the same language for your key messages, regardless of the constituency.

▸ If you receive feedback that people feel they're getting mixed messages from you, ask for more details. Pinpoint what is giving them this impression so you can improve your communication.

▸ Determine whether you limit or share information as a method of gaining power. Doing this may work in the short term, but it will ultimately undermine your integrity.

▸ If you decide to share different levels of information with different groups, tell each group why you made this choice. They are likely to understand and accept your decision if you have a viable rationale.

Address questionable business practices

▼

In the last few years, there have been many examples of leaders all over the world involved in questionable, unethical, and illegal activities—a reminder that questionable behaviors and practices need to be challenged, stopped, and avoided. Consider the following suggestions:

- Ensure that your organization has a clear code of ethics.

- Confirm that there are escalation procedures in the code of ethics, so that issues can rise to the appropriate level of the organization.

- Talk with your team about the code of ethics, so they know what it is and how to use it.

- Understand the investigation process, so that you have confidence that issues will be addressed.

- When people report concerns about ethics, take them seriously and ensure that they do not get into trouble for raising such issues.

- Study the ethics standards and practices for your industry and your profession. Familiarity with them will help you recognize when issues or situations are in gray areas or outside accepted practices.

- Study your organization's ethical codes for the business, its practices, and its employees. Determine your role in implementing and monitoring the codes.

- Recognize the difference between ethical practices and legal practices. An action may be legal and still violate your organization's ethical codes. Hold yourself to the stricter standard.

Talk with people about ethical issues you have encountered and how you handled them.

- When you face an issue that falls into a gray area, seek guidance from a colleague who is discreet and whom you trust. Choose your confidant carefully. Someone who is not discreet may potentially alarm people or tip them off before you're ready.

- When you encounter questionable business practices, focus on facts, not personalities. Don't assume people are trying to be unethical. They may be acting with incomplete information, or there may be circumstances you don't know about. Learn more about the situation.

- Practice talking about ethics with your team. Discuss situations that appear in the news or ethical dilemmas you hear about. Analyze what people did, why they did it, the consequences, and alternative actions.

Confront actions that are or border on the unethical

▼

Leaders are responsible for ensuring ethical behavior and for pointing out when others are behaving in inappropriate ways. To respond appropriately to unethical actions, consider the following suggestions:

▸ Request that an investor relations or communication group conduct a survey that investigates how the organization is seen in the community from an ethical standpoint. Take action on the findings.

Ask people what they think about others who do not take action on issues of ethics. Challenge them by asking: Do we have our own issues to address?

▸ Review press coverage of your organization. How comfortable are you with how the organization is seen? Are you proud of this image? Decide whether the organization needs to make changes or pay more attention to external relations and communication.

▸ When you encounter inconsistencies, investigate why they are happening. Then develop a solution that addresses the issues.

▸ Be sure all employees understand the organization's ethical standards and principles. Distribute copies and discuss them often with the group.

▸ Remember that silence implies consent. Don't sit by when you see actions that are or border on being unethical. Objecting is critical to maintaining ethical standards in the organization.

▸ When you speak to someone about unethical behavior, begin by learning more about his or her motives and intentions. Phrase your concerns in terms of the principle involved and indicate your personal discomfort with his or her actions. For example: "I'm uncomfortable that you are using the money in this budget for another project without alerting the manager, who has asked us to give up unused budget dollars."

▸ Depending on the situation, consult with HR, legal, or other appropriate internal resources to investigate and clarify the extent of the problem.

▸ It can be difficult to confront someone, especially someone you admire or someone who has control over your career. You may be afraid of appearing disloyal or ungrateful. Plan carefully how to approach the person. Talk to your mentor, an experienced HR representative, or another adviser you trust.

Encourage discussion of ethical considerations before decisions are made

▼

Ethical considerations are a part of business life. They range from the obvious, such as whether you will pay for a favorable decision or access to a decision maker, to the subtle, such as whether you will meet only the legal standards on an environmental or regulatory issue, or whether you will exaggerate what a product can do. Making ethical decisions challenges leaders to decide how they will follow through on their values. Consider the following suggestions:

- Identify ahead of time the common or expected ethical questions you might encounter in your organization. For example, you might need to make decisions about:
  - ▷ Working conditions.
  - ▷ Using child labor.
  - ▷ Paying bribes.
  - ▷ Environmental issues.
  - ▷ Advertising claims.
  - ▷ Hiring practices.
  - ▷ Selecting vendors.
  - ▷ Going along with cultural practices with which you disagree.

Ask people about the ethical challenges in their jobs. What is their process of thinking through how the issues should be handled?

- Decide ahead of time how you will make an ethical decision or what process you will use to come to a decision. In making a decision, consider:
  - ▷ What values are involved?
  - ▷ How do different constituencies view the issues?
  - ▷ What do your organizational values or code of ethics tell you about what decision you should make?
  - ▷ What are the consequences of the choices you have?
  - ▷ How comfortable are you with everyone in the organization knowing your decision?
  - ▷ How comfortable are you with people in the communities in which your organization operates knowing your decision?

- ▸ Review the organization's code of ethics. Ensure that it provides a clear understanding of what is deemed unethical, how it should be handled, and a process people can use to ensure it has visibility and is addressed.

- ▸ Encourage people to bring up what they see as unethical. Recognize that you may not agree with people about what they consider to be unethical.

  - ▷ Listen to the concern and seek to understand how it is an issue for this person.

  - ▷ Refer to your organization's code of ethics for guidance on how the organization sees this issue.

  - ▷ If it is an organizational issue of ethics or you think it should be, follow the code of ethics.

  - ▷ If it is a personal issue, work with the person to determine how to handle the situation. Sometimes accommodation can be made so individuals can act consistently with their personal values; other times this is not possible. In extreme situations, it may be most appropriate for you to help the person find a job in another organization more consistent with his or her values. For example, a person who objects to drug tests on animals would not be comfortable working in a medical research laboratory. On the other hand, an attorney in a law firm might be able to decide not to represent a particular client.

- ▸ When you encounter an issue of ethics, ask the following questions:

  - ▷ What is the issue? How important are the consequences in the short term? In the long term?

  - ▷ How does your organization's code of ethics apply in this situation?

  - ▷ Are your needs, or the needs of those you report to or advise, keeping you from seeing the full reality of the problem?

  - ▷ Is this situation harmful or dangerous to others?

  - ▷ Could this information damage your reputation or that of the company or your clients?

  - ▷ Do you need to take immediate action?

> ▷ Would you be comfortable with your decision if it were reported by local or national news media?

> ▷ Whom can you consult about this issue?

Align the organization's systems and processes with its ethical standards

▼

Ethical standards and values should be the foundation of and the touchstone for the organization's vision, strategies, practices, and policies. Periodically reviewing consistency between the code of ethics and values and the organization's systems and practices is important. They can be out of sync or become unintentionally inconsistent, and therefore not support one another. Consider the following suggestions:

▶ Ask a cross-functional team to identify any inconsistencies between the code of ethics and real-world practice.

> ▷ Do standards for vendor selection include an evaluation of working conditions or compliance with environmental regulations?

> ▷ Are people who violate the code of ethics rewarded or promoted?

> ▷ What happens to people who report unethical behavior?

> ▷ What happens to people who harass or ostracize others for reporting what they consider to be unethical behavior?

▶ When unethical behavior is discovered, review systems and processes to determine how they may have played a role. Solicit suggestions for solutions, and make the necessary changes.

Provide examples of ethical issues the organization has dealt with in the past. Explain how they were handled, and why.

▶ Because people focus on what gets measured and rewarded, include measures of ethical behavior in performance appraisals. Realize that accountability can be a measure of ethical behavior. For example, a salesperson who makes unrealistic claims regarding a product in order to make a sale often is measured only on total sales, not on negative consequences due to questionable ethics. An ethical measure in this case could be the number of customer complaints.

Understand community issues relevant to the business

▼

Every organization operates within a community and is affected by internal and external factors associated with that community. Successful leaders address community issues that have an impact on their business or profession. Consider the following suggestions:

▶ Locate and read long-range plans made by community or government agencies. Note projections made by demographers and by organizations and agencies regarding the future of your region and state.

▶ Be aware of long-range community plans and their likely effect on your business—on your present or future employees, customers, and so forth.

▶ Read publications from government, civic, and neighborhood groups. Check "state of the city" and "state of the state" reports to identify strengths and weaknesses of the areas in which you do business.

Ask people to identify community issues relevant to their organization. Discuss ways people could get involved in addressing these issues.

▶ Identify community factors that help and hurt your business, and work with community leaders to address issues. Examples include:
  ▷ Business climate, including taxation policies.
  ▷ Housing availability and affordability.
  ▷ Traffic congestion.
  ▷ Transportation options.
  ▷ Crime rates.
  ▷ Quality of schools.
  ▷ Overall infrastructure.

▶ Encourage your employees to serve in the community in some capacity through public or private initiatives and organizations. Ask them to share what they learn, through either informal presentations or short articles in the company newsletter.

Develop collaboration between business and community

▼

Because businesses exist within a community, smart leaders seek and create opportunities for learning, cooperation, collaboration, and synergy between and among business and community groups. Consider the following suggestions:

Pay attention to your organization's record for community responsibility. Take appropriate action to influence the organization to be more responsible.

▸ Get to know political and community leaders in your area. Learn about their issues, agendas, and concerns. Do this by reading local papers, attending community events, becoming involved in trade associations and the chamber of commerce, networking, and other activities.

▸ Find an area in which your organization can use and complement the resources of a community agency. For example, many communities have excellent child care, family counseling, and food shelves. Use available community resources and build your organization's programs around them.

▸ Encourage involvement in all the communities in which the organization is located, not just at corporate headquarters.

▸ Work with local high schools and colleges. Invite administrators, instructors, and students to visit your organization. Describe some of the opportunities, common concerns, needs, and constraints your organization faces. Offer internship and scholarship opportunities.

▸ Create or sponsor a speaker's bureau—people who can go to community meetings and talk about issues of concern to the organization, industry, and community. Service groups are often looking for speakers.

▸ Show commitment to the community by ensuring that your employee demographics are diverse and representative of the community.

▸ Participate in a community outreach program that helps individuals learn marketable skills. Make it fun as well as educational.

▸ Arrange for schoolchildren and community groups to tour your organization to learn more about what you do and how you contribute to the community good.

Contribute to community organizations

▼

Contributions to community organizations can take several forms; they may be financial, or they may involve donating time, energy, and skills. Consider the following suggestions:

▶ Identify organizations that have a significant positive impact on your community—schools, parks and recreation centers, charities, nonprofits, health care centers, day care or elder care facilities—and find out what kind of support they need.

▶ Develop the future leaders in your community. Become involved in a group that works with young people. Develop friendships with young people and provide internship opportunities.

Ensure that people include community involvement as a goal in each of their employees' development plans.

▶ Consider seeking an elective political or community position. Even if you have a demanding career, you may find that you can carve out time for positions on the school board, city council, or planning commission.

▶ Encourage and support the involvement of your employees in community service. Work with other leaders in the organization to determine how this will work and how formal you would like it to be. For example, if leaders find it difficult to give individuals time off, it might work best to have people volunteer as a group. Check with your HR group to see if they already coordinate activities with community groups.

▶ Determine at least one concrete thing the people in your group can do to improve community life. For example, sponsor a family around a holiday, participate in a fund-raising event, or collect clothes for needy children.

▶ If your organization has a corporate foundation, learn more about it. Find out whether it needs help and how your group could participate.

Encourage responsible use of resources

▼

Resource conservation efforts are good for the physical environment as well as for public relations, employee morale, and your organization's financial bottom line. To encourage your organization to use resources responsibly, consider the following suggestions:

▸ Challenge your team and organization to use resources wisely.

Ask people how they can promote the use of recycled products and environmentally safe practices.

▸ Understand how your organization uses resources on both a macro and a micro scale. For example, on a macro scale, understand what types of raw materials you need, how they are produced, and whether you're using the most responsible methods. On a micro scale, study how individuals use resources in your organization.

▸ Consult with your facilities manager to learn more about what your organization currently recycles. Also learn about best practices at organizations similar to yours.

▸ Develop small habits that conserve resources. For example, reduce the amount of paper you use by copying documents on both sides of the paper. Turn off lights when you will be gone for more than 10 minutes. Use fluorescent rather than incandescent lightbulbs.

▸ Invite an energy expert (from inside or outside the company) to talk with people about personal conservation measures at work and at home.

Support efforts to improve stewardship

▼

Encourage people to have a discussion with their team about good stewardship and how they can practice it in their group.

Stewardship means carefully and responsibly taking care of something that has been entrusted to you. As a leader, you have been entrusted with the personal resources represented by your team, organizational resources, community resources, and, depending on your role, global resources. Consider the following suggestions:

▸ Are you proud of how you spend your time? Is it consistent with your values of family, community, and respect for the environment?

▸ Reflect on the type of steward you are for your employees. As you work together, look for opportunities to discuss how people use their time, talents, and energy. Do this casually—as a way to discuss the issue in general, not to judge how people are choosing to spend their time.

▸ When you are involved in community groups, look for opportunities to improve their stewardship. For example, are people using their talents well? Does an adequate percentage of funds go toward serving the group's primary purpose?

▶ Look for ways to apply the stewardship principle to business decisions. For example, one commercial developer, instead of using 50 percent of the space in a large-scale suburban development for buildings, streets, and parking ramps, and 50 percent for grass, trees, and water, an 80/20 pattern was used. The developer used 80 percent for "green and blue" and 20 percent for bricks, mortar, and blacktop. The developer creatively retained more of the natural setting while providing an aesthetically pleasing and functionally effective area.

Seek alternatives to business practices that are harmful to the environment

▼

Depending on your industry, your organization affects the environment in some way, as either a producer or a consumer of goods or materials. To develop awareness of your organization's practices and viable alternatives, consider the following suggestions:

▶ Take the risk that your customers will care about your business practices and prefer that you support sustainable use of resources.

▶ Stimulate the creativity of your group to find alternatives to practices that harm the environment.

▶ Don't just follow regulations; do what is right.

▶ Analyze the real costs of "shortcuts."

▶ Fully understand the impact it will have in the marketplace if customers believe you damage the environment.

Determine if people are considering environmental factors when they make purchases or consider proposals from vendors.

▶ Use a range of information sources to learn more about your organization's business practices and how they affect the environment. For example, read your organization's annual report or web site to see how your company's environmental policies are described there. Also read environmental reports by government or independent agencies, media accounts, and industry or trade magazines. You might not agree with all the perspectives, but it will useful to know them.

▶ Learn more about the broad and narrow-range factors—worldwide prices, scarcity of materials, government regulations, entrenched practices and processes, highly competitive markets—that govern your organization's practices.

► If your organization has harmful practices, rest assured that you are not the first person to notice them or to want to change them. First, find out what people have tried in the past and what the results were. Also, become familiar with best practices in your industry and others, and consider whether they could work at your organization.

► If you suggest alternatives, try to quantify them. Turn them into "must haves" instead of "nice to haves" by showing that they could have a positive effect on the bottom line.

27

Show Adaptability

The ability to accommodate change in a positive manner—adaptability—is a survival skill for managers. Not only business climates but also people, strategies, and objectives change in response to the marketplace. You'll need to adapt quickly, smoothly, and appropriately when you deal with others or experience shifts in priorities and changes yourself.

Keeping a flexible, open mind and valuing versatility allows you to see potential and possibility in the face of change. You'll be able to change your leadership style as situations evolve and respond to unexpected opportunities with creativity, insight, and courage.

Show Adaptability

In this chapter, we will cover the following areas:

▼

- ▸ Adapt readily to different ways of doing things
- ▸ Be flexible when you're working with others
- ▸ Adapt appropriately to competing demands and shifting priorities in your personal and professional lives
- ▸ Show versatility in response to a wide range of situations
- ▸ Adapt your leadership style to fit situational needs
- ▸ Project an appropriate degree of self-confidence
- ▸ Maintain a positive outlook and a sense of humor in difficult situations
- ▸ Demonstrate an appropriate level of patience
- ▸ Work effectively in ambiguous situations
- ▸ Deal constructively with mistakes and setbacks
- ▸ Respond constructively to rejection or frustration
- ▸ Live according to your preferred life balance
- ▸ Use a support network to cope with life's challenges
- ▸ Work constructively under stress and pressure

Adapt readily to different ways of doing things

▼

When people aren't willing to adapt to something, ask what they need to see or hear to convince them. Make adapting their responsibility.

Change jolts people's comfortable habits and patterns, and makes people uncomfortable. But change also compels people to learn new skills, push beyond their comfort zones, and approach situations in fresh ways. Consider the following suggestions:

▸ Expect that you will frequently change processes, procedures, and other methods for work. Most organizations want to do things better and faster; this means that everyone's work will be affected at times.

▸ When you first encounter a new way of doing something, don't react immediately. Give the new approach some time before you express your opinion. Concentrate on the potential benefits of the new approach, not on how difficult it will be to adapt to it.

▸ Attempt to understand the change, what is driving it, and what it will do for your area and the organization. For example, attend all meetings and training sessions, and discuss the new approach with your colleagues and your manager. As you learn the reasons for new ways of doing things, you might become more willing to adapt to them.

▸ View yourself as a role model. Although it may be difficult to adapt to different ways of doing things, encouraging others to adapt can make it easier for you, too. Helping others make the transition is as important as making it yourself.

▸ Examine why you might be unwilling to do things differently. For example, is it because you are comfortable in a routine or because the original approach was your idea? If you have personal motivations for keeping things the way they are, admit to them and concentrate on the business reasons for the change.

▸ Stop saying "That's the way it has always been done." Don't defend an approach simply because it has been used before. The best solutions answer the demand or the challenge, and new challenges often require new solutions.

Be flexible when you're working with others

▼

One of the joys (and problems) of working with other people is their conviction that each individual knows the best way to get things done. When ideas and methods clash, a flexible approach can help you leverage your group's combined strengths. Consider the following suggestions:

▶ Be flexible in how you view a situation. You might be so accustomed to seeing it from one angle that you are literally unable to see other possibilities. Open the issue up for discussion and focus on listening, especially when you hear ideas that you would typically dismiss immediately.

Ask people who need to be more flexible to identify more than one way to see a situation. This can help them develop a habit of seeing multiple views.

▶ Recognize that there are several ways to achieve a goal. If you insist on micromanaging, you will lose the chance to learn from your people. Instead of telling people how to achieve a goal, invite them to tell you how they want to pursue it.

▶ If possible, allow other people to play a part in defining deliverables. Their ideas could result in a richer outcome than you had envisioned.

▶ Deadlines are sometimes negotiable. Ask the group or individuals to make a case for the deadline they propose and be willing to consider it if the reasoning is sound. Make sure they consider all the downstream consequences of their deadline.

▶ Ask trusted coworkers when they think you tend to be inflexible. Be prepared to hear some surprising answers. Plan how you want to respond in the future under similar circumstances.

▶ Be willing to adapt to others' working styles and schedules. For example, conduct conference calls with colleagues in different time zones during a time that is convenient for them rather than convenient for you.

Adapt appropriately to competing demands and shifting priorities in your personal and professional lives

▼

Leaders often face competing demands as they try to balance their professional and personal lives. Everything from shifting market conditions to personnel issues can affect their workloads. As you go through your day, consider the following suggestions:

▶ Change your expectations about the work environment. Instead of hoping for a quiet, stable workplace, expect things to be hectic, untidy, stressful, and fast-paced.

▶ Instead of dreading change, anticipate it. Pay attention to what is happening in your organization and in the broader marketplace. How might your priorities shift? What can you do now to get ready?

▶ Ask trusted coworkers how you typically react to shifting or competing priorities. Compare their perceptions to your own assessment of your adaptability. This will point out areas in which you could improve.

▶ Avoid snap reactions to a new priority or proposed change. Give it time and try to understand why it is necessary. Think about the impact it will have on your group.

▶ Identify what will help you manage a situation. For example, if you want more information, talk to your manager or other leaders about the importance of a new priority. Stress that you are not challenging the priority, but simply want to understand it better.

▶ When you face competing priorities, do two things: clarify what is expected of you and clarify what you can get done within the time frame. This will help you understand the parameters.

▶ Be straightforward with others when you must change priorities. Sometimes people dread telling their direct reports that there has been a change in plans. Talk to a more experienced colleague about how to communicate changes in priorities.

Recognize that people's priorities change. Do not assume that they want increased responsibility, a geographic move, or some other change. Ask them.

▶ Think of times in your life when you successfully responded to shifting priorities. Spend 15 minutes writing about the emotions you experienced, the strategies you used, and the results.

▶ Talk with your manager if competing priorities are making it difficult to juggle demands at work and at home. For example, discuss whether you could temporarily shift some responsibilities.

▶ Respond resourcefully to new demands and challenges. Look for opportunities to develop new skills and use old ones in new ways.

Show versatility in response to a wide range of situations

▼

In a dynamic business environment, you are likely to face a wide range of constantly shifting situations. Each may require a different approach. As a manager, you must assess the circumstances and the people involved, and show versatility. Consider the following suggestions:

▸ Analyze the general level of versatility in your organization and in your area. Observe how people react to new situations and new solutions. Also assess your team's typical attitude. Do they see versatility as an asset or a risk not worth taking?

▸ Determine the business reason for being versatile in your area and identify the driving force behind the new demand or priority. Your team members will be more likely to adapt if they understand the business need for a new approach and if they can see a bottom-line benefit.

▸ Consider how you typically handle situations. Ask objective people who see you in a range of circumstances. Find out if you generally treat all situations the same and apply the same solutions, or if you tailor your response to events. Do you see nuances, or do you like to view things as clear-cut?

▸ When you face a new situation, compare it to others you have faced. How is it similar or different? What familiar approaches can you build on? In what ways do you need an entirely new solution?

▸ Become a role model for versatility. Begin with low-risk situations, such as changing the setting or structure of your staff meetings. Let people know that you are trying something new and tell them why. Ask for their reactions and comments.

Provide people with feedback when you believe they should increase their versatility. Ask whether they see this as an issue.

▸ Pay attention to what's on the horizon, especially if you don't like change or are tired of it. A key part of being versatile is seeing what's coming and preparing for it. Keep an eye on business conditions and on the competition, and look for clues that you may need to change your priorities or your approach.

▸ Put yourself in as many new situations as possible and take on a wide range of responsibilities. For example, volunteer to work with areas of the business that you are unfamiliar with. Learn to adapt your skills to accommodate new situations.

Adapt your leadership style to fit situational needs

Every business situation requires slightly different skills and approaches. As a leader, you must assess the circumstances and the people involved, and lead appropriately. Consider the following suggestions:

▶ Watch how several people lead and how others react to their leadership styles and behavior. Incorporate leadership behavior that works and that makes sense for you to use.

Provide assignments for people to work with leaders who intentionally adjust their leadership style to a specific situation.

▶ Determine how to lead by considering the needs of your people, team, task, and situation. Consider the personalities and skill levels of the people involved, the time frame for the work, the complexity of the work, and your organization's culture and values.

▶ Ask people how you can improve as a leader. Also, talk individually with your direct reports and ask them to describe what they consider an ideal leader for them.

▶ Be willing to adjust your leadership style. Adapting your style to individuals shows that you understand them and want to help them perform at a high level. Some people want to figure things out for themselves, some want clear direction, and some want to be left on their own.

▶ Be careful about when and how you adjust your style. If you adjust it too much or too often, you may seem unpredictable. This can make your team anxious and ineffective. When you change your style significantly, explain why.

▶ Learn from the leaders around you. Observe how and when other leaders in your organization use particular leadership styles. If you can, ask them how they choose their approaches and which are most successful.

▶ Take diversity issues into account when you choose a leadership style. People will interpret your style in light of their culture and background. If you have team members from cultural backgrounds different from yours, talk to them about what they value in a leader. Be open and accommodating.

Project an appropriate degree of self-confidence

▼

If you have struggled with confidence, tell people what you did to make it less of an issue for you.

Many leaders have a great deal of confidence and strong egos; in fact, it is unlikely they would have achieved their position without them. The challenge is to act confidently without stepping over the line into egocentrism. Consider the following suggestions:

▸ Analyze how you currently show confidence and self-assurance. What behaviors do you use? In which circumstances are you likely to show confidence? What would you like to improve?

▸ Understand how confidence is expressed in the culture in which you are working.

▸ Use good posture and expressive gestures to create a confident impression.

▷ When you speak, use a strong, steady voice and state your views clearly.

▷ Avoid diluting your comments with verbal take-aways such as "don't you think," and "maybe I'm wrong, but."

▸ If you feel a lack of confidence, try not to focus so much on yourself. Instead, focus on the issue and the other people involved. This will help you be less anxious.

▸ Resist negative self-talk. Sometimes people think "I never handle those situations well." As the adage suggests, whether you think you can or you think you can't, you are probably right.

▸ Ask for feedback on whether you come across as arrogant. If you find that you do, learn which behaviors give this impression. For example, you may criticize ideas, frequently interrupt people, show no interest in ideas that aren't your own, or use humor to put people down. Arrogant people are often so focused on themselves that they don't notice or care how their behavior affects people around them.

Maintain a positive outlook and a sense of humor in difficult situations

▼

A positive attitude can help you manage challenging situations. Humor can draw people together, lighten a tense situation, increase job satisfaction, and relieve stress. Consider the following suggestions:

▸ Decide to see the positive side of things and assume that people have good intentions. Identify positive aspects of your work. This can be difficult, especially if you have gotten into a pattern of negativity. Focus on positive experiences and try not to magnify negative events.

▸ Anticipate successful results, which will increase your chances of success. When you hear yourself being negative, consciously substitute positive language.

▸ Realize that how you view a situation often determines how you approach it. Develop a more positive mind-set. Instead of believing that things just happen to you, think of what you can do to respond.

▸ Avoid personalizing. It is unlikely that anyone is deliberately making work difficult.

▸ Be thankful for the positive elements of your life. Make a list of all of the material and nonmaterial aspects of your life for which you are thankful, and add to this list regularly.

▸ When you face adversity, look at the broader context and find a humorous angle. If you can laugh, you can make it through.

Discuss the importance of having a positive outlook and ways to build resilience.

▸ Spend time with friends and colleagues who have a good sense of humor. Note how they use humor, and adopt some of their techniques.

▸ Use humor when you need to put people at ease, such as when you are building a new relationship or beginning a presentation. Remember to use humor that does not put down any group and is culturally appropriate.

▸ When you find yourself losing your sense of humor, rely on someone else's. Take time to read a humorous book or watch a comedy.

Demonstrate an appropriate level of patience

▼

Recommend employee assistance resources to people who are not able to maintain an appropriate level of patience.

When you're under stress, you may find that you react more quickly and more intensely. This can make it challenging for you and your colleagues to work together effectively. Consider the following suggestions to help you remain calm and reasonable:

▸ Catch yourself before you say something you might regret.

▸ When you are angry, think before you speak. As you choose your words, be clear about their impact and how they fit with your goals around relationships and the work you need to do.

▸ Avoid burning bridges, offending people, and blaming others. Remember that in organizations, friends come and go, but enemies accumulate.

▸ When you are angry, buy yourself time by saying things like "That's an interesting perspective," "Let me think about that," and "Tell me more." The idea is to choose the best response given your need to have an effective working relationship.

▸ Ask your manager or a coworker to observe you in a trying situation and to describe how you show impatience. For example, you might use a sarcastic tone, frequently interrupt people, or become irritable.

▸ Make a list of personal signals—a rapid pulse, shallow breathing, a clenched jaw, nervous gestures—that you are losing your patience.

▸ Plan tactics you will use when you feel emotional. For example, you could excuse yourself from the room, ask to reschedule the discussion, or remind yourself that the situation is difficult for everyone involved.

▸ When you cannot remove yourself from a trying situation, talk to yourself to calm down: "I'm getting angry about this. I don't need to take it personally; I'll just take a deep breath and calm down."

▸ Look to colleagues, friends, and family for support, especially during extended periods of stress. Talking with them will give you a chance to vent your feelings and ask for their help.

▶ Maintain a healthy skepticism about the rumor mill at your organization. Rumors create anxiety, especially when the organization is experiencing problems. Make an effort to obtain accurate information, but don't spend so much time chasing down rumors that you get sidetracked from your work.

Work effectively in ambiguous situations

▼

Ensure that people seek out unstructured situations in which they can practice dealing with ambiguity.

In today's fast-paced business world, you may often find yourself in ambiguous situations. Many people become uncomfortable when they do not know exactly what is expected of them or when there is no clear leader or structure. To work productively in these circumstances, consider the following suggestions:

▶ Analyze how you typically view uncertainty. Do you feel:

   ▷ Angry about a lack of direction?

   ▷ Frustrated that you can't get answers?

   ▷ Anxious to gain control?

   ▷ Fearful of failure?

▶ Try to see the possibilities in an ambiguous situation. For example, you might have an opportunity to take on more responsibility. You may be able to try new approaches because there are no time-honored precedents.

▶ Seek out opportunities to work in unstructured situations, such as informal problem-solving groups or task forces. Rather than avoid them, look at them as opportunities to practice being more flexible.

▶ Use your expertise and experience to make an educated guess about unknown factors. Also talk to more-experienced colleagues. You may find that a situation is clearer than it first appears.

▶ Stay productive, even if you feel a lack of clarity. Don't use ambiguity as an excuse to procrastinate. Focus on the areas in which you can move forward, set some goals, and take action.

▶ Remember that things change over time. Keep learning by asking questions and being persistent.

▶ Agree with your direct reports that as a group, you will keep a positive attitude. Use humor when things seem especially ambiguous. Don't develop a negative attitude.

Deal constructively with mistakes and setbacks

▼

Successful people don't fear mistakes and setbacks; they learn from them. They examine what happened, acknowledge their part, and determine what they could do differently next time. Consider the following suggestions:

▶ When you make a mistake, focus on what you can learn from it.

▶ Focus on the process rather than the outcome to help you understand what changes you need to make. For example, you might have neglected to build relationships, failed to prepare, tried to push people too far, or displayed an arrogant attitude.

▶ Discuss the mistake or setback with trusted colleagues to get additional perspectives. This will help you understand how other people viewed your behavior and understand the broader context of the situation.

Help people deal with mistakes by encouraging them to talk about the situation, what they intended, what they would do differently, and so on.

▶ Understand the political environment in which you work. Review the aspects of the business climate or culture that may have contributed to your setback so you can address them more productively in the future.

▶ When you feel confident that you know what led to the mistake or setback, decide how you want to respond. For example, plan how you will alter your attitude or behavior the next time you are in a similar situation.

▶ Don't dwell on the past. No one is perfect. Everyone makes mistakes and occasionally fails. Dust yourself off and move forward.

▶ Continue to take risks, try new things, and take on tough goals. Even if you feel burned by a negative experience, you need to push your boundaries.

Respond constructively to rejection or frustration

▼

You may experience rejection and frustration from time to time due to competing opinions, priorities, agendas, and personalities. As you work with individuals and groups in your organization, consider the following suggestions:

▸ Remember that you *can* control your emotions. You can decide how you will feel about what happens, what others say, and how you are treated.

Investigate whether people are able to talk about frustrations without getting into a negative pattern of constantly complaining.

▸ When you are frustrated, figure out what you can do.

▸ Adjust your expectations. It's unreasonable to expect that others will always agree with you, think your ideas are great, or give you a job you want.

▸ Try to extract lessons from every situation. Even adverse experiences are worthwhile if you learn something from them. Remember, this encounter may be preparing you for a more important challenge in the future.

▸ Practice patience. The time may not be right for your idea, but your idea may still be right for the organization. Keep building a foundation of support.

Live according to your preferred life balance

▼

Different people seek a different balance between work and personal life. Use your values and life goals to focus your time and energy.

Talk with people about their life balance goals. Help them identify roles that would help them meet those goals.

▸ Use the following process to help you focus on what's most important to you:

1. Identify the values, principles, and life goals that are most important to you. Too often people get into trouble trying to do it all because they have not thought through what is most important to them. If you have difficulty completing this step, ask yourself "What do I want my legacy to be?"

2. Determine your most important priorities, both at work and in your personal life.

3. Keep track of how you currently spend your time. Use a grid with spaces for noting how you spend your time each hour of the day for seven days.

4. After tracking your time for a week, analyze how you spent it (work, family, leisure, spiritual pursuits, and so on) and compare this with your list of values and goals. Look for areas where you are consistent and inconsistent.

5. Create an action plan to further align how you spend your time with your values and goals:

   ▷ Set your priorities according to your values and goals.

   ▷ Spend less time on low-priority goals.

   ▷ Periodically revisit your priorities and goals, as they may change over time.

▶ Approach this process as a gradual redesign rather than a major overhaul of your life.

Use a support network to cope with life's challenges

When you're feeling pressured, talking with other people can help. They can commiserate, listen to you vent, and help you think of potential solutions. Consider the following suggestions:

▶ List the people on whom you currently rely to give you candid answers, provide support, discuss ideas, and so on. Review your list and determine whether it is adequate. Do you have people who can help you in both work and personal challenges?

When people feel stymied by a challenge, encourage them to consult individuals who are known for their adaptability.

▶ For areas in which you require a stronger network, create a plan for building one. Keep in mind that building long-lasting support relationships takes time and requires a lot of give and take.

▶ Ask trusted friends and coworkers where they've found support and help.

▶ Build a stronger professional network by becoming more involved in professional and industry associations, where you can meet your peers in other organizations. Build a stronger personal network by becoming more involved in community organizations, religious organizations, health clubs, and so forth.

Work Life	People Who Can Provide Support	Personal Life	People Who Can Provide Support
Information Training		Relaxation	
Advice		Advice	
Relief from Overload		Relief from Overload	
Discussion of Issues/ Values/Problems		Discussion of Problems/ Sharing of Consequences	
Industry Trends		Companionship	
Other		Other	

Work constructively under stress and pressure

We all feel stress and pressure from time to time. (Some of us feel it all the time.) As a leader, you can count on experiencing the entire continuum of stress, from the energizing stress that gets you excited about an initiative to the debilitating stress that interferes with both your personal and your professional life. Consider the following suggestions:

▸ Develop your ability to handle pressure by exercising, using relaxation techniques, and eating well.

▸ Identify situations and people that cause you stress. Then find out what causes the stress in each circumstance.

▸ Develop a plan to reduce the intensity of your reactions or to remove the stress if you can.

▸ Work off stress through physical activity. Choose an activity that you can do each day and schedule time to do it.

Show Adaptability

Find opportunities for people to talk with individuals who work in stressful professions in order to learn how they handle stress.

▸ Examine your expectations as a source of stress. For example, if you expect interruptions during your day, you will be less upset when they occur.

▸ Set aside a few minutes each day to practice positive visualization:

1. Find a comfortable place to sit or lie down. Close your eyes and take four slow, deep breaths.

2. Imagine a pleasant and relaxing scene. Solitary images work best for most people. For example, picture yourself fishing on a beautiful, calm lake or sitting in a comfortable chair in front of a warm fire on a cold winter day.

3. Make the scenario as detailed and vivid as possible. Use all of your senses to imagine what it would be like in that situation— what it would look like, the sounds you would hear, and the aromas in the air.

▸ Limit your intake of caffeine, alcohol, and nicotine. These can all help you work constructively under stress in the short term, but they reduce your ability to function effectively in the long term.

28
Learn Continuously

Many leaders get so busy that they neglect to make time for conscious learning. It's amazing how fast information becomes out of date. Unless you make a decision to incorporate continuous learning into your daily life, you'll soon find yourself out of touch with what your competitors know and what new generations of employees bring to the market.

Even spending small amounts of time learning, if you do it regularly, can help you develop yourself professionally and personally—and give you the satisfaction of knowing that you are keeping up with trends, information, and current discussions in the industry.

In this chapter, we will cover the following areas:

▼

- ▶ Identify your core values and motivators
- ▶ Convey a clear sense of your core values and motivators
- ▶ Keep current on changing work expectations
- ▶ Demonstrate awareness of your own strengths and weaknesses
- ▶ Set development priorities
- ▶ Pursue learning and self-development
- ▶ Make your learning more efficient
- ▶ Get the most out of readings and seminars
- ▶ View mistakes as learning opportunities
- ▶ Anticipate roadblocks that could sidetrack your development
- ▶ Involve others in your development efforts
- ▶ Seek out and learn from others who are different from you
- ▶ Seek feedback to enhance your performance
- ▶ Accept criticism openly and nondefensively
- ▶ Work to understand and resolve conflicting feedback from multiple sources
- ▶ Work to understand feedback that conflicts with your self-perception
- ▶ Demonstrate willingness to try new things, even at the risk of failure
- ▶ Willingly accept challenging assignments and new career opportunities
- ▶ Know the job
- ▶ Keep up to date on professional/technical development
- ▶ Increase your knowledge of specific processes
- ▶ Increase your knowledge of functional areas
- ▶ Stay informed about industry practices

Identify your core values and motivators

▼

Effective leaders know who they are and what they value. They recognize that values are at the heart of their being and hold the purpose for what they do. Effective leaders do not just hold the title of leader or manager; they have a leadership purpose and a vision they are trying to achieve. Consider the following suggestions:

Ask people what gives them the most satisfaction at work. Discuss accomplishments they are most proud of and why.

▶ Reflect on the values and motives that drive you as an individual and as a leader. Regularly set aside time to think about, identify, and clarify your values, motives, and priorities:

▷ What brings you the greatest satisfaction?

▷ What do you want to accomplish?

▷ How would you describe your life mission? How can you most powerfully express your life mission in your work?

▷ What sparks your interest and energizes you?

▷ How can you best serve others and make a meaningful contribution in their lives?

▷ What truly motivates you to do your best work?

▶ Write down your values and beliefs. The process of writing them will help you clarify them further.

▶ Determine for each of the following:

	I try to avoid this	This would be nice to have	This is essential to me
Achievement or sense of accomplishment			
Financial security			
Recognition from others			
Professional growth			
Family			
Spirituality			
Adventure			
Other:			
Which would you give up first? Which would you give up last?			

- List your current age at the top of the page. Then list your age in five-year increments down the left-hand side. Write what you would like to accomplish in each five-year period. Include professional, personal, family, and community aspirations, priorities, and goals. Then answer the following questions about your list:

  ▷ How can you accomplish each objective?

  ▷ What sacrifices or trade-offs are you willing to make?

  ▷ Whose support do you need in order to get where you want to go?

  ▷ Are you satisfied with the work and life balance represented on your list?

Convey a clear sense of your core values and motivators

▼

Personal integrity is the foundation of trust. Your actions must flow naturally from who you are. It is important to have a strong core of guiding principles and to make a consistent and well-intentioned effort to demonstrate them. Consider the following suggestions:

- Be aware of your motives. If you are honest with yourself about what you really want and need, you will act more consistently.

Observe people to see if their actions are consistent with their values.

- Audit your personal consistency. If the following statements apply to you, people probably trust you and count on you to protect their interests.

  ▷ You keep your promises.

  ▷ You take responsibility for your mistakes and limitations, and you avoid making excuses.

  ▷ You respond appropriately to constructive criticism.

  ▷ You treat confidences with respect and discretion.

  ▷ You don't routinely shortcut procedures and policies in the name of expediency.

  ▷ You don't placate people by giving in to their demands or complaints.

  ▷ You put the interests of others on the same level as your own.

  ▷ You say no when you know you cannot deliver.

▸ Share your values and motivators with people you trust, and who have opportunities to see your behavior in a range of situations. Discuss whether your behavior is consistent or inconsistent with your values and beliefs. You may find that your intentions are not translating into actions.

▸ Realize that actions speak louder than words. Even if you share your values and motivators with others, it is your actions that will truly convey to them what you deem most important both at work and at home.

▸ Regularly assess how much time you're spending on issues and activities that support your most important values and priorities, both at work and outside of work. Plan how to close up inconsistencies between your actions and your values.

▸ Talk with someone whose actions are consistent with his or her values to learn more about aligning values with actions.

▸ Make an agreement with your peers that you will challenge each other when you don't act according to your expressed beliefs or keep your commitments. Peer accountability can be a powerful motivator.

Keep current on changing work expectations

Help people identify learning opportunities when work expectations change. Tell people what you believe they will learn from an opportunity.

Changes in organizations, in industries, in the marketplace, and in roles mean new and different expectations. It makes sense to regularly review and update the expectations for your current role and those in which you are interested for the future. Consider the following suggestions:

▸ Review the expectations for your current role. Have they changed recently? How have they changed within the past two years? If you do not believe the expectations have changed, talk with others and see what they think. Expectations for most roles continue to increase over time.

▸ Talk with your manager about current and anticipated future expectations of you.

- Find out who has a similar role in the organization. Periodically exchange information regarding expectations for your roles. This will help you stay on track with your peers in other areas in the organization.

- Note which individuals are most valued and respected in your unit and the organization. Determine the skills and characteristics that they bring to their jobs and the organization.

- Given what you know about the goals and strategies of the organization, how do you see expectations changing?

- If you want to be in a critical role in the organization in the future, what knowledge, skills, and abilities will be valued? Consider increasing your competency in these areas.

Demonstrate awareness of your own strengths and weaknesses

Before you can decide the priorities for your learning and development, you need to demonstrate awareness of your goals, strengths, and development needs. A GAPS grid can help you make informed decisions about your development by comparing (1) your perceptions with the perceptions of others, (2) your goals with your abilities, and (3) your goals with the perceptions of others and the future direction of the organization.

At least once a year, ask people to identify their strengths and areas for improvement. Provide your feedback, too.

A GAPS grid illustrates how you see yourself, how others see you, what matters to you, and what matters to others.

- The left side of the grid shows where you are now; the right side of the grid shows where you want to go.

- The top half shows your perceptions and goals; the bottom half shows other people's perceptions and expectations.

GAPS Grid

Where you are	Where you are going	
Abilities: *How you see yourself.* What I already know: What I need to learn:	**G**oals and Values: *What matters to you.* What I already know: What I need to learn:	**Your view**
Perceptions: *How others see you.* What I already know: What I need to learn:	**S**uccess Factors: *What matters to others.* What I already know: What I need to learn:	**Others' views**

To complete your GAPS grid, gather data from as many sources as you can. Then fill in the boxes as follows:

Identify your **G**oals *and Values.* You can do this through career discussions, value clarification exercises, meditation, and discussions with friends.

▶ What opportunities or experiences do you want to have in your work?

▶ What are your career goals?

▶ What are your important goals, values, and interests?

▶ What do you care about most in your work and your life?

Identify your **A**bilities and performance.

▶ How do you see your strengths and development needs?

▶ Where have you been successful? What skills have contributed to that success?

- Where do you believe you need to increase your knowledge or abilities?

- In what areas do others turn to you?

Look at the **_P_**_erceptions_ of others. You can get this information from feedback you have received, performance appraisals, 360-degree feedback, assessments, and customer feedback.

- Based on feedback, how do others view your skills?

- What do others see as your strengths?

- What do they see as your development needs?

List the **_S_**_uccess Factors_ for your role and your organization. Get this information from your manager, the organization's strategy, industry trends, and competency models.

- What are the criteria for success in your current job or position?

- What are the expectations for roles you are interested in?

- How are expectations in the organization or for your role going to change?

- Who is most valued and respected in your organization? Why?

- Which competencies are in greatest demand in your organization right now? Which will be in the future?

To interpret your GAPS grid:

- Look for common themes and patterns. For example, all groups may agree that you have strong interpersonal abilities, which will help you achieve your goals.

- Try to make sense of discrepancies, or "gaps," between the four boxes. Ask yourself the following questions to better understand your gaps:
  - ▷ _Abilities and Goals:_ Do you have the abilities you need to reach your goals?
  - ▷ _Goals and Success Factors:_ Will your goals get you to where you want to go in the organization?
  - ▷ _Perceptions and Success Factors:_ Do other people have confidence in your capability to succeed?

> ▷ *Abilities and Perceptions:* Do you have a blind spot? Do you need to do something more frequently? Do you need to market your skills better?

▶ Realize that both you and your environment will change over time. Update your GAPS grid and reevaluate your portfolio regularly, especially after you complete a major development goal or when significant changes occur in the organization, your profession, or the industry.

Set development priorities

▼

Skill development and continuous learning are essential to your success as a leader. While it might be comfortable to focus only on your strengths, most jobs require that you also use skills that aren't your strengths. You can increase your effectiveness by improving your skills. Consider the following suggestions:

▶ Look at your current work goals along with an accurate assessment of your skills and capabilities. How could you improve your effectiveness through development? Which improved skills would help you achieve your goals better, faster, or with more buy-in from others?

If you are concerned about a lack of skill, say something about it. The sooner people are aware of an issue, the sooner they can change.

▶ Focus first on developing skills for your current job; then focus on the future.

▶ Consider putting a high priority on development needs that affect your ability to get results and to work effectively with others. For example, if direct reports do not believe you listen to their ideas, address this need. It will have a great impact on your success.

▶ Ask your manager to list one or two areas in which he or she believes you should concentrate your development efforts.

▶ Ensure that your development efforts are focused on what you believe will make a difference.

▶ After you establish your priorities, be aware of your behavior. If you're not actually working on your development, you need to reset your priorities, because development does not appear to be important to you.

Pursue learning and self-development

▼

The most effective way to develop your skills is to make it a part of your daily routine. You are more likely to succeed if you pursue learning and development with a series of activities than if you attend one intensive training program a year. Even five minutes a day, used wisely, can make a tremendous difference. Consider the following suggestions:

▸ Link your learning goals with something you are already doing. Take a moment each day to examine the development opportunities that are right in front of you.

▸ Each day, identify where you can practice new skills and behaviors.

Treat development goals as seriously as you do work results. Review progress regularly. Hold people accountable for learning and development.

▸ Compile a list of people who can support your development. Share your development plans and goals with them and ask for feedback. This will make you more accountable for attaining the goals and will involve others in your development.

▸ Ask for support when you get frustrated or feel discouraged. Find two or three people who can act as a sounding board for you when you face barriers or when your progress is slowed.

▸ Test your assumptions and conclusions to ensure that you are on the right track. Involve other people in this exercise. Choose people who will give you candid feedback and encourage you to take risks.

▸ Observe people who are skilled in the areas you are trying to improve. As you observe their behavior, note what they do well and what they emphasize. Follow their example.

▸ Expect to feel discomfort from time to time. As you go through change and development, you may feel uncertain or ambiguous at times. Be patient and realize that real change takes time. Change will feel natural and easy only with persistence and practice.

▸ Redefine failure and success by separating what you are learning from how you are performing. Ask "What did I learn?" rather than "What did I do?"

Make your learning more efficient

To move forward in an organization, you need to continue learning. Sometimes the not-so-obvious experiences turn out to offer the most powerful learning opportunities. Training yourself to take advantage of a broad variety of experiences can accelerate your learning and development. To increase your learning quotient, consider the following suggestions:

- Get involved in a variety of experiences to maximize your development. High-quality learning most often comes from a wide range of life activities, not just a few.

- Admit your weaknesses and compensate for them by surrounding yourself with people who are skilled in those areas. For example, hire people who have strengths that you lack. Not only can you learn from them, your team will become more synergistic and well rounded.

- View your strengths as development opportunities. Typically, your greatest successes will come from leveraging your strengths. Broaden and improve your strengths by finding new ways to use these skills, by teaching them to others, and by pursuing assignments that stretch them even further.

- Experiment and take intelligent risks each day. Seek out high-voltage situations, such as projects that are highly visible to others or ones that give you an opportunity to work with new people.

Let people know if they are overusing any strengths, which turns those skills into weaknesses.

- Determine how effectively you handle your emotions. Successful learners tune in to their emotions and use them to help guide their decisions and enhance their effectiveness. Answer these questions:

    ▷ Do you worry too much about what others think and, as a result, allow your actions to be unduly influenced by their opinions?

    ▷ Do you tend to be out of touch with your emotions and take action without tuning in to your feelings or considering the feelings of others?

    ▷ Do you express too little or too much emotion?

    ▷ Do you learn new information quickly? Managers must pick up new skills and information rapidly. This increases your capability as a manager and your value to the company.

Get the most out of readings and seminars

▼

While the most powerful development experiences often occur on the job, readings and seminars are also good ways to gain knowledge and skills for your current and future job responsibilities. Consider the following suggestions to ensure that you get the most out of readings and seminars:

▸ When you are reading or are attending a seminar, take notes. Highlight ideas you might want to use and changes you could potentially make.

▸ After the course is over or you finish a book, decide what you will do differently.

▸ Rather than reading an entire book, scan the table of contents to determine which sections are most relevant. Then read just those sections. Look for downloads of free chapters and excerpts.

▸ Search for one insight or application in everything you read. It is more beneficial to read one article and learn from it than to skim five articles and take away nothing of substance. Work hard when you are reading by drawing conclusions and searching for meanings that are relevant to your development.

Frequently ask people "What did you learn?"

▸ Choose learning experiences that are relevant to your learning objectives. Be open to new ideas and innovations. When you learn something, determine how you can apply it.

▸ Build in time to reflect on what you learned and how to apply it to your job. Your behavior will not change simply because you have learned something from a book or a training program. You need to decide what you will do differently.

View mistakes as learning opportunities

▼

Mistakes often prompt people to look inward and evaluate their limitations and shortcomings, helping them learn more about themselves in the process. Mistakes are a problem if you repeat them or don't learn from them. Consider the following suggestions:

▸ Even if a mistake has not been made, get into the habit of thinking "How could I improve or do something better?"

▶ When you make a mistake, ask yourself what you can learn from it.

When people make mistakes, ask them to reflect on what they learned from the experience and what they could do differently next time.

▶ Consider talking about your mistake with others to increase your understanding of the situation. Solicit ideas about what you might do differently in the future. Sharing your mistakes with others will help them become more comfortable about sharing their mistakes with you, which will give you opportunities to learn valuable lessons from their mistakes as well.

▶ Focus on your role in the mistake instead of looking at what others did or didn't do. Avoid the temptation to blame others. Instead, examine what you did or failed to do so that you can learn from your actions to create more success in the future.

▶ When you make a mistake, ask yourself (and others, if it is appropriate) if you made a similar mistake in the past. You can gain powerful insights by studying patterns of behavior that result in repeated mistakes, miscalculations, or misreadings of a situation. For example, you may consistently underestimate how long it takes to do something.

▶ If you have not made a mistake lately, ask yourself:

▷ Am I challenging myself in my job and outside of work?

▷ Am I requesting feedback and hearing feedback from others?

▷ Am I taking any risks?

Anticipate roadblocks that could sidetrack your development

▼

Help people determine how they will handle potential roadblocks that keep them from growing or taking risks.

People have a natural tendency to learn, yet there are many roadblocks that can derail progress. If you anticipate possible barriers to your development, you will be better prepared to address them. Consider the following suggestions:

▶ List the obstacles you are likely to face as you pursue development. Beside each one, write down one or two actions you could take to counteract the obstacle.

▶ Show your development plans and goals to others. This will increase your commitment to attaining the goals and involve others in your development. Specifically, ask for support and feedback in the areas you find toughest to master.

- Keep the development process simple. Complexity can make development feel intimidating rather than motivational.

- Lean into your discomfort. Accept that change and development may feel frightening or ambiguous at times. Remind yourself that this feeling is temporary.

- Be patient and realize that change takes time. Real behavioral change feels natural and easy only with persistence and practice.

- Be aware of what happens when your progress begins to slip. Keep track of situations that cause you difficulty and figure out how to address them.

Involve others in your development efforts

Effective development rarely happens in isolation. Instead, successful learning occurs through a continuous process of feedback and support from others. Consider the following suggestions:

- Ask others for feedback on your progress. Choose people who have opportunities to see you practicing new skills.

- Tell people what you are trying to do differently. Ask them to watch for the new behavior and let you know how it is working.

- Involve other people in testing your assumptions and conclusions to ensure that you are on the right track. Choose people who will give you candid feedback and encourage you to take risks.

Involve your people in your development. It sends a powerful message about the priority of development and how you value their involvement.

- Realize that no single person will fill all of your development and feedback needs. Colleagues, direct reports, managers, team leaders, HR staff, role models and mentors, and family and friends can all support you in various ways.

- Learn from people outside of work. Leaders from other professions and organizations as well as community leaders can serve as effective coaches and role models. They may be able to introduce you to skills, styles, and techniques that you have not found in your current situation.

You need support to sustain your learning progress, to stay committed when your enthusiasm fades, and to persist when the going gets tough. A development support network can keep your learning pursuits alive. Consider the following suggestions:

- Choose development partners who can help you learn and who care about your development. Actively search for partners you trust who:
  - ▷ Are willing to help you.
  - ▷ Are willing to be candid with you.
  - ▷ Understand what you're trying to do differently.
  - ▷ Are good at something you struggle with.
  - ▷ Can help keep you on track.

- Share your development strategies and activities with your development partners. Talk about the support you want.

- Find ways to provide mutual encouragement and to be accountable to each other.

- Consult your development partners when you find yourself straying off course.

Seek out and learn from others who are different from you

Getting input and advice from a wide range of people will provide you with new ideas. Consider the following suggestions for seeking out and learning from others who are different from you:

- Develop a habit of identifying what you can learn from each person you meet.

- Realize that to keep learning, you need to put yourself into unfamiliar situations. People who view problems and issues differently than you do open up your mind to a new range of possibilities.

- Be open to learning from people at all levels and from all types of organizations. Always have your antennae up. Learn from direct reports, managers, colleagues, team leaders, support staff, family and friends, and role models and mentors.

▸ Put yourself into situations in which you are the "odd man out." For example, look for situations in which you are the only person from your department or organization. Pay attention to what the issues are, people's attitudes toward those issues, proposed solutions, and how they work as a group.

Talk about what you have learned from others and from whom you have learned.

▸ Set a goal for learning from others, or it won't happen. It's easier to stick with your current routine than to break out of it.

▸ Determine how you will approach the people from whom you want to learn. Depending on the situation, it may range from a single conversation to asking someone to consult with your team.

▸ If you're hesitant to learn from people who seem different from you, examine why you're reluctant. You may be afraid to test your assumptions, or you may fear that your methods are wrong. Instead of viewing a situation as right or wrong, think of it as a chance to add dimensions to your thinking.

Seek feedback to enhance your performance

▼

Getting feedback is like finding your location on a map. While you need to know where you've been and what your destination is, it's also critical to have an accurate picture of where you are now. But many people are reluctant to give feedback, especially negative feedback. It's up to you to actively solicit the feedback you need in order to grow and develop. Consider the following suggestions:

▸ Seek feedback from your manager regularly. Ask for specific comments, suggestions, and feedback in areas you are attempting to improve or enhance.

▸ When your boss gives little feedback or feedback that is too general, ask specific questions: How did the new agenda work? What do you think I did better in the presentation? How could I improve?

▸ Encourage your employees and peers to provide feedback. Ask them how you can be more effective in your job. Also ask what you might change to help them be more effective in their jobs.

▸ Solicit feedback at the end of projects. Ask others what you did that was effective and not effective. Decide how you'd like to do things differently the next time. Ask people to observe you in this specific area on a future project and provide you with additional feedback.

▸ When someone gives you vague feedback, either positive or negative (for example, "nice job"), ask for specifics.

▸ Express your appreciation to those who give you feedback. Then put relevant feedback to visible use. If others see that you act on the feedback you receive, they will be more willing to give you constructive, honest feedback in the future.

▸ Obtain comprehensive feedback on your skills using multi-rater or 360-degree feedback instruments available through Personnel Decisions International or through your organization.

▸ How you ask for feedback can determine whether you receive honest, useful information. Tell people why you're asking and what you intend to do with the information. Make sure your tone of voice and body language convey your sincerity and your desire to put the information to good use.

Give people specific, positive feedback so that they understand which actions and behaviors are effective.

▸ When you solicit feedback, ask specific questions so people can give you relevant answers. Examples include:

  ▷ How would you describe my leadership style?

  ▷ What do you think I do particularly well? What areas do I need to develop?

  ▷ Think of situations in which you have observed my behavior and performance. What can I do more effectively (for example, motivate others, manage meetings or groups, coach coworkers, delegate, handle crises)?

  ▷ What could I do to influence people more effectively?

▸ Seek constructive criticism instead of waiting for others to give it to you. More often than not, people are reluctant to provide negative or controversial information. You need to solicit this information.

▸ Guard against asking too many follow-up questions at one time, especially "why" questions. People may perceive your behavior as defensive instead of inquisitive.

Accept criticism openly and nondefensively

▼

Criticism can evoke an automatically defensive response. Defensiveness interferes with your ability to hear and understand the information others give you. More important, it can cause others to stop giving you the honest feedback and information that you need to learn and grow. Consider the following suggestions:

▸ View defensiveness as your worst enemy. Don't argue, don't explain, and don't debate the criticism. If you become defensive, others will be reluctant to give you feedback in the future, and you will cut off a critical information source.

▸ Check your response patterns for phrases such as "Yes, but . . ." and eliminate them. Whenever you catch yourself explaining why, stop talking and listen. Explanations are often perceived as a defensive response.

Identify the area people feel most defensive about and monitor them carefully when they hear feedback about it.

▸ When you are feeling defensive, stop and ask yourself a fixed set of rational-analytical questions, such as the following, to help diminish your defensiveness:

▷ Do I understand what is being said?

▷ Is the criticism about a situation or behavior I could change if I wanted to?

▷ What would happen if I acted on the feedback?

▸ Avoid seeking feedback when you are emotionally on edge, when you are upset with the feedback giver, or when you do not intend to use the feedback.

▸ Use discretion when you respond. Summarize the feedback to ensure that you fully heard and understood it. State your point of view only if the other person has expressed an interest in hearing it.

▸ Ask trusted colleagues to tell you when you are being defensive. Eliminate or change the behavior they have labeled defensive, even if you do not agree with their point of view. Their perception of your behavior is reality; it is what they believe to be true.

▸ When someone disagrees with you:

▷ Wait until the person has finished speaking.

▷ Restate the person's main points and try to understand his or her perspective.

▷ Ask the person to verify or clarify the accuracy of your understanding.

▷ Identify the points with which you sincerely agree.

▷ Then, and only then, state specifically which points you disagree with, and why.

Work to understand and resolve conflicting feedback from multiple sources

▼

Individuals often interpret the same events in different ways as a result of their unique perspectives. This can affect the type of feedback they give you. While your goal is not to get everyone to see your behavior in exactly the same way, it can be helpful to understand differences. Consider the following suggestions:

▸ Assess the degree to which you behave differently in various situations. Most people vary their approach according to the situation and the person. You may find that you are altering yours to an unusual degree.

▸ Realize that people from different functions, business units, and levels may observe different aspects of your performance. As a result, their feedback may not completely match. For example, your direct reports may frequently observe you leading meetings while your peers may frequently observe you participating in meetings.

▸ Consider personalities and attitudes when you assess conflicting feedback. An extrovert is likely to size up a situation differently than an introvert, for example.

Encourage people to ask clarifying questions when they receive feedback.

▸ Sort conflicting feedback into areas that you understand and areas that you don't. For example, you may understand why your direct reports would like you to delegate more and give them more autonomy but not understand why your manager wants you to be more hands off. This will help you pinpoint areas where it may be helpful to get clarification.

▸ Ask yourself if the feedback is important enough for you to seek clarification. Asking for more feedback creates an expectation that you will do something with the information.

- ▸ Find people who can help you make sense of conflicting feedback. Choose people who meet one or more of the following criteria:
  - ▹ People you respect and trust.
  - ▹ People who hold a point of view different from yours.
  - ▹ People who have a vested interest in your success.
  - ▹ People who know your work.
  - ▹ People who are good at giving feedback.

- ▸ Find ways to ask people for more information without putting them on the spot. For example, you might say to your direct reports, "I am trying to improve my ability to operate as a team member and there are some aspects of my behavior that I do not fully understand. I would like your assistance so I can improve in this area."

Work to understand feedback that conflicts with your self-perception

One of the reasons feedback is so valuable is that it allows you to see yourself as others see you. Sometimes the message is not what you expected or hoped to hear. You may hear information that is inconsistent with how you view yourself. When this happens, consider the following suggestions:

- ▸ Remember that people can observe your behaviors, but they cannot see your intentions. Reflect on the situation and determine whether you truly did something or just intended to do it. Maybe you had grand plans but executed only 10 percent of them. People can judge only the 10 percent.

- ▸ Determine the amount of energy that you want to expend to resolve the conflicting feedback. Ask the following questions:
  - ▹ Is the feedback important? Is this information tied to the critical success factors of your job?
  - ▹ Are the feedback givers' perspectives and opinions valued by the organization?
  - ▹ Is the feedback valid and accurate? Have the feedback givers had a chance to observe your behavior? (If not, it may be a public relations issue rather than a skill deficit.)

▷ Do you plan to do anything with the information once you understand it? (If not, it may not be worth your time and energy to understand it.)

▶ Realize that people often go through the SARA process when receiving feedback: shock or surprise, anger, resistance to or rejection of the feedback, and acceptance. In general, wait until you are in the last phase before you seek clarification.

Help people go through the SARA (shock, anger, resistance, acceptance) process when they receive tough feedback.

▶ If you are upset by the information, wait until your emotions settle before you attempt to resolve the differences. Your emotions are likely to get in the way of your ability to be objective, and it is difficult to talk with others in a constructive way when your emotions are not in check.

▶ Once you have decided that the feedback discrepancies are worth resolving, consider the following questions:

▷ When and where is a good time for you to solicit this information?

▷ Who is able to observe your behavior in this area?

▷ What specific information do you need to help you improve your behavior?

▷ What information is not necessary?

▶ Realize that if you seek clarification on feedback that others have provided to you, you are sending a message to them that you intend to do something in response to the feedback.

Demonstrate willingness to try new things, even at the risk of failure

Doing new things and taking risks does not come easily for many people because they fear the potential consequences. If this describes you, consider the following suggestions:

▶ Determine what you would like to try at work but haven't done. Discover what prevents you from trying. Then figure out how to minimize your concerns. For example, if you know you need to take stronger stands but don't because you are concerned about conflict, find someone who can help you learn additional influence skills.

▶ When you are concerned about doing something new, find a way to practice. For example, you could rehearse what you want to say by role-playing with a colleague. You could also discuss your approach with someone and ask for feedback.

▸ Assess how well you recover from mistakes. You may be able to take greater risks if you are good at recovery.

▸ Reflect on how you generally view risks and failure. Some people immediately view a situation in terms of what could go wrong instead of what they could learn.

▸ Identify your personal and organizational obstacles to trying new things and taking risks. For example, you may fear that you will lose hard-won ground, be singled out in case of failure, have an inadequate contingency plan, or lose credibility.

Encourage people to see possibilities for themselves. Express your confidence and trust in them.

▸ Look for patterns in situations in which it is most difficult for you to take risks. For example, you may readily take risks having to do with people issues but hesitate to take risks that might affect the bottom line of the business.

▸ If you work in a risk-averse organization, take smaller risks at first to create a positive track record, then move on to larger risks.

▸ Try to learn the right lessons from failure. Otherwise, you might simply learn that you don't ever want to take another chance again. Talk about the failure situation with a more experienced colleague. This will help you get past your immediate reactions and see the situation in context.

▸ If you failed in a similar circumstance, analyze what happened. Compare the situation to the one you're currently facing. Chances are that there is some learning you can take advantage of.

▸ Model risk taking. Describe to your team how you arrived at your decisions in various situations. Discuss the risks involved and the issues you considered as you made your decisions.

▸ Talk to people within and outside of your organization who regularly try new things and take risks. Find out how they prepare, how they handle discomfort, and what they have gained from these experiences.

Willingly accept challenging assignments and new career opportunities

Taking the initiative to seek out new work challenges demonstrates your commitment to the organization and increases the variety and scope of your job. Consider the following suggestions:

▸ Talk with your manager about your willingness to take on challenging assignments and your desire to expand your career. Indicate your interests and ideas, and discuss possible action steps.

▸ When you identify an assignment you would like, interview people who are currently doing that work. Learn what is required in terms of knowledge, time, and skills.

▸ Watch for opportunities to help out in other functions or areas, such as participating in special projects or task forces. This will broaden your skills, build your cross-functional knowledge, and help you learn about further opportunities.

▸ Identify issues critical to your organization's success and develop expertise in those areas. Watch for opportunities to share your knowledge and skills and demonstrate their usefulness.

▸ As you take on additional assignments, make sure that you still manage your current job capably. Your manager, direct reports, and coworkers depend on you to continue to do your current job as you take on new responsibilities.

▸ Be realistic about your commitments. You may become so enthusiastic about taking on a new challenge that you take on more than you can handle. Set challenging goals, but don't set yourself up for failure.

Tell people what is needed for advancement to other roles.

▸ Identify obstacles (lack of time, fear of failure) that would keep you from seeking new work challenges. Weigh the obstacles against what you will gain by expanding your skills. Look at your time and effort as an investment in your future.

▸ Realize that new situations may make you feel uncomfortable or cause you to question your ability to succeed. These are natural reactions to growth. If necessary, ask for additional help or support. Be persistent.

Know the job

▼

To perform at your best, you need to clearly understand the requirements and objectives of your position and the unspoken expectations of your manager and others. Consider the following suggestions:

▸ Discuss the expectations for your role with your manager. Talk about nuances of the role as well as broad responsibilities. Check in every six months to ensure that the expectations are current and on track.

Ensure that people periodically review the requirements and objectives of their positions. Discuss new expectations.

▸ Describe the purpose of your current role in the organization. You may want to discuss this with your manager. The following are helpful questions to ask:

▹ Why does your position exist?

▹ How does it fit into the broader leadership structure of your group and business unit?

▹ How do you see your role changing over the next year?

▸ Look for three to five key result areas in which effective performance is critical. Determine how you will measure performance in each area. Clarify with your manager if you are uncertain how to measure your performance.

▸ Set specific objectives for each indicator. For example, "Our group will respond to 95 percent of customer complaints within 24 hours, and 100 percent within 48 hours." Share your objectives with your employees and others in the organization with whom you work closely.

▸ Periodically review your performance against your objectives. Ask your manager for feedback on your performance and for input on how to achieve objectives more effectively.

Keep up to date on professional/technical development

▼

Although successful managers do not need the same amount of professional/technical development as their employees, they do need some. The amount of expertise and knowledge you need depends on your role in the organization, the level of your position, and the expertise available from others. Consider the following suggestions:

► Assess the level of professional/technical knowledge and expertise you need in your position. In general, the more expertise that is available from others, the less you need yourself. Leaders at high levels in an organization often need less technical expertise because they have many others on whom they can rely.

► Understand why you need the technical information. Reasons may include identifying and addressing strategic issues, making sound decisions and investment choices, hiring the right people, or developing others. This will help you determine (and potentially limit) what and how much you need to monitor in order to stay up-to-date.

► Identify the resources for professional expertise available to you. These may include your team members, cross-functional team members, other managers and peers, and trusted external consultants.

► Look for areas in which you don't personally have knowledge and you also don't have the technical resources you need. Gain the expertise you need by finding resources in other areas of the organization or by charting a path for increasing your knowledge.

► Look to company and industry best practices to quickly provide a basic level of standard information, knowledge, and practices.

Hold a regular discussion time to review current trends and information on issues relevant to your business.

► Network with others to learn needed information.

► Use resources available through professional associations, Web sites, marketing information, and so forth.

Keeping up-to-date with the technical advances in your field is important for your own and your organization's continued growth and development.

► Ask your management staff and their teams to keep you updated about the trends and developments in their areas of expertise. Discuss the implications of these new developments.

► Build an informal network of peers in your own organization and from similar organizations for exchanging ideas and discussing relevant technical advances and changes in your field.

► Ensure that you and your employees attend conferences and take advantage of educational opportunities to learn about new technology and technical developments.

- If your strategy team has identified potential competitors from other industries, make a point of learning about the technical foundation of those industries and potential new developments in them.

- Ask customers to educate you and your team about technical developments they see in their industries.

- Support funding for team members to develop their skills and become acquainted with new developments.

- Aim to take on at least one new project each year that will challenge you to search out new ideas and information.

- Hire people from outside the organization to build capabilities quickly in a particular area.

- Remember that as you advance in your career, you will need to move from a position of highly defined expertise to one that encompasses a broader view of a functional area. Learn from others in your function who have expertise different from your own. Try to gain a working knowledge of how each function in your area works so you get a broader view.

Increase your knowledge of specific processes

Have people draw a flow chart of a process as they understand it and review it with them.

Because of specific strategic issues, limited resources, or employee shortages, you may find yourself needing to gain knowledge and expertise outside your own area. You may need to learn about other functions or develop expertise about particular processes. Consider the following suggestions:

- Arrange for a coach in the content or process area who can help you on an as-needed basis.

- When you know what expertise you need, ask the leader of that area to recommend activities that will help you learn efficiently, including what you should read, observe, and do.

- Ask to see process flow maps or documentation. This will help you learn what exists now.

- Find out whether a colleague can lend you a resource for a short period of time to cover the need. Express your willingness to reciprocate in the future.

- Read about best practices in this area so you will become familiar with them and can understand why they are recommended.

- Seek opportunities to observe, work with, and get feedback from individuals who are highly skilled in the process, such as your supervisor, a colleague, or someone from another part of the company.

Increase your knowledge of functional areas

Today's business environment demands that organizations work and think more and more across functional areas. Increasingly, managers need to know how their function fits with others in the organization and how each adds value to the organization's core business processes. Consider the following suggestions:

- Talk with individuals inside and outside your organization who have expertise in functional areas. View committees, task forces, and department meetings as chances to increase your understanding of functional areas.

- Observe the actions and practices of people in positions similar to or related to yours. You may want to ask them if you can work with them on tasks, interview them formally or informally to learn their secrets for success, or check in with them regularly.

- Read reports and documents that describe procedures, practices, and other information related to your area and other functional areas.

Have people meet with peers in other functional areas to learn about their key priorities for the year.

- Attend courses and seminars that can give you a broader perspective of how your position fits into the functional area and how your functional area fits into the process.

- Join professional organizations. For example, a materials manager might want to get involved in a professional organization that includes additional areas of manufacturing.

Stay informed about industry practices

▼

Beyond the specific technical aspects of your work, which could apply to several industries, you also need to keep up-to-date on developments in the industry in which you work. Industry practices and standards can change. What was considered the norm as you started your career may be outdated. Consider the following suggestions:

▶ Visit other companies and talk with people in similar functions. Also talk with their customers. After each visit, detail what you have learned and how it adds to your knowledge of the industry.

▶ Attend industry or professional meetings, conferences, and seminars. Work on program committees. Actively involve yourself in the group.

Encourage people to ask seasoned colleagues in your industry to describe how things have changed and what they see for the future.

▶ Read professional newsletters and trade journals to stay up-to-date on new developments in your industry.

▶ Join (or form) an informal group of professionals from other organizations who get together to discuss technical advances and other issues of common interest. Affiliations can be based on type of business, organization size, manufacturing processes, market, or other common bonds.

▶ Attend university and industry association educational events to keep abreast of developments.

Resources

Knowledge is of two kinds: we know a subject ourselves or we know where we can find information upon it.

—Samuel Johnson

Knowing is not enough; we must apply!

—Goethe

An investment in learning pays dividends for years. In this section, you'll find books, seminars, and Web sites to get you started.

We've found books that will make you think, provide new perspectives, and give you the latest thinking in the field. You'll also find some classics, because good ideas never go out of style.

Seminars and programs are a great option when you want to immerse yourself in a topic or issue. Web resources grow exponentially every day. Start with our list, then follow their links to discover new experts and ideas.

Dig in—challenge yourself! You will never regret your investment in learning.

Chapter 1 – Analyze Issues

▼

Books

Fook, Jan, and Fiona Gardner. *Practising Critical Reflection: A Resource Handbook.* **Maidenhead, England: Open University Press, 2007.**

Critical reflection in professional practice is a way to ensure ongoing scrutiny and improved practice skills. The authors describe and analyze theoretical input as well as the approach involved in critical reflection.

Hurson, Tim. *Think Better: An Innovator's Guide to Productive Thinking.* **New York: McGraw-Hill, 2007.**

Think Better demonstrates how you can start with a difficult problem, an unmet need, or a flaw in your business strategy and, by following a clearly defined, practical thinking process, arrive at a solid, innovative solution.

Martin, Roger L. *The Opposable Mind: How Successful Leaders Win Through Integrative Thinking.* **Boston: Harvard Business School Press, 2007.**

Martin shows you how to think in a more integrative and expansive way, outlining the methods and benefits of an "opposable mind."

Nightingale, Jim. *Think Smart—Act Smart: Avoiding the Business Mistakes That Even Intelligent People Make.* **Hoboken, NJ: John Wiley, 2008.**

Nightingale describes misguided and erroneous thinking patterns, such as wishful thinking, mythical thinking, and royal thinking, and provides a plan for you to improve your thinking in life and on the job.

Schmitt, Bernd. *Big Think Strategy: How to Leverage Bold Ideas and Leave Small Thinking Behind.* **Boston: Harvard Business School Press, 2007.**

Schmitt shows how to bring bold thinking into your business by sourcing big ideas and executing them creatively.

Seminars

Business Analysis for Everyday Projects
Terry College of Business, University of Georgia

www.terry.uga.edu

Participants learn underlying principles of business analysis and how to successfully collect, confirm, and manage requirements while minimally affecting the business customer.

Critical Thinking and Strategic Problem Solving Skills for Leaders
Schulich School of Business, York University

www.elc.schulich.yorku.ca

Participants learn a problem-solving methodology that utilizes critical thinking approaches, prioritizes problems, and establishes practical and achievable action plans.

Innovative Thinking and Problem Solving
Sauder School of Business, University of British Columbia

www.sauder.ubc.ca/exec_ed

This course provides a comprehensive process for solving complex problems, including creative and integrative thinking, identifying problem scope and causal interactions, framing the problem, prototyping, and business model development.

System Thinking: Navigating through Complexity
Weatherhead School of Management, Case Western Reserve University

www.case.edu

Managers learn "system thinking," which focuses on the interrelationships and dynamics of a situation, and develop a more global perspective that can open up the possibility of new and more effective solutions.

Understanding and Solving Complex Business Problems
Sloan School of Management, Massachusetts Institute of Technology

http://mitsloan.mit.edu

This course is designed for leaders with decision-making responsibility who are looking for fresh ideas to resolve organizational problems. Participants gain a new way of thinking about and resolving complex, persistent problems that emerge from change.

Chapter 2 – Make Sound Decisions

▼

Books

Blake, Chris. *The Art of Decisions: How to Manage in an Uncertain World.* **New York: Prentice Hall Financial Times, 2008.**

Blake outlines the fundamental issues of business decision making, drawing from business case studies, poker, probability and game theory, and decades of psychological research.

Finkelstein, Sydney, Jo Whitehead, and Andrew Campbell. *Think Again: Why Good Leaders Make Bad Decisions and How to Keep It from Happening to You.* **Boston: Harvard Business School Press, 2009.**

Using examples from business, politics, and history, the authors deconstruct bad decisions as they unfolded in real time, to show how you can avoid the same fate.

Shaw, Peter. *Making Difficult Decisions: How to Be Decisive and Get the Business Done.* **Chichester, England, and Hoboken, NJ: Capstone, 2008.**

Shaw sets out a tested framework for making difficult decisions that has been used successfully by senior leaders in public, private, and voluntary sectors.

Thaler, Richard H., and Cass R. Sunstein. *Nudge: Improving Decisions about Health, Wealth, and Happiness.* **New Haven, CT: Yale University Press, 2008.**

Using colorful examples, the authors demonstrate how "choice architecture" can nudge you in beneficial directions without restricting freedom of choice.

Zeckhauser, Bryn, and Aaron Sandoski. *How the Wise Decide: The Lessons of 21 Extraordinary Leaders.* **New York: Crown Business, 2008.**

The authors share wisdom gleaned from their conversations with 21 major business leaders about crucial decisions they made during their careers.

Seminars

Critical Thinking for Decision Making
J. Mack Robinson College of Business, Georgia State University

http://robinson.gsu.edu

This interactive program, employing a mix of academic and practitioner knowledge, helps participants incorporate different viewpoints so they can act decisively and effectively in complex business situations.

Critical Thinking: Real-World, Real-Time Decisions
Wharton, University of Pennsylvania

www.wharton.upenn.edu

Participants reframe issues to address the right problems, distinguish systematic patterns from random events, and identify acceptable risks. They also learn how to make better decisions within network-oriented and decentralized organizational structures.

Negotiation and Decision Making Skills
Booth School of Business, University of Chicago

www.chicagoexec.net

Participants survey a range of negotiating and decision-making styles, learning to interpret and comfortably use the latest advances in the field of negotiation in their daily decisions.

Strategic Decision Making
Darden School of Business, University of Virginia

www.darden.virginia.edu

Participants deepen their decision-making skills, learning how to break down decision "problems" into more manageable parts; consider alternatives, available information, and relevant preferences of decision makers; and avoid common decision-making mistakes.

Chapter 3 – Act Strategically

▼

Books

Champy, James. *Outsmart!: How to Do What Your Competitors Can't.* **Upper Saddle River, NJ: FT Press, 2008.**

Champy discusses how you can consistently outsmart the competition in an environment where even the best strategies rarely prevail, and he explains how to generate strategy organically.

Gilbert, Xavier, Bettina Büchel, and Rhoda Davidson. *Smarter Execution: Seven Steps to Getting Results.* **Harlow, England: Pearson Education, 2006.**

The authors identify seven key steps that you must take to obtain the full benefits of your strategic initiatives.

Gottfredson, Mark, and Steve Schaubert. *The Breakthrough Imperative: How the Best Managers Get Outstanding Results.* **New York: Collins, 2008.**

The authors present four core laws of business, drawn from interviews with more than 40 CEOs and the authors' combined 50 years of management consulting.

Kanazawa, Michael, and Robert H. Miles. *Big Ideas to Big Results: Remake and Recharge Your Company, Fast.* **Upper Saddle River, NJ: FT Press, 2008.**

In discussing steps for success and practical solutions, the authors share their number-one insight: many obstacles occur when you make situations and decisions more complex than they really are and take too much time to prepare.

Mathur, Shiv Sahai, and Alfred Kenyon. *Creating Valuable Business Strategies.* **Boston: Elsevier/Butterworth-Heinemann, 2008.**

The authors make the case that each value-adding offering needs a competitive strategy, and they describe how an offering can be competitively positioned against rival offerings.

Seminars

Competitive Strategy
Kellogg School of Management, Northwestern University

www.kellogg.northwestern.edu/execed

Participants learn to identify their organizations' competitive strengths and turn them into profits and customer value, and learn how to analyze their business to identify when and in what form cooperation and competition are appropriate.

Growth Focused Business Strategy
Leonard N. Stern School of Business, New York University

www.stern.nyu.edu

Implementing competitive strategy requires an understanding of the fundamentals. This course covers economic principles and provides quantitative tools for evaluating strategic business choices in fast-changing markets.

Moving from an Operational Manager to a Strategic Thinker
American Management Association

www.amanet.org

Participants develop a broader view of their companies, gain insights and ideas into the core skills of strategic thinking, and take steps to take on a more strategic role.

Strategy: Building and Sustaining Competitive Advantage
Executive Education Programs, Harvard Business School

www.exed.hbs.edu

Participants formulate and evaluate new competitive strategies, lay the groundwork for change, and put their action plans to work for their companies.

Chapter 4 – Leverage Innovation

▼

Books

Duggan, William R. *Strategic Intuition: The Creative Spark in Human Achievement.* **New York: Columbia University Press, 2007.**

Duggan provides the first full treatment of strategic intuition, the flash of insight in which an idea for action changes a field—or starts a new one.

Fenn, Jackie, and Mark Raskino. *Mastering the Hype Cycle: How to Choose the Right Innovation at the Right Time.* **Boston: Harvard Business School Press, 2008.**

Drawing on company examples and Gartner's STREET (scope, track, rank, evaluate, evangelize, transfer) framework, the authors show how to orchestrate the key steps in the innovation-adoption process.

Förster, Anja, and Peter Kreuz. *Different Thinking: Creative Strategies for Developing the Innovative Business.* **London and Philadelphia: Kogan Page, 2007.**

Different Thinking contains practical tools and strategies—such as creating new markets, and inventing price and profit models that bring a competitive advantage—to increase the value of your business.

McKeown, Max. *The Truth about Innovation.* **Harlow, England, and New York: Pearson/ Prentice Hall, 2008.**

Drawing on 15+ years of research, consulting, training, and writing, McKeown outlines a set of bedrock principles for managing innovation and improving results.

O'Connor, Gina C., Richard Leifer, Albert S. Paulson, and Lois S. Peters. *Grabbing Lightning: Building a Capability for Breakthrough Innovation.* **San Francisco: Jossey-Bass, 2008.**

The authors recount how 12 companies developed a capability for sustainable breakthrough innovation and outline best practices for your organization, introducing the Breakthrough Innovation management system.

VanGundy, Arthur B. *Getting to Innovation: How Asking the Right Questions Generates the Great Ideas Your Company Needs.* **New York: AMACOM, 2007.**

Getting to Innovation details the critical first step in formulating creative and useful ideas—asking the right questions to define the challenges facing your organization.

Seminars

Creativity and Innovation in the Organization
Executive Education at the Anderson School of Management,
University of California, Los Angeles

www.anderson.ucla.edu

During an intensive week in a think-tank environment, participants learn approaches and tools to tap into the power of creativity to better create, innovate, and convert ideas into successful business solutions.

Full-Spectrum Innovation: Driving Organic Growth
Wharton, University of Pennsylvania

http://executiveeducation.wharton.upenn.edu

This innovative workshop provides a full-spectrum view of innovation and a challenging environment in which to test and adapt strategies.

Implementing Innovation and Change
Booth School of Business, University of Chicago

www.chicagoexec.net

Participants gain strategies for setting and maintaining the course of change, for overcoming resistance and maximizing learning and innovative thinking, and for anticipating and coping with the repercussions of change.

Leading Product Innovation
Executive Education Programs, Harvard Business School

www.exed.hbs.edu

Participants explore new approaches to align product development with corporate strategy, reinvent strategic innovation systems, assess disruptive technologies, and manage risk.

Strategic Intuition: The Key to Innovation
Columbia Business School, Columbia University

http://www4.gsb.columbia.edu/execed/

Based on his groundbreaking research and teaching, Professor William Duggan illustrates how to capture the benefits of strategic intuition and apply it to real-world business situations.

Chapter 5 – Use Financial Data

▼

Books

Berman, Karen, and Joe Knight with John Case. *Financial Intelligence: A Manager's Guide to Knowing What the Numbers Really Mean.* Boston: Harvard Business School Press, 2006.

The authors not only teach the fundamentals of finance, they also take you behind the scenes and show where the numbers come from and how estimates, assumptions, and judgment calls can skew the numbers in one direction or another.

Callahan, Kevin R., Gary S. Stetz, and Lynne M. Brooks. *Project Management Accounting: Budgeting, Tracking, and Reporting Costs and Profitability.* Hoboken, NJ: John Wiley, 2007.

This guide helps you determine how project revenues and expenses affect a company's financial results and make decisions about whether to continue with a project, find an alternative solution, or bring the project to an end.

Epstein, Lita. *Reading Financial Reports for Dummies,* 2nd edition. Hoboken, NJ: John Wiley, 2009.

Epstein's guide provides tools and accounting basics for understanding financial reports. This second edition includes information on reporting standards for private/small versus public/large businesses, and the impact of corporate communications and new technologies.

Koomey, Jonathan. *Turning Numbers into Knowledge: Mastering the Art of Problem Solving.* 2nd edition. Oakland, CA: Analytics Press, 2008.

Koomey focuses on how people use information, addressing the importance of ideology, the art of storytelling, and the distinction between facts and values.

Stutely, Richard. *The Definitive Guide to Business Finance: What Smart Managers Do with the Numbers.* 2nd edition. Upper Saddle River, NJ: FT Press, 2008.

Many managers fear finance, which prevents them from doing their job effectively. Stutely makes finance fun with a wry, commonsense approach and takes you through all essential aspects of business finance.

Seminars

The Essentials of Budgeting
American Management Association

www.amanet.org

From the basics of budgeting through planning and implementation, participants develop the capability to identify the costs and characteristics of budgeting systems.

Finance and Accounting for the Non-Financial Manager
Wharton, University of Pennsylvania

www.wharton.upenn.edu/execed

Participants gain knowledge of financial data and financial statements, the process that generates financial data, and significant concepts and terminology in finance and accounting.

Finance for the Non-Financial Manager
Goizueta Business School, Emory University

www.goizueta.emory.edu

This course is designed for leaders who have minimal knowledge of and/or experience with finance. Participants examine how financial data are generated and reported, as well as how data are used for organizational decision making.

Financial Analysis for Non-Financial Executives
Haas School of Business, University of California, Berkeley

http://executive.berkeley.edu/programs/fanfe/

Participants improve their ability to use financial information in decision making, to evaluate the financial performance of a business and its people, to understand financial statements, and to communicate persuasively and confidently about financial issues.

Chapter 6 – Manage Globally

▼

Books

Bloch, Susan, and Philip Whiteley. *How to Manage in a Flat World: 10 Strategies to Get Connected to Your Team Wherever They Are.* **Upper Saddle River, NJ: FT Press, 2009.**

The authors present realistic, proven techniques for leading and motivating teams in today's flattened and globalized business environment.

Friedman, George. *The Next 100 Years: A Forecast for the 21st Century.* **New York: Doubleday, 2009.**

Friedman, a renowned expert in geopolitics and forecasting, offers a lucid, thoughtful forecast of the changes we can expect around the world during the 21st century.

Ghemawat, Pankaj. *Redefining Global Strategy: Crossing Borders in a World Where Differences Still Matter.* **Boston: Harvard Business School Press, 2007.**

In-depth examples reveal how companies such as Cemex, Toyota, Procter & Gamble, Tata Consultancy Services, IBM, and GE Healthcare managed cross-border differences.

Lojeski, Karen Sobel, and Richard R. Reilly. *Uniting the Virtual Workforce: Transforming Leadership and Innovation in the Globally Integrated Enterprise.* **Hoboken, NJ: John Wiley, 2008.**

The authors introduce the concept of virtual distance—geographic, operational, and affinity distance—and show how to measure and manage the costs of working in a virtual environment.

Spulber, Daniel F. *Global Competitive Strategy.* **Cambridge: Cambridge University Press, 2007.**

Globalization has fundamentally changed the game of business. Managers and business students require new approaches to understand and cope with the far-reaching changes. *Global Competitive Strategy* provides a unique set of strategic tools for international business.

Seminars

Certificate in Global Business Strategy
School of Business Administration, University of San Diego

www.sandiego.edu

Through discussion and a strategic framework, participants develop international business strategies to resolve business problems faced by companies and individuals.

Global Leadership 2020
Tuck Executive Education at Dartmouth

www.tuck.dartmouth.edu

Designed to develop the global leadership skills of high-potential managers, the program incorporates sharing of experiences, cultural immersion, and active collaboration on real-world projects.

Global Strategy and Leadership
Foster School of Business, University of Washington

www.foster.washington.edu

Participants gain ideas and tools for leadership, corporate entrepreneurship, and international strategy. The program includes a visit to a major Seattle corporation with worldwide operations to provide insight into the development and execution of a successful global strategy.

Globalization: Merging Strategy with Action
Thunderbird School of Global Management

www.thunderbird.edu

Participants study the characteristics of corporate strategy, human resource management, cross-cultural communication, and operations management in a complex, competitive world.

Chapter 7 – Meet Customer Needs

▼

Books

Beemer, C. Britt, and Robert L. Shook. *The Customer Rules: The 14 Indispensible, Irrefutable, and Indisputable Qualities of the Greatest Companies in the World.* New York: McGraw-Hill Professional, 2009.

The authors share lessons on how to achieve strong customer loyalty, based on extensive market research and close studies of 14 companies that excel in customer service.

Blackshaw, Pete. *Satisfied Customers Tell Three Friends, Angry Customers Tell 3,000: Running a Business in Today's Consumer Driven World.* New York: Doubleday, 2008.

Blackshaw shows managers, marketers, and business leaders how to establish and maintain credibility for your brand by being authentic, listening and responding to customers, and forming relationships built on openness, transparency, and trust.

Fleming, John Howland, and Jim Asplund. *Human Sigma: Managing the Employee-Customer Encounter.* New York: Gallup Press, 2007.

Six Sigma changed the face of manufacturing quality; Human Sigma aims to do the same for sales and service. The authors introduce a new method for managing customer-employee relations that increases both productivity and profitability.

Goldenberg, Barton J. *CRM in Real Time: Empowering Customer Relationships.* Medford, NJ: CyberAge Books, 2008.

Goldenberg demonstrates how the right mix of people, process, and technology can help you achieve a superior level of customer satisfaction, loyalty, and new business.

Stull, Craig, Phil Myers, and David Meerman Scott. *Tuned In: Uncover the Extraordinary Opportunities That Lead to Business Breakthroughs.* Hoboken, NJ: John Wiley, 2008.

The authors present a guide to understanding and meeting the needs of consumers. Their six-step process helps you address unsolved problems, recognize buyer personas, quantify impact, and create breakthrough experiences.

Ulrich, Dave, and Norm Smallwood. *Leadership Brand: Developing Customer-Focused Leaders to Drive Performance and Build Lasting Value.* Boston: Harvard Business School Press, 2007.

Ulrich and Smallwood show how branded leadership delivers unique value for your firm's investors, customers, and employees; elevates market value; and creates a competitive edge.

Seminars

Building and Leading Customer-Centric Organizations
Executive Education Programs, Harvard Business School

www.exed.hbs.edu

Through lectures, interactive case studies, and small-group project work, participants learn how to align an organization's processes, incentive and control systems, leadership and culture, and formal organizational structures to attain customer centricity.

Customer Experience Management
Columbia Business School, Columbia University

http://www4.gsb.columbia.edu

Participants gain practical tools and knowledge to create powerful experiences for their customers, and to change the culture of their organization from a product and sales focus to a customer focus.

Excellence in Strategic Customer Management
Henley Business School, University of Reading

www.reading.ac.uk

Aimed at service-oriented organizations, this program helps participants who are launching a customer-management strategy and those who wish to maximize the potential of their existing customer-management programs.

Managing Customer Relationships for Profit
Kellogg School of Management, Northwestern University

www.kellogg.northwestern.edu

Participants will learn state-of-the-art techniques for acquiring new customers, enhancing the value of existing customers, and retaining profitable customers.

New Strategies for Creating and Managing Customer Loyalty
McCombs School of Business, University of Texas at Austin

www.mccombs.utexas.edu

This session examines what customer focus means, why customer retention is vital, and what it takes to achieve customer loyalty.

Chapter 8 – Manage Execution

▼

Books

Allen, David. *Getting Things Done: The Art of Stress-Free Productivity.* **New York: Penguin, 2002.**

Allen shares his breakthrough methods for stress-free performance. His premise is simple: productivity is directly proportional to the ability to relax. Only when your mind is clear and your thoughts are organized can you achieve effective productivity and unleash your creative potential.

Harpst, Gary. *Six Disciplines Execution Revolution: Solving the One Business Problem That Makes Solving All Other Problems Easier.* **Findlay, OH: Six Disciplines Publishing, 2008.**

Based on breakthrough research, field testing, and proven best practices, Harpst describes how small and midsized businesses can meet the challenge of executing strategy.

Morgan, Mark, Raymond E. Levitt, and William A. Malek. *Executing Your Strategy: How to Break It Down and Get It Done.* **Boston: Harvard Business School Press, 2007.**

The authors present six imperatives—ideation, nature, vision, engagement, synthesis, transition (INVEST)—that enable you to focus on the right strategic projects and to do those projects right.

Shapiro, Ronald M., with Gregory Jordan. *Dare to Prepare: How to Win Before You Begin.* **New York: Crown Business, 2008.**

The authors share stories from successful individuals—wine guru Robert Parker, pianist Leon Fleisher, firefighter Ann Marie Tierney, New York Mets manager Willie Randolph—illustrating how they apply discipline in preparing for career-changing games, deals, meetings, and interviews.

Tulgan, Bruce. *It's Okay to Be the Boss: The Step-by-Step Guide to Becoming the Manager Your Employees Need.* **New York: HarperCollins, 2007.**

Tulgan challenges you to spell out expectations, tell employees exactly what to do and how to do it, constantly monitor and measure performance, correct failure quickly, and reward success even more quickly.

Wilson, Susan B., and Michael S. Dobson. *Goal Setting: How to Create an Action Plan and Achieve Your Goals.* **2nd edition. New York: AMACOM, 2008.**

This revised and updated edition of *Goal Setting* features worksheets, quizzes, and other practical tools, providing effective techniques for setting goals, creating plans, and accessing the resources you need to achieve your objectives.

Seminars

Creating and Executing Breakthrough Strategy
Columbia Business School, Columbia University

http://www4.gsb.columbia.edu

Participants learn practical frameworks for planning and executing implementation and develop an action plan for their organizations' specific challenges.

Implementing Organic Growth Strategies
Kellogg School of Management, Northwestern University

www.kellogg.northwestern.edu

This program deals explicitly with the challenges and issues confronting any business trying to implement new growth strategies. Participants gain powerful, market-tested implementation tools and methodologies they can use immediately.

Implementing Strategy: Leading Effective Execution
Wharton, Aresty Institute of Executive Education, University of Pennsylvania

http://executiveeducation.wharton.upenn.edu/

Participants develop a broad view of implementation and a thorough understanding of the process. They learn how to align corporate structure with corporate strategies and how to integrate strategy formulation and implementation.

Operational Excellence: Keys to a Competitive Advantage
Carlson School of Management, University of Minnesota

www.carlsonschool.umn.edu

Participants study operations planning, Lean, Six Sigma, Kaizen Blitzes, activity-based costing, benchmarking, supply-chain cost reduction, self-managed teaming, change leadership, and other approaches to becoming a high-performance organization.

Chapter 9 – Build Realistic Plans

▼

Books

Aucoin, B. Michael. *Right-Brain Project Management: A Complementary Approach.* Vienna, VA: Management Concepts, 2007.

Aucoin views project management from a fresh perspective, exploring intuitive right-brain approaches that capitalize on natural human thinking and activity.

Campbell, Clark A. *The One-Page Project Manager: Communicate and Manage Any Project with a Single Sheet of Paper.* Hoboken, NJ: John Wiley, 2007.

Campbell's practical guide explains how to capture a project in a simple, one-page document and use it to communicate essential details to upper management, other departments, suppliers, and audiences.

Lock, Dennis. *The Essentials of Project Management.* 3rd edition. Aldershot, England: Gower, 2007.

Lock provides a concise, straightforward account of the principles and techniques of project management, using examples and illustrations to introduce key procedures.

Shenhar, Aaron, and Dov Dvir. *Reinventing Project Management: The Diamond Approach to Successful Growth and Innovation.* Boston: Harvard Business School Press, 2007.

Based on a study of more than 600 projects in businesses and organizations across the globe, the authors provide a new and adaptive model for planning and managing projects to achieve top business results.

Young, Trevor L. *The Handbook of Project Management: A Practical Guide to Effective Policies and Procedures.* London and Philadelphia: Kogan Page, 2007.

Young's handbook is particularly useful for individuals who need to build their skills, start a new project, or train others in project management.

Seminars

5-Day Project Management Training
Mendoza College of Business, University of Notre Dame

www.nd.edu

Designed around the six domains of competent performance in project management identified by the Project Management Institute, this program offers a faster rate of knowledge transfer and enough credits to sit for the PMP® (Project Management Professional) Examination.

Project Management
Industrial Relations Center, California Institute of Technology

http://irc.caltech.edu

Participants obtain tools and skills to deliver projects on time and within budget, and gain the information they need to pass the PMI® exam and earn PMP® certification.

Project Management Certificate Programs
Graham School of General Studies, University of Chicago

http://iil.com/university_chicago

IIL offers premier certificate programs for all levels: associate (CAPM) in project management for fundamental knowledge; the project management certificate for those achieving the PMP®; and the advanced mastery (APMC) designed for senior practitioners.

Project Management: Planning, Scheduling, and Control
Wisconsin School of Business, University of Wisconsin–Madison

www.uwexeced.com/

Participants learn to set up a project plan and notebook; estimate project costs, resources, and time; employ network scheduling and allocate time-critical resources; establish feedback systems for project control; and use project status reports.

World-Class Inventory Planning and Management
Supply Chain and Logistics Institute, Georgia Institute of Technology

www.scl.gatech.edu

This course addresses a broad range of inventory management issues, including measurement, data mining, forecasting, procurement, and deployment.

Chapter 10 – Manage and Improve Processes

▼

Books

Madison, Dan. *Process Mapping, Process Improvement, and Process Management.* Chico, CA: Paton Press, 2005.

Madison explains the evolution of work management styles and introduces the tools of process mapping, the roles and responsibilities in an organization, and a 10-step redesign methodology.

Melik, Rudolf. *The Rise of the Project Workforce: Managing People and Projects in a Flat World.* Hoboken, NJ: John Wiley, 2007.

A practical tool for managers, directors, and executives, this book offers guidelines and foundational basics for project-based work, standardized work processes, and better collaboration across the workforce.

Milosević, Dragan, Russ J. Martinelli, and James M. Waddell. *Program Management for Improved Business Results.* Hoboken, NJ: John Wiley, 2007.

The authors present a holistic view that describes program management as a critical business function and provide an approach to successfully define, plan, execute, and control programs.

Schonberger, Richard J. *Best Practices in Lean Six Sigma Process Improvement: A Deeper Look.* Hoboken, NJ: John Wiley, 2008.

Schonberger, a renowned process improvement pioneer, outlines the Golden Goals: better quality, quicker response, greater flexibility, and higher value, all with a focus on customers.

Sharp, Alec, and Patrick McDermott. *Workflow Modeling: Tools for Process Improvement and Application Development.* 2nd edition. Norwood, MA: Artech House, 2008.

Extensively revised and expanded, this edition provides proven techniques for identifying, modeling, and redesigning business processes, explains how to implement workflow improvement, and helps define requirements for systems development or systems acquisition.

Seminars

Excellence through Analytics
Center for Executive Education, University of Tennessee

http://thecenter.utk.edu

For over 30 years, the University of Tennessee has pioneered the field of process improvement and Six Sigma; they also "wrote the book" on improving industrial processes. This program equips participants with the ability to improve systems, deliver value, and maximize the bottom line.

Increasing Office Efficiency
Fisher College of Business, Ohio State University

http://fisher.osu.edu

Participants learn how to link operational excellence to organizational strategic competitive advantage and how to use value stream mapping to explore process improvement in an organization.

Logistics Short Course
Supply Chain and Logistics Institute, Georgia Institute of Technology

www.scl.gatech.edu

The Logistics Short Course provides an overview of contemporary logistics management and technology issues, and serves as the foundation for SCL's professional certificate in logistics.

Process Value Analysis
Project Management Institute, University of Florida

http://leadership.dce.ufl.edu

Participants develop a thorough understanding of the value chain, including who their customers are and how they define value. Topics cover customer expectations, processes and activities, and how to maximize the value produced.

Chapter 11 – Champion Change

▼

Books

Clark, Timothy R. *Epic Change: How to Lead Change in the Global Age.* **San Francisco: Jossey-Bass, 2008.**

Change rarely fails for lack of strategy. Clark shows that only the discretionary efforts of people, requiring leadership and energy management, can make change happen.

Cohen, Dan S. *The Heart of Change Field Guide: Tools and Tactics for Leading Change in Your Organization.* **Boston: Harvard Business School Press, 2005.**

This guide provides a practical framework for implementing each step in the change process, as well as a new three-phase approach to execution: creating a climate for change, engaging and enabling the whole organization, and implementing and sustaining change.

Fullan, Michael. *The Six Secrets of Change: What the Best Leaders Do to Help Their Organizations Survive and Thrive.* **San Francisco: Jossey-Bass, 2008.**

To help you navigate change, Fullan shares six secrets—love your employees, connect peers with purpose, capacity building prevails, learning is the work, transparency rules, and systems learn—designed to help with large-scale reform.

Herold, David M., and Donald B. Fedor. *Change the Way You Lead Change: Leadership Strategies That Really Work.* **Stanford, CA: Stanford Business Books, 2008.**

Because change is never a stepwise or easily prescribed process, the authors advocate that you develop and utilize realistic frameworks for organizational change, account for the abilities of those who will lead and implement the change, and understand the context in which the change is to occur.

Salerno, Ann, and Lillie Brock. *The Change Cycle: How People Can Survive and Thrive in Organizational Change.* **San Francisco: Berrett-Koehler, 2008.**

Salerno and Brock outline six predictable and sequential stages that accompany any sort of change, equipping you to cope with change by understanding and predicting your own behavior and the behavior of others.

Seminars

Leading Change in Complex Organizations
Sloan School of Management, Massachusetts Institute of Technology

http://mitsloan.mit.edu

This program presents innovative perspectives on managerial problems and offers practical ways to solve them. The issues examined apply across organizations, national boundaries, and technical domains.

Leading Change and Organizational Renewal
Executive Education, Stanford Graduate School of Business

www.exed.hbs.edu

This program delves into the challenges of organizational change and renewal from the diverse perspectives of innovation, organizational structure and culture, leadership, and risk management.

Leading Strategic Growth and Change
Columbia Business School

http://www4.gsb.columbia.edu

Participants will learn how to thrive in rapidly changing and highly uncertain environments, gain insight into a current change initiative within their organizations, and immediately begin to apply their learning to make rapid progress with current issues.

Managing Individual and Organizational Change
Darden School of Business, University of Virginia

www.darden.virginia.edu

This program begins with a focus on individuals in managerial roles who are trying to lead, manage, and deal with the change process. The focus then shifts to groups and perspectives around the total organization.

Chapter 12 – Show Drive and Initiative

▼

Books

Colvin, Geoff. *Talent Is Overrated: What Really Separates World-Class Performers from Everybody Else.* **New York: Penguin, 2008.**

Colvin offers new evidence that top performers in any field are not determined by their inborn talents. Greatness comes from practice and perseverance honed over decades. The key lies in practice, analyzing the results of your progress, and learning from your mistakes.

Forster, Mark. *Do It Tomorrow and Other Secrets of Time Management.* **London: Hodder & Stoughton, 2008.**

Forster shows that prioritizing tasks is never a sufficient approach to organizing a schedule, and is rarely helpful. Instead, he proposes new ideas, including closed lists, the *mañana* principle, and the will-do list.

Lowe, Tamara. *Get Motivated!: Overcome Any Obstacle, Achieve Any Goal, and Accelerate Your Success with Motivational DNA.* **New York: Doubleday, 2009.**

Every individual is hardwired with a unique motivational matrix. Grounded in eight years of research with more than 10,000 people, Lowe reveals how to decode your "motivational DNA" for maximum achievement.

Seldman, Marty, and Joshua Seldman. *Executive Stamina: How to Optimize Time, Energy, and Productivity to Achieve Peak Performance.* **Hoboken, NJ: John Wiley, 2008.**

The authors provide tips and tools to maximize your career potential while maintaining your health, staying in touch with your values, and avoiding costly trade-offs in your personal life.

Whitelaw, Ginny, and Betsy Wetzig. *Move to Greatness: Focusing the Four Essential Energies of a Whole and Balanced Leader.* **Boston: Nicholas Brealey International, 2008.**

Both success and failure originate in the use or misuse of four fundamental patterns: driver, collaborator, organizer, and visionary. Whitelaw reveals the strengths and weaknesses of each.

Seminars

Corporate Athlete Course
Human Performance Institute

http://hpinstitute.com/training-ec.html

Unlike any other executive training program, the Corporate Athlete Course is designed to strategically help participants become more productive and effective under pressure by managing their energy more effectively.

GTD Mastering Workflow
David Allen Company

www.davidco.com

This course provides a dynamic, systematic, five-phase approach to dealing effectively with the incoming "stuff" of our lives (e-mail, memos, meetings, notes, to-dos) and provides a practical methodology for utilizing paper-based and computer-based systems to organize it.

High Performance Leadership
IMD International

www.imd.ch

Participants examine their leadership roots and foundations, diagnose leadership tasks, advance leadership skills, and develop a personal leadership path that provides inspiration and resilience.

Time Management
American Management Association

www.amanet.org

This seminar helps participants make the best possible use of time. Topics include using a systematic approach to time control, accomplishing more with fewer meetings, and getting teams involved in time management.

Chapter 13 – Lead Courageously

▼

Books

Clawson, James G. *Level Three Leadership: Getting Below the Surface.* **4th edition. Upper Saddle River, NJ: Pearson/Prentice Hall, 2009.**

Clawson provides a comprehensive introduction to the practices and theories of values-based leadership, showing how you can get below the surface of simply influencing others' behavior and lead in a more profound way.

Godin, Seth. *Tribes: We Need You to Lead Us.* **New York: Portfolio, 2008.**

A tribe is any group of people who are connected to one another, a leader, and an idea. Thanks to the Internet, new tribes are forming and growing. Godin discusses who is leading these groups and how they're making a difference.

Nye, Joseph S. *The Powers to Lead.* **New York: Oxford University Press, 2008.**

Nye uses the concept of smart power to shed light on leadership types and skills, the needs and demands of followers, and the nature of good and bad leadership in terms of ethics and effectiveness.

Owen, Jo. *Power at Work: The Art of Making Things Happen.* **Philadelphia: Trans-Atlantic Publications, 2008.**

Power means more than formal authority—it is the art of building alliances, networks, influence, and control. Owen focuses on practical skills you can learn and use to your advantage.

Palmisano, Donald J. *On Leadership: Essential Principles for Success.* **New York: Skyhorse, 2008.**

Each chapter contains an example of positive or negative action. The author analyzes each situation, mining detailed, practical methods and strategies for becoming a true leader.

Seminars

Assertiveness Training for Managers
American Management Association

www.amanet.org

This seminar covers effective assertiveness techniques such as managing assertively, achieving objectives, resolving conflicts, and developing a self-improvement plan.

Authentic Leadership: Courage, Coaching, and Ethics
Carlson School of Management, University of Minnesota

www.csom.umn.edu

This program explores both the depths and the dimensions of authentic leadership. Participants gain a better understanding of the ultimate leadership task: self-leadership.

Courage to Act
Kathleen Howard & Associates

www.couragetoact.com

This intensive course is designed for women who are ready to enhance their impact in their organizations, their communities, and their own lives. Participants develop new perspectives and deeper insights about their strengths and talents.

Driving Vision, Action, and Results
Darden School of Business, University of Virginia

www.darden.virginia.edu

By developing a broad understanding of the enterprise and the connectivity of business activity, this program provides an opportunity for participants to focus on and drive actions that will enhance organizational effectiveness and drive superior bottom-line results.

Chapter 14 – Influence Others

▼

Books

Brady, Chris, and Orrin Woodward. *Launching a Leadership Revolution: Mastering the Five Levels of Influence.* **New York: Business Plus, 2008.**

The authors guide you through a five-step plan to create and maintain strong leadership in any organization.

Dilenschneider, Robert L. *Power and Influence: The Rules Have Changed.* **New York: McGraw-Hill, 2007.**

Dilenschneider offers 10 universal principles for success in a technology-driven economy and relates anecdotes and insights that illustrate how to acquire and amplify power.

Jones, Frances Cole. *How to Wow: Proven Strategies for Presenting Your Ideas, Persuading Your Audience, and Perfecting Your Image.* **New York: Ballantine Books, 2008.**

Knowing how to market yourself in any situation is vital. Jones, who has helped numerous CEOs and public personalities, shares her strategies for positively influencing others.

Mortensen, Kurt W. *Persuasion IQ: The 10 Skills You Need to Get Exactly What You Want.* **New York: AMACOM, 2008.**

Mortensen has sought out and studied the world's top persuaders. He describes the essential habits, traits, and behaviors necessary to cultivate your natural persuasive abilities.

Shell, G. Richard, and Mario Moussa. *The Art of Woo: Using Strategic Persuasion to Sell Your Ideas.* **New York: Portfolio, 2007.**

The authors present their systematic, four-step process for strategic persuasion. Starting with self-assessments to help you find your "Woo IQ," they show how relationship-based persuasion works.

Widener, Chris. *The Art of Influence: Persuading Others Begins with You.* **New York: Doubleday, 2008.**

Widener asserts that influence is not something you do to other people, but something that starts with how you shape and transform your own life. True influencers change themselves first.

Seminars

Advocacy: Championing Ideas and Influencing Others
McCombs School of Business, University of Texas at Austin

www.mccombs.utexas.edu

Participants gain knowledge to construct and deliver their message; position and differentiate their ideas; generate loyalty and commitment; and handle objections, problem people, and difficult situations.

Changing Minds: The Power of Persuasion
Sauder School of Business, University of British Columbia

www.sauder.ubc.ca

This course looks at the strategies and skills of effective persuasion. Participants explore the ethical use of persuasive techniques, learn what tactics to employ in a variety of situations, and practice various forms of persuasion in a nonthreatening environment.

How to Influence without Direct Authority
Wisconsin School of Business, University of Wisconsin–Madison

http://exed.wisc.edu

Participants examine characteristics and skills of influential people to understand the sources of informal power. They analyze situations requiring influence and learn how to build effective relationships upward, downward, and laterally.

Influence and Negotiation Strategies Program
Executive Education, Stanford Graduate School of Business, Stanford University

www.gsb.stanford.edu/

This program teaches effective negotiation strategies and influence tactics, and helps participants to analyze the ethical issues that arise as they negotiate to achieve objectives.

Negotiation Skills for Effective Managers
Kenan Flagler Business School, University of North Carolina

www.kenan-flagler.unc.edu

Participants learn the critical steps needed in planning for a negotiation and approaches used by successful negotiators, including how to create a win-win solution.

Strategic Persuasion Workshop: The Art and Science of Selling Ideas
Aresty Institute of Executive Education, Wharton, University of Pennsylvania

http://executiveeducation.wharton.upenn.edu/

This program provides critical tools for leaders to sell their ideas at work. The program is complementary to the book *The Art of Woo: Using Strategic Persuasion to Sell Your Ideas,* written by the academic directors, G. Richard Shell and Mario Moussa.

Chapter 15 – Motivate Others

▼

Books

Arussy, Lior. *Excellence Every Day: Make the Daily Choice—Inspire Your Employees and Amaze Your Customers.* **Medford, NJ: CyberAge Books, 2008.**

Drawing on the results of a 23,000-participant study, the author details the keys to expanding leadership skills, improving employee satisfaction and job performance, and securing customer loyalty.

Jones, Pam. *Managing for Performance: Delivering Results through Others.* **New York: Pearson/Prentice Hall Business, 2007.**

Jones's definitive guide helps you appraise and enhance both your own and your team's performance and successfully tackle the issues affecting performance.

Kerr, Steven. *Reward Systems: Does Yours Measure Up?* **Boston: Harvard Business School Press, 2009.**

Many reward systems actually discourage desired behaviors while they reward the very actions that drive you crazy. Kerr describes the steps necessary for creating an effective reward system.

Kotter, John P. *A Sense of Urgency.* **Boston: Harvard Business School Press, 2008.**

In this concise guide, Kotter illustrates how to create a sense of urgency by getting people to actually see and feel the need for change.

Magnuson, Debra S., and Lora S. Alexander. *Work with Me: A New Lens on Leading the Multigenerational Workforce.* **Minneapolis: Personnel Decisions International, 2008.**

The authors apply a generational lens to challenges of attracting, engaging, and retaining talent. Focusing on four areas of common ground—flexibility, respect, development, and coaching—they provide practical actions to help you address generational issues in your company.

Seminars

Building Engagement: What Leaders Do to Build Allegiance and Motivate Others
McCombs School of Business, University of Texas at Austin

www.mccombs.utexas.edu

Participants learn specific steps to enhance their interpersonal effectiveness and generate high levels of engagement among those who work with them.

Creating a High-Performance Organization
Carlson School of Management, University of Minnesota

www.carlsonschool.umn.edu

Participants develop a systemic view of the organization and learn to assess the needs of their work environment on several dimensions: capabilities, competencies, teamwork, empowerment, systems thinking, and leadership.

Energizing People for Performance
Kellogg School of Management, Northwestern University

www.kellogg.northwestern.edu

Participants develop intercultural competence and work with peer coaches on work/life integration, the politics of effective communication at the top level, and personal wellness. The program is especially suitable for those who work with global product lines or manage complex lines of business across borders.

Positive Leadership: Building Extraordinary Personal Leadership Capabilities
Ross School of Business, University of Michigan

http://execed.bus.umich.edu

In this course, participants learn principles and concepts that are fundamental to developing positive leadership capabilities in themselves and others.

Chapter 16 – Build Talent

▼

Books

Bryan, Lowell L., and Claudia I. Joyce. *Mobilizing Minds: Creating Wealth from Talent in the 21st-Century Organization.* **New York: McGraw-Hill, 2007.**

The authors assert that a company's workforce is the key to growth. Tapping into underutilized talents, knowledge, and skills, you can earn tens of thousands of additional dollars per employee and manage the interdepartmental complexities and barriers that prevent real achievements and profits.

Cappelli, Peter. *Talent on Demand: Managing Talent in an Age of Uncertainty.* **Boston: Harvard Business School Press, 2008.**

Drawing from state-of-the-art supply chain management and numerous company examples, Cappelli presents four principles for ensuring that an organization has the skills it needs, when it needs them.

Charan, Ram. *Leaders at All Levels: Deepening Your Talent Pool to Solve the Succession Crisis.* **San Francisco: Jossey-Bass, 2008.**

Charan shows how top companies approach leadership development as a core competency, recognizing that an adaptable leadership pool is a competitive advantage and focusing on bringing out the best in the leaders they have.

Lawler, Edward E. *Talent: Making People Your Competitive Advantage.* **San Francisco: Jossey-Bass, 2008.**

In this follow-up to *Built to Change*, Lawler shows how organizations can combine the right organization design, management practices, and talent to gain a critical performance edge.

Smart, Geoff, and Randy Street. *Who: The A Method for Hiring.* **New York: Ballantine Books, 2008.**

The average hiring mistake costs a company $1.5 million or more a year and countless wasted hours. The authors present their hiring method, which stresses fundamental elements and has a 90 percent success rate.

Seminars

Building Engagement: What Leaders Do to Manage Talent and Build Allegiance
McCombs School of Business, University of Texas at Austin

www.mccombs.utexas.edu

This program provides specific steps that will enhance participants' interpersonal effectiveness as well as generate high levels of engagement among those who work with them.

The New Realities Facing Talent Management
Marshall School of Business, University of Southern California

http://marshall.usc.edu

This course helps participants and their organizations address the new realities facing talent management, including the troubled global economy, generational changes, shifting talent dynamics in emerging markets, the rise in technology's role, and new workplace demands.

Smith-Tuck Global Leaders Program for Women
Smith College Executive Education, Smith College

www.smith.edu

Participants focus on three transformations that are key to global success: industry transformation (shape the future of your industry), organizational transformation (encourage productivity, innovation, and growth worldwide) and individual transformation (become a more effective leader for a rapidly changing global environment).

Strategic Talent Management
London Business School

http://www.london.edu

The Strategic Talent Management program process builds four core capabilities required for competitive success: enterprise and business strategy, the brand promise, organizational culture, and leadership team composition.

Talent and Retention Management
Ross School of Business, University of Michigan

http://execed.bus.umich.edu/

Participants explore strategies for hiring, executive training, and succession planning, and learn how to develop and implement integrated solutions to drive top talent to achieve both personal and organizational goals.

Chapter 17 – Coach and Develop Others

▼

Books

Goldsmith, Marshall, with Mark Reiter. *What Got You Here Won't Get You There: How Successful People Become Even More Successful.* **New York: Hyperion, 2007.**

Small transactional flaws (for example, not saying thank you enough) lead to negative perceptions that prevent you from moving up in a company. Goldsmith offers straightforward advice on how to change this behavior.

Loehr, Anne, and Brian Emerson. *A Manager's Guide to Coaching: Simple and Effective Ways to Get the Best out of Your Employees.* **New York: AMACOM, 2008.**

Emerson and Loehr guide you through every step of the coaching process, from problem solving to developing accountability.

Peterson, David B., and Mary Dee Hicks. *Leader As Coach: Strategies for Coaching and Developing Others.* **Minneapolis: Personnel Decisions International, 1996.**

Coaching improves the bottom line because it goes to the heart of what makes people productive. The five high-impact strategies outlined in this book help you form strong partnerships, accelerate learning, and make a solid investment in people's growth and development.

Underhill, Brian O., Kimcee McAnally, and John J. Koriath. *Executive Coaching for Results: The Definitive Guide to Developing Organizational Leaders.* **San Francisco: Berrett-Koehler, 2007.**

Offering practical learning, best practices, and illuminating case studies, the authors provide a definitive guide to the effective use of executive coaching in the corporate environment.

Whitworth, Laura, Karen Kimsey-House, Henry Kimsey-House, and Phillip Sandahl. *Co-Active Coaching: New Skills for Coaching People Toward Success in Work and Life.* **2nd edition. Mountain View, CA: Davies-Black, 2007.**

This revised edition equips you to design and maintain successful, collaborative, and empowering coaching relationships. Dozens of exercises, tools, sample coaching conversations, checklists, and forms are included.

Wilson, Carol. *Best Practice in Performance Coaching: A Handbook for Leaders, Coaches, HR Professionals and Organizations.* **London and Philadelphia: Kogan Page, 2007.**

Wilson offers a practical guide to the "what" and "how" of performance coaching, covering topics from both a personal and an executive angle, and explaining the structure of a coaching relationship.

Seminars

The Art and Practice of Leaders Coaching Leaders
Carlson School of Management, University of Minnesota

www.carlsonschool.umn.edu

This program offers a perspective and best practice from Richard Leider, a top executive coach. It provides leaders with a proven approach to develop and retain key people through effective coaching practices.

Coaching for Leadership Excellence
Sauder School of Business, University of British Columbia

www.sauder.ubc.ca

Participants gain understanding of the coaching role, learn to structure a coaching conversation that sets the right tone and context, and get feedback from professional practitioners on their skills.

Coaching for Performance
London Business School

www.london.edu

This program focuses on the day-to-day aspects of coaching all employees, utilizing a comprehensive model of the coaching and developmental feedback process, and a newly developed coaching 360-degree assessment.

The Leader as Coach
Haas School of Business, University of California, Berkeley

http://executive.berkeley.edu

Participants learn dynamic coaching strategies for building commitment and sustaining and fostering growth in their people, including new ways to motivate and inspire teams, and how to provide one-on-one coaching to both emerging and current leaders.

The Leader as Coach
Jesse H. Jones Graduate School of Management, Rice University

www.jonesgsm.rice.edu

The program focuses on the process of diagnosing development needs, using job experiences as a developmental tool, and best practices in performance management and succession planning.

Chapter 18 – Promote Teamwork

▼

Books

Guttman, Howard M. *Great Business Teams: Cracking the Code for Standout Performance.* Hoboken, NJ: John Wiley, 2008.

Guttman explores teams at top-management, business-unit, and functional levels and isolates five factors that drive team performance.

Kemp, Jana M. *Moving Out of the Box: Tools for Team Decision Making.* Westport, CT: Praeger, 2008.

Kemp offers tested methods and tools that you and your team members can use to increase performance.

Page, Scott E. *The Difference: How the Power of Diversity Creates Better Groups, Firms, Schools, and Societies.* Princeton, NJ: Princeton University Press, 2008.

Progress and innovation may depend less on a solitary genius than on diverse people working together and capitalizing on their individuality. Page shows how groups with a range of perspectives outperform groups of like-minded experts.

Rath, Tom, and Barry Conchie. *Strengths-Based Leadership: Great Leaders, Teams, and Why People Follow.* New York: Gallup Press, 2008.

The authors identify three keys to being a more effective leader: know your strengths and invest in others' strengths, get people with the right strengths on your team, and understand and meet your team's four basic needs.

Sawyer, Keith. *Group Genius: The Creative Power of Collaboration.* New York: Basic Books, 2008.

Sawyer shows how people can be more creative in collaborative group settings, how to change organizational dynamics for the better, and how to tap into reserves of creativity.

Wageman, Ruth, Debra A. Nunes, James A. Burruss, and J. Richard Hackman. *Senior Leadership Teams: What It Takes to Make Them Great.* Boston: Harvard Business School Press, 2008.

Wageman describes how to create and sustain a leadership team whose members learn from one another while collaborating to pursue a company's objectives.

Seminars

Creating and Leading High-Performing Teams
Wharton, University of Pennsylvania

www.upenn.edu

This program places participants in team challenges in diverse settings—from rowing crew shells to the performing arts—that will change the way they create and lead their own high-performing teams.

Leadership Development for Building High Performing Teams
Marshall School of Business, University of Southern California

www.marshall.usc.edu

Business organizations rely on effective teams to enhance company performance and execution. Through assessments and in-class exercises, this program will analyze individuals' leadership styles and provide methods for facilitating high-performing teams.

Leading High-Impact Teams
Kellogg School of Management, Northwestern University

www.kellogg.northwestern.edu

Highly experiential and collaborative, the program focuses on internal team dynamics (leadership roles, communication skills, and conflict) and external team dynamics (distance teamwork and networking), plus topics such as compensation and networking.

Mobilizing People
IMD International

www.imd.ch

Participants will experience leadership situations and experiment with their role as a leader, and elevate their leadership skills to the next level through intense individual feedback and coaching.

Chapter 19 – Foster Open Communication

▼

Books

Booher, Dianna. *The Voice of Authority: 10 Communication Strategies Every Leader Needs to Know.* **New York: McGraw-Hill, 2007.**

Booher, one of the world's foremost authorities on public speaking and business communication, discusses how you can communicate effectively and present yourself credibly.

Denning, Stephen. *The Secret Language of Leadership: How Leaders Inspire Action through Narrative.* **San Francisco: Jossey-Bass, 2007.**

Denning introduces the concept of narrative intelligence, connects it to the central task of leadership, describes its dimensions, and shows you how to measure it.

Locker, Kitty O., and Stephen Kyo Kaczmarek. *Business Communication: Building Critical Skills.* **Boston: McGraw-Hill Irwin, 2008.**

Grounded in solid business communication fundamentals, the authors anchor their work in workplace activity, helping you connect learning to what you do on the job.

Showkeir, Jamie, and Maren Showkeir. *Authentic Conversations: Moving from Manipulation to Truth and Commitment.* **San Francisco: Berrett-Koehler, 2008.**

The authors explain how to hold conversations that increase commitment and accountability, and improve business performance. They include examples of workplace conversations and provide sample scripts and other practical tools.

Weeks, Holly. *Failure to Communicate: How Conversations Go Wrong and What You Can Do to Right Them.* **Boston: Harvard Business School Press, 2008.**

Dodging issues, appeasing difficult people, and mishandling tough encounters carry a high price. Using proven techniques and detailed examples, Weeks illustrates how to get through the hardest conversations and keep reputations and relationships intact.

Seminars

The Art of Facilitation
Sauder School of Business, University of British Columbia

www.sauder.ubc.ca/

Leaders need to cultivate people and help them share their ideas in productive ways. In this course, participants will learn to facilitate dialogues, foster a collaborative environment, and increase accountability.

The Articulate Executive: Mastering High Performance Communication Skills
David Eccles School of Business, University of Utah

www.business.utah.edu

Through a highly interactive format, participants develop skills in several areas including coaching, speaking, and group facilitation.

Communication Strategies for Improving Performance
Moore School of Business, University of South Carolina

http://mooreschool.sc.edu

Participants study the power of persuasive speaking and active listening, which are essential to shaping performance, both through interaction and coaching.

Increasing Your Communication Effectiveness
Robins School of Business, University of Richmond

http://business.richmond.edu

Participants expand and develop communication skills through group exercises and a self-inventory tool.

Leader as Communicator
Haas School of Business, University of California, Berkeley

http://executive.berkeley.edu/programs/communicator/

Using an innovative approach, this workshop applies skills from theater arts to help participants project energy, confidence, and clarity with physical and vocal expressiveness.

Chapter 20 – Speak Effectively

▼

Books

Duarte, Nancy. *Slide:ology: The Art and Science of Creating Great Presentations.* **Sebastopol, CA: O'Reilly Media, 2008.**

Duarte provides a practical approach to visual story development, combining conceptual thinking and inspirational design with insightful case studies from the world's leading brands.

Reynolds, Garr. *Presentation Zen: Simple Ideas on Presentation Design and Delivery.* **Berkeley, CA: New Riders, 2008.**

Garr combines principles of design with the tenets of Zen simplicity to help you create simpler, more effective presentations.

Roam, Dan. *The Back of the Napkin: Solving Problems and Selling Ideas with Pictures.* **New York: Portfolio, 2008.**

Roam argues that everyone is born with a talent for visual thinking, even those who swear they can't draw. Used properly, a simple drawing on a napkin can help you crystallize ideas, think outside the box, and communicate in a way that people "get."

Simmons, Annette. *Whoever Tells the Best Story Wins: How to Use Your Own Stories to Communicate with Power and Impact.* **New York: AMACOM, 2007.**

Simmons shows you how to use personal stories to convey your ideas and create meaningful connections to your audience.

Tracy, Brian. *Speak to Win: How to Present with Power in Any Situation.* **New York: AMACOM, 2008.**

One of the world's premier speakers, Tracy reveals time-tested ways to present powerfully and speak persuasively, whether it's in an informal meeting or in front of a large audience.

Seminars

Develop Your Speaking Style
Speakeasy, Inc.

www.speakeasyinc.com

Extensive videotaping and individualized coaching and critiques help participants develop a more effective speaking style and feel more in control of both formal and informal speaking situations.

Presentations: Coaching for Executives
Carlson School of Management, University of Minnesota

www.csom.umn.edu

This program explores key communication challenges faced by senior managers and provides an opportunity to receive executive-level, strategic coaching to further develop communication abilities.

Presentations That Work®
Booher Consultants

www.booher.com

This course focuses on instruction and practice in content organization, presentation, delivery skills, visual design and use, and question-and-answer models. Participants receive personalized, confidential feedback and develop an action plan to improve their skills.

Powerful Presentations
Jesse H. Jones Graduate School of Management, Rice University

www.jonesgsm.rice.edu

Participants develop communication strategies for their presentations, tailor presentations to achieve the greatest impact, and learn how to use graphics effectively and present with greater confidence.

Slide:ology Workshop
Duarte Design

www.duarte.com

Participants engage in a series of fun, hands-on exercises in which they apply the principles in slide:ology using real-life examples. The session is held at the Duarte office, a creative workspace that allows them to break away from their traditional surroundings and conventional train of thought.

Chapter 21 – Listen to Others

▼

Books

Collins, Sandra D. *Interpersonal Communication: Listening and Responding.* 2nd edition. Mason, OH: Cengage South-Western, 2008.

The author explores how successful companies and effective managers use listening as a strategic communication tool at all levels of the organization and discusses common barriers to listening and strategies for overcoming them.

Donoghue, Paul J., and Mary E. Siegel. *Are You Really Listening? Keys to Successful Communication.* Notre Dame, IN: Sorin Books, 2005.

In this insightful guide, the authors explore the reasons people don't listen and provide a helpful approach for hearing others and being heard.

Downs, Lisa J. *Listening Skills Training.* Alexandria, VA: ASTD Press, 2008.

Downs's complete resource for developing listening skills includes a training guide; sample half-, full-, and two-day agendas; classroom handouts; tools; assessments; and PowerPoint slides.

Reiman, Tonya. *The Power of Body Language: How to Succeed in Every Business and Social Encounter.* Riverside, NJ: Simon & Schuster, 2008.

Reiman analyzes the components of body language and introduces the Reiman Rapport Method, a system for building an instant connection with anyone, in any situation.

Seminars

Dynamic Communication
H. Wayne Huizenga School of Business and Entrepreneurship, Nova Southeastern University
www.huizenga.nova.edu

Two-way communication is critical to a participative management style. Participants examine obstacles to effective communication and learn to facilitate supportive communication with diverse individuals and groups.

Dynamic Listening Skills for Successful Communication
American Management Association
www.amanet.org

Participants learn to use encouragement and praise to build rapport; separate message content from feelings; ask questions to expand knowledge and bring out new ideas; give directions effectively; and criticize performance rather than people.

Listening and Writing: Building a Foundation for Better Communication
American Management Association
www.amanet.org

Participants learn how to analyze a situation and audience; listen both actively and passively; listen for understanding; determine the proper channel or medium for communications; and organize and write concise, understandable messages.

The Power of Listening: Unlocking Your Communication Potential
School of Industrial and Labor Relations, Cornell University
www.ilr.cornell.edu

In sharing information, coordinating projects, working in teams, and coaching and empowering others, listening is a critically important, vastly underdeveloped skill. This participatory workshop explores the knowledge, attitudes, and skills necessary to become more effective in verbal communications.

Chapter 22 – Write Effectively

▼

Books

Camp, Lindsay. *Can I Change Your Mind?: The Craft and Art of Persuasive Writing.* **London: A. & C. Black, 2007.**

Drawing on his long experience as a leading copywriter, Camp shows how to argue a case effectively in writing.

Marsen, Sky. *Professional Writing: The Complete Guide for Business, Industry and IT.* **New York: Palgrave Macmillan, 2007.**

Marsen offers a comprehensive introduction to professional writing, synthesizing methods and ideas developed in linguistics, journalism, public relations, and marketing.

Moon, Jon. *How to Make an Impact: Influence, Inform, and Impress with Your Reports, Presentations, and Business Documents.* **Harlow, England and New York: FT/Prentice Hall, 2009.**

Moon provides ideas, tips, and principles that are easy to implement, guiding you through the most effective ways of presenting information, including tables, charts, slides, and flowcharts.

Sant, Tom. *The Language of Success: Business Writing That Informs, Persuades, and Gets Results.* **New York: AMACOM, 2008.**

Sant explains how to write more effectively in a professional setting, producing documents that ask and answer questions; provide information people need for their jobs; communicate opinions; and persuade, instruct, or update.

University of Chicago Press. *The Chicago Manual of Style.* **15th edition. Chicago: University of Chicago Press, 2003.**

The Chicago Manual of Style is an essential reference, providing answers on style, grammar, usage, and publishing.

Seminars

Business Writing for Professionals
H. Wayne Huizenga School of Business and Entrepreneurship, Nova Southeastern University

www.huizenga.nova.edu

Participants review grammar and punctuation rules; structure powerful and efficient sentences; practice proofreading techniques; and learn how to avoid misinterpretations, numerous edits, and re-work.

Business Writing Workshop
Center for Continuing and Professional Education, Georgetown University

www12.georgetown.edu

Participants learn a six-step writing process to energize their writing, eliminate rounds of editing, and get results.

MPW Weekend Writers Conference
College of Letters, Arts, and Sciences, University of Southern California

http://college.usc.edu/mpw/experience/process.cfm

Participants reconnect with their creative side, learn how to freshen corporate writing, meet one-on-one with noted creative writers, and attend keynote addresses and readings by literary notables.

Strategic Writing™
Booher Consultants

www.booherdirect.com

Participants learn effective techniques and processes such as the MADE Format®, the Idea Wheel, and the Five-Step Writing Process to improve productivity, achieve results, increase clarity, and present the appropriate image to clients, colleagues, and the public.

Chapter 23 – Establish Relationships

▼

Books

D'Souza, Steven. *Brilliant Networking: What the Best Networkers Know, Do, and Say.* Harlow, England, and New York: Pearson/Prentice Hall, 2008.

Networking is an important aspect of many jobs, but few individuals learn how to do it effectively. D'Souza provides tips and techniques to help you network confidently and effectively.

Gostick, Adrian, and Scott Christopher. *The Levity Effect: Why It Pays to Lighten Up.* Hoboken, NJ: John Wiley, 2008.

Based on ten years of extensive research, the authors argue against business tradition to reveal the powerful bottom-line benefits of leading with levity. With interviews, exercises, and case studies, the book reveals how humor in the workplace will help you communicate messages, build camaraderie, and encourage creativity for a better workplace and bigger profits.

Libert, Barry, and Jon Spector. *We Are Smarter than Me: How to Unleash the Power of Crowds in Your Business.* Upper Saddle River, NJ: Wharton School Publishing, 2008.

The authors explain which business functions are best suited for communities, how to be an effective moderator, and how to balance structure with independence, manage risk, define success, and implement effective metrics.

Nour, David. *Relationship Economics: Transform Your Most Valuable Business Contacts into Personal and Professional Success.* Hoboken, NJ: John Wiley, 2008.

Nour views business relationships as a platform for long-term business growth and success, going far beyond simple networking. He introduces new concepts in relationship management, including relationship currency, reputation capital, and professional net worth.

Sanders, Tim. *The Likeability Factor: How to Boost Your L-Factor and Achieve Your Life's Dreams.* New York: Three Rivers Press, 2006.

The more you are liked, the happier your life will be. Sanders shows how to build your likeability factor by enhancing four critical elements of your personality: friendliness, relevance, empathy, and realness.

Wall, Bob. *Working Relationships: Using Emotional Intelligence to Enhance Your Effectiveness with Others.* Revised edition. Mountain View, CA: Davies-Black, 2008.

Wall's tool kit helps you master the personal characteristics and social abilities of emotional intelligence (EQ) to manage conflict, develop teamwork, and get along with colleagues.

Seminars

Building Relationships That Work
Wharton, University of Pennsylvania

www.wharton.upenn.edu

This seminar focuses on three essentials of relationships: know yourself, understand others, and develop trust and credibility. Participants strengthen the impact of their relationships, both inside and outside their companies.

Cross-Functional Communication: Strategies for Workplace Effectiveness
American Management Association

www.amanet.org

This highly interactive seminar shows participants how to develop win-win professional relationships that lead to organizational effectiveness.

Leveraging the Power of Emotional Intelligence
David Eccles School of Management, University of Utah

www.business.utah.edu

Participants examine the qualities of great leadership and build the competencies needed to create a culture of cooperation and commitment, foster productivity, generate new ideas, and improve the bottom line.

Strategic Business Leadership: Creating and Delivering Value
Graduate School of Business, University of Chicago

www.chicagoexec.net

Participants learn to manage cross-functional, cross-organizational relationships; develop social capital; and create and manage organizational strategic partners. They also gain an understanding of how a savvy manager moves into a leadership role and how to create an environment where creativity is the norm.

Chapter 24 – Manage Disagreements

▼

Books

Doherty, Nora, and Marcelas Guyler. *The Essential Guide to Workplace Mediation and Conflict Resolution: Rebuilding Working Relationships.* London and Philadelphia: Kogan Page, 2008.

Doherty and Guyler discuss mediation, analyze reasons for conflict, and suggest useful communication skills to help defuse anger and aggression.

Maravelas, Anna. *How to Reduce Workplace Conflict and Stress: How Leaders and Their Employees Can Protect Their Sanity and Productivity from Tension and Turf Wars.* Franklin Lakes, NJ: Career Press, 2005.

Maravelas shows how you can deal effectively with the disabling emotions of hostility, desk rage, and workplace incivility. You will learn how to handle daily frustrations, handle cynicism and conflict, respond to anger, and create an emotionally resilient workforce.

Scott, Gini Graham. *Disagreements, Disputes, and All-Out War: 3 Simple Steps for Dealing with Any Kind of Conflict.* New York: AMACOM, 2008.

Scott provides powerful and practical ways to identify reasons for conflict, recognize and control the emotional factors, and find the best solution.

Smith, Diana McLain. *Divide or Conquer: How Great Teams Turn Conflict into Strength.* New York: Portfolio, 2008.

Smith argues for changing the patterns of interaction between people rather than focusing on attitudes and blame.

Seminars

Conflict Resolution Skills
Sprott School of Business, Carleton University

www.sprott.carleton.ca

Participants gain knowledge of essential skills, techniques, and tools for conflict resolution; increase their awareness of how to prevent conflict; and develop abilities to resolve conflict with greater ease and effectiveness.

Leadership Essentials: Conflict Resolution
Opus College of Business, University of St. Thomas

https://cbecrm.stthomas.edu

Effective leaders know that how they handle conflict affects future relationships and organizational progress. This program provides an understanding of what triggers conflict and focuses on practical strategies and skills for effectively managing difficult interpersonal situations.

Managing Conflict and Creating Consensus
Darden School of Business, University of Virginia

www.darden.virginia.edu

This program is designed specifically for managers facing recurrent climates of individual and institutional conflict. Participants learn to deal effectively with daily and systemic conflict so they can build and maintain strategic alliances, support creativity and innovation, and foster a collaborative culture.

Responding to Conflict: Strategies for Improved Communication
American Management Association

www.amanet.org

This program teaches communication strategies for resolving conflict and building trust. Topics include establishing clear outcomes for resolving conflict, expressing anger in a constructive way, using effective nonverbal behavior, and understanding gender differences and group dynamics that lead to conflict.

Chapter 25 – Increase Cultural Competence

▼

Books

Carté, Penny, and Chris Fox. *Bridging the Culture Gap: A Practical Guide to International Business Communication.* 2nd edition. London and Philadelphia: Kogan Page, 2008.

The second edition of *Bridging the Culture Gap* contains case studies, cultural awareness scales, communication tests, and practical tips to help you become a better communicator.

Gurian, Michael, with Barbara Annis. *Leadership and the Sexes: Using Gender Science to Create Success in Business.* San Francisco: Jossey-Bass, 2008.

The authors develop a new vision of gender diversity by combining brain science and gender studies with examples from top business leaders.

Kennedy, Debbe. *Putting Our Differences to Work: The Fastest Way to Innovation, Leadership, and High Performance.* San Francisco: Berrett-Koehler, 2008.

Using the latest research and real-world examples, Kennedy illustrates how putting differences to work accelerates innovation and contribution.

Klein, Freada Kapor, Martha Mendoza, and Kimberly Allers. *Giving Notice: Why the Best and the Brightest Leave the Workplace and How You Can Help Them Stay.* San Francisco: Jossey-Bass, 2008.

The authors explore causes and dynamics of bias in the workplace, offering a psychological, political, and societal analysis of the actual cost of bias to the bottom line.

Seminars

Communicating and Negotiating with a Global Mindset
Thunderbird School of Global Management

www.thunderbird.edu

Global Mindset is a set of individual characteristics that can enhance the ability to influence people from other cultural backgrounds. In this program, participants learn their own Global Mindset profile and develop an understanding of their negotiating preferences.

Cultural Differences and Communicative Practices
Loyola University Chicago

www.luc.edu

Participants develop a fuller understanding of the paradox that cultural differences may be subtle or almost imperceptible but have a profound, often negative, impact on communication, creating missed opportunities, unnecessary complications, wasted time, and bad feelings.

Leadership and Change Management in a Multicultural Context
Tepper School of Business, Carnegie Mellon University

www.tepper.cmu.edu

This seminar helps participants better understand how to manage intercultural differences amid change, and works specifically on the levels of managing multicultural teams and the communication among them.

Leading Global Teams: Understanding How Leadership, Culture and Team Create Organizational Effectiveness
Pitt Business Center for Executive Education, University of Pittsburgh

www.business.pitt.edu

This course focuses on what it takes for leaders to be effective when they are managing global teams. Participants gain insight into the challenges and opportunities of designing and managing cross-cultural teams, and assess their own leadership competence in cross-cultural management situations.

Mastering Management: Skills and Vision for Women on the Move
Ascent, in partnership with the Tuck School of Business at Dartmouth

www.ascentleadership.org

How multicultural women interact with corporate organizations often determines their career achievement. Communication, influence, coalition building, championing, teamwork, and networking are a large part of the program's content, helping participants see the organization as a networked system requiring continual management and development.

Chapter 26 – Establish Trust

▼

Books

Culbert, Samuel A. *Beyond Bullsh*t: Straight-Talk at Work.* Stanford, CA: Stanford Business Books, 2008.

Culbert describes straight-talk as the product of thoughtful, caring relationships built upon trust and a commitment to look out for one another's success. This brand of truthfulness enhances personal and organizational productivity.

Frankel, Tamar. *Trust and Honesty: America's Business Culture at a Crossroad.* New York: Oxford University Press, 2008.

Frankel asserts that fraud and the abuse of trust could have a widespread impact on the American economy and American prosperity, and argues that the culture of business dishonesty can be reversed.

Hall, Vanessa. *The Truth about Trust in Business.* Austin, TX: Emerald, 2009.

Using everyday examples and insights from leaders, Hall makes the connection between trust and its critical role in business. Leaders who build trust benefit from increased results and retention, and improved relationships.

Lukaszewski, James E. *Why Should the Boss Listen to You?: The Seven Disciplines of the Trusted Strategic Advisor.* San Francisco: Jossey-Bass, 2008.

Lukaszewski identifies and explains seven disciplines to gain influence and become a key trusted advisor to top-level executives.

Seidman, Dov. *How: Why How We Do Anything Means Everything—in Business (and in Life).* Hoboken, NJ: John Wiley, 2007.

Information and unprecedented transparency have changed the rules: it's no longer what you do that sets you apart, but how you do it. Seidman shares his unique approach to helping companies build "do it right" cultures.

Simons, Tony. *The Integrity Dividend: Leading by the Power of Your Word.* San Francisco: Jossey-Bass, 2008.

Simons's research reveals that businesses led by managers of high integrity enjoy deeper employee commitment, lower turnover, superior customer service, and substantially higher profitability.

Seminars

Donchian Seminars in Professional Values Program
Institute for Practical Ethics in Public Life, University of Virginia

www.virginia.edu/

Participants study ethical conflicts that arise in professional and public life and engage in critical reflection about their ethical responsibilities.

Institute on Corporate Citizenship
Boston College Center for Corporate Citizenship

www.bcccc.net

Trust in business is low, even though expectations of business are rising. This course examines how leading companies respond to this dynamic using corporate citizenship as a tool to create new value for all stakeholders.

Leading with Integrity: Ethics in Action
Brookings Institution Executive Education

www.brookings.edu

Participants create their ethical framework, using new tools to audit and manage their behavior. Developing moral reasoning skills will enable them to handle daily dilemmas in a way that enhances organizational integrity.

Leading the Value-Driven Organization
Olin Business School, Washington University in St. Louis

www.olin.wustl.edu

During the course, participants focus on why values matter to leaders, including how value clarity, value prioritization, and value integration enable greater effectiveness for individual leaders. In addition, they focus on how those values align with organizational values, and how organizational values align with corporate strategy.

Chapter 27 – Show Adaptability

▼

Books

Friedman, Stewart D. *Total Leadership: Be a Better Leader, Have a Richer Life.* Boston: Harvard Business School Press, 2008.

Total Leadership provides a blueprint for performing well as a leader by finding mutual value among four key areas of your life: work, home, community, and self.

Hamel, Gary, with Bill Breen. *The Future of Management.* Boston: Harvard Business School Press, 2007.

Hamel argues that organizations require management innovation to compete in a world where adaptability and creativity drive long-term business success.

Loehr, Jim. *The Power of Story: Change Your Story, Change Your Destiny in Business and in Life.* New York: Free Press, 2008.

For decades, Loehr has examined the power of story to increase engagement and productivity. Fortune 500 companies have paid millions to send employees to his program at the Human Performance Institute; those principles and methods are now available in this book.

Maruca, Regina Fazio. *The Way We Work: An Encyclopedia of Business Culture.* Westport, CT: Greenwood Press, 2007.

Maruca provides background and context for business and management concepts, discusses proponents and detractors, and considers the long-term impact on business and culture.

Pfeffer, Jeffrey. *What Were They Thinking?: Unconventional Wisdom about Management.* Boston: Harvard Business School Press, 2007.

Pfeffer uses examples, data, and insights to challenge assumptions and conventional management wisdom. He offers guidelines on how to think more deeply and intelligently about critical management issues.

Tappin, Steve, and Andrew Cave. *The Secrets of CEOs: 150 Global Chief Executives Lift the Lid on Business, Life, and Leadership.* Boston: Nicholas Brealey, 2008.

Tappin and Cave reveal what motivates and drives the world's top business leaders, how they lead their businesses, which leadership skills and experience are needed, and how businesses and leaders will evolve in the future.

Seminars

Leadership as a Daily Challenge: An Integrated Approach
Tepper School of Business, Carnegie Mellon University

www.tepper.cmu.edu

The course covers a range of topics, including negotiation skills, star performance, change management, and leadership using informal networks. Participants evaluate, practice, and improve their personal leadership skills by applying new techniques and strategies in group work.

Leadership That Shapes the Future
Foster School of Business, University of Washington

http://bschool.washington.edu

Participants gain strategies and methods to help others go beyond self-interest and act for the common good of the organization. As leaders, they will become more influential; link personal, team, and organizational goals; overcome leadership gaps; and leverage strengths to reach career goals.

Leading a Resilient Organization: Achieving Results During Challenging Times
Wharton Executive Education, University of Pennsylvania

www.wharton.upenn.edu/

Participants build resilience at the organizational, team, and individual level. They work on current business challenges, learn proven energy management models for managing with intensity, and develop leadership and coaching skills that blend realism with optimism.

The Looking Glass Experience
Center for Creative Leadership

www.ccl.org

Participants gain insights into their own strengths and weaknesses through feedback from other participants, from Center for Creative Leadership staff, and from a feedback instrument completed by their coworkers back home.

Managing Emotion in the Workplace®: Strategies for Success
American Management Association

www.amanet.org

Participants learn to identify their personal trigger points, develop techniques for staying calm in tense situations, practice receiving criticism in a positive manner, and find ways to reenergize at the end of the day.

Chapter 28 – Learn Continuously

▼

Books

Eikenberry, Kevin. *Remarkable Leadership: Unleashing Your Leadership Potential One Skill at a Time.* **San Francisco: John Wiley, 2007.**

Eikenberry describes the most important leadership competencies, offers a proven method for learning leadership skills, and shows how to apply the skills in the work world.

George, Bill, with Peter Sims. *True North: Discover Your Authentic Leadership.* **San Francisco: Jossey-Bass, 2007.**

True North shares wisdom from 125 top leaders, gleaned from research and first-person interviews, and shows how individuals who follow their internal compass become authentic leaders.

Gordon, Jack. *The Pfeiffer Book of Successful Leadership Development Tools.* **San Francisco: Pfeiffer, 2007.**

Gordon selects the most successful leadership development tools from three decades of the Pfeiffer Annuals and Handbooks, which provide resources for training and organizational development.

Peterson, David B., and Mary Dee Hicks. *Development FIRST: Strategies for Self-Development.* **Minneapolis: Personnel Decisions International, 1995.**

Development FIRST outlines five concise strategies that help you focus on what you want to learn and develop, implement action every day, reflect on what you learned, seek feedback, and transfer what you learned as you work on new goals.

Thomas, Robert J. *Crucibles of Leadership: How to Learn from Experience to Become a Great Leader.* **Boston: Harvard Business School Press, 2008.**

Drawing on insights and stories from accomplished leaders, Thomas offers self-assessments and innovative tools to help you develop a personal learning strategy.

Seminars

Emerging Leader Program
Gonzaga University

www.gonzaga.edu

The program comprises five interactive sessions focusing on leadership identity and vision, effective communication, conflict management, developing employees, and implementing change. Participants are matched with mentors and complete a strategically aligned initiative at their companies.

Experienced Leader Certificate Program
Division of Continuing Education, University of Florida

http://leadership.dce.ufl.edu/

Middle managers face multiple organizational challenges and work both strategically and cross-functionally. This program draws from organizational development, marketing, operations, human resources, and other functions to present an enterprise-wide approach to leadership.

Successful Manager's Leadership Program
College of Continuing Education, University of Minnesota

www.cce.umn.edu

This program, incorporating learning from *Successful Manager's Handbook,* addresses managers' need for understanding their roles as leaders; applies sound leadership principles; and provides participants with the skills, behaviors, and tools for success.

Women in Business: Transitioning to Leadership
Kenan Flagler Business School, University of North Carolina

www.kenan-flagler.unc.edu

Women commonly face a unique set of challenges as they rise to senior ranks. During this seminar, participants learn how to navigate the transition from managing to leading successfully and develop practical skills to enhance their impact as leaders.

Resources

Web Sites

800CEORead	http://800ceoread.com/blog/
All Things Workplace	http://www.allthingsworkplace.com/
American Productivity & Quality Center	www.apqc.org
American Rhetoric	www.americanrhetoric.com
American Society for Quality	www.asq.org
Ask a Manager	http://askamanager.blogspot.com/
The Back of the Napkin Blog	http://www.digitalroam.typepad.com/
The Balanced Scorecard Institute	www.balancedscorecard.org
Barron's Online	www.barrons.com
The Benchmarking Network, Inc.	www.well.com/user/benchmar/ tbnhome.html
Bloomberg.com	www.bloomberg.com
Bob Sutton: Work Matters	http://bobsutton.typepad.com/my_weblog/
Brand Autopsy Marketing Practice	http://brandautopsy.typepad.com/ brandautopsy/
BRINT Institute	www.brint.com/press
The Business Blog at Intuitive.com	http://www.intuitive.com/blog/
Business Ethics	www.business-ethics.com
businessLISTENING.com	www.businesslistening.com
Business for Social Responsibility	www.bsr.org
BusinessWeek Management IQ	http://www.businessweek.com/careers/ managementiq/
Business Writing	http://www.businesswritingblog.com/ business_writing/
CareerJournal.com	www.careerjournal.com
CEOExpress®	www.ceo-express.com
Chicago Manual of Style	www.chicagomanualofstyle.org
Chief Happiness Officer	http://positivesharing.com/
Chris Brogan	http://www.chrisbrogan.com/
Church of the Customer Blog	http://customerevangelists.typepad. com/blog/
ClimateBiz	www.climatebiz.com
CommLog	http://craweblogs.crainfotech.net/commlog

Web Sites

Communication Nation	http://communicationnation.blogspot.com/
Conversation Agent	http://conversationagent.typepad.com/ conversation_agent/
The Courage Institute	www.courageinstitute.org
Creative Class	http://www.creativeclass.com/
Creativity at Work™	www.creativityatwork.com
Critical Thinking Consortium	www.criticalthinking.org
Customer Care Institute	www.customercare.com
Dan Pink	http://www.danpink.com/
David Allen Company	http://www.davidco.com/
DiversityInc.com	www.diversityinc.com
Economist.com	www.economist.com
Fast Company	www.fastcompany.com
Financial Times	www.ft.com
Fistful of Talent	http://www.fistfuloftalent.com/
FORTUNE	www.fortune.com
Great Leadership	http://www.greatleadershipbydan.com/
Guy Kawasaki	http://blog.guykawasaki.com/
Harvard Business Review	http://harvardbusinessonline.hbsp. harvard.edu
HR.com	www.hr.com
Influential Marketing Blog	http://rohitbhargava.typepad.com/weblog/
InnovationTools	www.innovationtools.com
Institute for Global Ethics	www.globalethics.org
International Coach Federation®	www.coachfederation.org
International Herald Tribune	www.iht.com
International Listening Association	www.listen.org
Investors.com	www.investors.com
John Moore	http://brandautopsy.typepad.com/
Kiplinger.com	www.kiplinger.com
Knowledge@Wharton	http://knowledge.wharton.upenn.edu
KR Connect	http://krconnect.blogspot.com/

Resources

Planning Templates

Your time is valuable. When it comes to learning, you need to spend time planning and taking action on your plan, not designing a form. To give you a head start, here are four templates you can use for yourself, your direct reports, or the people you're coaching.

Learning plan

When you need to learn something quickly, use this form. Be as specific as possible, especially about your action steps and deadlines. To get the best results, include activities that you can do each day.

Development plan

Use this form for medium-term goals, such as yearly goals stemming from a performance review or from a 360-degree feedback process.

Career plan

This form can help you explore career goals and determine which strengths and development needs you will want to address in order to reach your goals.

Coaching plan

This form will help you keep track of individuals' learning objectives and determine how you can support them and create learning opportunities.

Learning Plan

Name _____	Date _____

1. FOCUS on critical priorities.
What do I want to change or develop? What development priorities give me the greatest leverage?

2. IMPLEMENT something every day. What situations, people, or events signal that right now is the time to put new behaviors into action? **Every time I see the following situation(s) . . .**	What new behavior will I try? Where will I push my comfort zone? **. . . I will take the following action:**
1.	
2.	
3.	
4.	
5.	
6.	

Learning Plan

3. **REFLECT on what I learn.**
   What will I do each day to consider what worked, what didn't work, and what I want to do next time?

4. **SEEK feedback and support.**
   How will I draw on other people to track my progress, gather advice and feedback, and support my learning?

   Seek feedback and information

   Seek resources, support, and opportunities

5. **TRANSFER learning to the next level.**
   How will I evaluate my progress? Considering my goals and organizational priorities, how will I update my development strategy and learning plan? How will I leverage what I learn?

Development Plan

Build on Strengths

Step 1 Strength	Step 2 Action Plans	Step 3 Involvement of Others	Step 4 Target Dates
Strength:	1. 2. 3. 4.		
Strength:	1. 2. 3. 4.		
Strength:	1. 2. 3. 4.		

Development Plan

Address Development Needs

Step 1 Development Need	Step 2 Action Plans	Step 3 Involvement of Others	Step 4 Target Dates
Development Need:	1. 2. 3. 4.		
Development Need:	1. 2. 3. 4.		
Development Need:	1. 2. 3. 4.		

Career Plan

Personal Mission Statement

Short-term Career Goals (1–2 years)

Long-term Career Goals (3–5 years)

Short-term Development Goals

Strengths to Leverage:	*Development Needs to Address:*

Long-term Development Goals

Strengths to Leverage:	*Development Needs to Address:*

Coaching Plan

Person's Name:	
Person's Learning Objective:	**My Involvement as Coach:**
Person's Criteria for Success:	

Working One-on-One	Time Frame
Orchestrating Learning Opportunities	
Enhancing Self-Reliance	
Recommended Resources:	
Overcoming Obstacles:	

Index

Index

Index

Index

Index

About the Author

PDI Ninth House is a premier global leadership solutions company with distinctive expertise in accelerating leadership effectiveness to maximize organizational performance. We have over 40 years of experience in helping clients identify, manage, develop, and promote superior leaders across all levels of client organizations. We serve thousands of clients on six continents, including 70 percent of the BusinessWeek Top 100 Global Brands, 75 percent of the Forbes Global 100 and 80 percent of the FORTUNE 100 firms in the United States.

PDI Ninth House partners with large global organizations to solve a wide range of leadership challenges, using a unique combination of innovative, field-tested strategies, state-of-the-art technology, and proven processes to tailor specific solutions for clients.

We help organizations:

- Identify, place, and maintain leadership talent at all levels

- Assess performance, potential, readiness, and fit for leadership transitions

- Develop and train current and future leaders at all levels from individual contributors to managers, executives, and CEOs

- Coach individuals to improve their leadership effectiveness

- Drive a human capital strategy that aligns talent with business and organizational strategy

- Plan for succession to promote and deploy the right people at the right time

- Provide stellar change management programs that create lasting behavior change in organizations

- Use technology to deliver rapid, cost-effective training to address the learning needs of all demographic groups globally

- ▶ Drive behavior change through highly engaging learning experiences that speak to the hearts and minds of today's learners

Leaders make or break organizations at all levels. We look forward to exploring how we can help you. For more information, contact PDI Ninth House at 1.920.997.6995 (in the U.S. 1.800.633.4410) or visit our Web site at www.pdininthhouse.com.

About the Publisher

SHLPreVisor, a leading provider of pre-employment assessments and employee selection solutions, helps organizations by connecting employment decisions to business results. Following the rigorous standards of industrial-organizational (I-O) psychology, SHLPreVisor's assessment content accurately predicts on-the-job performance and supports fair hiring practices. SHLPreVisor's solutions help streamline hiring, reduce recruiting and training costs, and improve corporate performance for over thousands of organizations worldwide, including more than 100 of the Fortune 500 as well as government agencies.

SHLPreVisor is the union of best-of-breed assessment organizations including SHL, PreVisor, Qwiz, ePredix, PDRI, Brainbench, Talent Technologies (formerly PSL Australia), CraftSystems, Performance Technologies International (PTI), and ASE Solutions. With over 80 years of combined experience, SHLPreVisor offers nearly 1,000 pre-employment tests and selection tools covering most jobs in most industries, through a single platform.

SHLPreVisor's award-winning talent measurement products and services give employers the ability to Know in Advance a candidate's readiness for the job today and their performance potential for the future – for any job in any industry. We give employers the ability to screen, select, develop, and promote the employees who will be the most productive moving forward.

Our offerings include:

Assessments

SHLPreVisor's employee assessment tests deliver measurable results and include nearly 1,000 titles. Our pre-packaged Job Assessments include pre-employment test solutions grouped for specific jobs and job types.

Interview Tools

SHLPreVisor's InterView and Interview Expert suites provide robust functionality, including real-time creation of a custom interview guide as well as interview training to ensure your process is consistent and legally compliant.

Skills Certifications

SHLPreVisor offers a valuable certification program, covering today's in-demand IT job functions.

Consulting Services

SHLPreVisor's Professional Services team leverages consulting expertise, online technology, and I-O best practice methodologies to address our clients' business needs related to all phases of the human capital life cycle.

Computer Adaptive Testing (CAT)

SHLPreVisor's PreView™ CAT technology is a method for administering tests that adapts to the candidate's ability level. It is one of the most accurate and secure methods of measuring skills and job readiness. A computer adaptive test "adapts" itself to test takers by selecting the next item to be presented based on performance on preceding items, resulting in increased test accuracy, enhanced test security, reduced test time and an improved applicant experience.

For more information on SHLPreVisor's predictive employment solutions, please contact us online at www.previsor.com or call 1.800.592.0977.